Verlaine: Fool of God

Verlaine: Fool of God

by LAWRENCE *and* ELISABETH HANSON

RANDOM HOUSE

New York

First Printing

Design: James McCrea

The translations of Verlaine's poems on pages 168-169, 215 and 287 are by Ernest Dowson; on pages 99, 169, 177-178, 187, 216-217 and 285, by Gertrude Hall; on pages 92-93, 96, 119, 212, 217-218, 328-329 and 329-330, by Arthur Symons, and on pages 90, 100-101, 111, 213-214 and 224-225, by Ashmore Wingate.

To Roland de Margerie

in gratitude for his help and encouragement

"*I have loved much in my life. Too much? Oh no! Decidedly not! For love, you see—and believe me instead of condemning me out of hand—love is the sole motive power of almost all, if not absolutely all actions worthy of the name. Don't speak to me of other things, ambition, wealth, glory! At the very most, perhaps, of Art. And yet, and yet, Art quite alone . . . ?*"

Contents

Illustrations

Preface

Almost all biographies of Paul Verlaine have praised the work and condemned the man. We find this attitude incomprehensible. We do not understand how a biographer can write a book about someone he despises, and still less do we understand how, if Verlaine is solely the kind of person some of these biographers would have their readers believe, he could have written the poems they admire so much. We are convinced that this man, who had dark passages in his life and was maligned for them, possessed the elements of greatness.

As a result this study of Verlaine approaches his work as an inevitable result of the man and the man, conversely, as an inevitable begetter of the work. Though Verlaine does not cut a heroic figure in the usual sense of those words (and we have not attempted to make him appear so), let no one forget that the great man is larger than life in every direction, in his faults, his virtues and his talents.

We have been greatly helped during the preparation of this book. Our dedication indicates one of the chief sources of indebtedness, with whom we gratefully join that kindest and most stimulating of hostesses, Madame Roland de Margerie. We also owe much to our friend Frédéric de Heeckeren's magnificent readings of Verlaine, Rimbaud and Baudelaire and to his promptness in answering difficult questions; to Madame Renée Modot, who first introduced us to the nineteenth-century French poets; to Madame Joly-Segalen; to Mademoiselle J. Gallagher; to Madame Marie Dornoy; to Monsieur Jean Adhémar; to Monsieur Bernard Dorival; to Mr. and Mrs. J. Baljeu; to Miss B. Carpenter; to Monsieur Jean Loize; to Councillor W. J. Whitelock, J. P., Mayor, and to Mr. Francis Pepin, Librarian, of Bournemouth; to Mr. C. L. Hoffrock Griffiths, Town Clerk of Boston; to the Town Clerk of Nottingham; and to Mr. Short of Stickney.

We have another and very pleasant sort of acknowledgment to make, to all those relatives of Verlaine, descendants of his friends and others who have helped us during our visits to the Verlaine-Rimbaud country. These kind people have not merely given us photographs and letters rarely and sometimes never before printed; they have more importantly provided direct evidence of Verlaine's movements and behavior at certain periods of his life. This has often enabled us to correct inaccuracies and malicious gossip which have been repeated in book after book these last sixty years. It is not possible to include the name of every interested and helpful person in these districts, since this would involve printing the names of half the inhabitants in many villages and small towns, but certain acknowledgments must be made, in addition to our general indebtedness to those in the Gendarmerie Nationale and the various Maries; Madame Veuve Prévost and Monsieur Jean Imbert of Juniville; Monsieur Jules Rigot and Monsieur and Madame Decloux of Coulommes; Madame Veuve Fricoteau of Roche; Professor Verdelot and Monsieur Charles Namur of Rethel; Madame Veuve and Mademoiselle Evrard of Jehonville; Monsieur Grandjean and Monsieur Charles Péture of Bertrix; Monsieur Jean Barras of Paliseul; Monsieur Tante and Monsieur Deshayes of Charleville; and Monsieur Prunis of Reims.

Finally, among those who have written about Verlaine we are especially indebted to V. P. Underwood for his indispensable work on Verlaine in England; to Harold Nicolson for his account of Verlaine's place in French poetry; and to Y.-G. le Dantec, whose edition of Verlaine has been a pleasure to use.

The bibliography of Verlaine is enormous; so much so that some kind of selection has been essential. In our bibliography, therefore, we have omitted all articles and have confined our list of books almost entirely to those written by Verlaine's contemporaries.

Most biographies of Verlaine include a fairly full account of Rimbaud's life after he and Verlaine parted. We have not done so; partly because it is largely irrelevant to Verlaine's later life, partly because we are now at work on a study of Rimbaud which we hope to complete in due course.

It is a curious fact that the virtues of this most English of French

poets are lost in translation and we would advise readers neither
to judge him nor to confuse their impression of his work by other
versions. For those who do not read French, translations have been
provided by the publishers, whenever possible, not because they give a
corresponding effect but because they do approximate the mood and
subject matter of the poems. No reader need feel debarred from
enjoying Verlaine in the original, however. Since he is primarily the
poet of sound and feeling, even a person with limited French may
capture the essence of his work by frequent reading of a single poem.

Our thanks for permission to reproduce illustrations are due to the
Bibliothèque Nationale, the Louvre, the Bibliothèque Doucet, La
Direction de l'Architecture, the *Mercure de France*, Librarie Giraud-
Badin, Paris; the Musée Rimbaud, Charleville; the British Museum,
London; the *Illustrated London News* and the S.P.A.D.E.M.

Tourrettes-sur-Loup, France   L. H.
1957   E. M. H.

Verlaine: Fool of God

1.

THE CHILD

1844-1851

In what is now the Belgian Luxembourg is a village named Verlaine. In the centuries before the French Revolution the village was a part of northern France. In it lived the forebears of the poet. The family was not, so far as can be known, a part of the small but noble family which occupied the chateau in the hilly woods surrounding the village. It may have been connected with the Sieurs de Verlaine, but the probability is that the name came into common use when the family moved from the village, and the father, living for the first time near strangers with the same Christian name, discovered the necessity of a surname. This at least accounts for the origin of many hundreds of surnames and there is no reason to suppose that the Verlaines differed from others.

At all events, by the time this particular family entered the period of firm records in the late eighteenth century, it had settled in and about the village of Arville, still in the Ardennes but south of its name place. It was an unremarkable family of peasant farmers and small shopkeepers, with its counterpart by the thousand in every province of France; pious, hard-working, close, neither rich nor poor, respectable if at times given to heavy drinking, but so insignificant that one forgets that if these people never made history they allowed history to be made, since without them there would have been no France.

Insignificant the Verlaines indubitably were. There is a mention of one as student in the University at Luxembourg, then silence. Over them rolled wars, revolts, revolutions, but imperturbable, hard-faced, sparing of speech except in their cups, they cultivated their land, built and rebuilt their houses and shops, married, gave birth, sowed and harvested, sold their wares, saved every sou, attended Mass, and above all remained unshakeably ordinary, their small ambitions driving them almost imperceptibly to form an unthinking, inarticulate part of the *petit bourgeois*. One man fought in the Army but went back to the land and it was left to his son Henri to be the first Verlaine to make a small name for himself. He broke family tradition by setting up a lawyer's office in the large village of Bertrix, also in the Ardennes but some miles south of Arville, but for the rest he seems to have been a somewhat shifty (or politic) individual blowing hot and cold before the years of the Revolution much as he alternated between bouts of drinking and religionism. In the last years of his life, however, Henri Verlaine revealed, besides an ability to butter his bread, an unexpected sense of principle. The success of the Revolution swung him once and for all to the side of the people. When Napoleon seized power the *notaire* of Bertrix denounced him as a traitor: at first in the family circle; then, in 1804, indignation overwhelming caution, publicly. Critics of the new Emperor, however obscure, were marked men. Henri Verlaine was haled summarily to Luxembourg, the juridical center of the Ardennes, but died before he could be brought to trial.

His father's defiant end did not, it seems, greatly impress his one son Nicolas, not at least in the way one would prefer. This boy was destined to make a furor in the family that rendered his father's departure from precedent a bagatelle. In due course (he was only six when his father died), he was put into the office at Bertrix but did not like the little he saw of the law. In company with most of the lads of France at that time he worshipped the all-conquering Emperor, and in 1814, before his seventeenth birthday, he abandoned the office, ran away and enlisted.

The moment was scarcely propitious—Nicolas, like his father, was given to periods of "naïve folly" (which could, however, be more charitably described)—for within a year Napoleon had been finally beaten at Waterloo, the French Army humbled, Louis XVIII thrust uncertainly on the throne and (one minor result of the great man's collapse) the entire Verlaine family found itself on foreign soil when the canton of Bouillon, which included all their villages, was taken into the newly formed Kingdom of the Netherlands.

But Nicolas, again like his father, was ambitious and could rise to occasions. He rose to this one. He chose French nationality and decided, unlike his grandfather, to make his career in the Army, defeated and disorganized though it was. So well did he acquit himself that by 1828 he had won a commission in the Engineers. He was one of the first of the "rankers" whose appearance was an early sign of the social revolution of the century.

By this time Charles X was in the last stages of his brief, inglorious reign. Two years later came the mild revolution. France was once again "respectable" under the innocuous Louis Philippe, being governed by and for the upper middle class—few in numbers but making money with a scarcely decent speed—and the least reputable remnant of the aristocracy. It was an age of factories, experimental railways, excessively romantic poets and novelists; of a Paris given over on the surface(if the behavior of the elite was to be taken as guide) to gossip about the latest amours, clothes and manners; at the core, to the building and ostentatious spending of fortunes by the businessmen; and underneath, to the mutters of the "Reds" as they were called, making and collecting arms and biding their time. Not perhaps so respectable as the other European powers persisted in seeing it and certainly not "safe" but on the whole extremely dull and utterly undistinguished—a combination which can be mistaken easily enough for respectability. Her Army, outwardly respectable too, had accepted its new role of keeper of order within the reduced frontiers; it did not forget Napoleon. But Nicolas was in a fair way to forgetting his origins; he did not precisely state that he had gone through the Ecole Polytechnique yet he did not discourage the impression.

He did in truth cut an excellent figure. He was an upright man in every sense, well turned out, with a distinguished air. He was an efficient if not brilliant soldier, and at the soirees and balls of the garrison towns he must have seemed, to admiring girls, far removed from the popular idea of the enlisted man as a coarse upstart. Though ambitious and more than a trifle snobbish he was governed in many things by native caution. When, after serving with credit under Cavaignac in Algeria and at the regular garrison towns and having reached the rank of Captain Adjutant-Major, he finally married, the match was in every way sensible; indeed it was more, it was happy. He did not go outside his class but chose from the most prosperous part of it, the small manufacturers then springing up all over the North of France. The family of Dehée had originated, like the Verlaines, as peasant proprietors but around Fampoux in the Pas-de-Calais, that flat bare country whose dead straight roads lined with poplars, under wide and windy skies, contrast so violently with the terrain of the Ardennes. Their advance had been slightly the more practical since they had preferred hard cash to the social advantages of the law; they made the land work for them, setting up sugar beet factories to serve their great center of Arras.

Arras was one of the regular garrison towns, and there Nicolas Verlaine met Stéphanie Dehée. They made an eminently suitable, if not a striking couple. Nicolas, then in his thirties, was tall, rigid, clean-shaven but for the small mustache which was accepted then as military fashion; a notable figure in the brave colors of that day, with two clear blue eyes looking out of a hard, closely cut oval head. Every inch an Army man perfectly describes him; he was almost as stupid as most, as brave, quite as conventional, rather more honest and perhaps a shade kindlier. He may even have concealed unsuspected depths, as they are called, beneath that impassive exterior, but if so they remained concealed for the rest of his life. He was what he seemed, an occasional irrational impulse excepted.

Altogether he made a much more impressive figure than his wife. Stéphanie was far from beauty: her brown eyes were set at too acute a slant, her face was too long, her chin too heavy and her black hair no more than adequate. She was above medium height, slim, retiring, and would scarcely earn a second look in any company: not an obvious catch. But Captain Verlaine was in essence, whatever his trappings, a peasant; plain Stéphanie might be, and insignificant, but she cared for him and if her show of love was inclined to excess she remained respectable, she had manners which were almost too good, and she brought with her a substantial dowry, very substantial for her position in life. Indeed, since he too had been careful, the pair began life together with more than a sufficiency of money.

Appearances are not everything, and one wonders whether the Captain realized what lay behind the demure, not to say dull, exterior of his wife. His marriage to Stéphanie at the end of 1831 was, affection apart, a good piece of business; her marriage to him was, for a woman of such a family, a step in the dark, a delightful adventure. For she, stuffed with the romantic novels of the day (sprung up to counteract prosaic reality), lived one long dream in the big house at Fampoux. With a little more daring, a little less conscience and a lot more sexual attraction she could have become another Madame Bovary; as it was, true product of her not very happy age, she dreamed of romance, seized it when it appeared to have come miraculously her way and then spent much of her time inventing explanations for its habit of slipping through her fingers. Her husband in his regimentals was no doubt a cut above poor dingy Charles Bovary, and the frequent moves from one garrison town of France to another, the color and romance of parades and displays, not to speak of the occasional rumor and the ever living possibility of real action, all provided the adventurous element that this overnourished soul, like Emma Bovary, craved for and that the Captain, brought down to essentials, was incapable of satisfying.

On the surface all was well, all exemplary. If beneath her calm a certain mild restlessness persisted, Stéphanie was too much a creature of her station to reveal it. She remained a loving and dutiful wife, a good hostess in a conventional and somewhat embarrassingly ladylike way—a manner which did her no disservice in an age of parvenus when France, recoiling from revolution and dictatorship, presented to the world a front compounded of all the bourgeois virtues. The Verlaines in their small and limited way moved in an aura of approval; their teas and soirees were impeccably dull, their quarters filled with the appropriate knicknacks, they represented that most stable and satisfying of sights, the domesticated soldier. If they were not civilized in any real sense of the word, if they were three-quarters dead and their life all but purposeless, they would be the last to suspect it. Behind that façade which stood for France in the thirties and forties stirred all the dissatisfactions from hunger to intellectual disgust. But who would have guessed it? Not the Verlaines, not the circles in which they moved. There mild gossip and flirtation, incessant speculation about promotion, the regular bustle of transfer from one station to another every year or so made up a life that they and all about them found good, useful and indeed indispensable.

Yet all was not well even in this domesticated paradise. Stéphanie was dutiful and loving but her husband was eleven years her senior and physically almost inarticulate, so she was driven to invent her romance about him. Her son tells the story, which could be true, of Captain Verlaine, who did not always enjoy the best of tempers, opening the window of their dining room and ejecting an omelette as unfit to be eaten. His wife chose to think, dared not think otherwise in fact for fear of being thought dull, that this was an unconventional signal to another woman. The thought and her consequent agitation made her almost happy for a time. Thus her true passion (vocation it cannot be called) necessarily rose elsewhere. Passion would seem an incongruous word to use of this mild if pleasing nobody, this weak though amiable woman looking up to her ramrod of a husband, delighting in insipidities. But passion is the feeling that ruled the frail vessel. She revealed herself as maternal, above all. In this solitary capacity she was rare if not unique; she hungered for children with an intensity, a single-mindedness, that makes nonsense of a Florence Nightingale. Maternity, like all that runs to excess, can be a disease and in this Stéphanie was diseased.

It would be reassuring to think that she had intimations of greatness but in truth the poor woman simply wanted children, as many as possible and as soon as possible. They would, of course, all of them be unusual but their mere existence was the thing. This she had persuaded herself was her life's adventure, to bear them and to live through them an exciting and colorful life. There were, as there must always be, chinks in this self-protective armor. To satisfy oneself vicariously is no true answer to the demands that rise in every living being. Stéphanie was to "break out" from time to time in her own limited fashion. But as long as she had no children she could always believe that children were the answer.

And she had none. She conceived but she could not bear. Three times she miscarried and brought forth a dead child. Frantic in her mild way, she worshipped what she had brought forth. She could not bear to part with it. She preserved the foeta in spirits and, with them always before her in her room, lived as best she could the insubstantial relationship of mother and three children. Sterile she was not and that thin comfort she hugged to herself as she gazed surreptitiously but ardently at the bottles ranged in order of birth.

By this time she was thirty. Hope dwindled. Some live child she must have. She looked about. She had not far to seek; a sister had died leaving a boy and a girl to the care of a drunken indifferent father. Madame Verlaine adopted her little niece Elisa Moncomble.

This was in 1842. Elisa, eight years old, settled down happily and the family seemed at last complete. Madame Verlaine did not precisely lose hope of a child of her own—that was beyond her simplicity—but for the first time she felt something approaching the resignation that the Church had so long enjoined on her.

It was at this moment that she conceived for the fourth time.

And on March 30, 1844, she gave birth to her first and only live child, a boy who was christened Paul Marie.

The Verlaine family was then in Metz. It could have been in Montpellier, Arras or any other of the garrison towns. Nevertheless, it was of Metz that the boy and man was to think, talk and write with a fervor which has often been criticized as insincere. Verlaine was to invite such criticisms by willful though good-natured exaggerations to please an audience, but this feeling for his birthplace was neither excessive nor unbelievable; he spent his first two years in Metz and the years from five to seven, two vital periods for a child as observant and as affectionate as he; there he had his first love affair, there he first made friends, there he was something of a regimental pet. Of this place alone he was to have nothing but happy memories.

The other small years, of three and four, were spent at Montpellier in the South; the one really notable event there being that which brought them to an end—the flight of Louis Philippe, the proclamation of the Second Republic and the three-day massacre of May, when Cavaignac and his troops killed three thousand "Reds" (a convenient name even then) at the barricades, taking no prisoners. The regiment was recalled to Metz where the small boy enjoyed three blissful years before his father abruptly left the service—blissful not only for the reasons given above but also because the young Paul enjoyed absolutely uninhibited admiration and love at home. His mother inevitably worshipped him—this abused word is strictly relevant here—but with a gentle whole-heartedness and abandon that must have surprised even her husband: Paul was perfect, Paul could do no wrong, he was to be sheltered from every unpleasantness, to know only the best of an imperfect world.

All this could be foreseen in theory though not (and repetition is necessary in view of the future) in its unbalanced fact. But Elisa allied herself spontaneously with the adoring mother. This little girl who had enjoyed two years as the darling of the family might well have resented the newcomer. But not at all; she was an exceptionally nice child and a loving one though not perhaps very wise, and she abetted Madame Verlaine in spoiling the child with a thoroughness that ought to have proved disastrous; whether it did so in the long run must be left to the judgment of the reader. She welcomed a playmate who could also be treated as a living doll and she took up the role of second mother in a spirit of self-dedication and fervent love.

One would expect the victim of this twofold maternal assault to show early and unfavorable signs of it. Yet the truth is that the child Paul, doted on and protected to a near maniacal degree, was decidedly and deservedly popular. He did not take this popularity at second hand; his father had always been too reserved to be really well liked, his mother too insignificant in mind and public manner. He did not owe it to his beauty, for he had none. He was not perfect and he could do wrong with an ease, but he was outstandingly good-natured, he had next to no pride, he was never puffed up and for all his lack of good looks—to a point because of it—he possessed what has from time immemorial overridden the powers of physical beauty—a potent charm. No one has yet satisfactorily defined charm and doubtless it springs from different causes in different people. In Paul Verlaine, child, boy and man, it came explicably from a finely made body, an intriguing face, a lively sense of humor, a remarkable absence of conceit (which means the showing of a true interest in the affairs of others), an impish disregard of ceremony and at times even decency, and from a warm and generous nature— all this, and even more from a something on which one cannot lay a finger, a personality, a soul, call it what you will.

So, in the years 1848 to 1851, there was this small boy lording it lovingly over his mother and cousin, a little restrained by the occasional awe with which he regarded that undemonstrative man his father, but essentially no prig, not precocious, not anything in particular but a nice playful child. Yet even in these early years the shape of the man is to be seen plainly in the manner of the child's reception of devotion. For there are ways and ways: one can accept demonstrations of love without thought, with gratitude, in humility, as one's right, for instance, and one can return it or not return it as the case may be in a hundred different styles all indicative of the future. Paul did not give much thought to the matter but he reveled in the caresses he was freely offered and he returned them with a softly rapturous, dedicated yet curiously detached air. He was warm-hearted, as we say, and more than that. It is not in French children actively to dislike food, but there are degrees in this too; Paul relished food as he relished the caresses and could scarcely have enough of either. This could be dismissed as greed and no doubt there was something of that in his raptures; but what must strike anyone who examines the records of his childhood is the evidence of a strongly sensuous nature; even so early he had begun consciously to distinguish degrees of sensation and to respond to each with the appropriate alacrity. Not for him the love of the spirit; his bond was the flesh, the tangible and present. None, one might think, could adore it more; perhaps few could; but his distinction lay not in that but in his perception of its, and his, limitations.

In retrospect one can distinguish clearly the seeds of both poet and profligate, yet poetry and the life that the poet was eventually to lead seem far removed indeed from that protected, adored yet apparently ordinary child taking the air day after day on the fashionable Esplanade of Metz with the Rhine flowing below, the outward center of his and everybody else's world in that town; a child made much of, at ease even in first love, conscious of popularity but unspoiled by it. No wonder that he was to look back to that time with nostalgia. Not all, perhaps not many, are so blessed; and—but of this Paul Verlaine was incapable of thinking—not many have so well deserved it.

2.

THE BOY

1851-1862

[1]

Captain Verlaine's retirement from the Army though apparently sudden was inevitable (the man being what he was) from the moment in December, 1848 when Louis Napoleon was elected President of the Republic. By 1851 the whole of France and many outside France had come to realize that Louis Napoleon had no intention of giving up the presidency at the end of his four-year term; that, on the contrary, he would almost certainly try to establish himself as Emperor. Though the countries surrounding France regarded such a possibility with alarm and anger, most of the French people, disappointed with the vacillating and unspectacular record of the Republican government and still nourishing its memories of Napoleonic triumphs and grandeurs, were willing, were even anxious for the great man's nephew to try to restore greatness (as they saw it) to their country. But there were exceptions, distinguished ones. Cavaignac was such a man; he distrusted Louis Napoleon as a politician and despised him as a soldier; an old-fashioned patriot, he could see nothing but disaster for France if either the common man (epitomized by the Reds) or the careerist (in the person of Louis Napoleon) held power. He had tried to prevent Louis Napoleon from reëntering France after the abdication of Louis Philippe, and when this failed he fought him in the Assembly and stood against him as rival candidate for the presidency. But Cavaignac had a bad record; the "May massacre" alone had earned him the hatred of every Parisian working man and woman, every Communist throughout the large towns; he was rejected.

Captain Verlaine's retirement has been explained as pique on account of being passed over in the most recent batch of promotions. This certainly explains a part of the man: the soldier's stiff pride, based on an awareness of social and educational inferiority, taking offense. But the true interest lies not so much in his reaction to the event as in the reason for it. He was not passed over because of any failing as a soldier or (in the larger view) as patriot but simply because he was a Cavaignac man and would not declare for Louis Napoleon. Captain Verlaine's superior officer, Major Niel, thought much of him and urged him to change his mind; but Niel, like most of the Army, was solidly for Louis and was years later to become War Minister under him. The Captain refused; he had worshipped Napoleon as a boy, he had admired and served under Cavaignac as a man; he could not or would not transfer his allegiance a third time even for a Napoleon. So at fifty-three, abandoning the prospect of several years' profitable service, he retired to Paris; he had money, he had health and a small but devoted family; his principles would seem to have let him off more lightly than most.

A few months later, toward the end of November, the young Paul heard indignant mutters of "coup d'état" coming from the room in which his father entertained his friends, and soon afterwards the long-anticipated stroke took place and France once more had a Napoleon as Emperor. The event seemed to have made no difference to the Verlaine household; Captain Verlaine was not among the few, exhorted by Victor Hugo, who raised the barricades again in the name of liberty; he confined his opposition to verbal fireworks with like-minded Army men who had settled near him.

But Madame Verlaine, caught in a moment of dissatisfaction which was ready to show itself in any convenient guise, had read and listened with increasing excitement; increasing frustration too, because this moment of history with all its blood and splendor appeared only too likely to be passed by the Verlaines in their drawing room. It became clear that her husband would not move a step and was blind to adventure on his very doorsill. Madame Verlaine "broke out"; early in the afternoon of December 4, the day of the barricades, she left the peace and security of her house in the Batignolles, that suburb of high respectability stuffed with retired Army men, and began to walk eagerly downhill.

She was not alone; she took with her the eight-year-old Paul. They reached the Boulevard des Italiens just before three o'clock. From there or from one of the neighboring boulevards Madame Verlaine hoped that they might obtain a view of the fighting at the barricades to the south. Many others had had a similar thought; the street was crowded, the shop doors and apartment windows looking south were a mass of eager faces. Parading the street too were Canrobert's troops, but peacefully in this middle-class district of good repute. The one sign of troop-baiting was the occasional cry of Ratapoil! from some politically minded member of the crowd. Paul took up the cry—he had no idea of its meaning but liked the sound of the word—and his mother laughed at the childish treble piping out sedition. But she was a little alarmed too, and took him as quickly as she could into the Boulevard Montmartre where the crowds were thick. Too thick for comfort, in fact, and they moved on again, threading a way through the people massed in street and on walks alike, but had not gone more than a few paces down the Boulevard Poissonière when Paul, a timid child, took fright: the character of the crowd was changing as they moved eastward; it was rougher and it sang the Marseillaise and other revolutionary songs.

Paul had heard the Marseillaise sung in the streets once before, at Montpellier when the Republic was proclaimed, but this second outburst sounded threatening and alarmed him. As quickly as they were able, he and his mother retreated hand in hand to the respectable watchers of the Boulevard des Italiens. But no sooner had they returned than shots suddenly rang out. One or two soldiers fell. In an instant the street became a battleground; the soldiers returned the fire and killed outright some fifty civilians—the famous "massacre" of December 4.

Paul, too small even to see a soldier, shared the panic which seized all the survivors. The street was black with a struggling mass trying to escape in all directions: men, horses, filled carriages mixed inextricably in a shouting, screaming mob. At last the mother and child, carried on a wave of people, were sucked through the open doorway of a large store and into the half darkness beyond. There they remained willy-nilly, listening to the shouts and the galloping of horses as the troops cleared the street. Then all was quiet and they walked the long way home, shaken but cheerful too. Paul at an early age was thus given a view of politics which, happy-go-lucky though he was, he was not likely to forget. More importantly, the adventure demonstrated that the "protected" life of this child had its limitations. He was indulged in food, in caresses and, when his father was not about, which was often, in behavior; but he was always at the mercy of that despotic and disconcerting master, the romantic temperament. Here it had led his doting mother to subject her darling to obvious physical danger; in the future the danger was to be less obvious and he was not to escape so easily.

The grayness of Paris at first depressed the boy's spirits as it has depressed many; then, again in conformance with the majority, he saw its beauty and felt its charm. It was a Paris on the eve of considerable and beneficial change. Within two years of Paul's arrival Haussmann was appointed Préfet of the Seine and forthwith began the extensive pulling down and rebuilding that changed the face of Paris. By 1855, the year of the first Louis Napoleon Exposition, when Paul was a schoolboy of eleven, the grand new boulevards were already taking shape before the admiring eyes of visiting foreigners. Notre Dame and the Hôtel de Ville had been set free from clustering houses (whose narrow streets had been an invitation to the throwing up of barricades by the dissatisfied); the Bois laid out; the Louvre, the Palais de Justice and Saint-Chapelle completed and restored. On his walks with his parents—he and his mother in particular were great walkers—the boy must often have seen the fine new Boulevard de Strasbourg, which ran wide, straight and handsome through the old streets from the Gare de l'Est to the Châtelet.

The adult Verlaine nowhere comments on the work of Haussmann—a good unthinking bourgeois would be expected to approve of it—but something in him, something contrary to upbringing, common sense and even safety, retained a fondness for the old, narrow, twisty streets and ramshackle houses that at first had depressed him. The difference between his vision and the vision of a thousand other boys lay in this, that what he saw, one visual image after another, and what he felt (and he early gave proof of extreme sensibility) did not slip into the customary oblivion. The images were conventional enough up to a point, as he was to show—mist over the river, crowded rooftops, glaring gaslit cafés and the like—but the most lasting and most typical invariably concerned the look and behavior of the people and particularly of his reaction to them. He was, in short, during these next years building up an intensely personal and poetic reaction to life.

But no one except his infatuated parents and cousin would have believed such a thing to be possible. He was to all appearances so ordinary a boy, his one noticeable characteristic, besides the passion for physical pleasure, being a not very unusual shyness that showed from time to time in his almond-shaped eyes—eyes which were evi-, dently of an indefinite color, being variously described as blue, green, gray and brown.

Essentially he gave every outward sign of an unremarkable child whose affectionate nature alone afforded some excuse for the raptures of the family circle. Who, one might wonder, would have been other than unremarkable reared on food and love and generalities in that well-kept house in the orderly rue Saint-Louis (now rue Nollet) which looked down on Paris with a certain condescension? Such rare boys do exist and Paul was to meet the most remarkable of all, but Paul was not apparently of this kind. He leaned literally and metaphorically on the bosoms of his womenfolk and the decrees of his father. He enjoyed the cosiness, adored the calm and the raptures alike and accepted happily the comforting sense of security.

This sheltered, respectable existence was barely touched when with many a sigh from his mother and Elisa he was sent to school. The ordeal, which began early in the year following the December coup d'état at the insistence of Captain Verlaine (the boy's perpetual questions wearied him, he said), was in truth not severe since the school was no farther from home than the rue Hélène, and its single unpleasantness, as Verlaine recalled, was the startling sight of the master in tears after the death of his daughter. The round of Verlaine life continued: the rush home to the last stages of the afternoon receptions, with Madame Verlaine in her invariable black dispensing cakes and emotional but meaningless conversation; to the long, substantial meals decorously devoured, the scent of cigar smoke floating up to his bedroom at night with the occasional male laugh; and not least the visits to the many relatives, of the mother at Fampoux and neighboring villages, and of the father at Paliseul and Bouillon, where the boy was fed enormously and cosseted as befitted the little Parisian Verlaine with the amiable smile. He loved every moment of it, the petting, the rich food, the airless overfurnished rooms, even (for he was no country child) the heavy scent of the hay under the spare sun of the Pas-de-Calais, the sough of the trees in the Ardennes—loved and cherished it.

Scarcely a cloud disturbed the sunshine under which he lived; the nearest he ever came to a rebuff being his father's occasional sharp petulance when he still tried to acquire knowledge at home, his mother's too hasty offer of cake or confection if he turned to her, and Elisa's pained face after he had been caught in some petty deceit. He had therefore to think his own thoughts and conceal his peccadilloes the more carefully. All else was a sheer and mostly sensuous joy which extended uncritically to his regard for the outside world. All men, his mother held with an inherited optimism that verged on the credulous, were good and were to be treated as such. And to him as a child this must have seemed no more than obvious truth; it was to become second nature, a lovable, pathetic, ineradicable fallacy.

But he was growing in every sense and quickly. Within scarcely more than a year he had grown out of the little school in the rue Hélène; while he was ready to rest on his oars if given half a chance, his capacity for understanding and assimilating what he heard and his promise of a prodigious memory made him a formidable pupil even in spite of himself.

There were further family consultations. Captain Verlaine announced his decision to a shocked and unbelieving circle: Paul must go to a boarding school, prepare himself for a career. What shape the career was to take remained vague, Madame Verlaine inclining to the engineering profession, the Captain favoring the civil service and the boy wanting, so little did he know himself, to follow his father.

Nine-year-old Paul started off in character, gaily, proud of his new cap, filled with optimism; he would love all, all would love him. He was escorted by the family—hand in hand, an imaginative biographer declares. The Captain was unlikely to have lent himself to such an embarrassing demonstration, but in spirit the boy was unquestionably borne on the sad journey by three pairs of hands, even perhaps by four, since Elisa's brother Victor was then staying with the Verlaines. The walk was familiar to all, being one of Paul's favorites, along the Boulevard des Batignolles to the Place de Clichy, down the rue Ballu with a right and left turn—no more than fifteen minutes from the rue Saint-Louis; and the house they entered was familiar too, at least the ornate gold lettering on large black boards outside announcing the presence behind the high wall of the Institution Landry which prepared pupils for courses at the Lycée Bonaparte, for the *baccalauréat* and so on. Paul, chatting away on earlier walks, had, in effect, sealed his own doom for, impressed by the "pompous façade," he declared that if ever he had to go to school it must be to that one. His parents took him at his word. Again, however, his lot was less hard than it might have been; he was not only comfortably close to his home, he was granted the unusual privilege of being allowed to spend every Sunday there.

The rue Chaptal was to have another claim to fame—in the Goupil gallery there, managed by Theo van Gogh, was to come a few years later that message from the Louvre scrawled in chalk: "I'm here. Vincent"—but it is unlikely that Monsieur Landry would have conceded that; the Institution Landry was, in effect, its own raison d'être; he proudly indicated the roll of honor with Sainte-Beuve heading the distinguished list of past pupils. The roll remained incomplete; why should not the name of this latest little boy be added in due course? The good man did not know how woefully his polite gesture was to fall short of the truth, but his visitors were no doubt pleased and two at least would not have accused him of exaggeration.

But the partings had to be made and the boy—very small then— left to face the disadvantages of an arrival at school in midterm and halfway through the day. He was put temporarily in a class of older boys. The boys were not pleased and made their displeasure plain as boys do. By supper time Paul was in tears, every illusion shattered for the moment. The supper, which was neither better nor worse than a thousand such, was so far removed from the repasts of the rue Saint-Louis both in content and presentation that his wretchedness reached the pitch of action. The day boys trooped out after the meal was done. He joined himself to them as casually as he was able, then ran for home, hatless, breathless, beside himself.

There were no reproaches—one suspects that the Paul-less family was experiencing too much guilt and sorrow of its own to feel anything but rapturous relief. His mother flung her arms around him (the escapade was after her own heart), Elisa petted him, and he was set at table where they were sitting down to a meal of special delicacy with an extra glass of good wine to round it off.

After the meal his father (restrained until then by an unusually dominant Madame Verlaine) had his say. It was mild, its burden being the call of duty; but it was adequate and the boy, aflare with optimism again, was led back willingly the next morning by his cousin Victor who symbolized all the military virtues in his spotless uniform and erect bearing.

[2]

From this moment the Verlaine family passed into the background
of Paul's life. It formed an important background, from the ever
present awareness of its existence to the tangible Sunday reunions,
from the loving missives of the women to the daily appearance of
the Captain at school, producing invariably from a capacious
pocket some tempting or solid tidbit saved from the previous night's
dinner to supplement a school diet which he feared was insufficient
for a rapidly growing boy; but a background it remained. Paul, put
into a class of boys of his own age, quickly flourished—he was,
astonishingly, neither crybaby nor bumptious little beast—and, as
man can acknowledge only one good at a time, unconsciously allowed
his home to recede to second place; that nightmare of a false beginning at school did not so much vanish from his mind (he forgot
little) as drift equally into memory; he could laugh at it while
retaining an authentic vision of unhappiness.

In a boy so enviably gifted as to nature, failings were bound to
show themselves. It soon appeared that he could be swayed easily
from almost any purpose—one had only to appeal to his good nature.
He also had, as might be expected, a passion for popularity and could
be made instantly and desperately wretched by a cold shoulder.
Fortunately for him that rare combination, charm and a good heart,
carried him almost unscathed through the first year or so. After that,
all was easy: he was consistently cheerful, laughed easily and without
malice, was only too malleable and, a certain physical timidity apart,
a "good sport." He was also refreshingly generous, showing not the
faintest awareness of the value of money (or could it be that in his
feckless unwisdom he had stumbled on its true value?), which prime
preoccupation of the French nation had never asserted itself more
vigorously than in those palmy days of the mid-nineteenth century.
And if his credulity and good nature were frequently taken advantage
of, he reacted so amicably that he soon escaped the attentions of the
bully. He was in any event a big boy and strong, even if he had no
idea how to use his strength, and was not quite the guileless child
he appeared to be and sometimes liked to make out he was; this gave
him a secret pleasure well known to the young and harmless enough
if it goes no farther.

Despite a ready yielding to every available distraction, the young

Paul at twelve found himself walking twice every weekday except
Thursdays in the long line of uniformed senior boys down the rue
Blanche, round the as yet unfinished church of the Trinité, along the
rue St.-Lazare to the rue Caumartin, through a "monumental"
doorway, between "not less monumental" fountains into the Lycée
Bonaparte (as it then was) where he listened, not always with rapt
attention (he had discovered among other things the charms of the
sketch and the caricature), to lectures on the classics, on history,
geography, physics, mathematics and philosophy. His companion on
these walks was more often than not a certain Edmond Lepelletier.
No two boys could have differed more profoundly; outwardly Lepelletier was one of those people who exist everywhere, changeless from
cradle to grave, without a very specific face; it could not be called
pleasant or unpleasant, being nothing and forgotten as soon as out
of sight; and the emotions that registered themselves on it were no
deeper than the reflection of moonshine on a rock; inwardly he was
cold, vain, ambitious, masterful and had in himself less of the poet,
speaking broadly, than one would have believed possible. His attraction for a Paul Verlaine, dreamy, warm-hearted, indecisive and
absolutely without pride, is obvious; add the facts that his parents
lived in the rue Lécluse, which Paul could see from his bedroom
window at home, and that Lepelletier's maternal grandfather and
paternal uncle were both Army men and the intimacy was inevitable.
Inevitable and for a time much to Paul's benefit; he needed a strong
hand and a sense of direction, his own enthusiasms veering madly to
every breeze; he had affection enough for two, though it must be said
that Lepelletier was a good friend according to his lights. Paul's
charm worked its usual magic, no doubt; nevertheless Lepelletier's
principles (and he was a youth and later a man of almost insuffer-
able rectitude) stood admirably against the many shocks that Paul
was to give them.

Lepelletier, we have said, had no face to speak of. Paul had so
much face that Madame Lepelletier, dispensing tea with thankful
glances from her son's face to that of his friend, declared afterwards
in the quiet of the family circle that she thought when Paul first
entered the room that an ape had escaped from the zoo. Paul's
face became an obsession of the Lepelletiers, and Lepelletier, writing
as an old man, was to describe with eloquent inaccuracy the embar-
rassments and limitations his dead friend's hideousness had brought
upon him. Expecting an ogre, the reader regards with some bewilder-

ment the photographs of this monster; he sees a massive forehead and beautifully shaped head, thick black eyebrows curving comically at the far end, long slanting eyes separated by a broad nose, high and wide cheekbones, a prominent chin, fine black waving hair. No beauty; no horror either.

Faunesque, Silenetic, Socratic—the similes have often been made. Is a faun, was Socrates or even Silenus repulsive? Paul Verlaine we know, having other and better witnesses than Lepelletier, as well as our own eyes, was decidedly not so. On the contrary he was, the first shock over, engaging. Naturally enough, since as always, in men at least, the expression is the thing and Paul's expression was essentially attractive. His schoolfellows did not run from him or avoid him any more than his grown friends were to do. They drew spirited caricatures of him, fish-faced, as a Turk, as a pigtailed Chinese, as a nightcapped philosopher stargazing with eyes so oblivious of worldly matters that he ignores the open drain at his feet; for the rest, they clustered around him, laughing at and with him, and took him for granted. What was a face but a heaven-sent invention to inspire caricatures and to differentiate a Fauré minor from a Fauré major? Mothers of course compared his looks gratefully with their sons' but men and boys did not give them a second thought.

Lepelletier bases his theory on Paul's visits to the brothels. Paul was a month or six weeks from his seventeenth or sixteenth birthday (the date is not clear) when, having collected the sum of ten francs, he invented a summons home one Saturday and was granted an exeat. Some time earlier (he is naturally not precise) he had been broken in to the sexual underlife of the school. Not unwillingly we must assume, most boys inclining to homosexuality and his own tastes being what they were. Not unwillingly but—and this is the only point that matters—with so little lasting satisfaction that one May evening he is found timidly but determinedly knocking at the discreetly closed door of a house recommended by an older pupil, sitting in the red salon and choosing his partner for the night with what sang-froid he could muster. Others whispered of it, handed thumbed books under the desk, but he . . . He was anything but a bold creature, but in this matter then and hereafter he was a veritable lion.

It is difficult to imagine where Lepelletier thought that Paul was to satisfy himself if not at the brothels; it was not, as he implies, that nice girls were so appalled by the Mongol face that the wretched young Verlaine was driven to the sordid. There was never any possibility that nice girls of that day would be allowed to grant such a favor even to an Adonis, let alone a schoolboy of sixteen. Lepelletier, as cold as a fish, could and did meet these girls freely. When Paul excused himself he thought the worst. Yet given Paul's initiation into sex, his discovery of an enormous appetite in this direction, and his upbringing, the brothels were inevitable.

If Verlaine is to be understood, his exhaustless enthusiasm for a life of sensation, of which this was merely an inevitable stage, must be accepted. Every form of bodily pleasure pleased him, preferably but not necessarily when he could share in it, the act and feeling, imagined or real, being the main point. And one form of pleasure led to another. The Frenchman is sexually adult because he is a connoisseur of good food and wine; to Verlaine all sensation was received like the good wine that partly at least had induced it; he had begun early and was to end only with death. He spoke about copulation as an Englishman might speak about the fragrance of his roses. He would in any case see only a difference of degree in physical pleasure. He was later to adopt from time to time the "naughty boy" attitude because he understood that it was expected of him and he was always obliging, but he was not truly conscious of doing anything but obeying a dominant and right impulse. He has often been called a child of impulse and so he was if it be remembered that the child was in some respects much more adult than any adult of his time, in some respects exceptionally gifted and in every respect extraordinarily sensitive.

He was, in short, a poet of life, and to condemn his life and to praise his work is to ignore the reality that the one depends absolutely on the other; had Verlaine been, as we say, a less self-indulgent man, had he not savored the flesh (which with him ranged impartially from a well-spread table to a companioned bed, from a scent to a sigh, from touch to sound) with a fresh and perceptive joy, he could not have written the poems famed and loved throughout the world, for they spring from the same source.

By the time he was eighteen the young man was a regular visitor to the brothels and loved them. He looked forward to a more respectable method of enjoying himself in due course, but for the moment he was contented. What, after all, were brothels for if not for such as he?

In another direction he had also progressed fast by the age of

eighteen. Here Lepelletier was a strong influence for good. Not
Lepelletier alone—Paul was far too convivial a soul to be satisfied
with a solitary friend—but he chiefly, because bent on knowledge
and, through knowledge, advancement. Verlaine sat at the feet of
the great preachers and reveled in their oratory, at the same time
dispassionately feeding himself with the atheistic *Force et Matière*
of Büchner, and toured the museums and churches—these last chiefly
to study the Delacroix frescoes. But books were the obvious high-
way to knowledge and the two boys read ravenously and discussed
their reading without end. In his fifteenth and sixteenth years,
haunting the Bibliothèque Sainte-Geneviève, Paul raced through a
great medley of French and foreign literature and ephemeral rubbish. The compulsory classics apart he devoured the novels from
Balzac to Dumas, the books of travel, the macabre stories then in
vogue from Hoffmann to Poe, the historians, the philosophers, the
literary critics, translations from English, Spanish and German, the
religious books of the East and anything else he could lay hands on.
And every week he called at the bookshop to collect the latest part
of *Les Misérables*. A rite, this, as much as an enjoyment, for Hugo
had become his god as he was the god of practically the whole of
literary and Republican France. His first poem, following custom,
was sent to the hero in exile; he was then in his fifteenth year and
prayed judgment on "this first step on the stormy path of poetry."

It is unlikely—Verlaine in later life supports the theory—that
even the schoolboy Paul truly sympathized with the writings of
Hugo, their romantic blustering was so much the antithesis of his
own quietly personal vision. But Hugo was then much more than
the grand *maître* of French letters, he stood as a voluble symbol of
freedom. From his nearby exile in Jersey the bull-like little man,
when he was not sleeping with every woman he could find (or who
could find him, for he was the most famous lover of the age),
directed a stream of words into France: abuse of *"le petit Napoléon,"*
novels, poems, plays, invocations to the people to rise and destroy
the tyrant, approval at once patronizing, pompous and fulsome of
literary productions by the younger writers at home. Marine Terrace
was the Mecca to which almost all rebels looked; and when a man
could not make the pilgrimage in person he sent his latest poem,
book, play, whatever it might be, to obtain the sanction of the
master. Not all, perhaps not many, were whole-hearted in this admiration—Hugo, though he tried his hand at everything, was in

truth gradually becoming passé, a relic of the romanticism of the eighteen-thirties—but all or almost all trod the path whatever they might privately think or do; a symbol, a center was necessary, and Hugo with a curious but not unknown mixture of greatness, adroitness, bullheaded sincerity and undisguised volte-face had planted himself where none could or would dare to try to pull him down. He had been a great poet in his day; he remained a great character, and the character had substituted itself for the lost genius.

The young Paul eagerly followed the general example. In a schoolboy this was understandable, in grown men less so unless the state of intellectual France is borne in mind. By 1860, when Paul was sixteen and reading for dear life, Louis Napoleon had established himself firmly, as it seemed, in his uncle's seat; the victory of the Crimea (for as such, remarkably, it was then widely seen) followed by his success of 1859 against the Austrians, to his own secret surprise, for he was no general, had enabled him to make a triumphal ride through Paris when he was for once widely acclaimed. Men walked and drove along the noble new boulevards spanning and encircling the city, their wives shopped at the grand new stores; men and women talked of and traveled in the new railways covering France, attended sumptuous performances of opera and ballet, gazed admiringly at the beginnings of the ornate Opéra rising close to the Boulevard des Italiens to take the place of its humbler and more tasteful predecessor, watched the crowds of foreigners sightseeing with gaping reverence, and pocketed their share of the money the visitors lavishly expended. Paris was great again, the center of the World. France was great and respected once more. Industry boomed, wealth was made, theatres, cafés, every kind of entertainment flourished. The Church, placated, looked with a kindly eye on the Emperor. Truly he had done much and well.

But there was another side to the picture. The beautification of the city, the popularization of France cost money. Prices rose, the masses were sweated, many starved. In 1860, the year of Louis' triumphal ride through Paris, the number of arrondissements was increased from twelve to twenty; the workers displaced by the Haussmann clearances of the center, who had made new homes on the outskirts, automatically became liable to municipal taxation—the main reason for the extension—although sharing none of the benefits. This caused an outcry which the Government ignored and made new enemies of the regime by the thousand. There was altogether too much gold watch chain; the vulgar display of wealth in the capital and chief towns was a constant offense to the tasteful, the hungry and the envious, and rumors not without foundation of corruption in high places roused bitterness. Orsini's attempt to assassinate Louis outside the Opéra in 1858 had even then expressed the hatred of thousands, and the victimization of the revolutionaries that followed it increased the already widespread detestation of the Emperor. Nor did art escape: painters and writers of a kind were patronized but the forward-looking were frowned on and from time to time persecuted. The year before the assassination attempt Flaubert had been prosecuted for publishing an immoral work, *Madame Bovary*; Baudelaire's *Fleurs du Mal* was proscribed and the author fined; Renan was soon to arouse the enmity of the Church with his *Vie de Jésus* and to be driven from his post. There followed naturally an alliance between the artist and the revolutionary; numerous anti-Louis pamphlets and underground newspapers appeared; journalists (including young writers of distinction) were thrown into prison year after year. Underneath the prosperity of France and the popularity of Louis the spirit of dissatisfaction, disgust and revolt grew; the France represented by fat shopkeepers, overdressed manufacturers and a debased section of aristocracy was not, in the eyes of the intellectual patriot, the true France, and her leadership of Europe inasmuch as she did so was false and alien to her spirit.

In an English school all but the pageantry and the battles would have passed over the heads of the boys. In a French school where boys are taught to think for themselves such blindness, or innocence if one prefers the term, was impossible. The Institution Landry seethed with revolutionary fervor, and the well worn sheets handed surreptitiously about the school were not often the "smut" so beloved of the adolescent but free-thinking pamphlets: calls, as violent as they were ineffectual, to political action; abuse of Louis and the Church which bolstered him; glorification of the depressed workers and the persecuted elite of art.

To this last all the school intellectuals instinctively attached themselves. To be a modern reader and writer was to be a revolutionary; it was as simple and as attractive as that. Lepelletier was one of the most voluble of the band, but the leader was another school friend of Paul's, Raoul Rigault, an alarming representative of the revolutionary leader in embryo, single-minded to the point of insanity, blind to compassion, stupid, cold to all and everything but an impracticable idea, caring neither for his own life nor for the lives of others.

To find Paul in this gallery is not without its amusing side. Had he followed his inclination he would have concentrated on the "smut," for he was developing an absolute passion for the obscene, with this difference from the other boys, that he would shout, not whisper, the words which gave him increasing delight. Unlike Lepelletier and Rigault, who, as their lives showed, were politically minded, he lived simply for and in his particular sensation of the moment; and, lazy and easily led as he was, the sensation originated more often than not in other minds. The appeal of the Church to such a nature is obvious; the ritual pleases the senses, the discipline soothes and fascinates the mind, the infallibility relieves the conscience from the distressing necessity of making a decision. To become antireligious, to become at all politically serious, was for him to mock himself. Nevertheless spurred on by a fanatical Rigault, a purposeful Lepelletier and a longing to agree with those he loved, he did so with a will: none hotter than he, none wilder in speech and writing. He enjoyed himself immensely playing at revolution with these rather frightening schoolboys who called themselves his friends. And in this spirit he read the blustering prose and verse of Victor Hugo; to this extent and no farther Hugo was "his god."

[4]

Paul's true gods were very different from Hugo whose verses he had read, like those of other poets, only in "chosen morsels"—the choice being that of the master or compiler of the textbooks used at school. One day however he saw lying on a chair, forgotten by its owner, a first edition of *Fleurs du Mal*. He read and reread the poems with astonishment; it was a measure of Baudelaire's obscurity at that time that to the bookworm Paul his name conveyed nothing. The meaning of the poems for the most part escaped him—an interesting commentary on his persistent innocence in the midst of carnal pleasures —but two characteristics at once impressed him, the sonorous music of the lines and their austerity. The appeal of the first was inevitable to one who was to become the most musical of poets, but that it was possible to combine this musicality with a monastic condensation, that the sensuous could at one and the same moment be ascetical amazed him; how much so can be imagined when one remembers

that the work of the popular poets of the day and the whole conception of poetry praised in school and discussed by the boys were of
highly romantic not to say sentimental ideas expressed either in florid,
excessively "poetic" language or in a lifeless classical style.

It is perhaps not stretching a point too far to compare the boy at
this moment with one who had much in common with him, and to
see him as a Coleridge—a Coleridge brought up on and revering the
eighteenth-century formalists and who was with Wordsworth to bring
reality and romance back to poetry in the *Lyrical Ballads* or, if one
prefers it so, to bring poetry back to earth and the common reader.
The comparison is far from exact, however; Coleridge had no *Fleurs
du Mal* to inspire him and in any case the *Lyrical Ballads* and *Fleurs
du Mal* are as different as the nations to which the authors belonged; the poetry to which each was the reaction was also of a very
different order. And Paul Verlaine was not then a Coleridge, he was
a schoolboy of sixteen who knew no more than that he had discovered something exquisitely pleasurable and a something that he
longed to imitate. Had he understood better the nature of what he
read he might have hesitated, but the full stature of Baudelaire was
only to be revealed to him later. He plunged on, therefore; for of
course he, like most of his companions, would be a poet or, to be
precise, a writer.

The immediate and more important effect of *Fleurs du Mal* was
to fix part of his mind on poetry and send him in search of other
modern poets. He was, thanks to his parents, a good though leisurely
walker accustomed to the drop down to the center of Paris and the
return upward pull—a good hour or more—as all in the nature of
the day's work. He now extended his range, exploring the islands
and the Left Bank until the city was known to him, and he began,
with Lepelletier, what he called his "book searchings" whenever he
had an afternoon off, tirelessly tramping the lanes and river bank,
dipping into all the stalls and bargain boxes outside book shops. It
was at a shop on the Quai Voltaire that he found, on his first "book
searching," a copy of Théodore de Banville's youthful *Cariatides*.
Paul's excitement at this discovery greatly exceeded his reception of
Fleurs du Mal and that accurately places the two poets, for *Cariatides*
presented no miracle to the boy beyond the miracle of its appearance
at that time and place. It was wonderful to him naturally but, as he
read and read until he knew the poems by heart, an entirely explic-
able wonder; the technical devices which made the merit of the

book, skillful though they were, were visible to an acute eye, and Paul's eye even at sixteen was in this matter acuity itself. Hence his excitement as he plumbed the not very great depths and made the book his own, whereas with *Fleurs du Mal* the much that was above his head tempted him for self-respect's sake to underrate it.

To *Cariatides* he added during later journeys but at the same shop the *Vignes Folles* of Albert Glatigny and the *Philoméla* of Catulle Mendès, and began to get a reasonably accurate picture of the work of the younger generation of poets. He was enchanted. Not much of that enchantment is felt today but in the early sixties Mendès and Glatigny seemed advanced, charming, spirited rebels with all manner of comprehensible merits to a boy who loved to praise, yearned to write and who had had intimations that there was more to poetry than met the eye in school books.

He built himself a small library of "moderns" as his walks ended more and more often at the quayside, moderns which included the *Poèmes antiques* and *Poèmes barbares* of Leconte de Lisle, the *Ensorcelée* of Barbey d'Aurevilly and the *Emaux et Camées* of Gautier and, inspired by his many heroes, wrote passable imitations of all in bursts of poetic industry that carried him pleasantly to his nineteenth year. He did other things, plenty of them, including school work when that became unavoidable; he planned and perhaps began to write (few fragments exist today) a series of historical dramas, impassioned and bloodthirsty, on the "wise" and "mad" Charles V and VI and on the two Louis XV and XVII, a fairy play, and, with Lepelletier, he really did complete the first act of a fierily Republican tragedy, the *Forgerons* with a working-man hero. In all, it could be said with fair accuracy that he spent the greater part of these days, weeks, months and years in pleasing himself, and of his pleasures the reading and writing of poetry most satisfied him. Yet this poetry cannot convey to the reader the raptures that it presumably gave him. He early discovered a facility for the writing of verse, he was clever in catching the tone of a particular hero when composing, but not a trace, not a suggestion of the great or even the good poet can be found. Here was no born genius breaking out of insignificance but a charming, decidedly lazy and quite remarkably sensuous young man sipping honey from a variety of flowers. The result is youthful and tedious; a game whose pleasures have long since passed.

[5]

He was at school, however, with an aim toward which poetry played next to no part—to obtain in due course the *baccalauréat* without which in his father's eyes, and in the eyes of all good Frenchmen, the long years of schooling would be so much money thrown away. In that elaborately written parchment with its great seal and flowing signatures, its gold leaf and grandiose wording, was the order, tradition, rectitude, respectability so dear to the French heart, and (almost as though the prospect had been reduced to this) the entree to the civil service.

How reconcile the *baccalauréat* and all that was to follow with Paul Verlaine reading and writing poetry with a silent fury? It is not difficult. He was above all things amenable to suggestion; the line of least resistance (provided that it did not promise unpleasantness of any kind) was the line he favored. If asked why he gave so much time to poetry he would probably have replied that it pleased him. He would be a poet if he did not become playwright first, but that was not antipathetic to a safe job, a snug home and all the amenities; in the Paris of that time it could almost have been considered de rigueur. On the other side was the ugly vision of poverty, mean living, strife, even starvation, from which he averted his eyes with an incredulous shudder. Everything had become respectable—that was Louis Napoleon's achievement—and the arts not least. Had one suggested to Paul that he read or wrote poetry because he must, that it was as essential to him as the food and the embraces he loved, and that he would suffer for it, he would have laughed with that rather gruff engaging laugh of his. He a martyr to art! The thought was grotesque.

The *baccalauréat* therefore appeared a boring but essential stage toward security, the preservation of respectability and the perpetuation of all the pleasures including the composition of poetry, drama and anything else that came into the head in one's spare moments. There would be plenty of these moments, of course, because whoever's will prevailed as to the exact nature of his future—his father's, mother's or his own—the result would be a sinecure. And on August 16, 1862, having submitted himself to examination, he was duly granted the status of a Bachelor of Letters and, having to wait for

some months for the official diploma and being in any case wishful
to rest after unprecedented labors, withdrew himself, as soon as he
had secured Monsieur Landry's consent, to the supposed peace and
quiet of his relatives in the North.

In later years Verlaine, following custom, made light of his
passage through the examination; if he is to be believed, a combination of luck and cheek pulled him through. In fact, he is not to
be believed; every statement he makes about himself has to be taken
with a large grain of salt. His sense of humor and modesty are both
more English than French; the truth is there often enough but not
often the truth he would have the reader or listener believe. The joke
if carried to extremes can become a disease, and Verlaine's passion for
self-denigration was not far removed from this; it was a childish trait
he never threw off. In this case, though there is a considerable element of luck in every form of examination, a study of the questions
and of the fate of many of his companions, including Lepelletier,
and the "cramming" they found necessary before sitting again makes
clear that merit played its part and no mean part in his success. In a
letter of the time he tells a cousin that he is working very hard and
there is no reason to doubt it. Lucky he may have been, lazy he
certainly was, but only to the extent that he was sufficiently clever
to afford to be so; a fact borne out by the certificate from Landry
which shows him to have been one of the most promising pupils in
the school.

These questions needless to say did not concern him in the
least; he was conscious of virtue and of the reward that should follow
it; he was not averse to acting the successful city nephew and cousin
before admiring relatives; and by the late summer he was in the
North.

3.

THE YOUNG MAN

1862-1865

[1]

The boy who was soon lounging about the fields and farms and small factories of the Pas-de-Calais, then lying in the woods and fishing in the streams of the Ardennes, had turned six feet and was, for one so indolent, robust-looking, with an upright and beautifully proportioned body. Mentally he could have stood as symbol of ten thousand other boys of his kind; more amiable than most, perhaps, certainly gentler, but in essence a true product of his time and class and upbringing—the perfect young *petit bourgeois* with all the virtues and limitations of the species. His one ambition was to enjoy a good time; he was conventional, impractical, emotional and, if his words were to be accepted literally, hopelessly sentimental. He seemed bound for a blameless and utterly useless life.

Yet he was in reality neither all he appeared nor all he wished to be, and his future, could he have foreseen it, would have appalled him. The bourgeois in him, fostered so sedulously by his mother and father and by every recognizable desire in himself, was to be countered by the peasant heritage. Apparently he was his mother's son; actually he was to look back more and more, for good and ill, to his paternal grandfather and his forebears.

This did not mean, however, that he was a countryman *manqué* as Lepelletier afterwards claimed on the strength of a few sentimental passages in letters of this time. Quite the contrary; Verlaine was a city man from birth and his occasional raptures over the country and plans to settle there were the raptures and plans that most city men, and especially the self-deceivers, indulge in from time to time. He enjoyed himself in the north-country strongholds of his relatives because he took care never to stay at any place long enough to wear the pleasure thin. When he found himself temporarily trapped in the country his true feelings soon showed themselves. For the moment he extracted a sensuous delight from scenes, sights, smells, sounds, as only a poet and a city poet could do, but even this was incidental to his main pleasures. He could tickle the trout in the Semoy at Bouillon, lie in the fields at Fampoux, laze through the woods of Bertrix, take pot shots at rabbits across the marshes of Lecluse, but he was twice the man if he had company and could talk out his emotions.

And never more so than in this summer of 1862 when a new friend, the young Dujardin, was at his side. Dujardin was the son of a widowed sugar manufacturer who had just married Elisa; the Verlaines stayed with the Dujardins at Lecluse, near Douai, for some weeks, and the friendship between the young men ripened with a speed and ardor that was to be characteristic of all Verlaine's relationships; he could do nothing by halves and his friends had to be and were the soul of perfection. His extravagant praise of Dujardin and his hints years afterwards that this and other male friendships were not all that they might have been have led naturally to suspicions of his relationships with men. For this last Verlaine has only himself to blame; he loved to shock and to mystify. But beyond the juvenile wish to baffle others and blacken himself the truth is that he loved men and women indiscriminately as the Greeks did and could never reconcile himself to the distinction drawn between the sexes by the society of his time.

When facts are examined he and Dujardin are found to have shot together, fished together and danced not together but with every pretty village, town and city girl (for *Parisiennes* were on holiday there) they could find. They danced six nights running, they were for the time mad about dancing and their partners, they talked and wrote about them incessantly as boys do. No mention is made of Verlaine shunned, only of him dancing until he could have dropped.

Innocuous indeed. Then he and Dujardin found another way of passing their evenings and Verlaine was soon complaining not only of his legs (after the dancing) but of his stomach. His complaints were not serious; he felt like a dog: women and wine! Unfortunately he did not confine himself to wine, in fact scarcely tasted it. Young Dujardin was of course no more than a cipher; anybody would have done; the thing was inescapable. A later friend, Ernest Delahaye, has explained what happened. Delahaye knew his people—he too was from the Ardennes—and he knew Verlaine. The countryfolk were hard drinkers with good heads; hard workers too and shrewd; they kept their serious potations for special occasions, the birthday, fete day, first communion, marriage. And what better occasion than the arrival in their midst of the great Paul Verlaine, bachelor of letters at eighteen and with a future of such brilliance shining before him that the entire family (which in France extends endlessly through the realms of second, third and fourth cousins on all four sides) was anxious to acclaim him, that is to eat heavily and at length and to drink deep into the small hours; not the, in their eyes, insipid wines of the Center and South, but beer and spirits swallowed with grim relish and in alarming quantities.

It is not difficult to see the young Verlaine, the hero of hour after hour, tall, dark and dressed for the part in his borrowed rustic blouse and cap, small eyes glinting with mischievous good humor under their heavy brows, long arms waving, large mouth opening to emit a stream of words in the deep and rather husky voice. He would be a countryman! He would dress like one, smoke like one, puffing a clay pipe, and drink like one, tossing down one stiff potion after another nonchalantly; he would even, he declared, work like one, if common politeness did not insist on a round of "thank you" calls which demanded a drink or two and usually ended in another carousal. And then there was more stomach trouble; head trouble too, for Verlaine was not then of the caliber of his hosts nor was he given their chance of recuperation. They were in their fields the next morning none the worse for the night before unless to be a shade more short of speech, but he was continuing his triumphal tour of "calls" when he would "clear his throat" and his head with eggs swallowed raw, a row of *p'tits cafés* which with the lightest of pressure by his host became the less innocuous *bistoules* (half-coffee, half-spirits), rounded off by several *gn'niefs* (gins) or the most potent and soon most beloved *trois couleurs* composed of a cup of black coffee and glasses of rum, cognac and kirsch from which he drank in turn. The point came soon enough when the remedy was overtaken by the malady it had set out to cure. He would lie down for an hour or two. Having rested he would be too late in decency to leave and was persuaded without difficulty to sit down to another huge meal washed down with pots of *breune* and *chl-binque*, the dark and light beers of northern France, and followed by a repetition of the morning drinks.

For he was not only naturally gregarious, he had discovered a taste for liquor. The two things, he discovered happily, formed the perfect combination. During a night of drinking he felt godlike, his words golden, his thoughts wonderfully illumined. And if his stomach troubled him the next day, well, what better remedy than more of the hair of the dog that bit him?

His parents did nothing to stop him. His father who might have exercised a restraining influence, was in his own way being quite as foolish as his son and with much less excuse; succumbing to the passion of the day for speculation, he had begun to "play the markets." He had no need of extra money but boredom, vanity and a recrudescence of the "naïve folly" of his father led him to do his best to dissipate what he had. He did not see it like that—naturally, he saw himself as a financial Napoleon in a small way—but such was the effect; every speculation went wrong, the comfortable Verlaine fortune was dwindling and it was becoming a question whether Paul would inherit anything but debts. Immediately after his latest reverse some hint of this would dawn on the Captain and he would grow preoccupied and unwell. He was so then; his son's long absences were excused and the curious moods of elevation followed by biliousness were overlooked.

Elisa was also preoccupied by this first official visit of her beloved trio and thought more of making her new home fit for them than of the curious behaviour of the adored Paul outside the home. Madame Verlaine, fluttered by the festivities and enjoying her role as mother of the man of the moment (for although Paul's triumphs were as sure as day following night she did not disdain the world's acknowledgments), also had more of her time filled than was usual. However she had eyes for her son as always and could observe what escaped her husband and Elisa, that the soul of perfection had begun to sow quite a few wild oats. That was how the romantic woman saw it; when she worried (and she was always worrying about something) she could tell herself that not only was Paul virtually immune from the common weaknesses, but indeed the one weakness that he now patronized was the one most forgivable, natural and looked at in a certain light even a matter for pride. To drink on equal terms with hard-drinking men and at such an age to carry his drink (more often

than not) with an air—that was a thing! No serious reproof was to
be looked for from that quarter; the doting Madame Verlaine could
scarcely be expected to realize that her darling was not sowing his
own oats but reaping the oats of another.

[2]

He returned to Paris late that autumn with an appetite for drink,
but it is just possible that had circumstances been different he might
have remained one of those who only "take a drop too much" when
life does not run smoothly. At all events, to drink for the sake of
drinking seemed a far cry from the young man who came back to
Paris and a career—a young man with devoted parents, a sufficiency
of money (his father's efforts notwithstanding) and, if his headmaster was to be believed, with a fine future.

There was some delay before this future materialized, and it was
not until he had tried a snatch of law study, a few months' clerking
in an insurance office and the Marriage Registry Department of the
Ninth Arrondissement that soon after his twentieth birthday and to
the general family delight he was found sitting at his desk in the
Hôtel de Ville, a fully fledged civil servant with a good salary, excellent prospects and the promise of a pension.

This delay did not in the least perturb Verlaine; the one cloud
in his sky, the possibility of military service (so far had he moved
from his plan to follow his father), was happily blown away when he
drew a good draft number and spared his parents the search for a
substitute. For the rest he was so easygoing that nothing mattered
to him so long as he was enjoying himself; this included some drinking in company but depended more on the company than the
drinking. If he could be with a crowd, making music, making
rhymes, talking the wildest politics or the most romantic nonsense,
he was happy; and happy he was without serious interruption between that autumn of 1862 and the winter of 1865—three years of
"having a good time." Café lights blazing, the blare of argument
on every hand, the bustle of waiters, the comforting clink of glasses
on marble-topped tables, these were accessories to that good time.
Like all intellectual Frenchmen his set was intoxicated with words
and had no need of real drink though they sometimes took it in
passing. Some, such as Lepelletier, were practically nondrinkers;
almost all the others (including Verlaine for most of this period)

contented themselves with what, in comparison with the habits of
the North, were mild stimulants, wines and apéritifs for the most
part.

In short, anything less like a disreputable sot would be hard to
imagine than the Paul Verlaine of 1862 to 1865 and especially in his
first years as civil servant. Instead one must imagine a smartly (and
preposterously) dressed young man in frock coat, striped trousers,
light waistcoat, shining boots, tall hat and splendid cravat who
every weekday morning arrived not too early at the entrance to the
great building close to the river, jauntily swinging a cane and sur-
veying the world with sprightly benevolence.

[3]

His duties and behavior at the Hôtel de Ville have been, like his
youthful drinking, the subject of many inaccurate comments. Verlaine can so easily be made to appear a figure of fun—he being the
first to encourage the game—that it is not easy to resist the temptation. The facts are that by normal standards, which admittedly were
not high, he had plenty of work. To him, after the shortest of intervals, this work was insufficient to occupy his time, far less his talents.
He did not ask for more—he was the most human of beings—but
either dispatched what he had quickly and efficiently or tried to
spin it out through the day. His spare hours, which grew every month,
he devoted to more congenial subjects than the salary of priests (one
aspect of his official jobs): to the reading of newspapers without
which no Frenchman's day would be complete, to the writing of
poems, scenes for plays and anything else that came into his head
and, as he came to know the staff, to rewarding conversations with
like-minded members.

There were quite a few of these; since the practice of practically
no form of the arts paid its way, would-be painters, musicians and
writers sought the safety of the civil service; every branch of it was
sprinkled with them. In the Hôtel de Ville Verlaine was soon hob-
nobbing with Léon Valade, Albert Mérat, Armand Renaud and
Georges Lafenestre, would-be poets all, who gained their bread and
butter at the expense of the state, and to a lesser extent with the
elderly one-eyed Jules Andrieu, author of a book on the Middle
Ages and an anthology of famous love songs.

Verlaine quickly became intimate with the first two. Indeed, to become attached to one was to be attached to both, for the young men were inseparable, so much so that Valade was quickly Albert to his companions and Mérat Léon, the little group having a penchant for the juggling of names. Verlaine was particularly attracted to Valade, tall and thin, three years his senior, a gentle soul too. Valade was shy, however, as Verlaine was not, preferring quiet corners and walking noiselessly so that he should not draw undue attention to himself. He said little, and that in a high fluting voice, but his rare contributions to the conversation were listened to with some respect, not only because his silence was so extraordinary amid the hubbub but also because his ironical little asides were considered worth hearing. His pale bearded face, set off by black hair brushed over the forehead, soon became a dim but essential part of the midmorning gatherings which were even known to pause for his opinion. His poems faithfully echoed himself: "I am a milk drinker," he would say, speaking of his fear of excess. He was translating some Heine lyrics and writing with Mérat a selection of poems to be known as *Avril, Mai, Juin* in which his contributions were sad little songs of Paris and the Parisians, love lyrics from which passion or even a hint of it was carefully excluded.

The big broken-nosed Mérat, as would be expected, was his friend's opposite. He was nicknamed "the disdainful cigar" because he was rarely without one, walking slowly and majestically, head held high, cigar tilted, eyes raised and with an expression which suggested that he was determined not to acknowledge the existence of a world filled with stupid people. He threw explosive comments into conversations, smiling sardonically at the resultant clamor, and told delightful stories of a certain Hôtel de Pérou where he and Valade had huddled penniless, homeless but with plenty of spirit among a little group of would-be poets until they were snatched into the security of the civil service. He had a flaw, a serious one, he was envious. His envy of the slightest success of a comrade (and slight it would be then, no more than the acceptance of a poem by some nonpaying magazine) burst out in recriminations so naïve as to raise laughter, no one except Valade taking them seriously. Like so many young writers of these years Mérat had talent but it was neither original nor powerful. He was a city nature poet as his *Poèmes de Paris* was to show, but a derivative one, melancholy and sentimental. Eventually an unbearable sense of failure and the success of so many of his companions were to drive him to kill himself after many false reports of suicide. But this was far ahead; in the sixties he was a stimulating young man though not always a popular one.

Their discussions in the Hôtel de Ville were sometimes interrupted by those who having no more work than the talkative poets but less ability to dispatch it were irritated by this display of superiority, and Verlaine, leaving his hat on its peg to vouch for his presence, grew into the habit of adjourning bareheaded to the nearby Café du Gaz on the rue de Rivoli to continue the conversation. He relates this with the self-depreciatory gusto common to all his confessions: "See what a naughty boy I was—and am" his tone implies. But because it would spoil the story he omits to mention (as he always omits to mention commonplaces) the dampening fact that to leave one's hat on its peg was a widespread custom throughout the building as indeed it was and is in every civil service building in the world. Valade for one, and Mérat of course, would be found at his table in the café (that is, when the three young men had not sauntered out arm in arm) with others from similar resting places. The Treasury for instance had to make its way as best it could for half an hour or so while its clerk Armand Silvestre discussed his poems with his comrades. The burly Silvestre, older than "les trois" as Verlaine, Valade and Mérat came to be known, was accorded a certain respect because he was an occasional drinking companion of Baudelaire. The respect would have been awe had Silvestre been another man; as it was, his gross laugh riding high over the room is sufficient description of him, and for that matter of the poet, long forgotten except for an odd comic song or nonsense rhyme. He was addicted to the risqué joke more than most and Verlaine laughed with him, his sensuality tickled, but Silvestre was not to become one of his intimates.

The Café du Gaz was one of the centers of the arts that Verlaine was to know so well; respectable as some of his later haunts were not; jammed with frock-coated young men apparently vibrating unresolvedly between displays of childishness and the deadly earnest. The first fitted Verlaine like a glove, the last is not a word that sits easily on him at any time; his type of earnestness is better known to the Anglo-Saxon than to his own countrymen. Yet in these years, for all his fatuities and careful clinging to convention, he became aware that he was a writer and he thought, in quite the wrong direction, that he had something to say. That this would ever conflict with jokes and arguments in respectable cafés, with large and regular meals, and top hats on pegs, and frock coats and a comfortable home in the suburbs never occurred to him; he would have been dismayed, not to say terrified, at the mere thought. All he knew and cared to know was that he had a gift and that he was living at a moment when the gift could, in the most pleasant manner conceivable, bring him excitement and happiness. His idea of exercising the gift was modest indeed, no more than the writing of an occasional poem and the beginnings of bloodthirsty social dramas and broad farces more planned than written; but no matter, he was an author even if an unpublished one and—and this was more than half the attraction—in excellent company. He had as co-authors Lepelletier and a melancholy youth Lucien Viotti, first met at the Lycée Bonaparte; and as audience, whenever he could get a word in, the young hopefuls of the Café du Gaz. Even the death of Captain Verlaine at the end of 1865, though it roused him for a moment to a most uncharacteristic display of assertiveness (he forced reluctant authorities to give his father a military escort on a public holiday), could not deflect him for long from following with lazy ardor what appeared as a most delightful destiny, to be one of a crowd, a gay, sometimes elegant, sometimes raffish but always convivial crowd, which collected around the tables of the Café du Gaz and, when the day's work was nominally done, at the Café de Bobino in the rue de Fleurus.

Even when the French have nothing to say they say it at unbelievable length and with a vivacity and with more interest than one would think credible; and when, as with the young intellectuals of Verlaine's day, they feel a sense of creativeness in the air the result in sheer sound is deafening, bewildering, exhilarating too and not merely because of the magnificent music of the language. History is forever repeating itself. Today the huge American cars of profiteers aimlessly café-crawling, the gaping tourists, the swarm of beggars, the grasping shopkeepers, the torrent of useless oratory at the Palais-Bourbon, the endless talk of money, the whole sense of waste, decay, nothingness in a setting of superb loveliness, merely serve to whet the intellectual appetite. In one of the largest Paris theatres a full orchestra can be heard enthusiastically performing Monsieur X.'s variations on some themes of Monsieur Y. In France this composer is a dance-band leader, in England he would still be chiefly concerned by the newness of his gown in some Oxford or Cambridge college. The *maître* from whose work the themes have

been extracted is well on the tender side of thirty, but the themes
are original and excellent, the variations extremely clever. And
so in the closing years of Louis Napoleon the vulgarity, the corruption, the false morality, the emphasis on wealth, the atmosphere
of uncertainty and dissatisfaction provoked in the young a particular
enthusiasm for the arts. Many of the antics of these young men,
their rowdy fooling, their assumption of titles not their own, their
extravagances in speech, clothes and behavior appear pretentious,
juvenile, absurd, as they often were; but related to their day they
can be seen also as inevitable and justifiable protests against the
enveloping regime of Monsieur Prudhomme—the French version
of Babbitt, a regime which was eventually to overwhelm many of
the protestants. But that was in the future; in the present they reacted violently in act and in thought; Paris was intellectually alive
and hopeful and amid all the talk there was talent and more than
talent. The stimulus of political discussion had much to do with
it, since to be revolutionary in one thing was to be revolutionary
in all, music, poetry, politics appearing then as manifestations of a
single spirit.

The ambitions of Verlaine's friends reached no higher—though
seeming to them high enough—than the publication of the verses
all were pouring profusely onto paper. Mérat excepted, they felt no
envy; due partly on Verlaine's side to an innate laziness but more
to the lack of pretension that made him such a popular companion.
Neither then nor for that matter at any time did he see himself as
specially gifted, and the idea of genius never crossed his mind.
There were, in any event, leaders enough. The conversation was
thick with names reverently pronounced; one would have thought,
listening to them, that Paris was alive with poets, the streets chock-
a-block with men furiously composing.

The most frequently recurring of these names, apart from the
inevitable Hugo—"*le Père est là-bas dans l'île*" they would cry, after
Théodore de Banville—were those of Baudelaire, who was spoken
of as a man at once mysterious and a martyr (the proscription of
Fleurs du Mal being awesomely fresh in mind), a man somehow
withdrawn from life, immersed in the creation of his *frisson
nouveau*, as Hugo had well described the Baudelairean verse; of
Leconte de Lisle, mysterious too but in the sense of the formidable
rather than the inaccessible; and finally of Banville, whom one

could guess, by the tone of these young men, was a very different kind of hero.

All these heroes were the seniors of the café crowd by twenty years or more. Other names shouted across the table were those of true contemporaries, known and unknown, Glatigny and Mendès foremost. These names were pronounced with a special intonation, compounded of familiarity, envy, affection, jest and pride. The bright and shining light of this talkative company was evidenced in nothing more imposing than a genius for absurdity. Who could dream that the would-be dandy with his buttonholed and velvet-collared frock coat, his flowing spotted cravat, lazily twinkling deep-set eyes, cane twirling idly, was anything but an innocuous addition to the band, a useful listener who at times had begun to show a certain flair for the telling of questionable tales and who in expansive moments was given to the confession of improbable misdeeds? Not his companions, and certainly not he. To look at the long and languid figure sprawled as much as one can sprawl in the chair of a Paris café, to hear the queer gruff voice tell a doubtful anecdote, praise in wildly exaggerated terms some poet of the day, or to answer the ready smile of the large loose mouth and respond to the infectious good-natured laugh, was to think, when his companions bothered to think at all, what a nice chap the young Verlaine was; a bit of an ass, perhaps, rather a weakling, maybe, but definitely a good fellow.

One day not far in the future this amiable nonentity was to astonish the little coterie by appearing somewhat self-consciously with a large square monocle jammed uncomfortably before his right eye, a thick black silken cord dropping down the long face to a decidedly florid bow in the buttonhole. That ridiculous monocle was a sign and a symbol; it was to signify his adherence to a poetic school, even to a measure of seriousness and, if one proceeds sufficiently far ahead, to the poet himself. But that is another story, a story which began, if stories can ever be said to have a beginning, when the monocled one was still at school.

4.

THE PARNASSIAN

[1]
CATULLE MENDÈS
1861

At the beginning of 1861 a youth, Catulle Mendès, came up to Paris from Bordeaux. He was just eighteen, one year older than the schoolboy Verlaine, and had the intention in good provincial style of taking the capital by storm. He had much in common with Verlaine besides nearness of age; he possessed considerable charm, he was gregarious, excellent company of a kind, and was to become an omnivorous lover of women and strong drink. He also had that which Verlaine was utterly without, the wish and the will to "get on." He had Jewish blood in him, he was of Spanish extraction; but his appearance showed no trace of Jew or Spaniard; fresh-faced, blue-eyed, with a cloud of fair hair—much like the mane of Hugo when young—that he had an engaging way of tossing off his forehead when making a point. "Apollo in person" Louis Ménard was to say; a vulgar Apollo, often tasteless and on occasion obscene, but with undeniable vivacity and force of manner.

Perhaps his attractive looks proved irresistible, perhaps his drive, for he had a tireless tongue, a hide as tough as steel and a broad sense of humor that covered the occasional rebuff with a joke and a laugh. He had taken his first steps in poetry at the feet of Valade and possibly the decision to assault Paris, for both came from the same city; but was soon off on his own in a manner that Valade could not and did not wish to imitate. Within a month the boy, regally splashing the entire *dot* his fond parents had sent with him, was sitting in the editor's chair of the *Revue fantaisiste* in an opulent room in the passage de Mires receiving one of the greatest of French poets, one of the best known and most of the more interesting. His taste in decoration was imperfect, the office being hung with Persian tapestries in green and rose, cluttered with mahogany desks and tables, a leather armchair and a gaudy couch—"a room trying hard to be a boudoir"—but in another and more important respect his instinct was correct, for he founded the review "to tilt against the two great failings of the literature still revered by most Frenchmen—elegiac sentimentalism and defective French." Hugo, ignoring with Olympian blindness the presence in much of his own work of these failings and eager as always to proclaim his eternal youth, encouraged the venture with the customary flourish of eloquence.

Hugo's support was of symbolic value only; Mendès was merely taking the obvious precaution of the opportunist; the most regular visitor to the office and the most important by contemporary judgment was Banville. In fact, given Mendès' self-assurance, the existence of the office and of the *Revue fantaisiste* was due to Banville. He looked neither important nor a poet. He came from Moulins, the beautiful capital of the Bourbons, and was a typical *Bourbonnais:* chubby, round-cheeked, hairless face, plump and insignificant body, indeterminate nose, sharp but empty blue eyes, and he spoke between his teeth, clipping his words in a manner which had become the fashion in all advanced literary circles. For this man, just twice the age of his young protégé, who looked like an unprosperous commercial traveler, was the most successful and most highly regarded poet of his time. He was unquestionably one of the nicest men, generous, without envy or pride, good-natured and, allowing for contemporary taste, witty. No young men called on him in vain; he found them work, lent them money, introduced them to editors and, as with Mendès, even helped to set them up on their own. His Thursday soirees were famous and unlike some others—for every evening of the week was open house at the home of some leader of the arts—considered the stomachs, often empty enough, of the struggling poets, painters and musicians who were free to drop in at the rue de Buci and to step from the salon to the *salle à manger* where food was spread on the tables. Yet hungry though they might be, not a man would move when Banville was talking in his high-pitched voice. He had a gift of speech remarkable even for a Frenchman, bright with clever paradoxes, brilliant with caricatures of the famous and not so famous men and women in the Parisian art world, particularly of those on the stage. He exaggerated wildly, discovering a new genius weekly and having a fresh scandal or two up his sleeve for every occasion, but his manner was so joyous and so inoffensive that his hearers merely laughed and did their best to extract the grain of truth lurking below the stream of words. All the Paris salons and cafés had laughed at and loved the young Banville who at the end of an evening years earlier had said to Hugo, then the darling of society, that it was ridiculous for a man to play the lover after the age of seventeen—a typically provocative remark which put new life into the gathering, the great man replying with raised eyebrows and reddened face, "I should like to hear that extraordinary theory explained"; which Banville did for a twenty minutes so sparkling that the entire party began afresh.

Banville was not respected, having no dignity of person, but was immensely and understandably popular. "*Clown étonnant*" Verlaine was to call him, but contortionist would be nearer the mark. He was far too good a Frenchman even to think of breaking the strict rules which had governed French poetry for centuries; he employed his exceptionally agile mind in the playing of verbal games within the limits convention assigned to him; and certainly if verbal dexterity is the criterion he was a wizard and deserves all the admiration he received. Cleverness appealed to the French intellectual then as now, and from the moment when he published his first book of verse Banville was a made man; the fact that he had nothing to say was overlooked in admiration for the manner, or rather manners, in which he said it; the banality of his thought was overlooked for the optimism, facile but attractive, that sweetened it.

Here, then, was Banville, affable, successful, kind, coming day after day to the passage de Mires to see how his latest young follower was getting on, allowing him to print new verses and introducing him to his friends. Mendès soon took the measure of his master. He genuinely admired Banville's technical virtuosity—a natural *pasticheur*, he was to become just such another poet-journalist—and having an eye to the main chance as most of his contemporaries had not, he saw not only how Banville's popularity and kindness could be put to his own use but, more important, how from Banville's attitude toward his work a theory of poetry might be extracted. And there was nothing quite so advancing to a man, in Paris particularly, as the putting forward of a theory which was, or at least sounded, new.

But this last was to come later; the germ of it can be seen in Mendès' description of the aims of the *Revue fantaisiste*. Being firstly a practical young man, apart from women and his own temperament, he concerned himself lightheartedly and with fervor (the blend being fairly common then) with the question of filling his columns advantageously. In this Banville's patronage was all-important; Gautier and Daudet permitted extracts from their work to be printed and one after another of the friends of Banville came into the office with contributions. The first of these was Baudelaire, "slim, elegant, a little furtive, almost alarming because of his attitude of one with a secret fear which could be discerned from time to time beneath an hauteur of manner softened by a grave courtesy. He had the irresistible charm of beauty in distress and carried himself with the air of a fastidious bishop somewhat fallen from grace who had donned an elaborate lay costume to go on his travels—His Eminence Monseigneur Beau Brummel."

The description is by Mendès who describes even more of himself; if offensive, it accurately ticks off the manner in which the great poet was regarded. Baudelaire was then forty years of age, a disappointed man conscious of greatness denied, and a haunted man, haunted physically by his creditors from one mean lodging to another and by the disease that was to kill him, haunted spiritually by his consciousness of sin, and physically and spiritually by the dreadful attacks of despairing ennui that his loneliness induced. His dandyism, slightly decayed, and his perfect manners contrasted horribly with the ravaged face whose great burning eyes and majestic forehead bespoke the most obvious face of genius ever seen, but Mendès was more concerned to place his guest within a neat phrase than to comprehend his tragedy. If the spectacle of Baudelaire carrying his wares from one petty magazine to another, humbling himself before a youngster not out of his teens, was painful, Mendès was not the man to feel it; he was absorbed by pleasure in the prose poems that Baudelaire brought with him and by elation at his capture. His attitude toward Baudelaire's work fairly expressed the man, enthusiasm blending with a patronizing tone which is laughable or deplorable as one looks at it, freely criticizing, amending and rejecting—all done under cover of a genuine appreciation: "I have violently admired your verses" he was to write, in the act of cutting them. In any event, like the young Verlaine, Mendès' admiration for Baudelaire's work was confused by the poet's "martyrdom," but unlike Verlaine his sense of importance was unpuncturable even by close contact with genius.

In this, however, Mendès was, if not in good company, in a very numerous one, three men only in the whole of France (an uncertain four if the uncritical Banville be included) recognizing in Baudelaire one of France's greatest glories. Two of these form the main subjects of this history; the third was one of the many visitors to Mendès' office with copy. This was the long-forgotten Léon Cladel, "a damned Christ," said Mendès, looking and listening to the great hairy peasant who laughed through a life of unspeakable hunger and misery, "a Robinson Crusoe in the solitude of Paris, superb and terrible to see" with his long hair, wild tormented eyes and violent speech. Cladel had a penchant for horrors, Baudelaire's translation of Poe and the vogue for Hoffmann infecting a mind never stable. With Mendès he sketched out in one night a melodrama, the first act containing two duels, a fire and several kidnappings, and the final act showing the father of one of the kidnapped girls with his beard torn out by the roots "continuing his tirade with bloody chin before the shocked public." There was no public, of course, but the young men enjoyed themselves.

Then came another dealer in horrors, Villiers de L'Isle-Adam. Like others in Paris at the time he was entitled neither to the name nor to the aristocratic birth he advertised in and out of season. But remarkable in his own right he was, having a flair for the horror story with the ironic twist and loving "ferocious and funereal pleasantries." Again like other young men in Paris he had devoted parents who, believing him a genius, sold all they had and moved to a single furnished room in the capital so that their son should come into his own. This was two years earlier, when Villiers, to give him the only name remotely his, was twenty-one. He had acquired neither fame nor fortune by the time he arrived in the passage de Mires, his pockets stuffed with manuscripts, but a gift for picturesque speech and the twists of a strange imagination had brought him a certain notoriety, one critic even describing him as "the most magnificently gifted young man of his generation." He had already written two unactable dramas and a philosophical novel so obscure that the few who glanced through it were persuaded without difficulty that his genius was too profound for words.

He brought a story which Mendès quickly agreed to print and a

fiery enthusiasm for Wagner whose Tannhäuser had recently been
damned at the Paris Opéra. Hero worship of Wagner was to become a sine qua non among the young intellectuals, attaching itself
naturally enough to the revolutionary fulminations of the cafés.
Mendès, who had already determined to use the pages of the
Revue fantaisiste to propagate the Wagnerian gospel, greeted this
fellow spirit rapturously.

Another visitor, Sully Prudhomme, was of an age with Villiers
but in all else could not have been more different. He was big,
almost to stoutness, with a large wavy chestnut-brown beard, thick
brown hair and grave eyes of a mild blue. He had a look of Musset
but was far removed from Musset as poet, writing discreet and
chaste love lyrics and philosophical verses of considerable com-
plexity. Even at this early stage he had won a notice foreshadowing
his later fame, and Mendès, conscious of his own youthful appearance, affected "a grave, almost magisterial air" from his seat in the
editorial chair. But Prudhomme gave no indication of acting the
accepted poet to the boy editor; on the contrary he appeared shy
and sat almost silent. The one thing that could stir him was,
curiously enough, the work of a tall young man "thin to the point
of transparency" who bounded into the office a few days later; he
thought this work "indelicate and reveling in sensation" but his
was a lone voice.

This tall young man's entrance was too dramatic to be real; without a word he plumped into a chair, threw a manuscript on the
desk and followed it with two large and tattered boots protruding
from patched nankeen trousers which in turn merged into the
remnants of a shirt covered halfway up his chest by a small red
waistcoat shining out of a shrunken metal-buttoned blue jacket.
From a tie flapping wide rose a long thin neck on the top of which
was perched a small round head covered with fair hair falling
straight to the open collar. The face, worn and hollow, contained
two faunlike heavy-lidded eyes, glinting humorously under heavy
eyebrows, and a great gash of a mouth which opened to announce
in the hoarse voice of the heavy drinker: "Glatigny." This was
superfluous, Banville having warned Mendès of his approach, and
given "with his enchanting mixture of Orpheus and Balzac" an
outline of this protégé's career. Albert Glatigny looked the strolling
player who had spent his teens acting small parts throughout the
provinces. And so no doubt he would have continued had he not,

sleeping as usual in a barn, found one night an old volume of Ronsard, read, instantly adored and become an avid reader of poetry. At eighteen he discovered *Cariatides* and determined immediately that he must become a poet.

A little later Verlaine, wandering along the quays, made a similar discovery but his reaction was less violent; for Glatigny not only began feverishly to write poems but the moment he had saved a few sous made his way on foot to Paris. Paris took no notice of him. The next year he tried again, encouraged by Banville who found him a room and occasional journalistic work and showed his poems to Hugo and Sainte-Beuve. Again he was forced to go on tour leaving his manuscript poems with Banville who finally arranged their publication. This was *Vignes folles* of 1860 which, like the Banville, Verlaine came across on a riverside bookstall, learned by heart and proclaimed to his schoolfellows as a modern masterpiece.

The young Verlaine was not alone; in contemporary poetic circles Glatigny was hailed as a latter-day Villon. He had a gift; like Banville (and like Mendès for that matter) he displayed a verbal facility and juggled dexterously with rhymes. He even, in one or two fantastic pieces, showed a certain originality, but like Banville and Mendès he had nothing to say. He wrote because he loved words and thanks to a prodigious memory had acquired an enormous vocabulary, and because he panted to imitate his chosen master. This he did sufficiently well to confuse a critical sense then generally distrait.

He was besides, to bedevil the critics further, a "character." Whenever he had a sou to his name he took root in his favorite Buffet Germanique and there would hold spellbound two formidable habitués, Baudelaire and Silvestre. Both men, no mean talkers, would listen by the hour to one fantastic tale after another, punctuated by the teller's bull-like roar of laughter, the impish gleam in the bright eyes until, having drunk heavily on an empty stomach, Glatigny would stretch his legs on the table and instantly sleep. His largeness of heart was prodigious. His customary food in Paris was raw carrots but he would give half and the better half to any hungry poet, actor, painter, musician he happened to meet. Although he had never handled a pistol in his life outside the stage dummy, he called out the critic Albert Wolff for daring to speak slightingly of Banville and escaped miraculously with a graze.

Verlaine as a Boy

Barricades at the
Hôtel de Ville
Paris, 1871

Verlaine in 1869

He swam the Seine one cold autumn to borrow money for a friend in distress.

To think hardly of such a man was difficult, to mistake him for another Villon too easy. Superficially he was like Mendès who sat facing him for the first time; both had the gift of tongue, both were loud, boisterous, vulgar, both possessed charm to a high degree. But in another direction Glatigny was the antithesis of Mendès and a forerunner of Verlaine, a modest man thinking little of his achievement, without ambition to dominate, to acquire money or fame. He asked for nothing but company, absinthe if it could be had, conversation, laughter and more absinthe.

Hearing from Banville of the enthusiastic reception given to *Vignes folles* he had hurried back to Paris as soon as he could raise the fare, and wearing the preposterous stage clothes of his latest role (having no clothes of his own) had precipitated himself into the office of the *Revue fantaisiste*.

Mendès astutely took in this fellow spirit at a glance. He read a few lines of the manuscript on the desk, then exclaimed excitedly, "You are a poet!" "You too!" replied Glatigny ingenuously, and a bargain was quickly struck. Glatigny was not only to contribute to the magazine—he began at once with a laudatory article on Hugo—but also to act as assistant editor. The question of salary was not raised, Glatigny typically overlooking the need for it, Mendès purposely forgetting it.

But this job, like all the others he had taken in his twenty-one years of life, did not occupy Glatigny for long. Mendès was not content to "tilt against" the romantic writers of the first decades of the century by printing neoromantic poems and articles and preaching the gospel of form; he wished to expose the stuffy rules of the Second Empire regulating right conduct in contemporary literature, an equally admirable aim but one which he mistakenly tried to attain by printing in installments from the second number onwards his own sultry play *Le Roman d'une Nuit*.

The challenge was taken up by the police with some relish; in November the *Revue* was fined five hundred francs for publishing indecent material and since Mendès was unable to pay he was imprisoned for a month in the Sainte-Pélagie and the *Revue* came to an end. Released and in disgrace with his respectable parents, he joined Valade and Mérat at a fifth-rate hotel in a sunless passage off the rue Dauphine. This hotel (by name the Pérou but known

to posterity as the Dragon Bleu) had become the temporary strong-
hold of a few young poets existing on less money than one would
have believed possible, the proprietor being an optimistic man or
kindhearted (one of the most pleasant aspects of nineteenth-century
Paris is the generosity of the Montmartre and Montparnasse *hôteliers*
and café owners toward writers and painters), and for a time after
Mendès joined them they even enjoyed a sort of comfort. There
was some faint shadow of room service and—Mendès: "We were
consoled from time to time by our lady friends."

The poets were writing hard in the intervals between discussion but
it was a red-letter day when anything appeared in print and they
trooped out to eat a decent meal and, if they could find fifteen sous
apiece, to invade a Pasdeloup concert and applaud the rare Wagner
overture or aria. As the months passed piles of unsold manuscripts
littered the bedroom floors. No longer first-floor bedrooms; the
proprietor losing patience moved the poets to the second floor
where the rooms held only bare beds and a single chair, were
unvisited by the *femme de chambre* and, to the general chagrin,
by the lady friends. And there, stranded on the second floor of this
gloomy hotel, remained the little colony of poets, forgotten and
hungry men who often went thirty-six hours without food. "One
dined on a page of Ronsard," said Mendès, a remark with more
meaning in it than one might suppose.

From time to time an outsider penetrated the fastness bringing
a breath of encouragement with him, possibly leaving a little cash
behind and almost certainly treating them to a meal. One winter
day as Mendès, huddled in a blanket, was trying to urge his chilled
fingers across a sheet of paper, the door burst open and a hairy
young poet named Glaser threw himself into the room with a crash.
Behind him advanced timidly the neat Napoleonic figure of a small,
plumpish young man with the eye and the nose worn by ten
thousand Frenchmen. "François Coppée," announced Glaser in his
customary voice of thunder. "He has read your poetry." He added
that his friend was a clerk in the War Office but that he repented
of his ways and wished to become a poet.

Mendès looked at the impeccable black suit and overcoat of the
newcomer, his soft hands and clean nails, and began to bridle: the
War Office! But before he could let loose one of the caustic remarks for which he was becoming notorious, Coppée, who had
been gazing about him wonderingly, exclaimed in a queer deep

voice and with naïve and irresistible ecstasy, "Oh, Mendès, how I envy you your room!" Mendès, melting at this, motioned the visitor into his only chair, a dilapidated cane affair; Glaser stretched himself on the bed and Mendès sat on the floor. There was a moment's silence, the three looking around at the room Coppée envied so much; then all simultaneously broke into laughter. "We were friends at once," said Mendès, and wished at once to celebrate the friendship. Then he remembered that he had no coat. "That's nothing," airily remarked Glaser who had just collected a fee for an article in the Dictionnaire Bouillot; he scrambled off the bed, was gone for a few minutes, returned with an overcoat from a nearby second-hand clothes shop, and out they went to dine and talk.

To talk; and when all allowance is made for the nonsense habitual to high-spirited young men, there remained the solid kernel which Mendès, faced with a new disciple, duly developed with florid emphasis. He outlined the theory which was to lead Verlaine, just about to leave school, to his first book of poems and to settle him in his career as poet.

[2]

BEGINNINGS OF THE SCHOOL
1862

The regeneration of French poetry; that, with various excursions into less impersonal matters, was the grand theme of the discussions in the Hôtel de Pérou: away with the sickly romanticists prating nauseatingly of the state of their hearts, debasing a great language for unworthy personal ends, away with them and back to the pure beauty of Ronsard when the writer was nothing, a mere instrument, his verse all.

Neither Mendès nor those who sat on the bare bed with him, leaned their backs to the dirty wall or paced the bare boards gesturing were original thinkers; they expressed views heard in any literary café and they followed the lead of their seniors. They were original only as, disciplined by their forceful young leader, they attempted to put into practice on a large scale a theory so far restricted to a few individuals. Mendès used the dreary months in the hotel, womanless, drinkless months which covered the whole year of 1862, to try to reason and work out what he considered poetry should be and do. Much of the day and well into the night he and his followers read all the great poets, studied the practice of meter and rhyme and declaimed poems based on their study. Often enough they barely heard one another speak; all had something to say, some observation that could never wait to be said even if it had to be shouted, and each believed with a fervency invariably overcoming modesty that the poem he had just written contained the imperishable germ of the doctrine that all burned to express.

This doctrine did not take the form, as one might have expected, of a reversion to realism—that was far ahead. It consisted simply of an effort to express pure, as against personal, romanticism: created art was greater than its creator—this was their view, or rather, for all were exceedingly human young men, this was the view that for one reason or another they were determined to hold.

When Mendès a year earlier had explained the purpose of his *Revue fantaisiste* he was echoing the pronouncements of greater men, but he sensed correctly the prevailing mood of the young intellectual of the day and that his own advancement was best linked with the advancement of this cause which in turn was dependent on publicity; in a city where all talked, only the loudest, most persistent voice would be heard. He had failed, but, ever the opportunist, used the material at hand; he determined to propagate the gospel in the only way open to him, by a band of disciples.

The first man to express the new creed had been, curiously enough, one of the young hopefuls of the 1830 school of romantics— Théophile Gautier; in 1835 his preface to his novel *Mademoiselle de Maupin* contained the first mention of art for art's sake. At the time the preface fell flat, most of those who noticed it commenting acidly that Gautier deprecated subjective poetry merely because he had difficulty in writing it. Seventeen years later he published his *Emaux et Camées*, one of the schoolboy Verlaine's favorites, the poems of a traveled man, exotic descriptive verses written with great care and in which both personal feeling and references to contemporary events are absent. This book brought him the devotion of Baudelaire who declared, "there is no good and no bad in the ethereal regions of true poetry"—a conclusion which must have given Gautier some uneasy moments; and later Baudelaire dedicated to him the *Fleurs du Mal* of 1857.

Of more importance to Mendès and his young men was the attitude of Banville and Leconte de Lisle. Leconte de Lisle found the original Gautier preface agreeable to his mind, and in the same year as the Gautier volume of poems he published his own *Poèmes antiques* which as its name implies exalted the past ages of man and his pagan gods and included a nostalgic evocation of the author's native island of Réunion. His descriptions, particularly of wild life, were highly colored to the point of caricature but had an impersonal grandeur carried on lines which read like an incantation, and in stanzas marked by impeccable form and a strong rhythm. This, coming from a man reputedly difficult to meet, earned him a mysterious reputation with the young intelligentsia in the Hôtel de Pérou—a reputation enhanced by his preface, which said bleakly, "There must be no trace of personal emotions in a book" and deplored the vanity of parading one's feelings in public. The romantics he declared brusquely were without ideas because without a philosophy, "weaklings who can express nothing but their own insanity." These plain words were repeated with delight through the cafés, to be followed by recitations of extensive quotations from his *Poèmes barbares* of the same year as the Hôtel de Pérou period, which leaned backwards as far as the Eastern mythologies in the determination to be impersonal. Soon afterwards, the book having been criticized in the more reactionary journals, he wrote a letter expressing the utmost contempt for critic and public. This letter, the gist of which soon spread from café to café, settled the eventual ascendancy of Leconte de Lisle. To all the young writers who could not get published, to all who were published but criticized, to all who were published but not sold (that is, to virtually everyone) this open defiance of public opinion appeared godlike and, in lieu of success, to be immediately imitated.

But before this letter and *Poèmes barbares* had appeared the voluble Banville entered the lists with an ode to Gautier praising his return to classical values and rejection of the romantic view of life through an individual reaction to it and went about declaring joyously, "Art is my religion." A few months later Gautier marched red-waistcoated into the offices of *L'Artiste* shouting, "The idea is born of the form," a phrase which he had caught from Flaubert that morning, Flaubert declaring that "the artist should not express opinions, which change, but should confine himself to art which is for all time; let him be in his work like God in his creation, felt but not seen." The result of this conversation was seen in Gautier's

L'Art, published in *L'Artiste* late in 1863, in which he called for
"impassibility" in the poet "so that truth and feeling shall be conveyed through perfection of form."

Gautier, Banville and Leconte de Lisle, poets of substantial
reputations, had therefore been preaching for years, each in his
own fashion, and demonstrating in his work that the writer must
be impersonal, reason controlling feeling, devoted to impeccable
form, and should look for inspiration at least as far back as the
great days of Greece and Rome. And the man whose knowledge of
France and the French is limited may well wonder why, with this
volume of sanction behind them, Mendès and his followers should
do more than quietly follow their masters' example. But this is to
ignore both the ambition of Mendès and the peculiarities of the
French character. It is a paradox that the Frenchman, the most
independent of men, to whom for instance the notice *Défense
d'entrer* reads as a challenge to go in at once, is nevertheless the
slave of method. For him to receive an idea is not as it would be
with, say, an American or an Englishman, simply to possess a subject
for discussion; to him it appears as an immediate and even agonizing
demand to disseminate by organization. He must if humanly possible
collect and convert a group, give this group a name, acquire a journal
and propagate the idea. Until the idea is thus pigeonholed and
advertised, no young Frenchman worth his salt can enjoy a moment's
peace. In vain one asks, what's in a name? To the logical Frenchman
the name, in view of what follows, is everything.

In the eyes of Mendès and his youths the new movement, if it
could be called so, was no more than a series of isolated statements
over the years by men who for one reason or another had been
sufficiently un-French to let these straws blow in the wind instead
of collecting them neatly into an unmistakable haystack. It had
no name, no organized body of adherents, no journal and so no
future. It was, in brief, unregulated, than which no more damning
judgment could be found in the whole of France. Unregulated!
Unorganized! Unmethodical! That was a call to arms no good
French intellectual could resist, and certainly not an ambitious one.

The work, the discussion, the agitation, in the Hôtel de Pérou
thus becomes understandable, and, particularly in the eyes of
Mendès, essential. But read, talk, write though they might, they
had no conceivable chance even if they discovered and agreed on

a name, of purchasing a paper to exploit it. All they could do was to bide their time which they used to compose and recite poems increasingly "impassible" and remote from reality.

[3]

L.-X. DE RICARD
1863

On the Boulevard des Batignolles, a few steps from the homes of Verlaine and Lepelletier, lived a distinguished old soldier, the Marquis de Ricard, former aide-de-camp to Prince Jerome. He had one son, Louis-Xavier, a young man who could without difficulty have been mistaken for a thousand others of his type, long-faced with straggly black beard, pince-nez sitting on the bridge of a strong nose, long black hair brushed back smoothly to a long thin neck correctly cravated, long thin body attired elegantly à la mode of the sixties. As he resembled the common picture of the young intellectual in appearance, so in mind he was on a par with a thousand others then talking, gesturing, writing on both banks of the Seine. He had, however, an opinion of his talents which was strong (one could almost say monomaniac) even in days when genius by general consent flowered on every other bush; and since his parents had money, a good name and plenty of room in their house, the young De Ricard had every possibility of surrounding himself with company which for one reason or another accepted his pretensions.

And if allowance is made for a vanity impossible to substantiate, for more than a touch of envy and pigheadedness, he made a tolerably good companion as long as he could somehow be prevented from undue speech, this not being his forte. Some—Mendès for example, and Leconte de Lisle—were to wonder, not silently, precisely what his forte was; perhaps it consisted in optimism, for although only in his early twenties he had tried his hand without trace of originality at poetry, criticism, novel, journalism, plays, history, philosophy, theology, politics, this last with a certain ferocity. Only memoirs were to come, as in time they did. Meanwhile he had yet to edit a journal and in the beginning of 1863 he made this gesture, obligatory to every young Parisian with intellectual pretensions and the requisite financial backing. His *Revue du Progrès* ran for a year, thanks to his parents and to a

(for those days) curiously lax censorship or one reluctant to notice
a De Ricard; but it was notable finally only for a contribution
by Verlaine which the writer was to regret.

Not that the *Revue* lacked fire; it was predominantly political
and regularly tore the government to shreds, proposed utopian
remedies for all social problems (these were the days of Fourier
and Comte) and published much unpublishable prose and verse.
The running of a journal called for a weekly soiree, nominally a
gathering of contributors but in practice including their friends
and, soon, the friends' friends. For the guests were entertained
luxuriously. The Marquis, partially paralyzed, remained upstairs
writing indiscreet memoirs, but his wife, some years his junior and
with a passion for young people, made a hostess of much charm,
encouraging the shy and treating the far from shy with an admirable
tact. A good violinist with a taste for amateur dramatics, she and
not her rather stiff son was at the heart of the entertainment, her
white worn face with its heavy-lidded eyes and gently skeptical
smile seen and welcomed by all.

Lepelletier was soon in the thick of the fray, all caution leaving
him when he turned revolutionary; but he remained intrinsically dull.
With him came a Verlaine at first somewhat timid, a Verlaine
of nineteen, who had barely thrown off the last traces of the schoolboy
but who quickly became an habitué, with no more than a growl from
his father who could not resolve the dilemma of disapproval of the
De Ricard son and admiration of the old Bonapartist and superior
De Ricard father.

Verlaine had only to be let loose amid well-disposed men and
pretty girls, plenty of talk, music, food and drink to be in bliss.
Privately he was a little shocked by De Ricard's militant atheism,
considered his antichurch diatribes in indifferent taste and his
political rodomontades excessive—understood, that one disapproved
of the corrupt and effete Church, the government of the vulgar
and the reign of Louis Napoleon, but . . . However, he was far
too unsure of himself, too amiable and too anxious to stand well
with present company to do more than smile uneasily. Moreover, the
soirees were eminently respectable despite the occasional hot words,
all present being dressed well, reciting their poems to a reasonably
silent audience, listening with commendable patience to piano solos
and to ballads, a patience that turned to rapture if Wagner was
the composer, and flirting harmlessly, inspired by an innocuous

lemonade punch, with the demure young ladies invited from neighboring houses. There was nothing to disquiet the bourgeois in Verlaine and almost everything to please the gregarious youth, including the ever popular charades. Nevertheless, conscious of harboring a weakling, he grasped the chance to atone when De Ricard asked him later in the year for a contribution. He wrote a sonnet on Monsieur Prudhomme, the mythical archetype of the bourgeois provincial Frenchman who since the advent of Louis and the industrial revolution had invaded Paris. This display of satirical fireworks, the satire borrowed out of sheer good fellowship (the author having much in common with the type he attacked) appeared in the August number.

Until the end of the year the *Revue* miraculously survived; then De Ricard, desperate perhaps for the distinction of martyrdom, made an attack on Christianity too violent to be ignored, and was duly sent to prison. His parents did not, like those of Mendès, withdraw support from him. Moreover, his sentence was for three months, which insured a larger halo. He emerged in the Spring of 1864 the man of the moment in advanced literary circles and for the next year or two held something of the position he had dreamed of.

The change was quickly reflected in the attendance of his soirees which, although the *Revue* had been suppressed, flourished as never before. The big names were seen in the De Ricard salon approvingly watching an amateur performance of *Marion de Lorme*—Flaubert, the Goncourts, Gautier and other eminent gods in evening dress. More important, Banville was to be seen there occasionally, ever amiable, talkative, the plump center of a circle in which his round smooth head of fine fair hair could just be made out through the listening wall of frock coats; and following his example the young men of promise began to drop in.

Of the musicians Emmanuel Chabrier's work alone is still played, but at that time, a boyhood friend of Manet, he was wavering between music and painting. His small body could be distinguished from afar since whatever the weather he wore a mustard-colored ulster. On closer view his cravat was seen to be set at precisely the crooked angle then the height of fashion for he was something of a dandy. Although he was only in his early twenties, the fair hair was already beginning to recede from the round face, notable for its large forehead, protruding, heavy-lidded eyes and lips perpetually thrust forward in a childish pout; but when he laughed with a mouth all teeth his plainness was forgotten in his good nature. The wide hands and short thick fingers of the pianist were at the disposal of all, to accompany, to improvise by the hour. Even his restlessness—one agitated expression chasing another across his face, quick abrupt gestures of the short arms, foot-tapping whenever he was obliged to stand still for a moment, and a formidable range of humors from petulant to jovial succeeding each other at short notice—made him an excellent if at times embarrassing party man.

Sully Prudhomme, wearing with becoming modesty the distinction of the young contemporary poet who had been printed in book form, was induced to read his latest poems, standing back to the fireplace, grave, handsome, his low voice pronouncing each word with loving inflection. The reading done, he would repair to the dimmest corner confused by the applause and no one could get a word out of him.

Villiers made one sensational entry after another, a genius if looks and behavior were to be believed; one evening he would come into the room like a somnambulist, eyes glazed, alternately muttering and giving a high-pitched laugh as at some private joke. When a bold guest summoned courage to address him he did not answer for a minute or two, gazing at the speaker with startled blue eyes; then in a profound voice and as if terrified by his own words said, "It isn't necessary to have a great idea of God," a remark which would strike the company into temporary silence through incomprehension and the uneasy certainty that in that simple statement lay some tremendously important key to life. Another time he would declaim Poe's "*Raven*," acting it out with wild gestures and staring eyes and—for these were refreshingly unsophisticated days—leaving jangled nerves and chilled blood behind him.

A different kind of blood-chilling was practiced by a nebulous-faced young man attired after the manner of an undertaker's assistant who would glide discreetly into the room, giving occasional circumspect glances from cool, keen eyes, shake hands distantly, then stand aside and regard the crowd with a slight sneer. He always carried one or more large books under his arm. He too could scarcely be other than a genius. His name was difficult to come by but gradually he became known and slightly feared as Anatole France.

[4]
RUE DE DOUAI
1864

Then came Coppée, came and conquered. There was a something about Coppée, perhaps nothing more than a sparrowlike ordinariness, that endeared him to people; he was so obviously not out of one's reach that he came as a distinct relief after a run of geniuses. He was good-natured too, modest, yet showed a refreshing tinge of delicate malice when telling a story. He read one or two distinctly poor poems so unaffectedly that he became a general favorite. Sully Prudhomme fell into a strong friendship with him. Verlaine loved him practically on sight and immediately besought him to join the civil service group at the Café du Gaz, but then Verlaine was also highly taken by Chabrier and liked everyone else with a broad and indiscriminate good nature.

And with Coppée came the beautiful Mendès, a Mendès at last released from the Hôtel de Pérou, a Mendès whose first book of poems had been published. *Philoméla* showed promise; Mendès had a feeling for words, used alliteration skillfully and from time to time managed to convey sensual beauty. The emptiness of thought and feeling remained, however, and today only one poem *"Pudor"* possesses a certain historic interest. The sale of the book had not freed him—*Philoméla*, like *Vignes folles*, brought its author much praise within his own circle but next to no money—but the fact of its existence had convinced his parents that he would be a poet and presumably (since volumes of new poetry were scarce enough in Bordeaux) was one already. They relented, sent money, and Mendès soon established himself in the rue de Douai in an apartment which he measured by the number of fellow poets it would hold; eight to ten, he reckoned.

This Mendès of the De Ricard soirees was curiously subdued, his usual masterfulness absent, his scintillating wit in abeyance, a young man who could almost have been described as ordinary were it not that Mendès was incapable of passing unnoticed. He seemed, and was, out of place, and in due course explained why, as he explained everything. "At the De Ricards'," he said, "we narrowly escaped being fashionable, having to appear in black and looking for all the world like lawyers reciting sonnets."

At the rue de Douai the atmosphere was otherwise. There an afternoon, Tuesday, was set aside each week for a literary tea party commonly all-male; if a woman were seen there she was not of a kind that would be admitted to the Boulevard des Batignolles. The key to the tone of those Tuesdays was given by the reception of each guest. After he had knocked, the door was opened an inch or two, a sharp eye peered through the crack and a hoarse voice whispered, "*Qui est là?*" If the answer was anything but "*Tragalda-bus,*" the door slammed before a creditor's foot could be thrust into the opening. If the visitor gave the correct password, the door opened wide to reveal Mendès' valet, a Parisian gamin, sharp, thin, droll, whom Mendès had first seen selling rabbits and geese at a fair in Montmartre. He never failed to make money, Mendès noticed, although his goods were of the mangiest. Later, his sales made, the two young men met in the crowded street. The gamin jostled Mendès, the better to pick his pocket no doubt; Mendès threatened him with a box on the ear and, liking his intelligent grin, offered him a job straightway as man of all work. The association flourished; Covielle was a cool customer, more than a match for the creditors who hung about (Mendès being no respecter of his own or anybody else's money) and for the occasional obstreperous guest—for this was not a "reputable" gathering. "One brought champagne instead of tea if one could afford it," says Mendès, but little tea was drunk at the rue de Douai and champagne was by no means the most potent liquor. Nonetheless, these Tuesdays were not orgies though they might occasionally end rowdily; they were informal, as the De Ricard soirees were not, and they had, riding all the jokes and abuse and high spirits, a purpose also lacking in the Boulevard des Batignolles once the *Revue de Progrès* had collapsed.

At first sight the onlooker would see little but oddities. Villiers would make one of his famous entrances, walking unsteadily, chewing a cigarette, throwing back his fair hair with a shake of the head, twining his small fair mustache with nervous fingers and, after a wild glance about the room with pale blue eyes, shaking hands all around with a distracted air. "Villiers! Here's Villiers!" all would cry with delight. Then, noticing that the piano was open, he would seat himself at it and begin to play, singing in a quavering voice a song that he had improvised on his walk to the rue de Douai, a setting of one of the sonnets of Baudelaire. He was no singer and no pianist but he silenced the talkative roomful until before the song had ended he would strum the notes with an impatient hand, get up, close the piano, walk into the darkest corner of the room and, rolling another cigarette agitatedly, would regard the stupefied audience with a suspicious stare, "the kind of look Ophelia received from the Hamlet sitting at her feet."

The artist André Gill, "a fine looking fair-haired young man with an all-conquering mustache," was by comparison ordinary, his one peculiarity being the pleasant habit of laughing at his own vanity. Cladel stormed in occasionally, all hair and temperament, with "the false air of a Christ of the Midi"—Coppée's description this time. But Coppée also describes his book of poems as a perfect work of art. The two things are not necessarily incompatible but at this distance from the event one can see that Coppée was dazzled, as were most of his companions, by the unusual in speech, writing and appearance.

Glatigny had been in and out of Paris as funds permitted, usually out, and in 1864 reappeared momentarily with the publication of his second book of poems, *Flèches d'or,* was photographed by Etienne Carjat who had more genius than most of his poetical companions put together, then was not seen again for two years. His coming was announced by a thunderous beat at the door and a head-first entrance, the door being insufficiently high to let him pass freely. His trousers and his sleeves were as short as ever, and his hunger as insatiable; he had been living, he explained, on the crackers he was supposed to nibble in the second act of a current play. As a two-book man he was regarded with respect for a few moments, but respect could not live long after he had opened his great mouth to emit the "folle causerie" which, lewd, cynical, gay, foolish, suggested only "a Panurge in his naïve sensuality but honest as Panurge was not." Most of the company felt better for his zest for life, untouched by privations which made the Hôtel de Pérou seem paradisal. Verlaine, meeting him for the first time, liked him altogether too well. Of the rare dissenters Sully Prudhomme's fastidious revulsion took fresh impetus when he noticed the admiration of Coppée: how, he asked, could a man be considered a good poet who confused true feeling with sensual love?

The question fell flat, obtaining one not altogether welcome assenter. De Ricard too looked askance at the tattered giant. De Ricard enjoyed the teas only when they were teas; when they moved into something stronger and the talk grew broad he was a fish out of water, having little capacity for liquor or for fun, and his one idea of originality in conversation or writing being to choose a grotesque subject. Mendès, who was cultivating him with some care, succeeded after difficulty in preserving the dignity of the dedicated and persecuted spirit against the assaults of Glatigny humor and the general free speech and behavior as afternoon turned to night.

Another visitor out of his element was Stéphane Mallarmé, at twenty-two one of the youngest men present. He was rarely there, being of all improbable things a teacher of English in a provincial school, but even had he been free it may be doubted that he would have been seen more often. He was small, quiet, with calm and sacerdotal gestures, and he had a habit when speaking "of lowering his silky eyelids on the eyes of an amorous goat." Not an attractive picture, nor the image of one likely to be at home in the rue de Douai; yet Mallarmé, despite the airs of an old maid and the eyes of a lecher, was a pleasant as well as a highly intelligent man and had more in common with his opposite, the vulgar Mendès, than would have seemed believable. He was to bring to one kind of finality a development of the poetry Mendès was striving to define; and had even then begun to write *Hérodiade*—the poem symbolizing virginity —which was to occupy him at intervals for the rest of his life, an effort to rid a poem of every imperfection, every obviousness that Mendès and his crowd would heartily approve.

For although the rowdy company at the rue de Douai was mixed, as it was not at the De Ricards', it was, paradoxically, serious where the well-behaved, well-dressed visitors to the Boulevard des Batignolles were not; it says much for Mendès that he not only kept the group together but, in the intervals between fooling, kept its head pointed roughly in the direction which he hoped would exploit his talent for literature and leadership. As at the Hôtel de Pérou he and his friends read together, studied, discussed, theorized, experimented, not endlessly but with a persistence that went strangely with their outward irresponsibility. But their leader was of this nature: "he was," admitted one who had no cause to love him, "a great trainer of men, and directed on them all his irresponsible charm in the guise of an apostle of belles lettres—a charm from which I have never seen anyone escape."

Coppée provides a good example. One Tuesday soon after the meetings began Mendès recited an unsigned poem. Who was the author? all clamored to know. Mendès could not tell them; the manuscript had been put on the table unobserved. Coppée, sitting quietly as usual in the background, made a sign to Mendès to come outside. The poem was his, he explained. Mendès returned, announced the author, and there was vigorous hand-clapping. Mendès remained cautious. "But are you just a one-poem man?" he wanted to know. "Have you written other poems?" "Six thousand," replied Coppée calmly. "Show them to me tomorrow," said Mendès. He was shown the poems the next day, read some, then pushed the pile aside with a brief "*Exécrable!*" Coppée, still calm, put the whole into the fire. The story does as much credit to Coppée as to Mendès; Coppée also was a sensible young man determined to get on; but, Mendès, recognizing the talent in the one poem, took Coppée in hand and, as the latter afterwards freely admitted, made a successful poet of him.

This was the work of a leader of men. "Seductive but imperious," said Verlaine, which from him was positively harsh. For Verlaine was there, a minor figure, the youngest of the company, still in process of adjusting himself to the Hôtel de Ville, which he had recently joined, and a little alarmed as well as charmed by what he heard and saw of Mendès. He asked for a quiet and pleasant life but had an uneasy feeling that he would not get it if Mendès had his way. The Mendès program was too much like work. He therefore lay low. He was drawn to the quietly affable Mallarmé, and had begun to plan joint efforts with Coppée whom he had already persuaded to leave his hat on a peg at the War Office and join the Café du Gaz group for their mid-morning refreshment. He relished this new friend's sentimental suburban outlook, spiced by the saving grace of a quiet irony, and had been introduced to the Coppée home with its Balzacian mother and sister, who were convinced that their beloved François was a genius who would make a name for himself—this last supposition having more justification than most. But one suspects that he yearned after the De Ricard charades in which, suitably disguised, he could make an ass of himself. The musicians offered new attractions, the mercurial Chabrier and a youthful violinist Ernest Boutier foremost, and a yellow-haired, yellow-bearded Ernest Cabaner who kept life in himself by playing the piano in a third-rate Left Bank café every night, who was composer, poet, painter as the mood took him, and whose awareness of the outside world was so slight that Verlaine, a voracious reader of newspapers and periodicals, for some time suspected a hoax behind the sublime ignorance. Verlaine's ambitions began to incline toward the musical-comedy stage, and he discussed plots in vague terms with everybody who had a musical score to his name. He contributed no more than a dutiful enthusiasm to the Mendèsian hue and cry for verses in which the form should be all. Yet despite himself he learned much of his trade at the rue de Douai and was to be given by Mendès and company his first chance to display his true gift publicly. He was later to pay his tribute to the effect on him of *Philoméla*, quoting significantly from a poem that Mèndes had dedicated to Baudelaire.

[5]

LECONTE DE LISLE
1864-1866

The most obvious sign of Mendès' acuity was his realization that the movement which he was trying to bring to life needed a leader and that this leader could not ostensibly be himself. Who then? The malleable Banville would not do, for all his popularity and renown; he was not serious, he was too approachable and not at all impressive. Gautier at first sight appeared an obvious choice since the movement sprang from him, but he was handicapped by his public reputation as a romantic of the old school, he traveled often and had never become a Paris "figure." There was another objection; Gautier was beginning to look askance at the pushing young provincial, and Mendès' relations with him were to become singularly unfortunate. As also with the next man, Hugo, who disqualified himself by his exile, by his insistence on standing full in the limelight and by the fact, though no one would so much as breathe a hint of it, that his sincerity was suspect. Baudelaire, whom Mendès would have preferred, was a lone wolf; his reputation insofar as he had one was low with all but a few intellectuals, he was not respectable and that would never do: so Mendès, far from respectable himself, was obliged to reason.

This left Leconte de Lisle; his reputation though restricted stood high; he was serious, difficult of access, very much a man with a mission which he was too proud to prosecute in person, he was by all accounts dignified to the point of disagreeableness, his hauteur was a byword at the De Ricards' and the rue de Douai. Glatigny had dedicated his second volume to him (his first had been dedicated to Banville), a dedication claiming him firmly as the inspiration of all

that was "impassible" in the poems, and Mendès took this to be a
sign of the times. He exerted his charm to obtain an introduction.
Banville obligingly contributed to his own displacement; he introduced Mendès to Louis Ménard, one of the select visitors to the
Boulevard des Invalides and the strangest. Ménard had met Marx in
England, become a communist and fought at the barricades in 1848;
he was also poet, painter, philosopher, scientist and a naturalist devoted particularly to the study of snakes, coming home day after day
his pockets stuffed with these reptiles gathered from the country surrounding Paris. Above all he was a Hellenist, practicing a kind of
mystic stoicism, which he expressed in poems anticipating the Symbolists and which had contributed greatly to the formation of
Leconte de Lisle's outlook and style. In person he was a thin middle-
aged man, brown hair springing irrepressibly from a large head, a
wispy brown beard that looked as if it had been stuck onto the
bony chin, kind blue eyes, a pinched nose. He never had a penny to
bless himself with but, absorbed in his researches, seemed not to
notice the lack. His clothes were all but falling off his back but this
detail also escaped him.

This queer but attractive figure worshipping the gods as he did
was naturally much taken with Mendès: "Apollo in person!" was an
exclamation that had already been heard. He sought and obtained
the master's permission to introduce Mendès and his friends and
one Saturday evening the little cavalcade, Ménard, Mendès, Coppée,
De Ricard and Villiers climbed to the fifth floor of the house in
the Boulevard des Invalides where the great man and his satellites
awaited them.

The contrast between Leconte de Lisle and Ménard was extreme,
Ménard all affability and rags, Leconte de Lisle stiff, correct, impeccably clothed, sitting in a salon which had the air of a museum.
However he was gracious; though not admitting to the fact, he knew
the work of Mendès and had privately determined that he could
use the objectionable but undeniably go-ahead young man to forward
his own intention of becoming the foremost figure in the literary
world of Paris. Each imagining himself the spider to the other man's
fly, the meeting was cordial; that is to say, Mendès poured out all his
not inconsiderable powers of flattery ("Here is our Mecca!" was one
of his first remarks), which Leconte de Lisle accepted imperturbably
but with an expression that in another could have been described as
benign.

It was in fact not possible for Leconte de Lisle to look benign. How one regarded him depended on the angle from which one did so, for he had a blind eye in which he wore the famous square monocle. He was also on the short side and rather stout (he was then verging on fifty), and it was freely and correctly said that he could tell friends from enemies from the position they took up, facing him or content with a side view. He helped his friends by sitting sideways, and stationed thus he made an arresting figure, decidedly Lisztian with strong profile and long hair to the collar. "His brow has the mystery of a temple!" cried Silvestre, a somewhat unexpected devotee. "His eyes are those of an eagle!"

Leconte de Lisle was a strong poet and the effect of his work on the young poets is understandable. Nevertheless his work, like the man of the Saturday soirees and like the name he had assumed, was primarily a pose. He was in origin a Le Conte, a Norman family of no particular account (father a doctor, grandfather a druggist) who had allied themselves at several removes with a noble house. He would speak occasionally of his descent from the Vikings. As a young man he was politician rather than poet, pressing for the freeing of the slaves on which his family, who had become sugar planters in Réunion, depended, and, after his father had cut off his money, leaving the island and the quadroon cousin he had adored since boyhood to become one of the many antichristian Republicans in the Paris of Louis-Philippe. There he met Ménard and founded a club which had as its guiding principle the queer theory of the transmigration of the soul from star to star. From this to the socialism of George Sand and Fourier was no great step and the young Le Conte was soon preaching civil war and the inalienable right of the poor to happiness, an exemplary aim but coming strangely from a man fundamentally unfriendly, who could not bear contact with the multitude—strange, that is, were this not the case in nine examples of the social reformer out of ten. His family disowned him. He joined the Central Republican Club and was given the mission, in 1848, of "opening the eyes of Brittany." But Brittany preferred to keep its eyes closed, and gave the missionary, busily preaching against the evils of religions, such a hot reception that he barely escaped to Paris with his life. He took part in the revolution but as a matter of form only; like all idealists unblessed with a sense of humor he had become disgusted with politics and people; he arrived inevitably at a disillusioned middle age, a disillusion which he covered, effectively one must admit, by setting himself up as Leconte de Lisle, the poet-priest of the cult of impassivity, a mixture of the Hindu, Buddhist and Confucian philosophies.

Actually he remained a romantic, sentimental and bad-tempered man but had successfully imposed the veneer of "impassibility" on all but his young wife (in company "my child") and his several women friends. He was in truth, as so many idealists, a cold man and unsociable, and to this extent was able to believe in the person he presented to the public, but the sharp Mendès, his "Mecca" notwithstanding, was not deceived, not for one instant. "Leconte de Lisle," he said on his return home, "being one of those who claim to conceal their intimate personality from the vulgar eye, we had a pretty dull time of it; not one worthwhile story to repeat." Even De Ricard, who might have been expected, could he have kept envy out of his heart, to appreciate the great man, remarked acutely that "he always had a tinge of the barbarian in him."

In the great one's presence, however, Mendès played up to his company and launched into a dissertation on the difference between the chaste pagans and the licentious early Christians. He backed his argument by several Mendèsian examples, and one of the women present complained of such stories being told before her daughter. Whereupon the master "glaring at her through his terrible monocle and employing his redoubtable irony" replied coldly that "in my house friends are in their own home, and in any case the elevation of their thoughts places them above all worldly conventions."

Such was Leconte de Lisle. He has long since been relegated to histories of French literature, being notable now for a single fact, that he was the only poet and almost the only person to arouse Verlaine's dislike, a feat indeed and one which explains him better than many words.

Two of his disciples had distinction. Léon Dierx, also a creole from Réunion, was a tall fair young man given to the writing of melancholy poems. Pale-faced, sad-faced, quiet to the point of non-existence, his devotion to the master was embittered by Leconte de Lisle's immoderate passion for women and by what he saw as unfaithfulness, for he too had been separated from his first love in the island. Dierx had published his first volume of poems *Les Aspirations* five years earlier and was on the eve of his second. He was to become well known, but at that time his talent remained unacknowledged. Nevertheless, his somber black clothes, grave voice, tranquil but pensive expression, slow and hesitant gestures, exquisite politeness and even his distant manner, as though his thoughts were forever elsewhere, were being accepted at the various soirees of poets, painters and musicians as a necessary part of the atmosphere. "One of our saints. Never has he sinned against the dream and the ideal," declared Mendès who was to sin often enough. And even De Ricard could say no worse of him than that "he always seemed to be in a dream." He was a romantic writer persuaded by Leconte de Lisle into "impassibility" and with much the same result. To connect this eminently poetical figure with railways would seem a sacrilege, yet such was his fate. His poems did not pay, his family was ruined by the failure of the sugar crop, and, helped by Mendès "so that he could develop his talent in peace," he followed so many of his kind into a civil service clerkship, which in his case was to lead him incongruously to the baggage office of a provincial railway station.

He and the other staunch disciple, J.-M. de Hérédia, shared a common faith, both firmly remaining Catholic in spite of Leconte de Lisle's bitter anticlericalism, and a common courtesy. But Hérédia's manners were the ceremonious ones of a Spanish grandee —he was from Cuba—and they did not always include consideration for the feelings of others. He was rich, for instance, and was apt to forget the poverty of the poets he consorted with. Even the master, to whom he had begun to lend money, was to be affronted by him. When he complained one day that actors were taking liberties with a play he had written and would not listen to his criticisms, Hérédia replied in his loud confident voice: "Let me go to the theatre with you. These curs will soon see that you are with a man of the world and that will impress them. Then they'll listen to you." Man of the world was Hérédia's favorite expression and he lived up to it; he was big and handsome and spent a small fortune on his clothes, parading the streets and, less happily, marching importantly into the mean rooms of other poets with perfectly cut trousers and frock coat, swinging a gold-headed Malacca and fingering negligently the silk cravat, different every day, that shone with splendor on his thick neck.

On this particular evening he differed with Ménard who, his easily inflamed enthusiasm aroused by Mendès' defense of paganism, suggested impetuously that they make a ceremonial sacrifice of pigeons to Venus. Hérédia, after a prolonged stare through his monocle (all disciples wore the square monocle as a tribute to the master), said coldly, "I don't care for pigeon pie." The subject was dropped.

Hérédia was understandably not popular with the young poets of his age and there was much mockery of his mannerisms the moment he left the room and some spiteful remarks while he was still in it. Even Mendès, anxious to impress Leconte de Lisle and constitutionally unable to be downright disrespectful to a wealthy man, could not force himself to more than an oversmiling shadow of cordiality. Yet of all the poets of his time this loud, vain, overdressed creature was the one destined to write poems with the polished, and at times exquisite, craftsmanship which demonstrated to perfection the theory and the absurdity of art for art's sake.

Happily unaware of this irony in store, Mendès hurried back to the rue de Douai where a conclave headed by himself, Coppée and Villiers decided, with the blessings of Dierx and Hérédia, that Leconte de Lisle be acknowledged the head of the forward movement in poetry—or a return to essentials, as they would have it. Leconte de Lisle, the picture of gratified dignity, received his new disciples Saturday by Saturday at the Boulevard des Invalides. In mellow moments he even permitted young aspirants, such as Paul Verlaine, to be brought before him and to sit in goggling silence in a far corner; which gestures led to the immediate though hesitant sprouting of a square monocle in the Hôtel de Ville and at the Café du Gaz after preliminary trials before the bedroom mirror on the rue Saint-Louis. He did more; acceding to Mendes' importunities he gave his patronage to the *Lectures poétiques*, regular readings of poetry in a large hired room by young poets unable to get their work published, the poets carefully sifted by Mendès and the room filled with as many influential people as could be scraped together.

So far so good; this gave satisfaction and hope to the talented young men who then as now struggled vainly for a hearing; Mendès as a publisher-poet was genuinely concerned about their plight, remembering his own frustrations at the Hôtel de Pérou. But to that other Mendès, the Napoleonic Mendès, a journal it was not, a movement it was not, and nameless and paperless he looked about him hungrily once more; looked and, such is the reward of persistence, eventually found.

[6]

NINACUM
1864-1865

Twenty-one years before this first visit of Mendès to Leconte de Lisle a girl, Marie Anne Gaillard de Villard was born in Paris, daughter and granddaughter of well-to-do lawyers; and since their wives brought each of them a handsome dowry she grew up a wealthy young woman. Nina, as she was always known, was an only child and an unwanted one; her hardship was to be given her own way in everything. By the time she reached her twenty-first year her father, "a phlegmatic and nonchalant *Lyonnais*," had retired permanently to the third floor of their house in the rue Chaptal where Verlaine had spent so many years at school. The mother's interests in life were cats, dogs and a monkey which, pampered to the point of idiocy, reigned over the second floor; but being indulgent as well as indifferent she presided nominally at her daughter's soirees, "following her about like a shadow without ever risking the least observation."

For Nina had begun the soirees which were to become the most notorious in Paris. Late in 1864 she married the Comte Hector de Callias, a handsome, charming and penniless journalist and, unknown to her, a dipsomaniac. He married for money, she for a mixture of affection, kindness, and ambition; family love being denied her, she had thirsted after fame since her teens and hoped to win it by proxy. But the only genius this young man possessed was for the bottle, and although the marriage lingered on in law for three years, it ended, except for silent hopes on Nina's part, within a few months, early in 1865.

Unhappy and bored, Nina sought distraction; ambitious, talented (she was a good pianist) and generous, she yearned to reign over and encourage young and gifted men. The answer to everything was plainly an artistic salon; for, differing in this from other hostesses of her time, to her the important people of Paris were the artists: "*Sculpteur, musicien, poète sont ses hôtes*," Verlaine was to write.

The soirees began as musical afternoons then, reports spreading of Nina's brilliance on the pianoforte and of the sumptuous refreshments, blossomed into musical evenings. The star of afternoon and evening alike, the hostess excepted, was Charles de Sivry, a small black-haired young man with long drooping black mustaches that gave him a slightly oriental air. He was popular for several reasons: for his rank (he was a marquis, a fact to which he never referred); for his talent (he had arranged many folk songs and composed light music with contemptuous ease); but especially for his high spirits and affability. He never left his bed until early afternoon which may partly explain his increasing brightness as evening succeeded afternoon and night evening. By the small hours he was the life and soul of the party, any party; he was not particular so long as he was at one. At Nina's musical gatherings he would begin soberly enough, accompanying the singers, singing himself, and improvising dutifully, but as time went on and tea was followed by apéritifs the mischievous in him bubbled out and practical jokes became the order of the evening. The decorous disappeared and the rest gave themselves over to fun with the lively little De Sivry as ringleader.

So opened the soirees at the rue Chaptal. But the name soiree soon lost its meaning; there were no Tuesdays, Thursdays, Saturdays as at Mendès', Banville's, Leconte de Lisle's and elsewhere; from time to time as Nina's fame spread, formal receptions were held, but essentially the house became open house to all young, deserving, interesting and hard-working artists: "No one needs fine clothes to be received by me," she said. "A sonnet is enough." Such could come at any hour, leave at any time and if they had no bed—and Villiers, Cabaner, Dierx and Glatigny of the company we know were often homeless—were welcome to sleep on the sofa, on the great rug by the fire, in the hammock in the garden. Even on the nights of formal receptions the night truly began when the distinguished guests had gone, leaving Nina with her circle of intimates sprawled on the floor, declaiming from the hearth rug, perched on the piano. None had any notion of time; there were newly written poems to be read, newly composed songs to be sung, plans to be hatched against the Government and, that standard form of *jeu d'esprit* dispatched, the work of their great predecessors to be studied, analyzed and emulated: "all loved Nina's because there could be obtained not only food and wine but enthusiasm and encouragement for the most wretched and broken. Rich and poor they came to bewail the misery of their failures, to be consoled, to argue, to quarrel and above all to express their ideas, always having in common the supremacy of art."

The lines were Mendès', for of course Mendès was soon there.

De Sivry knew Chabrier, Chabrier knew Mendès, it was too simple in the Paris of those days. In no time at all Mendès and his assorted company had virtually taken possession of Nina's house and the preponderantly musical element of the gatherings changed as Nina discovered the charms of poetry and poets. Soon Banville, Leconte de Lisle, Gautier and other celebrities were to be seen at the occasional dinner, and Nina had been launched as a literary hostess. The memoir writers have found it difficult to take her seriously, indeed have not tried very hard; many stories have been told about Nina and her poets and musicians and almost all leave the impression of a bedlam. "The studio of cerebral disorder," reported the Goncourts; "My private Charenton," said Nina once, comparing it to the French asylum; and such sanction from the ringleader has been too great a temptation to resist. There was much fooling, some of it stupid, but there was also in these early days the sense of a mission, the one thing often so wrapped in the other that one would need to be young and creative and optimistic to distinguish and approve.

There was nonetheless a something in Nina's face even then, in her eyes particularly, which foretold her end and the end of her soirees. But no one troubled to see the unpleasant, obvious though it was, the present being altogether too attractive. Only one man, and he surely the last person one would expect, had not merely an inkling of the truth but indeed wrote it down at the time. The young Verlaine first came into his own in the *"Quartier Ninacum,"* as he called it; that is to say Nina drew him out. What she drew was not particularly impressive; he showed himself a good second or third to De Sivry, Chabrier and the other bright sparks, and he became even more active, verbally, in musical collaboration and in the condemnation of Offenbach which was de rigueur in that company. Sivrot, as De Sivry soon became, had a gift for musical pastiche and parody, and Offenbach, Delibes, Halévy, Lecocq and Hervé suffered at his hands; but for all that and for all the youthful scorn of his latest disciple, the book for an operetta which Verlaine was soon enthusiastically planning called for music of precisely that nature. Yet something else was stirring sleepily, for his sonnet to his hostess shows observation and ability. His opening line, *"Des yeux tout autour de la tête,"* puts a finger on her one beauty, the enormous black eyes, intelligent, emotional, with their alarming glint of irresponsible playfulness, of the willful, the reckless glowing from an excessively pale face and set off by

Ses cheveux, noir tas sauvage où
Scintille un barbare bijou . . .

As for the person behind those exciting, disturbing eyes:

Point très bonne. Un esprit d'enfer
Avec des rires d'alouettte. . . .

a picture that needs no explanation. "*Ange pervers*" Verlaine sums up, for there was little peace and no certainty where she was except the delightful-horrific knowledge that there could be no boredom and would probably be trouble. He also uses the nickname by which she came to be known: *La Pétroleuse:* and this characterizes her accurately: the incendiary, reveling in the stirring of revolt against the smug, the satisfied, the established. Verlaine does not mention her gift for putting the most disparate people at their ease, yet admirable hostess though she was, apparently shaping the company to her wishes, there was another and less obvious aspect of her that he saw through the glamour:

La font reine et la font fantoche

he says truly; for Mendès, while giving good value for his entertainment, was using her for his own ends. They were her ends too, regarded in the large, but this was incidental; she had money, she had influence, she could help the movement of modern poetry to its feet; to this extent she was the queen acquiescent in her puppetdom.

Mendès liked to describe himself as Porthos to Glatigny's D'Artagnan, the Aramis of Coppée and the grave Athos of Dierx but his charm aroused in Nina nothing more lethal than a mixture of admiration and amusement. In her house Othello was preferred to Apollo. Othello was Charles, the more remarkable of the Cros brothers. Henry Cros had just sketched Verlaine, a long-haired Verlaine with a slight Mongolian mustache—a faint effort to imitate the more luxuriant growth of De Sivry—but Charles was to be the chief glory of the family, a glory that Nina clearly perceived. In appearance he showed a Negroid origin, woolly hair parted in the middle, flat nose, tiny mustache ornamenting a long upper lip but with clear blue eyes contrasting oddly with swarthy skin. Not in repose a particularly attractive young man, but he was rarely seen in repose, seeming to be possessed by unrest. He spent his life searching after the unknown, said an admirer. He began as a small boy—"Father, I've discovered how to raise the dead. I'm beginning after breakfast." "Oh please don't, Charles, they would be so unhappy." And he continued to find it. He invented color photography, the telephone and the gramophone among other things but, hurrying on to the next discovery, forgot or could not raise the money to put his inventions into commercial use, a fact which still fills many Frenchmen with patriotic bitterness; and as poet he anticipated the later Rimbaud and the Symbolist school with his surrealistic prose-poems and fantastic, macabre verses. An original in his butterfly way, he was not a member of the Mendès–Leconte de Lisle school; he was to form his own group from which many of the lesser Symbolists emerged. His interest in the house was in Nina, and later in Verlaine, who even then regarded his mental and physical busyness with the admiration of the lazy; and it may be that Cros' imitations of Leconte de Lisle and mockery of his mystical pretensions did more than merely shock the younger man and that his penchant for plain speech and unloaded verses struck, dimly and half-heard, an answering chord in the one who was destined eventually "to wring the neck of eloquence."

Dierx was, next to Cros, Nina's favorite; desperately poor, he took to sleeping there every night; he regarded with wonder, being a perfectionist, the successful wager of a very youthful poet, Jean Richepin, that he would speak in verse throughout dinner; and neatly put one of the rare notoriety hunters in his place: "Do you write your verses to be read or to be heard?" "To be smelled," returned the melancholy Dierx. For the rest he remained quiet, statuesque, seen but never heard.

After Cros and Dierx the most regular visitor was Villiers who since the year of the *Revue fantaisiste* had been led to strange shifts to keep his head above water, teaching boxing in a suburban gymnasium, begging loans at the gates of the Benedictine monasteries in Paris and at last feigning madness so that he could get food and a bed in an asylum. By the time of Nina the monks had lost patience, the asylum doctors had come to the conclusion that all was not insanity that looked and behaved insanely, and Villiers muttering imprecations ("What a fuss about a cutlet or two!") joined Dierx, Cabaner and Glatigny when in Paris as one of Nina's permanent guests.

As clown-in-chief he did his duty. In worn black trousers, chimney-

pot hat, loose gray overcoat trimmed with fur, the pockets bulging
with manuscripts, he would enter the salon with his customary
chamoislike bounds, legs meeting the ground unsteadily, chewed
cigarette jerking between his lips, every feature of his face working,
and never failed to provide the expected sensation. Howling with
hysterical laughter he would tell how that morning he had seen an
acquaintance reading Hoeckel's *History of the Creation*, had asked
its price, and when told ten francs had replied, "The catechism costs
only two sous." Having related the story he immediately retold it
in a falsetto voice, again in a voice of deepest bass, and yet again in
a series of yodels. Then he would spring to the organ and sing it to
his own refrain; and from the organ to piano where it would be sung
again to a different accompaniment, all performances punctuated by
bursts of high-pitched laughter.

In another mood he bounded to the organ, pulled out every stop
and played the *Tannhäuser* overture, after which if he did not, as at
Mendès', subside into a corner, he would stand in the center of the
room and say mysteriously: "Plot for my next story. Scene, a room
with a bed, on the bed a woman, round about the bed everything
needed for an accouchement, doctor, midwife, bottles, jars, phials,
everywhere the atmosphere stale, stale. Then appears feebly the head
of a newborn child; he opens his eyes, looks round about, sniffs, then
cries: 'So this is it—life! Oh!' And he hurriedly dives back into the
womb."

Or having heard during the day some praise of a realistic novelist,
probably of Zola himself, a harsh critic of Mendès and company, he
would say impressively before he was well through the door: "Monsieur so-and-so? Very good. Excellent. I'm going to write an analytical
novel too. I have already studied my subject deeply. A rentier goes
into the country one Sunday but forgets to take his purse." Silence,
everyone looking at him expectantly. "Well?" a listener asks at last
as he remains silent, his eyes rapt. "Well, what of it?" "That's all,"
he replies absently. "If anything else happens in his life, which I
doubt, I'll write a second volume." Someone, changing the subject,
speaks of Vitu, the theatrical critic before whom the contemporary
theatre trembled. Villiers raises an imperious hand, says in the tone
of Lady Bracknell: "Vitu? No!" and Vitu is exterminated.

Like everybody at Nina's he read his poems, and once, reciting
to a large and fashionable audience, the guest of honor an Austrian
countess, he felt a twinge at his heart, dropped his manuscript and,

obeying his doctor's orders to the letter, undid his trousers, lay flat on the floor and rested his feet on the keyboard of the piano, reciting soulfully. On the few occasions when Leconte de Lisle attended a dinner at Nina's, Villiers was liable to take him up on some abstruse reference to the Hindu Scriptures; though whether this queer poseur, who would discuss Hegel, Kant and the Eastern mystics with impartial passion, was truly well read or whether the master had skimmed the surface too is a question.

The exuberant Hérédia, as much disliked as Villiers (familiarly "the oculist" as one perpetually with an eye to the main chance) was liked, would stride imposingly into Nina's of an evening patting his latest sartorial creation with a loud "Well, my friends! And what do you think of this thick pearl-gray cloth I'm wearing for the first time today in your honor? Admire it. Thirty-one francs, seventy-five sous at the Trois-Quartiers!" And the friends, most of whom would have been glad to put their hands on the odd seventy-five sous, would look hungrily and growl beneath their breath when he launched out for the thousandth time on an anecdote of his grandfather, bosom companion of the great Pizzarro. But when, later, he faced them from the fireplace resonantly reading his latest sonnet, the admiration was as genuine as the envy. One or two succumbed to the malice of the quiet individual who stood about, book under arm, in but not of the company, the man of whispers: "Didn't you know? Leconte de Lisle writes them all for him." Anatole France, one felt, was surely destined to be a power in the land; Leconte de Lisle, it was known, thought much of him, even listened to him; he was tolerated with a kind of regretful respect as when one watches a cat with a rat.

For the rest, the young men flocked to Nina's, much the same crowd as at the De Ricard and Mendès' soirees but showing little of the formality expected of them at the former and only an occasional trace of the license sometimes found at the latter; Coppée was a favorite as ever, Sully Prudhomme too, Valade remained obscure as usual, Mérat threw the expected stones into the pool, Cladel made his customary caveman entrance but subsided quickly into a watchful silence; Cabaner, swathed in a long and hairy cloak, bright yellow in strange contrast to his brick-red face, drifted in absent-mindedly after he had thumped his café piano until midnight, to discuss the setting to music of poems by Cros and Dierx and was occasionally persuaded to sing in an unmusical broken voice some of his own songs or to play a part of the oratorio he was writing. He was always good for a laugh, as when he described his father as "a man of the same type as the first Napoleon but less beastly" and, after his father's death, his comment to a friend at the funeral on observing the raised hats on all sides: "I should never have believed I was so well known."

Manet headed the painters, the hero of the scandalized reception of his *"Déjeuner sur l'Herbe"* at the Salon des Refusés before Nina's soirees had begun and of his *"Olympia"* soon after they were in full swing, and made a portrait of his hostess which gives some idea today of her extraordinary black eyes. And revolutionaries of another kind were there too, the "politician" Lepelletier reading blistering articles against the "tottering regime" as he prematurely described it, and the sinister Rigault whose suavity made the other hotheads appear somewhat childish, especially Nina and her friend, the fiery cigarette-smoking Augusta Holmes in her symbolical red-velvet dress. Augusta unlike her friend was one of the "modern" women with long cigarette holder perpetually between her teeth, close-cropped hair, curt masculine manner. She gave her own soirees, musical ones at which the presiding god was Wagner. Later, on the centenary of the Revolution, she was to publish a triumphant ode; for the present she played Wagner with a fervor.

But the hot speeches, like the fooling of De Sivry and his henchmen, did not give a true picture of Nina's in these years; for that one had to wait until most of the guests had gone and the select gathered in the walled crescent garden of the kind to be made famous by Proust. There, by a magnificent magnolia giving off thick night fragrance, Nina, wearing the Japanese dressing gown just coming into fashion with Eastern pots, paintings and fans, moved gently in a rocking chair, head back, meditatively blowing smoke rings as she listened to Charles Cros who stood under the great plane tree discussing magic with Villiers: for magic, like Japanese art, was then thanks mainly to Lévi an obligatory stage in the intellectual grand tour of the young Frenchman. The dark Spanish beauty, Manoel de Grandfort, lay prone on a couch working out the next of the "fantasies" she was contributing to *La Vie Parisienne* or the next chapter of *La Cousine d'André* by which she was soon to make a slender name. Augusta swung in the hammock, its faint creaks drowned by the splash of the ornamental fountain in the center of the paved walk; she was trying to pick snatches of the conversation between Mendès and Mallarmé who walked up and down trying to

thresh out the latter's creed: "Poetry must be an enigma; the charm
of it must lie in the attempt to divine the meaning. Describe things
only by their reminiscence. Suggest never state." Mallarmé had explained his theory at a Leconte de Lisle soiree, to be met at once by
a cry of "Do you know where this leads, this abuse of the indirect
and abstract? It leads to madness!" The timid young man, veiling his
eyes, had tried to appear as though he had heard nothing while the
master, sitting massive, profile Romanly to the light, had pinched
his thick lips joyfully to witness the snub of a disciple who dared
to think for himself.

Mendès did not officially take this view; on the contrary he told
Mallarmé that his poems were "miracles of dream, sensibility and
charm"; his "horrible vision of a pure work in trying to decipher
which I have nearly lost my reason and have entirely lost the meaning of the most familiar words" was to come; in Nina's garden in
the summer of 1865 he saw in this mild little spinner of words, this
careful avoider of the obvious, this fastidious shrinker from unclad
emotion a disciple beyond price. But he was on safer ground when
they moved to the familiar question, what name should the "art for
art's sake" movement bear, and was even more at home when,
pausing by the table on which stood glasses of champagne, he
raised one in toast to the three musketeers, Coppée, Dierx and
the absent Glatigny. Dierx, hearing his name spoken, shrank deeper
into the shade of the wall against which he leaned pensively eyeing
the stars; but Nina, noticing his movement, begged him to read
poetry appropriate to the night and the company. He rarely refused
her; after some moments of reflection he inclined his head and recited in his grave, sad voice:

> Le soir fait palpiter plus mollement les plantes
> Autour d'un groupe assis de femmes indolentes.

[7]

L'ART
1865-1866

Verlaine was not of this select company on Nina's lawn night by
night. His devotion to poetry had progressed little farther than the
enjoyment of hearing it discussed at the cafés and soirees. It was
not that he had lost interest in poetry, it was not even that his at-

tention was given largely to lighter matters, it was simply that he did little about his enthusiasms but indulge them. There was a reason for this beyond an inveterate laziness. None warmer than he in the "cause"; and if ever the suspicion flitted across his mind that the "art for art's sake" doctrine was diametrically opposed to his nature and talent he allowed it to flit. Nor can he be blamed; it was almost as difficult for a poet to get published then as now and he could not be expected to throw away the substance for a shadow. In any case his mind did not work that way; in a sense it scarcely worked at all; friendliness and pleasure were its driving force. It is scarcely surprising that the few poems he had actually written were not inspiring, and it is probably true that no less promising member of the group had come under the bright but meaningful glance of Mendès.

Fortunately for Verlaine, Mendès was human too, none more so. Verlaine drawn out by Nina made a companion very much to his mind; and when, toward the end of 1865 and with Nina's help and encouragement, another journal was launched with De Ricard as editor and Mendès his assistant, Verlaine was asked to contribute.

The new journal was called L'Art after Gautier's poem and devoted itself to the popularization of impassibility; poems by Leconte de Lisle, Coppée, Mendès, Dierx and De Ricard demonstrated the strict application of art for art's sake; articles explained why the personal must be cut out of poetry, castigated the emotionalism of Lamartine, the sensibility of De Musset and the lyricism of the Lake poets in England, and praised the importance of the form and the sovereign rights of art pure and simple. "The new generation of poets," the editors stated, "convinced that reverie and the neglect of form are the characteristic signs of infancy in art, devote themselves above all to the inflexible cult of this so greatly despised form and to the mathematical precision of ideas." And Villiers, doing the utmost violence to his nature, declared solemnly: "Poetry consists solely in the choice and juxtaposition of certain unusual words, bizarre sounds and suggestive assonances. The perfect sonnet is one in which the poet makes the most possible use of ingenious and exceptional epithets without the slightest hint of emotion or idea. When a so-called poet objects that I produce works of a glacial coldness and gives me a look of disdainful pity, I reply with an hieratical solemnity, 'Monsieur, marble is cold also!'"

After following this barrage of statement and example on the objective and intellectual approach to poetry, one reads with a certain stupefaction the two poems that Verlaine was permitted to print. One begins:

> Souvenir, souvenir, que me veux-tu?

and continues:

> Nous étions seul à seule et marchions en rêvant,
> Elle et moi . . .

while the second launches itself with a:

> J'ai peur dans les bois.

Both poems, indifferently good, are characteristic to this extent, that they are unrepentantly personal and defy the principles of impassibility. To some extent he redeemed himself by an article attacking Barbey D'Aurevilly, a tiresome romantic of the old school, living and dressing after the manner of the 1830's and, like so many others, pretentious, his name for instance being plain Barbey; and still more by an article praising Baudelaire. Mendès thought so well of the latter that he sent the three numbers in which it appeared (with apologies for the faulty grammar) to Baudelaire who had by that time embarked on his disastrous attempt to lecture in Brussels; and Baudelaire, though speaking of the "talent in the younger men, but how much folly and what exaggerated and youthful fatuity," was sufficiently pleased to forward the article to his mother with an "it seems there is now a *school of Baudelaire.*"

So Verlaine lived to fight another day in the ranks of the moderns and perhaps because of his narrow escape became excessively impassible, wearing his square monocle with a defiant and even haughty air insofar as he was able to assume an attitude so wildly out of character, and beginning at last to write poems with a will and a direction. One of these, he recited in Nina's drawing room, the now famous *Epilogue,* two lines of which (owing something to Villiers it would seem)

> L'Art n'est pas d'éparpiller son âme:
> Este-elle en marbre ou non, la Vénus de Milo?

brought him tumultuous applause.

Catulle Mendès

Charles Leconte de Lisle

François Coppée Léon Valade

Albert Mérat

Emile Blémont

Théodore de Banville

Auguste, comte de Villiers de L'Isle-Adam

[8]
LE PARNASSE CONTEMPORAIN
1866

For a moment the young Verlaine (he was still only twenty-two) seemed to have won a modicum of attention for nothing. Early in 1866 *L'Art* stopped publication; it had been bought only by enemies and by friends who had not succeeded in obtaining a free copy. The public lack of interest in modern poetry as in painting (the Impressionists were to suffer too) remained abysmal. Only Gautier, Banville and Leconte de Lisle were being published; the wretched Baudelaire, now near his end, had spent the past twenty years in one demoralizing attempt after another to beg, cajole and flatter editors and publishers into printing his verses; the younger and lesser poets faced the dismal prospect of writing endlessly for an audience of friends who would praise but not pay. The readings organized by Mendès and Leconte de Lisle had failed to spread their names beyond a small fashionable circle; no periodical could live for more than a few months; at Nina's, De Ricard's, Mendès' and the rest they were preaching to the converted, in no way did they seem able to reach the general reader.

At this depressing moment light appeared from an unexpected quarter. *L'Art*, all agreed, had been yet another failure. Yet it was not so; its readers had been few, but one of them, the least regarded of all, stamped into the disconsolate circle like a god, godlike in act and person, and saved the day. Preoccupied by the fortunes of the periodical they had overlooked the publisher, but it was he who, actually reading what he printed and liking it, gave the movement a new and this time lasting lease on life.

Alphonse Lemerre, a big autocratic Breton with fine gray eyes, friendly smile and great yellow beard, a blend of Viking and proconsul, Mendès and company thought, had taken over the business of Percepied in the passage Choiseul. Percepied had specialized in the lucrative printing and sale of *Première Communion* manuals and other religious books, but Lemerre had different ideas; he was ambitious and kind, and he wished to make himself famous through literature and to help the pleasant and talented young men he had met through *L'Art*. "Let the little poets come unto me!" he cried with his famous roar of laughter, large blond head thrown back. And the little poets came; came to the literary lunches in his apartment in the rue Claudin, flocked to his shop every afternoon where from five to seven he held open house as Theo van Gogh was to do with his young painters twenty years later. Eating good food and watching their host at the head of the table, seignorial, authoritarian and with all the mannerisms of a rich man, the poor poets felt themselves to be in an earthly paradise. And not only watching but listening, for this curious publisher was not interested simply in making a name from his connection with promising poets, he knew and appreciated their poems; he learned by heart all the sonnets of Hérédia which he declaimed in stentorian voice between mouthfuls, he spoke the verses of Leconte de Lisle with florid gusto. His generosity became proverbial; no poet of any reasonable pretensions should go hungry, he declared; all should eat and all should see their poems in print. Eat they did at his expense and plans were soon under way for the printing.

The small office and shop in the passage Choiseul became the headquarters of every progressive poet in Paris. Every afternoon the office on the second floor was jammed with gesticulating young men declaiming, arguing at the top of their voices; the entresol where books were stored and sold was packed by a kind of overflow meeting, and the iron corkscrew staircase connecting the two was perpetually cluttered with poets trying to thrust themselves into the heaven of the upstairs room where the great men were to be seen and heard. Gautier looked in from time to time, an imposing figure with his breadth of red waistcoat, and received the plaudits for his every scarce word with a sleepy benignity—a benignity that did not extend itself to Mendès who had had the temerity to glance admiringly at his beautiful young daughter, Judith, still less to Villiers whose parents, when they heard of his engagement to another of Gautier's daughters, promptly forbade it on the grounds that Gautier, master or no master, was a commoner.

Banville bounded up the corridor cleared for him on the staircase and immediately began to bandy words with Lemerre, whose invariable greeting was a huge "Ah! Here is Théoville de Bandore coming to breathe a breath of fresh air." To which Banville would reply with a sparkle, "Yes, my dear Lephonse Almerre, I have come to the celebrated Choisage Passeul of which you are the Fudot Mindi—oh, what am I saying?—the Zereriel!" This form of wit seems never to have failed to please, but Banville remained too accessible for worship

and far too amiable; he criticized only one man, the money-making
Scribe; for the rest, he would shrug plump shoulders with a "They
too are condemned to live."

Leconte de Lisle made no such error; he paid short visits two or
three times a week, aloof, majestic and on occasion "acrimoniously
Olympian" as when overhearing a eulogy of Lamartine he said
with a pontifical frown, "Yes, a fine man but what a boring poet!"
In his wake came the book-laden Anatole France, silent, distastefully
observing and with the look of one who really read his books and
intended to profit by them; the timid Dierx trying to make his bulk
appear as if not belonging to him; and the thunderous Hérédia el-
bowing a broad path up the stairs so that his clothes should not be
harmed and who, breathing heavily, would accost Mendès with a
"I say, old boy, I can't understand a word of this man Mallarmé's
work, can you?" To which Mendès, with a toss of the golden curls,
would give in his smooth, caressing voice a conciliatory, nebulous
reply.

De Lisle then, taking Lemerre's place at the desk, sat monocled,
stern, the monumental profile slightly lifted to the light. A dozen
square monocles flashed in his honor before eyes having no need of
their assistance; his slightest word was greeted with acclamations
from poets astride the corners of the desk, balancing on piles of
books, sitting tailorwise on the floor, propping up the door, occupying
every step of the staircase; even the silent Dierx was once heard to
exclaim in a voice broken with emotion after someone had attempted
to praise him, "I am only a lover of poetry, a humble disciple of
him who will carry the scepter so majestically when Hugo passes
it on."

Villiers and Mallarmé were notable absentees at these moments.
The master had been heard to tell Hérédia that Villiers' recent poems
were "banal nonsense"; and his treatment of Mallarmé's theory of
poetry had not been forgotten. But Mallarmé, being considered the
most trustworthy member, was chosen as treasurer when, Villiers
being absolutely penniless, every man voluntarily gave him five francs
a month. Not that shortage of money or even of food could keep
Villiers down; he would claw his way through the crowd and,
chewing the stub of a cigarette, relate his latest story with all the
appropriate gestures and disappear leaving Sully Prudhomme with
the feeling that "he had just seen a ferocious crocodile in the
garden where he had expected to find a lizard." Prudhomme would

edge his way to Coppée, always the center of a little group, and whisper warnings in his soft voice, for to him Glatigny (then mercifully on tour) and Villiers were equal menaces to his friend's muse.

The masters gone, the meetings grew noisier and the atmosphere steadily more stifling. Across the room Silvestre's indecent laugh would burst out in contrast to the delicate chuckle of Émile Blemont, a coming light who had just met Verlaine at a Banville soiree and had been introduced with éclat as a man with a book of poems soon to be published. In one corner stood the pale Valade so silent that eventually the men around him would turn to ask his opinion. Mérat's coming was announced by the sound of his stick trailing from step to step; he entered puffing the inevitable cigar and, if he thought the atmosphere too peaceful, would interject a "Surely a little passion wouldn't hurt?" or, even more effective, "the *Prunes* of Daudet are admittedly infantile but there are one or two pleasant lines," a saying which brought imprecations about his head, Daudet having declared himself an enemy. And Mérat would take himself off happily, cane clattering, cigar at an angle, with Valade silently following like a shadow.

Painters led by Manet formed their own little group within a group of which Feyen-Perrin (now remembered only because Van Gogh admired him) and the floatingly fair-haired Fantin-Latour, painter of attractive flower pieces, were the main supports. Nina was once seen there supported by Charles Cros (she was then busily composing passionless poems) and Gill, Chabrier and their like filled any available space.

All except Dierx and Valade talked ten to the dozen, acceded with alacrity to the slightest hint that they should read their latest poem, tell their latest story, hum their latest tune or sketch their latest picture, and all but one had to be thrust out of doors after seven o'clock had struck. This one was De Ricard. He was the kind of man who hugs a grievance and he had found a good one. Had he not begun the soirees three years earlier, edited two of the three periodicals and, finally, discovered Lemerre? This last was a little wide of the mark, since Lemerre had actually been introduced to Lepelletier and Verlaine by the ephemeral Boutier then playing second violin in a theatre orchestra, but De Ricard had made the first approaches. Yet where was the respect, the hush when he spoke, the deference to his opinions? Through his pince-nez he observed with increasing rancor that Lemerre was undisputed king of the passage Choiseul except when he made way for Leconte de Lisle, and that of the younger group, much swollen, which first came together in his father's house, Mendès was now foremost, having finally thrown off the fiction of leading reins.

No doubt this rebuff sharpened the revolutionary in De Ricard; in this (Rigault not attending) he remained unchallenged leader and, supported by Lepelletier and Verlaine, made bloodthirsty speeches which produced roars of laughter from Lemerre. Lemerre might well laugh; anything less formidable than this fierceness would be hard to imagine. De Ricard looked and acted like a museum curator imitating one of his livelier exhibits, and sure enough, as men always meet their deserts, this was what he was to come to. Lepelletier presented the depressing (or laughable as Lemerre wisely thought) picture of a suburbanite conscientiously having his fling, writing plays, poems and republican articles with a fervor that deceived himself but few others. As for Verlaine in tub-thumping mood, he had little to recommend him but charm and a good heart. All three seemed booked for a comfortable maisonette and, if lucky, a ribbon across the chest.

Verlaine had come out of his shell with a vengeance, Nina, Mendès and the monocle all having had their effect, not to speak of the two published poems. Lepelletier or De Ricard about, and he preached revolution; absent, and he preached Leconte de Lisle with loud assurance, swallowing against every instinct the general worship and imitation from monocle to Buddhism. "*Pa Indra!*" he exclaimed one day. "How beautiful! And how it disgusts one with the Bible evangelists and all the *vomissement* of the Fathers of the Church!" For which he was given a resounding cheer. And he was soon declaiming with enormous emphasis a jingle he had just completed, of which two lines will be more than enough to repeat:

> *Ils marchaient droit dans la stricte observance,*
> *Les chers, les bons, les braves Parnassiens!*

Parnassians: for at long last they had a name. Lemerre had proposed that, periodicals being unprofitable and unable to popularize a poetic theory, the theory should be made public by an anthology of poems, the anthology to be published in parts week by week. The offer, joyfully accepted, reopened the battle for a title; the chief run-

ners were *fantaisistes, stylistes, formistes* and *impassibles* as opposed
to the abhorred *passionistes*. Of these *impassibles* was most favored,
Glatigny having written a much admired poem to Gautier, *L'Impassible,* and it being widely known that Leconte de Lisle liked to be
referred to in similar terms. Yet the debate continued, the years
having possibly given the subject such glamour that no one had the
heart to end it, and all showed signs of enjoying themselves in perpetual indecision when a chance visitor blowing into the midst of
the discussion and no doubt becoming bored by it, said hastily,
"Why not *Parnasse contemporain?*" a suggestion which Lemerre instantly adopted.

The number of contributors and the order in which they should
appear was an even more ticklish decision to make and Mendès,
throwing a sop to De Ricard and giving himself one by the way,
took over the job without so much as a by-your-leave. "L.-X. de Ricard,
that absurd but divine man, has founded with me *Le Parnasse contemporain,*" he wrote to Baudelaire in a letter seeking contributions;
and continued, Mendès in business mood, "I have put all useless
people outside and hope to conduct the *Parnasse* in a serious way."

And to a point he did so. De Ricard wished the editors' contributions to be published first; Mendès' vanity, though it had the
better excuse, was neither so tactless nor unbusinesslike. Gautier
opened the first part at the beginning of March in company with
Banville and Hérédia, Leconte de Lisle occupied the second and
Baudelaire the next. Then, having leaned back so far in abnegation,
the editors let themselves go; each had a part to himself, printing
sixteen pages of poems, twice the space given to Leconte de Lisle,
Banville and Coppée, four times as much as Gautier and Hérédia and
many times more than the selections of the remaining thirty contributors which were thrust into thirteen issues.

The series finished at the end of June. It brought no money to
thirty-five of the contributors—only Baudelaire and Leconte de Lisle
were paid—but it justified Mendès' hopes, put the Parnassians on
the map and, perhaps somewhat to the astonishment of that easy-
going young gentleman, made a poet of Paul Verlaine.

5.

THE POET PUBLISHED

[1]
POÈMES SATURNIENS
1866

Considering the obscurity in which the Parnassians had lived for the past five years, if one dates the movement no farther back than the *Revue fantaisiste*, the stir caused by *Le Parnasse contemporain* is astonishing. True they had formerly walked in the darkness of no name and certainly the name when it came provided a temptation that no comedian worth his salt could ignore; nor did he; the music halls and cafés soon rang with skits and songs and sketches. The general effort to discredit the movement by abuse and laughter on the stage and in print appears in retrospect as a rehearsal by the Philistines and the reactionary intellectuals for their longer lasting and more virulent attack on the Impressionists eight years later, the difference being that the first was in part deserved, the second not at all.

Some surprising developments followed the anti-*Parnasse* attacks, including a duel fought by Mendès which he lived through, and, more noteworthy, the slapping of Daudet by Verlaine—in the back. This followed the publication of the *Parnassiculet contemporain*, a skit largely written by Daudet making cruel fun of the denizens of the Hôtel de Pérou under the alias of the Dragon Bleu. Zola, who had ridiculed the Parnassians' struggles to get into print— "these reviews of theirs never last long, but as one succeeds another the little army marching after Monsieur Mendès doesn't lose heart at all and falls into step once again with the utmost conviction"— now said briefly but unkindly, "like the fakirs of India absorbed in contemplation of their navels, the Parnassians pass the evenings admiring each other."

Another lance was broken by a would-be Parnassian rejected by Mendès, the young Jean Richepin, who promptly published an anti-Parnassian periodical which he named *Les Vivants* on the assumption that the Parnassians were moribund. But the main attack, and the one that really made the movement, was launched by Barbey D'Aurevilly. Annoyed both by Parnassian criticisms and by their omission of a young friend of his, he published in the *Nain jaune* in the late autumn a series of *Médaillonets*, reviews of every contribution to the *Parnasse contemporain*. Barbey was a hard-hitting critic and mingled truth with virulence. He dispatched Verlaine quickly, quoting a line of one of his eight poems

> *Elle a*
> *L'inflexion des voix chères qui se sont tués*

with a "when we listen to Monsieur Paul Verlaine we could wish that his voice had a similar inflection"; instead, one read "a puritan Baudelaire, a droll and unhappy combination, with none of the brilliant talent of Monsieur Baudelaire, and with reflections here and there of Monsieur Hugo and Alfred de Musset."

This last was a cruel cut and the whole had more substance than was comfortable; substitute "Batignolles" for "puritan" and there apparently is Verlaine, an infelicitous echo of better men. If this was not the exact truth it was close enough to rankle, and nothing more so than the puritan.

On the other hand this was fame, one was abused, discussed, one was an acknowledged poet. Verlaine, essentially a happy soul, soon regarded the affair entirely from the sunny side, and strong in the belief that he must after all be a man of consequence, a belief nourished by the acceptance of three poems by *La Revue du XIX*⁰ *Siècle*, began busily to prepare a volume for publication side by side with Coppée. He had moved into a friendship with Coppée, collaborating with him on a poetic skit in eleven scenes and an epilogue—*Revue de l'année, 1867*—which occupied three of the four pages of a little review *Le Hanneton*, a skit containing two lines

> *Nous mendierons la soupe aux portes des casernes,*
> *Monsieur, et nous irons coucher dans les plâtras!*

which Verlaine twenty years later was to find "almost prophetic."

But at the time it was a game; nothing he liked better than collaboration which combined company with a not too serious exercise of a gift, and nothing better than collaborating with a young man on whose common sense one could rest gratefully while relishing the loving atmosphere of his home. And if Coppée had an adoring mother and sister convinced of his genius, why so had he, the sole difference being that his mother and Elisa substituted for faith in him as poet an all-embracing wish to give him what he thought he wanted. He now wanted to publish a book of verse and Elisa, following his every move with loving interest from her home at Lécluse, offered to pay for it. The printing of the *Parnasse contemporain* had cost the contributors two thousand francs and the money had to come from the pockets of those who could scrape it together. Though well paid at the Hôtel de Ville, Verlaine was sufficiently un-French to allow generosity to outweigh prudence, of which he had slender store. He was, in short, chronically hard up, and gratefully accepted Elisa's offer. On October 20, then, appeared simultaneously under Lemerre's imprint Coppée's *Le Reliquaire* and Verlaine's *Poèmes saturniens*.

Coppée's book had a succès d'estime after the manner of Glatigny's and Mendès' first volumes; Verlaine's fell flat, only two journals reviewing it, one scathingly. The critics of those days have since been blamed for blindness, but the truth is that Coppée's poems deserved notice, Verlaine's with one exception did not; Coppée did adequately what he set out to do, Verlaine did not. No man, given such a framework as Verlaine had put together, could be expected to extract a single poem from it, still less to deduce from a few hints here and there in versification and melody that a genius had arrived and with him a true revival of French poetry.

In any case the genius had not arrived. *Poèmes saturniens* began with a motto in the form of a poem explaining that he, like all those born under Saturn must suffer and die:

> Les Sages d'autrefois, qui valaient bien ceux-ci,
> Crurent, et c'est un point encor mal éclairci,
> Lire au ciel les bonheurs ainsi que les désastres,
> Et que chaque âme était liée à l'un des astres.
> (On a beaucoup raillé, sans penser que souvent
> Le rire est ridicule autant que décevant,
> Cette explication du mystère nocturne.)
> Or ceux-là qui sont nés sous le signe SATURNE,

Fauve planète, chère aux nécromanciens,
Ont entre tous, d'après les grimoires anciens,
Bonne part de malheur et bonne part de bile.
L'Imagination, inquiète et débile,
Vient rendre nul en eux l'effort de la Raison.
Dans leurs veines le sang, subtil comme un poison,
Brûlant comme une lave, et rare, coule et roule
En grésillant leur triste Idéal qui s'écroule.
Tels les Saturniens doivent souffrir et tels
Mourir,—en admettant que nous soyons mortels,—
Leur plan de vie étant dessiné ligne à ligne
Par la logique d'une Influence maligne.

* * *

Sages of old as wise as ours to-day
Thought—'tis a riddle dark as formerly,
To read men's good and evil fates in heav'n,
Each soul being to some planet's influence giv'n
(And much we scoff: ridicule none perceives
The more ridiculous, as it deceives,—
At this reply unto the Sphinx of night).
But those whose birth occurred by Saturn's light
To wit, wild star, to necromancers dear,
Share, if my reading of old words be clear,
Misfortunes many, jealousy most black;
And morbid Fancy ever on the rack
To Reason's labours gives a fierce denial;
While in their veins like poison from a vial
The subtle blood, as lava, raves, then roll'd
In ice-drops, strikes their dim Ideal cold.
Thus the Saturnians suffer, thus must die,—
(Unless you grant man's immortality).
Their chart of life Fate figures line by line,
More accurate she the more she is malign.

Nearly all the poems which follow adhere to the declared pattern, the first section, *Melancholia* having in it *"Résignation," "Nevermore," "Lassitude"* and *"L'Angoisse"* and the rest of the volume being only a little more cheerful. The mood of the book and the Saturnian explanation has led to the conclusion that Verlaine at the ripe age of twenty-two was after the manner of genius foretelling the course of his life. The idea is at once too obvious and too subtle; Verlaine was to remain a happy man through most of his miseries and in 1866 the miseries existed in print only: the marriage of Elisa (whom he could see whenever he cared to make the journey and from whom he heard regularly) and the death of his father (the effect of which was not, understandably, lifelong) were the sum of his sorrows to date. He had a doting mother, many friends and no enemies, security, ample means and hopes without end, varied and changeable though they might be.

The motto was merely an expression of the melancholy then de rigueur with the young poets who wrote—with Baudelaire well in mind and with hearts bounding with hope and happiness—of doom, death, wretchedness without end and all the horrors their imaginations could compass. The mood of the volume as a whole was a blend of this youthful hankering after morbidity and of Verlaine's wish to be a true Parnassian.

He tried hard. The Prologue ranges dutifully through the glories of the mystic East, the classical Aegean, the southern troubadours, to the unhappy lot of the modern poet; in the volume proper one finds the expected nature pieces, historical poems, barbaric names, and the inevitable slighting reference to De Musset; and the Epilogue winds up the whole with an explanation, very well done for a task completely against the grain, of the Parnassian conception of poetry. If one overlooks the occasional un-Parnassian intrusion of the personal *"mon pauvre coeur"* and the like, and if one does not scan it too searchingly, the volume passes muster as in the main an obvious imitation of Baudelaire. But since a man cannot be kept down indefinitely even if he does his utmost to stay under, Verlaine emerges occasionally as a very human being and as poet expressing that individuality. The very first poem

> *Tout enfant, j'allais rêvant Ko-Hinnor,*
> *Somptuosité persane et papale*
> *Héliogabale et Sardanapale!*
>
> *Mon désir créait sous des toits en or,*
> *Parmi les parfums, au son des musiques,*
> *Des harems sans fin, paradis physiques!*
>
> *Aujourd'hui, plus calme et non moins ardent,*
> *Mais sachant la vie et qu'il faut qu'on plie,*

J'ai dû refréner ma belle folie,
Sans me résigner par trop cependant.

Soit! le grandiose échappe à ma dent,
Mais, fi de l'aimable et fi de la lie!
Et je hais toujours la femme jolie,
La rime assonante et l'ami prudent.

sets off in good Parnassian style, the personal note excepted; but even in this best-forgotten sonnet the essential man will intrude, and there he is plain enough in the last line of the first quatrain.

The poet is discovered inexplicably in the middle of the little volume, in the section dedicated to Mendès.

Les sanglots longs
Des violons
*   De l'automne*
Blessent mon coeur
D'une langueur
*   Monotone.*

Tout suffocant
Et blême, quand
*   Sonne l'heure,*
Je me souviens
Des jours anciens
*   Et je pleure;*

Et je m'en vais,
Au vent mauvais
*   Qui m'emporte*
Deçà, delà,
Pareil à la
*   Feuille morte.*

*　*　*

When a sighing begins
In the violins
Of the autumn-song,
My heart is drowned
In the slow sound
Languorous and long.

Pale as with pain,
Breath fails me when
The hour tolls deep.
My thoughts recover
The days that are over,
And I weep.

And I go
Where the winds know,
Broken and brief,
To and fro,
As the winds blow
A dead leaf.

Nothing like *Chanson d'automne* had been written since Ronsard, and it was not Ronsard, it was Verlaine. Only the irony and the unself-consciousness are missing; for the rest the intimate, unstudied, personal note, the quiet expression of a mood that comes to all from time to time, the economy and the musicality, an exquisite feeling for words and above all for the placing of words so that the mood is recreated not only in the mind but by its actual physical sensation—all this anticipates the mature poet.

The critics did not detect the originality buried in the book and one does not blame them. Of his friends, the praise of Mallarmé alone was more than mere friendliness. The great men to whom Verlaine, as was the custom, had sent copies did not detect it either. Four replied. Neither Hugo nor Banville had bothered to read the book, the latter declaring with usual exaggeration that he had read it through ten times at a sitting, the former saluting the author as the dawn to his sunset. Verlaine and his friends laughed at this typical Hugoism, but it is possible that Verlaine faintly hoped, as who would not, that the master for once in his life meant what he said. The third man, Jules de Goncourt, praised the wrong poem, a juvenile effusion, and the fourth, Sainte-Beuve, said, "We should not take poor good Baudelaire as our starting point and try to outdo him," which was well said if one overlooks the patronizing reference, but for the rest praised the historical pieces—the weakest in the book—and the nature poems and urged Verlaine to concentrate his attention objectively on the descriptive type of verse which of all things was least suited to his genius.

Verlaine was to take his advice, yet such is the protection given to the instinctive artist, that he was to make, beginning from a false premise, a thing nearly perfect. But first was to come a different kind of publication.

[2]

LES AMIES
1867-1868

It is typical of the career and character of Verlaine that his first book should be eminently respectable, the most decorous of revolts conforming to every conventional requirement, and that his second could not be mentioned in polite circles and had to be passed surreptitiously around a selected group of friends. Verlaine, in most things anything but French, was French to the core in his reaction to physical appetites; he not only enjoyed his meals, his drinks, his sexual excursions with a voracious and uncomplicated relish but even found an enormous exhilaration merely in contemplating the various manifestations of physical pleasure. He was absolutely without the moral sense that society has found it necessary to adopt in self-preservation; to him the body, no matter whose body, was fair game. It was also, as were the millions of scents, sounds and sights in his world, an experience to be transmuted into a work of art. He who had played at poetry was finding himself, thanks largely to the Parnassian springboard, a born poet; a man who wrote poetry as he drew breath, and being what he was must write about any and everything that impinged on his senses. Hence one good reason for the unusual charm of his work: for in this he was absolutely un-French, his fellow poets being conscious artists to a fault, closer to the English and blood-brother to the Russians.

One result of the *Parnasse contemporain* was to open the columns of some ephemeral periodicals to its contributors, and in 1867 Verlaine published a number of poems (including the joint effort with Coppée) in *Le Hanneton*, a satirical journal edited by Eugène Vermersch, a young and unbalanced man who was well on the way to fancying himself a second Robespierre but whose chief claim to notice then was the challenge he sent to the editor of the journal which had belabored the *Poèmes saturniens*. To those who know their Toulouse-Lautrec the title will strike a chord, for some twenty years later the painter was to make one of his second homes in this Lesbian café of Montmartre. But Verlaine did not need the example of Lautrec; he had in his room at home a much prized drawing in red chalk of two women embracing in the manner of Lautrec's "*Le Baiser*"; one of the poems published by him that summer was a sonnet to Sappho and a month or two later he was sending a group of six such sonnets to Poulet-Malassis in Brussels, introducing himself as a friend of Coppée. Poulet-Malassis, the publisher of Baudelaire and the man who had introduced Glatigny to Banville, was known privately among the Parnassians as Lemerre's John the Baptist and it is true enough that French poetry would have suffered without his courageous help. He was then printing the last of the poems of the lately dead Baudelaire, printing them in Brussels for the good reason that Louis Napoleon's censors would have clapped him in jail if given half a chance. He replied gaily that since Coppée wished it he would become the godfather of *Les Amies* (the title Verlaine had given the group) and would treat them like his godmothers and goddaughters: "I'm just the man to fit out these foolish creatures."

The foolish creatures did not get far. In May of the next year the little book was intercepted by the French customs on its way to Paris and in company with Baudelaire's *Les Épaves* was condemned as indecent literature by *le tribunal correctionel* at Lille and the whole consignment destroyed. Verlaine, who had prudently signed himself Don Pablo Maria de Herlañes (his nom de plume for the Prudhomme sonnet), received by roundabout means only eight copies which he distributed among his friends. These sonnets, very youthful works all but the last, are derivative to a degree; in them Verlaine is first a revolutionary doing his bit to *épater le bourgeois* and defy the Government even if only by cocking a snoot at the censor; secondly, a Parnassian writing of times far away; and lastly the young worshipper leaning heavily on Baudelaire, using throughout a Baudelairean vocabulary, once even borrowing from De Musset, and in the example below owing more than a little to the "*Erinna*" which Banville had just published in a new book of verse. Nevertheless, Verlaine can never quite be someone else; the borrowing is well done, the objectivity is given life by a genuine interest in the subject, and the coming poet is observable.

But the reader will wish to know whether or not the censor was justified; was *Les Amies* indecent literature or simply literature? He can judge for himself by a reading of "*Sappho*," last and best of the six.

Furieuse, les yeux caves et les seins roides,
Sappho, que la langueur de son désir irrite,
Comme une louve court le long des grèves froides,

Elle songe à Phaon, oublieuse du Rite,
Et, voyant à ce point ses larmes dédaignées,
Arrache ses cheveux immenses par poignées;

Puis elle évoque, en des remords sans accalmies,
Ces temps où rayonnait, pure, la jeune gloire
Des ses amours chantés en vers que la mémoire
De l'âme va redire aux vierges endormies:

Et voilà qu'elle abat ses paupières blêmies
Et saute dans la mer où l'appelle la Moire,—
Tandis qu'au ciel éclate, incendiant l'eau noire,
La pâle Séléné qui venge les Amies.

* * *

With hollow eyes and breasts rigid, furious,
Sappho, irritated by her supreme desire,
As a she-wolf by the sea runs ravenous.

Dreaming of Phaon, not of her own heart's fire,
She, seeing to this point disdained her caresses,
Tears with angry hands at her tragic tresses.

Then unrepentant for herself she evokes
Her passionate desires to satiety,
Where lust turns lust and dies as ardently
In sleeping virgins spirits she invokes:

She lowers her weary eyelids where hill smokes
And leaps into the depths of the Red Sea:
Pale in the sky Silene intolerably
Avenges the Virgins that her madness strokes.

[3]

FÊTES GALANTES
1867-1869

Here was objectivity of a kind, referring the ever present to the past. But at the same time Verlaine, obeying Sainte-Beuve literally as he thought, was writing another kind of objective poem, and between 1867 and the early part of 1869 two of these were printed in *La Gazette rimée* and eight in *L'Artiste*, which with twelve others were published by Lemerre in February, 1869 as *Fêtes galantes*.

The genesis of these poems, Sainte-Beuve's injunction excepted, is uncertain. In fashionable circles there had been for some time a rage for the eighteenth-century painters, a rage begun by the De Goncourts' *L'Art du XVIII° Siècle* which began to appear in 1859 and culminating in the opening in 1867 of *la salle Lacaze* at the Louvre with its great collection of Watteau, Fragonard, Chardin, Boucher and Lancret. Verlaine read the De Goncourt publication and went often to look at the pictures in the new gallery. He also admired, to the point of memorizing, Hugo's *"La Fête chez Thérèse,"* a poem which set out to recreate the spirit of the lost age, and discussed it with the master in Brussels. For there was a meeting, Verlaine taking his mother for a holiday to his paternal aunt at Paliseul and traveling beyond to Brussels. Hugo was in great form, still fresh from the overwhelming success of his new novel *les Travailleurs de la mer* in the year of the *Parnasse contemporain* and, the year following, the year of the Exposition Universelle, the triumphant restaging of *Hernani*, the first Hugo play to appear in the Paris theatre since the coup d'état. He was therefore more than ordinarily the plain old countryman bending the knee to the young hopeful. He took seriously the cultivation of disciples, to the point of learning one or two stanzas from *Poèmes saturniens* which he repeated to the author with every sign of profound admiration; and although in after years Verlaine was to remember only the "crafty look" in the "beady" eyes of the "sublime and smooth old fox," there is reason to believe that he was flattered by such attention and that when Hugo went on to "tell his fortune" as one of the foremost young poets he quite forgot in his delight that this fortune had been told many times before to others.

Whether the two men discussed *Fêtes galantes*, about half of which was written, does not appear from their correspondence and is of no more importance than any other part of the supposed genesis of the volume, for there comes a moment in the creation of every work of art when the creator throws off all his beholdenment and strikes a path for himself. This the young Verlaine (a month under twenty-five when the book was published) achieved with a charm, an originality and a skill, as well as a successful battle against every natural inclination, that still arouses wonder.

It was a Parnassian shibboleth that one art should be expressible in terms of another ("Poetry only lives through its images," declared Leconte de Lisle, and "All that the poet says in verse must be translatable into a design by the painter," said Banville), and Verlaine was no doubt trying conscientiously to write with these commands in mind: *Fêtes galantes* are superficially an evocation in words of the age painted by Watteau and his fellow painters. Had he succeeded he would have produced a little masterpiece but one without much raison d'être, an exercise in skill merely. Remarkable enough in all conscience, but what he actually did because he was incapable of absolute objectivity and could not suppress a sense of the ludicrous, was much more so: he recreated the eighteenth-century scene by one delicate touch after another—the mood, the air, the manner, all are there to perfection—and then with a delightfully humorous and kindly irony exposed in a word or two the silliness, insincerity and essential worthlessness of the thing he had brought back to life and which so many Parisians were sighing over sentimentally in their boudoirs. The whole thing is done in the lightest imaginable fashion with a mastery of words and phrasing and an economy (the twenty-two poems occupying less than twenty pages) that is past praise. Even the title is a stroke of genius, for all is in those two words. The book is a tour de force, written by perhaps the most unlikely choice in the whole of France.

Examples are better than words, the difficulty being that every poem is such a little treasure that one hesitates to prefer one to another. However, the last poem *"Colloque sentimental"* is more favored than others and possibly with reason.

> *Dans le vieux parc solitaire et glacé*
> *Deux formes ont tout à l'heure passé.*

> *Leurs yeux sont morts et leurs lèvres sont molles,*
> *Et l'on entend à peine leurs paroles.*

> *Dans le vieux parc solitaire et glacé,*
> *Deux spectres ont évoqué le passé.*

—Te souvient-il de notre extase ancienne?
—Pourquoi voulez-vous donc qu'il m'en souvienne?

—Ton coeur bat-il toujours à mon seul nom?
Toujours vois-tu mon âme en rêve?—Non.

—Ah! les beaux jours de bonheur indicible
Où nous joignions nos bouches!—C'est possible.

—Qu'il était bleu, le ciel, et grand, l'espoir!
—L'espoir à fui, vaincu, vers le ciel noir.

Tels ils marchaient dans les avoines folles,
Et la nuit seule entendit leurs paroles.

* * *

In the deserted park, silent and vast,
Erewhile two shadowy glimmering figures passed.

Their lips were colourless, and dead their eyes;
Their words were scarce more audible than sighs.

In the deserted park, silent and vast,
Two spectres conjured up the buried past.

"Our ancient ecstasy, do you recall?"
"Why, pray, should I remember it at all?"

"Does still your heart at mention of me glow?
Do still you see my soul in slumber?" "No!"

"Ah, blessed, blissful days when our lips met!
You loved me so!" "Quite likely,—I forget."

"How sweet was hope, the sky how blue and fair!"
"The sky grew black, the hope became despair."

Thus walked they 'mid the frozen weeds, these dead,
And Night alone o'erheard the things they said.

The book, which Verlaine had paid for, fell even flatter than *Poèmes saturniens;* only a handful was sold and he received only two notices of moment, from Hugo and Mallarmé. The latter learned *Fêtes galantes* by heart and twenty years later was recommending the young leaders of the Symbolists to do likewise with this and *Lèvres closes* of Dierx published in 1867. Hugo, back in Marine Terrace, reminded Verlaine of his fortune-telling at Brussels and proclaimed roundly: "You are one of the first, one of the strongest, one of the most charming of the new and sacred legion of poets which I, the old thinker of the solitudes, salute and love." This was gratifying if not novel, but there was a postscript which makes one love the man and which must surely have given the author a moment of real pleasure, for there is no mistaking the enthusiasm: "What delicate and ingenious things you have put into this fine little book! . . . 'Les Coquillages!' What a jewel of a last line!"

So Hugo had read the book! and how well he had chosen even though one knows why he loved that last so-Verlainean line.

> *Chaque coquillage incrusté*
> *Dans la grotte où nous nous aimâmes*
> *A sa particularité.*
>
> *L'un a la pourpre de nos âmes*
> *Dérobée au sang de nos coeurs*
> *Quand je brûle et quand tu t'enflammes;*
>
> *Cet autre affecte tes langueurs*
> *Et tes pâleurs alors que, lasse,*
> *Tu m'en veux de mes yeux moqueurs;*
>
> *Celui-ci contrefait la grâce*
> *De ton oreille, et celui-là*
> *Ta nuque rose, courte et grasse;*
>
> *Mais un, entre autres, me troubla.*

*   *   *

Each shell that doth incrusted lie
Within the cave where we loved well
Hath its peculiarity.

One hath our souls' bright cardinal,
When stripped to the heart's inmost vein,
When thou'rt afire, and from me fall

Sparks. One affects thine idle strain,
The pallors which, in tired sloth wound,
Thou'dst lend to eyes that give thee pain.

Another mocks the grace profound
Of thy sweet ear. And that one, see,
Thy rosy neck so short and round;

But most of all one troubled me.

A modern French scholar has said that *Fêtes galantes* is Verlaine's most original, purest and justly his most famous work. It is certainly his most famous work; beyond the millions who prize the poems in print, millions more know and love them because they attracted the genius of Debussy. *Fêtes galantes*, like some of the music of Debussy, is near to perfection, the nearest that Verlaine, or any other poet for that matter, was to reach. But the originality and the "justly" most famous, are true only if each volume of Verlaine's verse is to be considered as a whole; and for a poet whose strength lay normally in the occasional poem this is not the best method of comparison. It is difficult to resist the charm of the book and there seems no point in trying, but all the same if the irony—which is part of the charm—the light touch and the technical virtuosity are excepted, one is left with something that any clever young man might have done. It is not the true Verlaine; he was to become preëminently a personal poet, his work expressing his life; there is his abiding charm and there his power; and it is with his life that we must now concern ourselves.

6.

"VILE SORCERESS"

1867-1869

The young man Verlaine worked without enthusiasm at the Hôtel de Ville, taking protracted office breaks at the Café du Gaz where the talk was nine-tenths poetry, sitting the night out at De Ricard's, Mendès' or Nina's where he sang, acted, recited, flirted and talked, and having in general what he would describe as a very good time. Although he was not one of the leaders in the various assemblies and cafés he frequented (and there was rarely a night that he was not found at one or the other), his curious but likeable face, with its sharply angled eyebrows, deep slits of eyes between wide cheekbones and fine hair already thinning above his high brow, had long since become a looked-for feature in the landscape; his laugh was heard often, deep and hoarse, he was an excellent listener, a natural comic, obliging to the point of folly and absolutely without envy or pride. His one trouble, if trouble it could be called to one so easy-going, had been that his schoolboy passion for poetry showed signs of going to seed and dissipating itself in footling directions. Then more by luck than judgment he found himself a Parnassian and his natural genius thrust itself through Parnassian rules and a sluggish temperament with an ease that would have puffed up a more self-centered man.

It might reasonably be thought that with two volumes of poetry behind him, a growing reputation among the young literati (for they, though penniless, were exceedingly vocal) as one of the coming writers of the day, with a safe if boring job, an adoring mother, a comfortable home and friends by the dozen, his lot was a happy one and his future rosy. But in 1867 in the midst of this undeniably pleasant existence and at the moment when his true vocation was being demonstrated with such power, three events—the death of Elisa, the reappearance of a successful Glatigny in Paris, and the legal separation (divorce then not being permitted) of Nina from her husband—threatened to wreck his life.

He had acquired a taste for drink in 1862; that is to say, he discovered the pleasures of drinking in company, which is not quite the same thing; but for several reasons the taste was kept within bounds during the next few years: the presence of his father until the end of 1865 and a carry over of filial respect after Captain Verlaine's death; the necessity for putting in regular and respectable appearances at the office; the fact that his first poet friends were comparatively abstemious and in any event were too short of money to overdrink; the strong bourgeois element in Verlaine himself—the puritan that Barbey had talked about; and finally and most obviously, the lack of motive or leader.

Then, in February 1867, when the reins of his dead father had slackened, the motive appeared. Elisa fell ill suddenly, Verlaine was sent for and, arriving at her home in driving rain and an icy wind, was told brusquely that he was just in time to attend the burial. Drenched to the skin he followed the cortege and, the ceremony over, stumbled, crazed with grief and shock, to the nearest inn. He stayed there for three days stupefying himself with beer. He had a large capacity for love, he had been shielded from birth from all unpleasantness and, meeting it abruptly, could find no consolation; he had no religion and his mother was too busy with her own grief to comfort him. His one thought was oblivion; it was, he knew, at the bottom of every glass, as easy as that; pleasant too, the dead playmate no longer dead but a hazy sentimental memory. So, in Paris again, he continued the treatment and at once fell foul of his chief in the Hôtel de Ville; he had exceeded his leave and he began to be unpunctual to an extent which could not be covered.

At this moment, in March, Glatigny returned to Paris with a novelty which he sold to the owner of the Alcazar café-concert in Montmartre, that he should do an act every evening as an improviser of sonnets and ballads. The idea caught on and in no time he had become one of the minor rages of Paris—which then included the crowds for the Exposition. The Alcazar was crammed night after night waiting for the moment when, between Theresa's song and a trapeze act, the long thin form of Glatigny dressed in black from head to foot came on with a piece of paper in one hand, a pencil in the other, bowed, and asked the audience to suggest a theme and to give him twenty words to rhyme in a forty-line poem on that theme. Suggestions were shouted from every corner of the room; he wrote them down and, the moment he had written the last of the twenty rhyming words, began to recite the poem he had improvised. "There were no stops, no hesitations, never a moment's silence," said a fascinated onlooker. "It was prodigious." It soon became a matter of pride for the erudite to trip him by insisting that he rhyme the most intractable words and use the most intangible themes, but he strode over all obstacles, glibly reciting execrable poems which fulfilled all the conditions.

To his friends he was apologetic: "It isn't pleasant, but nothing having gone right for me I've had to become an *équilibriste*, a nightly spectacle. Don't blame me too much for I must eat a little. I assure you my heart beats with shame under my black suit when the people applaud. The muse must pardon me these exercises if I can see ahead for the first time because of them." At any rate for the first time in his life he walked the streets in a suit of his own, the long legs covered to his smart boots, the long arms clad to the fashionable gray gloves, striding gloriously about like a millionaire.

Gill made an excellent caricature of him at the Alcazar, and the Parnassians despite the frowns of Leconte de Lisle, the emphatic shoulder-liftings of Hérédia and the pained appeals of Sully Prud-homme came in a body to hear their comrade display a technical virtuosity that many of them coveted. In his splendor after the show Glatigny collected them and splashed his money on them with a childish delight; he paid cash down for the publication of his next book of poems, but that done and clothes on his back he had no more need of money, being so unused to it as to feel happier when it was flung away. Verlaine was there, clinging to company, and Verlaine was at the café chosen for celebration (usually the Café de Suède where he had first met Glatigny) long after most of the band had gone home. Mendès remained often, having a capacity for assimilating drink harmlessly that Verlaine might have envied; Coppée sometimes, De Sivry always, busily turning night into day.

Years later when Glatigny had been long dead Verlaine looked back to these nights at the Café de Suède with an absence of bitter-ness extraordinary even for him: "My poor friend! What a droll spirit and in what a droll body, long and lithe as an eel, wide-eared

like a faun with sharp, impudent nose, peasant's laugh . . . and
noble heart, the best that ever beat." Extraordinary because Glatigny,
backed by De Sivry, persuaded Verlaine to change from beer to
absinthe.

From that moment Verlaine was in trouble. Beer merely dulled
the senses, the "vile sorceress" raised the devil after killing every
resistance to it. What it could do has been shown comprehensively
by Degas and Toulouse-Lautrec. "The source of folly and crime,
of idiocy and shame, which governments should tax heavily if they
don't abolish it altogether"; that is Verlaine's description written
with a glass of absinthe in front of him. It has long been recognized
as a deadly drug and suppressed. In his day, the day of a prudish
literary censorship and a cult of respectability, it was free to all.

Until he began to drink absinthe none suspected that the mild,
good-natured Verlaine had a devil; it was not easy to imagine. His
mother protested feebly, his better friends forcibly, he listened,
promised, reformed, then fell again. He would quarrel, become
violent, was actually thrown out of one café, but though repenting a
thousand times he drank on, for the sorceress promised forgetfulness
of grief, of incessant trouble with his chief, of lack of notice for his
poems, of every trouble great or petty.

In June Glatigny vanished from Paris as abruptly as he had re-
entered it, the brief vogue having expired. "I didn't leave the Alcazar,
it left me," he explained laughing; and once again went on tour.
But he had done his work and De Sivry remained to carry it on, an
able lieutenant if ever there was one. Verlaine had recovered from
the shock of Elisa's death but the absinthe habit had been formed
and excuses were easy to find. Not that he ever became the absinthe
addict that the reader of his confessions or those of the teetotaler
Lepelletier might reasonably imagine. To him absinthe, like every
other drink, was just a social act, a stimulation in company; its
advantage, that by the time the company had dispersed and he
was alone the stimulation had given way to a merciful state of
no-thinking. One cannot even say that he could not do without
absinthe; precisely, he felt the need for it but could abstain on
occasion. There are signs that he began to put up some sort of
fight after Glatigny went away; he certainly forced himself back to
his poetry from time to time.

But if he could have controlled himself unaided—and this is
unlikely—Nina made sure that he did not. She gave up hope of

her husband, separated legally from him and, her father dying soon afterwards, moved to the rue de Londres with her mother. There the soirees continued but with a difference; some attempt was made to preserve the decencies, the tea-time concerts continuing for instance, but by 1868 Nina was plunging into plots against the Government, her house becoming a notorious rendezvous for Communards, and the soirees—the *Parnasse contemporain* having been launched and the second number settled—lost most of their artistic purpose and were given over to the wilder spirits. They reminded him, said an onlooker, of students' reunions. He was thinking perhaps of the night when, a dozen fiacres bringing back a theatre party, Nina organized a quadrille with Cros at the organ, De Sivry at the piano and a third wielding a cornet. Then, peals at the bell unheard in the din, appeared an agitated figure in nightgown and nightcap asking, "Are you ever going to end this mad life?" only to be at once set on by four dancers and paraded around the room in triumph until Nina, helpless with laughter, managed to gasp, "The owner of the house!" Whereupon he was dropped on the carpet, the cornet player blew a blast, De Sivry cried, "To the fields!" and the roomful emptied into the dawn. Or perhaps the onlooker thought of the evening when Hérédia came in with his wife to find everyone perched on sideboards, sitting on the tops of chairs and bookcases, sprawled on the carpet and making such a racket that he walked out disgusted and, with Leconte de Lisle, Banville, France, Valade, Mérat and Mallarmé, struck the place off his visiting list.

The staid element banished, the parties degenerated, absinthe appeared and

> *Dieux, quel hiver*
> *Nous passâmes! Ce fut amer*
> *Et doux. Un sabbat! Une fête!*

A witches' sabbath with Nina stirring the pot was an invitation to Verlaine to take part in the revels, silly enough as a rule but always liable to end in some sort of explosion. Even so, he did not lose his sense of humor; after an excursion with Lepelletier to the less savory quarters of Montmartre he produced a novelty at Nina's in the shape of an argotic song after the apache manner.

This was a notable moment, and one or two of the applauding

crowd might have had a dim idea that the modern Villon was not Glatigny after all—might, if they were not more concerned with egging on the poet who was at first rather fun in his cups. In any event, this was the only good to come out of Nina's—Nina de Villard now, having abandoned her title. Verlaine had already been informed that his presence was no longer welcome at the Leconte de Lisle Saturdays, he having in the heat of liquor contradicted the great man to his face. In Lemerre's bookshop he was earning a reputation for bad temper.

Nevertheless five new poems were chosen for the 1869 *Parnasse contemporain*, which is interesting for two reasons: that he could still be classed as Parnassian and that opinion of his poetry was sufficiently high to outweigh the master's personal disapproval. In the rue de Londres Nina's gift for putting people at their ease had become a menace; the last thing Verlaine needed was to feel himself free (encouraged would scarcely be too strong) to misbehave himself, and more than once he was escorted out after making free with the sword stick he habitually carried.

He rarely left alone; his nighttime companions were often the ringleaders at Nina's, De Sivry, Charles Cros and Mendès, who took him with them to Mendès favorite brothel. Mendès was nursing a severely wounded vanity. Leconte de Lisle and France had finally outmaneuvered him, the *Parnasse* appointing a selection committee of three, Banville, Coppée and France, to take the place of De Ricard and Mendès as joint editors. After some hours at the brothel they would end up at the Café de Suède or some such, and Verlaine, roused from the table at which he slept by a bottle of water being poured over his head, would shamble off to the Hôtel de Ville. Gone were his fine clothes, smart monocle and impeccable top hat; he was dirty, unshaven, bedraggled, his speech surly. When he was not refreshing himself at the Café du Gaz he sat at his desk feeling ill and looking hangdog, for he was not one who could fall from grace attractively.

After such nights his days were dizzy with good resolutions; he continued in spurts to collaborate with Lepelletier in a verse drama of no merit, and with Viotti in comic opera, and he wrote *Fêtes galantes* which seems a near miracle but is actually just what one would expect, for, disgusted with himself, he grasped at that past century of mannered repression as at a haven. But in general he felt hopeless because no one was sitting at the helm. His mother's

reproaches hurt him but did no more than overload a bad conscience. One can love second fiddles without respecting them; the
years of adoration and compliance were having their reward. He
had in any event been brought up in the romantic tradition which
called for a rescuer of another kind. But what hope had he, unable
to carry off the life he led with a devil-may-care air, of the fair hand
outstretched to save?

However, even the novelettish can come true when eyes are
tightly closed. A year earlier, coming as usual to the rue de Londres
from the office, he had passed some people leaving one of Nina's
afternoon amateur recitals. Keeping his head bent as usual he el-
bowed rudely past the little crowd in the doorway, but a girl on her
mother's arm noticed him, gave one glance at the tall repulsive figure
in its dirty raincoat and battered soft hat jammed over the eyes and
drew away in an instinctive movement of disgust.

He had hit his wife for the first time.

7.

LA BONNE CHANSON

1869-1870

In the first *Parnasse contemporain* Verlaine published a poem, "*Mon Rêve familier*," which he reprinted in *Poèmes saturniens*. It has become well known not so much for its poetical merits—it is excessively Baudelairean—as for the light it throws on Verlaine himself. He was to show that there is tragedy as well as comedy in the life of every man and beauty in the superficially ordinary thought or sensation, and it is his distinction that he gave what is contemptuously dismissed as small beer its true value as legitimate material for great poetry. He showed that poetry could be grand without the grand manner. He wrote down every mood, every thought that entered a mind of peculiar sensibility; he withheld nothing; and the form of his poems perfectly suits the subject.

This last, which seems so obvious, is the reason why he appeals to the reader in English, accustomed to the intimacy of lyrical verse; it is equally the reason why his work even today is acknowledged with a certain reservation by so many of his own countrymen. To the occasional visitor the French often appear embarrassingly unreticent; they are forever talking, forever gesturing and they will talk to anyone of what seems to be their inmost thoughts. Yet it is not so. The error arises from the Frenchman's complete unself-consciousness and his passion for ideas; shyness is virtually unknown to him, awkwardness in society of any kind is a thing undreamed of, as undreamed of as entertaining an idea which he does not at once try to define. The misconception is placed exactly in the saying "the café is the Frenchman's home"—this because he seems to be almost always there and always talking. In truth the café is the protector of the sanctity of his home; if one listens to the spate of talk there it is found to be nothing more personal than exchange of ideas. Sit at that café for five years and you will know their ideas to the point of boredom but you will not know the men. And even if after five years you secure an invitation to their houses the polite formality there will baffle all attempt at intimacy.

That is the Frenchman, the most enlivening and exhausting companion in the world and the most reserved of men. And the French poet of the young Verlaine's period, to take the matter a stage farther, was yet more limited; for in his poetry, thanks to its formal setting and his passion for meticulous design—a man's thought being governed by his language—he was never permitted unself-conscious expression of his ideas, let alone his personal feelings; he was mesmerized by the national insistence on correctness of utterance within the most rigid bounds—a fact which had driven the Parnassians to mere word play.

But Verlaine was like the Englishman who after traveling from London to Edinburgh in silence will tell a complete stranger his life story between Edinburgh and Aberdeen. Except that Verlaine would not wait until he reached Edinburgh. He would sit at a café and tell anybody, everybody who would listen, about his latest infatuation, his inability to control his passion for absinthe, anything and everything dearest to his heart or burdening his mind at that particular moment, and especially the ever growing longing for a stable influence to rescue him from debauchery; and how if that influence could take the shape of a beautiful young bed companion the world would be perfect indeed.

Nor did he simply talk, he told everybody then in the world and everybody to come in the future who wished to read; luckily for posterity, reticence either humanly or poetically was not in him. Hence we read "Mon Rêve familier."

> Je fais souvent ce rêve étrange et pénétrant
> D'une femme inconnue, et que j'aime, et qui m'aime,
> Et qui n'est, chaque fois, ni tout à fait le même
> Ni tout à fait une autre, et m'aime et me comprend.
>
> Car elle me comprend, et mon coeur, transparent
> Pour elle seule, hélas! cesse d'être un problème

Pour elle seule, et les moiteurs de mon front blême,
Elle seule les sait rafraîchir, en pleurant.

Est-elle brune, blonde ou rousse?—Je l'ignore.
Son nom? Je me souviens qu'il est doux et sonore
Comme ceux des aimés que la Vie exila.

Son regard est pareil au regard des statues,
Et, pour sa voix, lointaine, et calme, et grave, elle a
L'inflexion des voix chères qui se sont tues.

*   *   *

This strange and thrilling dream is often mine,
Of woman whom I love and who loves me,
And who each time half different seems to be
Yet half the same, and to me there incline
Her heart and wit, and all my soul doth shine
Transparent unto her alone! None see
Aught but enigmas there, and only she
From my wan forehead drives the dew malign
With tears. She seems nor dark, nor red, nor fair,
Her name I know not,—save 'tis rich to hear,
Like their lov'd names, long sever'd by Life's stream.
Her glance is calm as lovely statues shed,
Her voice far off, and still, and grave, doth seem
The echo of dear voices that are dead.

Familiar indeed; but unlike most who write or think so, Verlaine had actually bumped rudely against the ministering angel and did not recognize her, which could have been taken as a warning but of course was not. Nor was his instinct any brighter a few weeks after the first encounter when he deputized with considerable comic success for an absent tenor in an amateur performance of a De Sivry and Chabrier operetta. The girl was in the small audience, but he never so much as noticed her.

She however had noticed him and this time favorably; she said so much to De Sivry as they walked away together and he praised his friend enthusiastically, his good nature, goodness to his mother, intelligence and poetic gift. He lent her Verlaine's two published volumes when they reached home: "He's sure to be famous one day," he told her, a remark which she did not forget.

There was then a gap of nearly a year until, on a certain afternoon of June, 1869, Verlaine walked up the hill to see De Sivry; he knew this part of Montmartre well enough (it was no more than a fifteen-minute walk from the Batignolles and just as respectable), for here was the studio of the Bertraux, sculptors both, where De Sivry was a familiar at the musical and artistic soirees, and here the Chôtel troupe performed on alternate Saturdays, Verlaine watching the plays from the orchestra pit next to his violinist friend Boutier. And here in the rue Nicolet was the house of Monsieur Mauté, a retired lawyer with the mutton-chop whiskers, gold-rimmed eye-glasses and well-filled watch-chained waistcoat of the old school. It is not easy to reconcile Monsieur Mauté and De Sivry as room-mates, yet De Sivry had an apartment in the same house. The explanation was not the marriage of his widowed mother to Monsieur Mauté but Monsieur Mauté's *snobisme*; in the name of a title he would overlook, under his very eyes as it were, goings on which he spent much of his later life denouncing.

Verlaine and his friend were sitting together, De Sivry having as usual just risen from his bed, talking over one of their projects for an operetta when the door opened and a girl came in. She hesitated when she saw a visitor and was going to retreat when De Sivry called her back and introduced her to Verlaine.

The half sister of De Sivry, Mathilde Mauté de Fleurville as she signed herself (the de Fleurville being a picturesque addition with-out warrant), was an attractive girl of sixteen. She had only two faults of moment, being stupid and vain, and it was hard luck that weaknesses which are practically the form in physically at-tractive women should have led her to so much suffering. Although a *Parisienne* of sixteen was far removed in age from an English or American girl of sixteen and although Mathilde had already won a local renown for her singing, she remained young—young enough to have the literary pretensions which contributed to her undoing. She was very young, yet, following the career which ended with the divorced woman of the early years of this century boring the guests of her pension at Nice with eternal reminiscences of herself and the great ones, one wonders whether her age really mattered quite as much as one at first naturally assumes.

However this may be, Mathilde worshipped poets and wrote poetry in their image. Her poems were not good but the contents are instructive. Here is one:

How powerful is a woman's tear!
A signal to the feeling heart
That takes the lovely, weak one's part
Of danger drawing near.

A dreadful weapon 'twixt the lids
Of an indomitable She,
That makes deep wounds, as you will see;
Unless you do everything she bids.

Just to begin with, angry looks,
Tho' this is nothing but a skirmish,
'Neath frowning brows her clear eyes burnish
With anger and gleam bright as hooks.

Then bitter tears rain from her eyes,
True tears of mystery are these,
Soon swelling into floods and seas
Broken by sobs and storms of sighs.

But to dry up these brackish springs
Ask pardon as she understands
By pouring in her dimpled hands
Jewels, ribbons, flowers and pretty things.

This, then, was the girl who came timidly back into the room
at De Sivry's call. Verlaine, who had been searching with a hungry
hopelessness for his good angel for the past three years, did not
see her exactly as she was. In fact he saw nothing at all essential,
the superficial being far too much for him; he saw perfection in a
gray and green dress.

> En robe grise et verte avec des ruches,
> Un jour de juin que j'étais soucieux,
> Elle apparut souriante à mes yeux
> Qui l'admiraient sans redouter d'ambûches.
>
> Elle alla, vint, revint, s'assit, parla,
> Légère et grave, ironique, attendrie:
> Et je sentais en mon âme assombrie
> Comme un joyeux reflet de tout cela;

Sa voix, étant de la musique fine,
Accompagnait délicieusement
L'esprit sans fiel de son babil charmant
Où la gaîté d'un coeur bon se devine.

Aussi soudain fus-je, après le semblant
D'une révolte aussitôt étouffée,
Au plein pouvoir de la petite Fée
Que depuis lors je supplie en tremblant.

He saw too "*Ses yeux, qui sont les yeux d'un ange*" and, putting angels aside, the fine shoulders, the breasts promising a delicious fullness, "the almost imperceptible pulsing of the bluish veins below her eyes and of the faint violet veins at the side of her forehead, the chaste tip of her tongue appearing and disappearing quickly from time to time as it moistened her lips."

For at once the thought had come to him, could this celestial young creature with her "ethereal body a little disposed to plumpness" (just as he liked them)—could she possibly be the answer to his prayers? And she had no sooner replied to De Sivry's introduction with an "Oh! I like poetry very much, Monsieur" than certainty came on him and he was struck dumb with rapture, proving if proof is needed that deathless words can be of any quality as long as they are spoken at the right time and by the right speaker.

The conversation languished, Verlaine remaining tongue-tied until Mathilde murmured that she had heard of him and had read his poems: "They are perhaps a little too . . . strong for me, but I like them very much all the same."

The repetition did not daunt Verlaine, nothing would have daunted him then, having taken the bit between his teeth. He bowed, with a muttered "You are really too kind, Madamoiselle" and added, "But I hope that I shall soon write poems more deserving of the honor."

And that was all; a few platitudes on the weather and Verlaine got himself somehow out of the room, leaving the reader to wonder whether the only child present on that June day of 1869 was not the twenty-five-year-old man shuffling uneasily in his chair before the adorable spectacle of girlish innocence and charm.

As for the Mathilde of that afternoon and the later weeks, she was at first confused by the admiration of this man with the bad reputation and brilliant future, confused but not displeased, flattered rather. And if, as quickly became obvious, he wished to place his whole life at her disposal, to be guided back into respectability and virtue, who was she to tell him that she was not in fact all that he so fervently believed her to be, the pure, strong, intelligent guiding star and lovely besides—if, that is, she could by then see herself as anything but the saint in his mirror? Verlaine behaved as men have always behaved when physically attracted and conscious (though never conscious enough) of their shortcomings. He too was to suffer in his way and for long after Mathilde was contentedly remarried; and this accurately points the difference between the two.

At the time, he retired in a daze from the rue Nicolet, his mind a blur, at one moment seeing heaven ahead, at the next trying to face the hell of a Mathildeless future; and when that evening De Sivry sought him at their regular haunt he found Verlaine meditating on "that almost impalpable something which blossoms in the young girl in the roseate glory and mystery of innocence" (a form of meditation which fortunately he did not then put into words), sitting over an untasted glass of absinthe which no pleasantries would induce him to drink. The next morning after a night which can be left to the imagination Verlaine absented himself from the office and rushed with his mother to Fampoux where, having decided to think no more of a being so far above him, he drank himself silly in the bars of Arras and, the morning afterwards, offered his hand to Mathilde by way of De Sivry.

This change of front was typical even to the improper approach through the half brother. The negotiations dragged on until the late autumn and the engagement for almost another year. Monsieur Mauté regarded his daughter's suitor with disfavor; he did not care for his face, his manner, his absence of aristocratic connections, and most of all for his poetical pretensions; the Hôtel de Ville was too plainly an excuse for foolery with a pen and piece of paper. The thought of a Verlaine being united to a De Fleurville offended him, and he in general liked nothing about the Verlaines, not even their home which, as he told his wife, was shabby and barely respectable, lacking the potted aspidistra in the drawing-room window. Madame Verlaine was also opposed to the match; she gave as her reasons the girl's age and lack of money; possibly she merely wished to keep her son to herself, absinthe and all. On the other hand, Madame Mauté, who had had first-hand knowledge of good blood and who rather fancied herself as an intellectual, took to Verlaine, and De Sivry was strongly partisan. Mathilde without any hesitation that we know of, allowing for conventional tremors, ranged herself on the side of her mother and half brother; she had three other suitors, she afterwards declared, including a vicomte, but she preferred to throw in her lot with the arts; certainly she could not resist the temptation of bringing the black sheep back to the Batignolles fold, a weakness which did her credit. It is not known whether De Sivry or Madame Verlaine opened her eyes to the picture of a Verlaine under the influence of absinthe; De Sivry may well have made a laughing remark which youth and vanity and affection would combine easily enough to dismiss—for Mathilde had come to be flattered into liking a man she had had no opportunity of knowing. Madame Verlaine is more difficult to judge; hints there too, probably, and with as little effect. Verlaine had drunk absinthe, had behaved badly under its influence, very well, but who could dream that he would ever touch the stuff again when he had received his heart's desire, as he called Mathilde? Mathilde could imagine nothing of the kind.

And to see Verlaine then was to see a man transformed; clothed again in spotless black, top-hatted, his breath innocent of all noxious fumes, he (after an engagement had been agreed to) would visit the rue Nicolet each evening at the appointed hour and sit stiffly exchanging polite nothings with a reluctant father and all but speechless girl (when she was allowed into the room) and when necessary play the appropriate game of cards. His mother also profited for the moment, for her reformed son now accompanied her to her favorite tea parties, playing cards and munching petits fours with a good grace. He had abandoned absinthe, brothels and all harmful companionships; he was, it seemed, the faithful suburbanite restored to his true trim path; and though he continued to write poetry it was for the most part of a kind acceptable to the rue Nicolet.

It is a moot point which is the more deplorable, the absinthe-sodden Verlaine of much of the past two years or the ultrarespectable Verlaine of the latter part of 1869. His account of this time and his letters make poor reading; he was earning his Aurora the hard way, and the dishonest way too, although he could scarcely be expected to recognize that in the heat of first love, and his sentimental references to Mathilde's perfections, and still more his sly references to future enjoyment of her charms, grate unpleasantly. It is interesting to notice how very much less admirable he is when painstakingly on the side of the angels than when just being himself.

For two months or more he and Mathilde were separated, her father keeping her out of Paris as long as he was able in the hope that the madness would pass. But Verlaine had allies in the camp and love letters reached the bewildered but excited girl—what a triumph, after all, to have a real poet at one's feet, and a poet who would become famous!—through the hands of the half brother who was himself courting a young actress he had met at Nina's. These letters consisted on Verlaine's part of the poems which were to form *La Bonne Chanson*; on Mathilde's, who was entering into the spirit of the romance with a will, of confessions that she too wrote poetry and of exhortations to her admirer to act like the knight of old who waited chastely and patiently for his lady, singing love ditties the while.

The poems continued—slipped into the hand of a Mathilde he was not allowed to see alone—throughout the winter and spring of 1870; for Monsieur Mauté, soothed by the substantial *dot* that Verlaine would provide, had agreed with an indifferent grace to a long engagement and was eventually brought to the idea of a wedding in June when Mathilde would be seventeen. Not all of these poems were to be printed in *La Bonne Chanson*; some were, as Verlaine puts it, "possibly a trifle passionate for a fiancé's engagement gift, but I think they are to the point." They are indeed and make one blush, not because they are indecent or indelicate but because of the unbearably coy approach to a natural physical function. One has to remember firmly that Verlaine, who was not accustomed to abstinence of any kind, chose this method of relieving himself, and that his tone, objectionable though it now appears, was the result of a genuine delusion that this girl was the goddess who would save him from himself.

Anatole France tells the story in a biographical novel of a moment shortly before Verlaine met Mathilde when, maddened by despair after one of his bouts of absinthe, he rushed into a church, hammered on the confessional box and shouted, "I must confess! I must receive absolution!" One need not doubt this story, maliciously though it was told; even Charlotte Brontë had been driven to the confessional a few years earlier, and she a rigid Protestant and a strong character; how much greater the need of the lifelong indulged Verlaine. He did not confess, being too much beside himself to join quietly the queue he had overlooked, but his instinct was sound—sounder by far than the elevation of the idol he set up in the rue Nicolet.

Verlaine is not the only man and not the only great man who has loved and worshipped on sight; he was merely unluckier than some. His sexual appetites apart (and he did not differ in this from any other lover except that his were larger and more difficult to suppress), Verlaine looked upon Mathilde as the drowning man regards the spar his hands touch at the last moment, and all the rest followed naturally—her purity, beauty, goodness, wisdom being elevated to fantastic heights just as to the drowning man the spar appears the most glorious object he has ever seen, a true gift of God. But Verlaine did not then believe in God although his god—love—was not dissimilar in essence, and Mathilde naturally became the high priestess of his temple.

With this and the quotation opening this book in mind, the poems of *La Bonne Chanson* take their place among the most charming love poems in the language. What, for instance, could be more delightful in this genre or more unaffected, and what more ironical than the occasion and the audience for such a poem as *"La lune blanche."*

> *La lune blanche*
> *Luit dans les bois;*
> *De chaque branche*
> *Part une voix*
> *Sous la ramée . . .*
>
> *O bien-aimée.*
>
> *L'étang reflète,*
> *Profond miroir,*
> *La silhouette*
> *Du saule noir*
> *Où le vent pleure . . .*
>
> *Rêvons, c'est l'heure.*
>
> *Un vaste et tendre*
> *Apaisement*
> *Semble descendre*
> *Du firmament*
> *Que l'astre irise . . .*

C'est l'heure exquise.

*   *   *

The white moon sits
And seems to brood
Where a swift voice flits
From each branch in the wood
That the tree-tops cover. . . .

O lover, my lover!

The pool in the meadows
Like a looking-glass
Casts back the shadows
That over it pass
Of the willow-bower. . . .

Let us dream 'tis the hour. . . .

A tender and vast
Lull of content
Like a cloud is cast
From the firmament
Where one planet is bright. . . .

'Tis the hour of delight.

Not surprisingly the formal visits, month after month, and the formal words in public with Mathilde soon weighed on Verlaine's spirits, but he displayed an admirable resolution for a near alcoholic, a sexually frustrated man of enormous appetites and a creature of impulse; he drank little, absinthe not at all, and in general succeeded in putting the years back. He was helped in this by Lepelletier, who despite a month in prison with Rigault for slandering the famous Haussmann then at the head of the Hôtel de Ville and despite a stream of violent revolutionary speech remained in his private life extremely proper; by Valade and Mérat, quiet souls at heart both of them; and by Coppée. His tendency naturally was to revert to those of whom he had memories more or less unclouded by a bad conscience; Viotti had shot off to Le Havre but whether jealous of Verlaine (as Mathilde claimed) or of Mathilde herself cannot be said, Verlaine's verses on this subject following his best fashion of mystification; for the rest he kept to the old friends, eschewing Nina's and all temptations and being drawn particularly to Coppée, a kind of Verlaine with the genius left out—simple, sentimental, humorous. Coppée had sown his wild oats at high speed and was already beginning the climb, one could almost say the leap, to popularity and rectitude. He had so far, like almost all the other Parnassians, restrained his true métier, but early in 1869, defying Leconte de Lisle's injunctions to despise the public, he succeeded in getting his one-act play *Passant* put on at the Odéon with Sarah Bernhardt in travesty and the famous tragedienne Agar for whom it had been written. The play was an immediate success and Coppée became practically a made man overnight. This led to two developments: to the suspicion of a split in the Parnassians, Leconte de Lisle, Hérédia, France and a few others, disapproving and envious in equal degree, sneering at "the popular poet of the *Parnasse*"; and to a new and delightful gathering of the faithful rump. All Coppée's friends turned up at the Odéon and saluted the piece with a storm of applause so prolonged that one of the critics, eyeing the motley crowd with distaste, wrote in his critique the following day, "Well, that was certainly a jolly meeting of the *Vilains Bonshommes!*"

No better excuse was needed; a regular dinner of the *Vilains Bonshommes* was at once arranged, with Valade as secretary and the young artist Felix Régamey as the designer of the invitation cards. It was first held at the Hôtel Camoëns near St.-Germain-des-Prés, then crossed the river to the Mille-Colonnes restaurant in the rue Montpensier and came to rest on the Left Bank at the café attached to the Bobino Theatre in the rue due Fleurus, a café well known to Verlaine from his early days at the Hôtel de Ville. At the opening dinner here Régamey first met Verlaine. He had heard much about him, of course, for the *Poèmes saturniens* and especially *Fêtes galantes* had already given Verlaine the name of "a master of the *belles funérailles*" among the anti-Leconte de Lisle Parnassians and their friends; and by the time they met in the winter of 1869 some of the poems that were to form *La Bonne Chanson* had also leaked out, Verlaine being incapable of keeping a good thing to himself.

Régamey was charmed by him and sketched him at the table, long-haired to counteract the thinning on his forehead, nose with its comical upward turn, small mustache and beard ornamenting the long upper lip and long chin, pipe belching smoke while Verlaine, no mean caricaturist Régamey thought, made a sketch of *"Les Trois,"* Valade gravely smoking the pipe protruding briefly from the black beard, Mérat with hair slanting over forehead, buttonhole of violets,' cigar angled heavenwards. The dinners were high-spirited affairs with much free speech and were not confined to men—they for a time changed their name to *Dîner des Cygnes* because the beautiful model Léda was guest of honor and were to change it again—but never quite lost sight of their purpose which, beyond eating a good and in many cases badly needed meal, was the exchange of information, display of sketches, playing of new melodies and the reading of poems.

Verlaine was one of the liveliest at table—it is not difficult to imagine the way in which he rebounded from the frigid civilities of Monsieur Mauté's salon—and Régamey never forgot the sight or sound of him as he stood, dessert over, "looking like a nice young monkey taking a pleasure in mystifying his audience." For instance, having improvised a poem during dinner he began reciting it in a tone of voice so completely at variance with the meaning that when the climax, a trick ending, came everyone was staggered. But his chef-d'oeuvre was the recitation of *"Les Coquillages"*—an exquisite treat, says Régamey—which Verlaine ended with an irresistible smiling grimace as he sighed

Mais un, entre autres, me troubla.

At this the company, who knew their Verlaine and his position vis-à-vis Mathilde, howled with laughter—an unmalicious reception which he received with more comical twists of the malleable face.

A visit to Sainte-Beuve with Coppée was less happy. This "whimsical pope" with a malign grin on his ugly face correctly warned Verlaine against long words beginning with *k*, *g* and *c*—the legacy of his Leconte de Lisle enthusiasm—but when Verlaine announced his engagement and began to expatiate on the great happiness awaiting him by the side of his pearl-without-price, all the cynic in Sainte-Beuve appeared, and he said "without enthusiasm" as Verlaine mildly reported and as one can very well comprehend, "We shall see. Wait and see."

Waiting, Verlaine was certainly doing and much against the grain; and he needed all the diversions which the *Vilains Bonshommes* and his quieter friends' inventions could provide. The contract of marriage had been drawn up after the usual haggling in which Verlaine, supremely uninterested, took no part, and the wedding was fixed for the third week in June. But as the day at last crawled near it appeared that he would wait endlessly and see nothing. The evening before he had to put up the banns, three weeks before the wedding date, he arrived at the rue Nicolet in great good humor to find the house in turmoil, Mathilde in bed, smallpox (which had been raging in Paris for some time) suspected. Verlaine's optimism collapsed with a bang and something of a whimper when, the next day, having uneasily put up the banns, he found Antoine Cros, the doctor brother of Charles, at the bedside with another doctor, smallpox confirmed and the marriage postponed, if all went well, to the middle of July. He insisted on seeing Mathilde, which for him was tantamount to a bayonet charge against a forest of machine guns, and left the house in considerable mental confusion, anxiety struggling with what he engagingly confesses as "a disappointment that one might almost describe as carnal."

His "wicked" disappointment was to last some time, for no sooner had Mathilde recovered than her mother became ill, and the despairing Verlaine was told that the wedding could not take place before the middle of August. He continued his "abstinence and fast" with an effort, but his nerves cried out for absinthe and his body for the brothels. Toward the end of July he reached such a pitiful state of nervous excitement and fear that the newly married De Sivry carried him off with Mathilde's younger sister to the Normandy house of the Marquise de Manoury, a friend of Nina, for an enforced rest cure in the country. Verlaine took with him the proofs of *La Bonne Chanson* which Lemerre had just printed but could scarcely bear to look at them; he had planned to give the volume to Mathilde as a surprise wedding present, but what hope, he moodily asked himself, was there likely to be of such an opportunity? Enemies raised themselves all about him: his mother still reluctant; Monsieur Mauté barely troubling to conceal his relief at the successive postponements; smallpox; and, as if smallpox were not enough, another little obstacle, war. For on July 19 France declared war on Prussia.

8.

THE COMMUNE

1870-1871

[1]

Verlaine described his new enemies comprehensively as "The *Corps legislatif*, the *Garde mobile*, the King of Prussia, the Emperor, the Prince of Hohenzollern." The war, he complained, "gave every sign of threatening my happiness in a horridly legal way." It was certainly hard, having suffered the double menace of smallpox, to be faced with a war in which he was not at all interested and in which he might even be obliged to take part. He, perhaps the least militaristic, least chauvinistic man in France at that moment, felt injured and apprehensive for his person as well as his marriage. What, he wondered dismally, were all these people about, interfering with peaceable poets who wished simply to be allowed to marry, enjoy themselves in bed, avoid obnoxious liquors and write love poems ad infinitum?

He was not alone nor, though he was supposed to be an active revolutionary, was his shocked surprise entirely without reason. Ever since the Prussian victory over Austria in 1866 it had been an understood thing in France that one day the Prussians would have to be put in their place. Paris had been stuffed with men in highly colored uniforms for as long as Verlaine could remember; almost every day he had seen the sky-blue steel helmets and cuirasses of the *Cent Gardes*, the bearskinned grenadiers of the Imperial Guard, the veterans of the first Napoleon in their white breeches and black gaiters, and the Zouaves swaggering romantically in baggy black and green trousers, broad white sash, tasseled caps and cutaway jackets trimmed with yellow lace. He saw—at first with a boy's excitement, then with the distaste of the Republican—because no one could live in Paris and fail to see. Scarcely a day went by without an imperial review, a spectacular parade on the Champ de Mars or the sound of a military band on the march.

But the inevitability of a war proclaimed by the Army and jingoistic press for the best part of four years lost its force when nothing untoward happened. The bands and uniforms and parades roused in him eventually nothing but a revolutionary growl as meaningless as the pageantry of dictatorship seemed likely to become. By the late sixties he, like a good half of the population, thought no more of it than of the circuses intended to preserve Parisians from pondering on the price of bread, the rising taxes, the unemployment which had jumped to alarming heights after the end of the Exposition and other shortcomings of everyday life: the *foires* with their gilt gingerbread, dancing and performing apes, the carnival masques in the Place de la Concorde, the congresses of *orphéonistes* bearing standards showing the great lyre, the marches of the *pompiers* with their enormous brass helmets glittering in the sun and the innumerable religious processions headed by choirs, followed by large bands of girls wearing blue sashes and the effigies of saints borne high by the priests and acolytes.

Yet war was coming nearer day by day, year by year. Like every dictator the wretched Louis Napoleon found himself, poor soldier though he was, obliged to take to the sword again and again in order to keep himself on the imperial throne. He had given much to France—prosperity, good communications, a beautiful modern Paris, tourists by the million and glory besides, but in the end nothing mattered but the glory, the most difficult and the only dangerous thing to come by. Let the trains run on time, no matter, the people had a short memory for benefits of this kind, they wanted more glory or . . .

The "or" was political and social reform which Louis dared not grant since it would make an end of him. Glory, then, it had to be, or so his wife Eugénie, the power behind the throne, decided. Opportunity came on July 2 when news reached Paris that Prince Leopold of Hohenzollern had accepted the vacant throne of Spain. Four days later the *Corps législatif* heard from the Prime Minister what amounted to an ultimatum to Prussia and responded with excited cries of "*Vive la France! Vive l'Armée! Vive l'Empereur! A Berlin!*" —cries which the Paris newspapers reported the next day.

For a moment war appeared to recede when Leopold withdrew his

name, but Eugénie and the Army, their heads turned by the shouts
of "A Berlin!" that greeted them everywhere, made certain of it by
a new demand, that the King of Prussia should renounce any further
support of Leopold's candidacy. The demand was refused and the
refusal announced in such a way by the adroit Bismarck's "Ems
telegram" that both in Paris and Berlin war was felt to be inevitable.
And on the 19th it came, with France in warlike mood if public
demonstrations were to be trusted, crowds parading every city in the
country singing the Marseillaise and chanting "A bas la Prussie! A
Berlin!", booksellers advertising French-German dictionaries "for use
in Berlin."

Verlaine did not buy a dictionary and was not among the demon-
strators; his thoughts were not on Berlin but the church of Notre-
Dame-de-Clignancourt where if he was spared (what a thought for a
peaceful man to have to entertain!) he would at last be joined to
his Mathilde.

Yet at first he was not unduly perturbed and, had his nerves been
steadier, would probably never have given a second thought to the
matter. War, though deplorable, could scarcely be said to touch
such a one as he; every Frenchman was agreed that a Prussian army
would collapse like a house of cards as soon as it clapped eyes on a
French soldier; this had been a foregone conclusion ever since
Verlaine could remember. On August 2, just before he left Normandy, came news of the first French success—Saarbrücken captured. And on August 6, when he was back in Paris, a victory by
MacMahon was announced, every window was beflagged and
crowds paraded the boulevards singing the Marseillaise. So the Army
was after all, as his father had said a thousand times, the greatest in
the world and would incidentally save him. Verlaine doesn't tell us,
but it seems exceedingly probable that, Republican and all, he joined
in the singing that day.

The rejoicing was brief. By midnight a telegram from the front
gave the facts; the French Army in Lorraine had been beaten in
three battles and was in a general retreat. Eugénie drove to the
Tuileries that night and ordered placards to be posted throughout
Paris the next day announcing the news. Verlaine, hearing of it in
the Place Vendôme, bought a newspaper and retired shattered to the
Café de Madrid to calm himself over a drink, his scruples automatically relaxed in the hour of need. Perhaps he had several drinks,

having run into several friends, mostly of the literary-political sort, because when a regiment marched by, the band playing the Marseillaise, and a cry of "*Vive la République!*" was set up, Verlaine was among the most vociferous. He even left his seat to shout "*Vive la République*" at the curbside; and conspicuous because of his height, was seized by police. His friends snatched him free and made a cordon while he slipped away and down the passage Jouffroy to safety.

To safety? Mockery was now in that word. That evening Verlaine had his first and last taste of the discomforts of being a true political prophet and, like every young revolutionary (or young anything for that matter) whose theories begin to come true, he felt shocked and unbelieving. What was Louis Napoleon thinking of, to prove himself in practice—and such practice—the hopeless bungler he, Verlaine, following Lepelletier, Rigaud, Vermersch and the rest, had always declared he was? Verlaine's indignation, fighting alarm, rose to a pitch. To endanger the innocent—no, that was too much—was not to be borne, was not at all what he had meant when he cried out on the dictator and demanded liberty. Naturally he had expected that Louis Napoleon would abdicate in due course and be succeeded by the millennium, whatever that might be; but here was the insane man still on the throne, fighting and busily losing a war that everyone had assumed he must win. The horrid possibility soon emerged that Verlaine, innocent of all violence except when under the influence of absinthe (and that had of course gone out of his life for all time), might be entrapped into at least a show of it because of the criminal incompetence of this fellow, might again have to endure a postponed marriage, might perhaps go so far as to lose, or say injure, an arm or leg, might even . . . That last thought rejected itself at once as impossible, but nevertheless what a situation for a man of peace and good will, and above all an engaged man, to find himself in.

Not that the position was utterly desperate; his age group had not yet been called up and there were only four days to go before the marriage. He was uneasy, however, and could not thrust from his mind's eye the distasteful series of pictures that had greeted him at every station on the way back from Normandy, of reservists crowding into the train, of wives, mothers, children weeping.

Wives? Alas, alas, if he were carried off to that cruel, that hopeless war, there might be no wife to bid him farewell, to weep over him.

These thoughts, and the possible shearing away at the last minute of
the wedding night on which he seems to have rested most of his
hopes of bliss (and in which he was wiser than he could have
dreamed) drove him nearly distracted.

As he was sitting in his office the next day moodily filling in
"orders for quarterly payment," a young friend burst into the room,
pale, disheveled. He pulled a revolver from his pocket and told the
startled Verlaine that he was going to shoot himself; his mistress had
just died in childbirth and he no longer wished to live. With this
he threw a bulky envelope on the desk and hurried out. Verlaine
pursued him but was given the slip in the crowded corridors. Returning, he opened the envelope, hoping that it would give an address;
it contained only a will.

This at least had the merit of disengaging his attention from
himself and his woes. The next morning, two days before his wedding, came a telegram summoning him to Passy. In a room there he
found his friend dead on his bed, a shot through his head. Horrified
and sick—for he shrank from every form of physical suffering—Verlaine forced himself to attend to the unpleasant details, breaking the
news to his friend's mother, interviewing the doctor, the police,
begging the priest to give his friend a church burial. Anyone who has
been unfortunate enough to interview French officials on some legal
but complicated matter will understand a little of what Verlaine un-
dertook in the wake of a suicide; for a supposedly lazy, cowardly and
inefficient man it was surprising.

He returned to his reward at rue Nicolet, passing through drunken
crowds despondently singing the Marseillaise, and little knowing
what was brewing for him at the Tuileries where Eugénie had given
orders for the garrisoning and provisioning of Paris for a siege.

The next day, August 10, he saw his friend buried and, in a state
of near collapse, returned to the center of Paris. He could not face
Mathilde so shaken; he sat at a café, the Café de Mulhouse (he
never forgot the name although in his memoirs he relates it to the
wrong occasion) on the site of which the Musée Grévin now stands
and, it being no time for half-measures, ordered an absinthe.

He had greater need of that drink than he knew. He picked up a
newspaper as usual and his horrified eyes fastened at once on an
official notice: "All unmarried men of the 1844, 1845 classes are
called to the colors."

[2]

The marriage took place as arranged—presumably the date of the contract, June 24, exempted him—and the scene of the previous night, with the last farewells of a distraught Verlaine on his knees before Mathilde, was wiped out. Valade was a witness and so was the fanatical *Communiste* Louise Michel, soon to be notorious as the Red Virgin, but who curiously enough had taught the bride in her school at Batignolles. Thereafter Verlaine disappeared from public life for a short period although he had to return to work after two days, to his indignation but not to the surprise of anyone else since he had done little but take days off since meeting Mathilde.

He is next found a week or two later nicely installed in an apartment hung with portraits of himself by Bazille and Cros, a Courbet landscape, a Monticelli and etchings of Dürer and Rembrandt, at the corner of the Quai de la Tournelle and the rue du Cardinal Lemoine with the Hôtel de Ville almost facing him across the river; and at the Hôtel de Ville on September 3rd he heard with the rest of Paris of the surrender of Louis Napoleon and his army at Sedan, and on the following day, the famous *Quatre Septembre*, he saw the Republic once more proclaimed. He, like all his friends, greeted the fall of Louis Napoleon with immense enthusiasm, believing that the millennium had come and that all men would now become brothers, an enthusiasm soon known as siege fever. For the Prussians were closing in on Paris which they surrounded a few days later.

Before then Verlaine's enthusiasm had carried him to the drastic length of volunteering for the *Garde nationale*. Had he wished he could have remained a civilian throughout the war, all married civil servants being exempt from the Army, but in any event Paris soon became the front. He did not go to the length of volunteering for the most dangerous part of the fortifications, being content with the 160th Battalion guarding the Issy, Vanves, Montrouge sector.

So, in September, there was the unmilitary Verlaine going out to the southern suburbs with his percussion gun every other day, as absurd a sight as Coleridge in the dragoons. Yet for a time he enjoyed himself, alarmingly so for a newly married man; the weather was superb as so often in Paris in autumn; the early rising held no horrors, he being an early-morning man; even the drill seemed a pleasant novelty to the bored clerk from a stuffy office; there were no alarms to stir a

timid heart, the enemy keeping their distance with admirable discretion; there was nothing more military than gossips by the hour
around a camp fire or in barracks for this most convivial and least
snobbish of men. For the moment all went well and better than well
because, as he explained, his absences from home were more than
made up by "double rations" every time he returned. That this new
form of an already old excitement could be the first stage of a mortal
wearying he would be the last man to suspect.

In the first days of December *La Bonne Chanson* was printed,
announced but not published, Lemerre holding it back for better
times, but Verlaine was able to distribute copies to friends, including
Hugo who had made a triumphant return to Paris. Hugo described
the book as a bouquet in a bombshell and it is true that its delicate
sweetness—too sweet some will think, lacking Verlaine's saving touch
of humorous irony—came like a breath of flowers into a Paris bom-
barded daily by the Prussians and moving into the rigors of the siege,
with rats and horses already a staple food and wood and coal unobtainable.

Lemerre did not show similar caution with the second *Parnasse
contemporain* which, having been withheld since 1869, he published
early in 1871. Perhaps he feared that the Parnassians would have disintegrated and have been discredited by the end of the war. If so he
judged wrongly, and the *Parnasse contemporain,* in which Verlaine's
Les Vaincus was not the least good thing, was thrown away, obtaining virtually no notice from the few critics still left in their jobs.

Physically disintegrated the Parnassian circle certainly was; Lepelletier was in the Army, De Sivry in garrison service outside Paris,
Hérédia had retired to Nice, Glatigny was in Corsica, Ménard in
London was writing furious letters to the press about the widespread
calumny of France. Only Gautier had come back to share in the
siege and at once to fall foul of Mendès who married his daughter
against his wishes. Gautier refused to attend the ceremony and publicly attacked the Leconte de Lislean poetry of the *"Crapule Mem-
bête"* as he called him: "This pundit pupil of the school of the
Brahmin Leconte de Lisle now explains the mysteries of the lotus
flower and worships the child Krishna." This sneer, not without justice, caused some trouble among the Parnassians once more, Gautier
and Leconte de Lisle not acknowledging each other's existence.

Leconte de Lisle had in any event fallen from his self-elevation. He
first astonished every Parnassian by writing strongly patriotic verses

in the newspapers before the fall of Louis Napoleon. It then leaked out that Louis had been paying him a pension of three hundred francs a month since 1864. When Hérédia who had himself been lending money to Leconte de Lisle demanded the reason, his former god replied haughtily, "When I go to the lavatory I don't boast about it." "No," said Hérédia, "but one can take a thing or leave it." And Leconte de Lisle retired into a deeper isolation, an isolation not lessened when, after serving like Verlaine but without Verlaine's camaraderie with the soldiers at the fortifications, he demanded the deportation of all Republicans, men, women and children.

The Parnassians continued to disintegrate in another sense although the name was to linger on into a third *Parnasse contemporain*; Coppée had become too successful to be popular, Mallarmé gracefully, Mérat cynically, Valade without a word had all retired from the Leconte de Lisle soirees, De Ricard was freely spoken of as no poet, Sully Prudhomme began to write poems which were nothing but philosophical treatises, and Verlaine—well, had *La Bonne Chanson* been published earlier he would have declared himself as fatally un-Parnassian but he was to be expelled for other reasons.

Happily unconscious of his fate he enjoyed his "double rations," his drink and games with the soldiers, his talks with other Parnassians turned home-soldier (Régamey sketched him again that autumn at the Café du Gaz on one of his office days, velvet-collared, beard rather long and wider, sitting with Mérat and Valade), and in spare moments, being a gourmand of no mean order, toured the city in search of beef that was beef, even, such was his appetite, braving Monsieur Mauté who had moved his family to the Boulevard St.-Germain to try to avoid the Prussian shells and whose larder was not to be despised. Here too—for Madame Mauté was hospitable and musical and her husband felt an obligation to Antoine Cros—came from time to time such of the Parnassians who sympathized with Coppée.

As always when men share a common danger the Coppée group felt a special bond, and these evenings revived something of past joys; even, when Monsieur Mauté was absent, the lightheartedness of the prewar soirees. But with a difference, the lightheartedness being close to a kind of desperate gaiety. Paris in the winter of 1870 was not a pleasant place, for the Parisians were not simply suffering the rigors of a siege, they were suffering it in disunity; after the first flare of enthusiasm it had become plain to many that September 4, far from being another July 14, had simply heralded the substitution of one form of reaction for another. Ugly crowd scenes took place week after week, the red flag of the Commune began to show itself, the *Garde mobile* was dissatisfied almost to the point of mutiny and it became a question whether the siege would not be broken by civil war rather than by the Prussians. By the middle of October the Government was building barricades in all the main streets—against the *Garde mobile*, not the Prussians—and Verlaine on his days at the Hôtel de Ville had to thread his way through a maze of obstructions. For the Hôtel de Ville had become the headquarters of rebellion; during October it was crowded by *Garde mobile*, many half-drunk; large red "*Vive la Commune*" and "Death to Thiers" were scrawled on the walls; there came Rigault, peering through his glasses, muffled in three or four overcoats against the cold, to talk significantly with the slovenly one-eyed Andrieu; and there were read the violent articles by Vermersch in *Le Père Duchesne* reminding the *Garde mobile* how the first Commune had dealt with its nobles and priests and other reactionaries eighty years earlier. During that month Verlaine eyed apprehensively the little flotilla of gunboats moored off the Pont Neuf, and on the 29th and the two following days his feelings pass beyond imagination, for then the Commune was proclaimed in the Place de l'Hôtel de Ville, the Hôtel de Ville was invaded and the rising put down only after a bloody struggle.

But in such an atmosphere the wilder spirits flourished and a group within a group began to form based on the members of the *Vilains Bonshommes* dinners (discontinued during the siege because no eatable dinner could be assembled) but having as their bond political and scatterbrained sympathies rather than the dubious poetical affinity with Coppée. They met at Nina's occasionally but Nina's for Verlaine at any rate, held awkward memories and had besides become one of the more notorious meeting places of Communist leaders; he much preferred the evenings in his own cosy apartment or at the Mautés'. The leading lights were Cros and his brothers, De Sivry, Villiers, Chabrier, Blémont, Silvestre, the tramp-like poet-composer Cabaner who had not yet noticed that France was at war, and the photographer Carjat. But Carjat was a poet too and a personality besides, a dandy who would not allow a mere war and bitter siege to disturb the symmetry of his smart velvet-collared frock coat, frilled waistcoat, top hat and shining monocle. He was accompanied by a man, boy rather, Louis Forain, a friend of Cros, who was learning to paint, who was to become one of the greatest caricaturists of the century, but who then was notable only for a spirit of devilment. Verlaine, the good mixer, the poet of repute and, trying hard to forget the violence he had seen and heard of, the ardent Communard, was not the least lively member of the gatherings; he had the gift of enjoying the passing minute, which made him good company. They by no means abandoned poetry, nor Charles Cros invention; he was busy between guard duties making artificial rubies at enormous cost, helped by a De Sivry convalescing after smallpox; and during one of the evenings he initiated a new type of ditty which was to become the latest craze in the *café-concert* some years later. Villiers, who had turned soldier in his spare time, arrived with a pickled herring (each guest bringing what food he could muster), exhibited his rare find with the air of a man presenting Madame Mauté with a magnificent bouquet, then sank onto the sofa and immediately slept. Cros suspended the fish by a string from a pair of steps straddling the sofa and chanted:

> *Il était un grand mur blanc, nu, nu, nu;*
> *Contre le mur, une échelle haute, haute, haute;*
> *Et par terre un hareng saur, sec, sec, sec.*

> *J'ai composé cette histoire simple, simple, simple,*
> *Pour mettre en fureur les gens graves, graves, graves,*
> *Et amuser les enfants petits, petits, petits.*

[3]

Verlaine, then, appeared to have good reason for happiness, siege and shortcomings notwithstanding. Yet before the winter was done, before even the year was over, he was in the thick of trouble. It began ostensibly with the coming of bad weather. The winter was late but severe. The pleasures of amateur soldiering faded abruptly when Verlaine found himself wet through or frozen night after night; he caught cold, rheumatism fastened on him (the effect of which he was never to lose) and he became utterly miserable. And when Verlaine was miserable he knew of one remedy only, to stop doing that which was causing the misery. This led to two days' detention which he endured philosophically, then to more guard duty which he was not prepared to endure at all. And if he must, then again only one remedy occurred to him; his friendly drink with his comrades, who included porters from the wine market, extended itself into prolonged drinking bouts, and from beer and wine he moved at last to absinthe. Paris was short of everything but drink; of this it had too much and the *Garde nationale* most of all.

The day came when he arrived home as he had arrived at his mother's house night after night before he had met Mathilde, quarrelsome, violent. He fastened a quarrel on her, struck her. She ran to her parents. He fetched her back. The quarrel extended into the night.

The next morning when the effect of the absinthe had worn off he was horrified, prostrated himself before the girl and there was a grand reconciliation. A few days later the scene was repeated. Their life together degenerated into a deplorable series of violent quarrels followed by the nauseating spectacle of a penitent Verlaine on his knees and of no less nauseating reconciliations—nauseating because all element of reality, such as there ever was, had gone.

In later years Verlaine reproached himself bitterly but in the matter of Mathilde he was never to become realistic or, to be exact, only when absinthe released the truth. The general explanation of this disastrous end, as it was, to the marriage has been that Verlaine was a dipsomaniac, but within a few years he was to show that, given the necessary incentive, he could fight the absinthe habit successfully for years. Rheumatism was merely a convenient excuse for him to return to absinthe; the truth came out when, brimmed with absinthe, he accused her of failing him: she had not the necessary patience, the necessary sweetness of disposition, she did not understand his "tigerish love," his simplicity, did not this, did not that; in short, she was not the inspiring saint who was to carry him on the wings of love to everlasting bliss.

All the poor girl had done to deserve such a charge was to be herself. Verlaine found himself in the position of every intelligent man who has married for reasons which nature disguises as spiritual. Out of bed Mathilde showed herself the naïve, vain and stupid Philistine that she really was. Illusion gone, every remark she made on poetry was an insult, every idiotic political enthusiasm jarred, every escape to her father became a bourgeois treachery; she stood revealed as a good-looking nonentity, a veritable wife of the Monsieur Prudhomme he had castigated years earlier, and he as a man who had made a ghastly error.

Even in bed she failed him though the fault was neither in her nor in him; they were badly matched, that was all. Verlaine, coddled from birth, wanted to be mothered in love as in life. Yet who would dream of such a thing to look at the tall, strong man with an excess of virility? Not Mathilde and not Verlaine himself, then. Later he understood, and that was the meaning, or one meaning, of his reproachful "You did not comprehend my simplicity."

But Mathilde comprehended nothing; her husband's attitude was bewildering and one which she could never understand to the day of her death. Why did he dislike or grow impatient with that which he had loved to the point of fatuity? She had not changed; and this indeed was the trouble.

Verlaine equally would not face the truth because he dared not. Few men will admit even to themselves that their marriage is a failure a few months after it has begun, but Verlaine did not fear loss of esteem, he feared the collapse of his life, the reversion to the horrors of the pre-Mathilde years, if he once confessed that he had married not a savior in mortal guise but a rather silly little girl. He would have been kinder to Mathilde and to himself if he had simply allowed her to stay with her parents but, feeling as he did, this was impossible. Instead he soaked himself with absinthe, and at the end of the year when his mother suggested that he come to her to recuperate after an attack of bronchitis, she having a good stock of food, he brought Mathilde with him.

During their stay in the rue Lécluse where Madame Verlaine then lived one can feel unalloyed pity for Mathilde. Verlaine had escaped the *Garde nationale* at last by the move and the bronchitis, and was less inclined to drink to excess, but his mother made sure that their life together was not the happier; in the worst tradition of the mother-in-law she was forever "getting at" the girl for failing to minister to Verlaine in the manner he was accustomed to. They were not there long, a few weeks only, but Verlaine had been given what he always sought, moral support.

In the Batignolles they were out of the worst of the excitements though chronically short of food and fuel, but on his way to the Hôtel de Ville Verlaine saw uncomfortable evidence of trouble ahead; the failure of the great Champigny sortie at the end of November led to widespread accusations of treachery and a few days later red posters appeared all over Paris overnight demanding the impeachment of the Government. On January 19 came the Buzenval sortie into which thirty thousand *Garde mobile* were thrown with the regulars to keep them out of mischief. The sortie failed with heavy loss of life. Two days later the communist leaders, imprisoned after the repulse of the October revolt, were rescued by a large and angry crowd. The next day a second attack was made on the Hôtel de Ville and the horrified Verlaine heard the frightening sounds of battle not a hundred feet from his room.

The revolt was again broken after much bloodshed but the Government soon afterwards capitulated to the Prussians, and civil war was suspended to await the result of a general election. Hugo was triumphantly returned as a Republican member for Paris but the elections as a whole showed a decided swing to the monarchists, and the situation in Paris looked so ugly, with vast unemployment the moment the war ceased, heavy drinking and continued shortage of food, that the Prime Minister, Thiers, decided to base his government on Versailles. Before the Prussians made their ceremonial entry on the first of March there had been calls for a Commune by an enormous crowd overflowing the Place de la Bastille, and cannon were seized and dragged from the center of the city to the *Garde mobile* headquarters on the heights of Montmartre. When the invaders marched in they were received in absolute silence by all and throughout their three-day occupation they were contemptuously ignored by the whole city. But the enemy gone, the unspoken truce collapsed; within a week the Communists had placarded Paris with an appeal: "Unite to save the Republic." Verlaine saw these posters as he walked to work from his apartment, for Mathilde had without difficulty persuaded him to return home after the signing of the armistice.

The next few weeks were too hectic for their differences to reappear. On March 18, following the failure of the Government attempt to disarm the *Garde mobile* and capture their cannon, the Commune was set up at the Hôtel de Ville and the remnant of the French Army retired to Versailles. Verlaine greeted the Commune as he had greeted the return of the Republic, with ecstatic joy. Rigault had been made public prosecutor, Andrieu Minister of Works, Vermersch placed in charge of propaganda; De Ricard, Régamey and Louise Michel were all fire-eating Republicans, and Verlaine believed with them that a second and more glorious revolution demanded his services. He felt himself to be in the midst of great events and supported by like-minded friends. Even such a man as Courbet, the friend of Vermersch and Gill, was staunchly on their side. He was not alone; thousands of men took literally the promises of the Communards that France should become a federation of free and independent communes in which all would live in peace and prosperity. Hence when the Thiers government called on every loyal civil servant to go to Versailles, Verlaine stayed where he was; not only stayed but, remarkable reversal of roles, when his alarmed mother sent Lepelletier to insist that he obey the order, he persuaded Lepelletier to stay also and soon got De Sivry a job in the Hôtel de Ville.

The millennium quickly showed itself to consist solely in free meals, open house being held at the Hôtel de Ville which was stocked to bursting point with food and wine. In all else the Commune proved a disappointment, his friends at each others throats, Paris filled with discontent, and his job, grandiloquently named Press Officer, little livelier than his old one, for all he had to do was to go through the daily papers and mark references for and against the Commune in red and blue chalk.

The job did not last long. The Versaillais laid siege to Paris at the beginning of April and on May 22 Verlaine was wakened by the maid, Louise, with the rumor that they had broken in and reached the Porte Maillot. The truth was even more unpleasant; MacMahon had captured the Trocadéro on the previous day, his troops were advancing along both sides of the river and the Palais Bourbon was on the point of falling. A few minutes after Verlaine had leaped hurriedly out of bed he heard drums beating, people began to run down the street, and the bells of Notre-Dame sounded the alarm. Then came the noise of artillery far too close and Verlaine, going onto his balcony, could see shells bursting over the Arc de Triomphe, aimed he thought at the center of the Champs Elysées, from the Garde mobile cannon at Montmartre. Mathilde begged to be allowed to see her parents who had returned to rue Nicolet and he saw her off with poor grace, feeling forsaken and worse than forsaken, obliged to do likewise. He therefore left the apartment in search of his mother but not with resolute step. The sight from the quayside understandably daunted him; the palace of the Tuileries, the Louvre, the Palais Royal and the Ministry of Finance had been set on fire with petroleum supplied by Andrieu and the shelling of the Champs Elysées was increasing; smoke, flames, noise, crash of timbers filled the air. He managed to force himself on despite his terror but was eventually turned back so brusquely—the sentry's rifle pointed directly at him and to his imagination on the half cock—that nothing would induce him to show his head again even on the balcony.

Alarm expresses itself in the human body in the oddest, the most disconcerting forms, but Verlaine's fear, rising to a pitch as the clamor increased outside, took a novel shape; he wanted nothing so much as to go to bed with the maid. No thought of disloyalty to Mathilde, still less of punishing her for leaving him came into his mind. With a desperation known only to the thoroughly frightened man he longed for company and for distraction, and where could he find both but under the sheets with Louise? They did not go to bed, however, because he could not be induced to use the bedroom, insisting after much heated argument that they retire to a tiny windowless closet. This, stuffed with mattresses, seemed to him to provide reasonable safety in a hideously unsafe world; at least the noise would be muffled. But when at last, arguments over and the mattresses dragged and pushed into place, he and Louise squeezed themselves into the closet they could move no farther; even the ingenuity of a roused Verlaine could not devise the means or the possibility of pleasure. And it seems that frustration still reigned—Louise or safety—when there came a thunderous knock at the front door.

Believing it to be Mathilde, Verlaine rushed downstairs, to find to his astonishment and dismay Lepelletier and a friend seeking shelter; they had been caught between Thiers' troops and the retreating Communards in the Boulevard St. Germain. They found Verlaine a bundle of nerves which they did not improve by telling him that Paris had become a battlefield, the *Versaillais* already at the Pont d'Alma, the barricaded streets filled with dead and wounded. The Hôtel de Ville was blazing, the arsenal in the Luxembourg had blown up with a terrific roar, the sound of street firing was growing ominously closer, and the guns at Montmartre thundered hour after hour. Nor was he reassured when Lepelletier predicted that his *quartier* would inevitably be occupied by Government troops within a few hours and that the Communards were fighting a losing battle; Verlaine, as a Communard sympathizer, was suspect, and he was now harboring two active members of the movement, one of them in uniform. Between them they stripped off and destroyed the stripes on the trousers of Lepelletier's friend and burned his kepi, and Verlaine was sufficiently relieved to eat a good meal but he absolutely refused to regard from the balcony the scene of a blazing, smoking Paris, the Seine glinting red; Lepelletier thought him in a highly emotional state, which would be scarcely surprising even in a bold man; and significantly he expressed greater fear for the fate of his mother than his wife.

They had one shock when the building was invaded by a crowd of people fleeing from the neighborhood of the Panthéon which they declared was about to blow up, but the rest of the day passed with nothing worse to endure than the incessant and alarming noises from outside. They slept, but early the next morning Verlaine was wakened by a knock at the door; his mother stood there, having crossed Paris during the night; the stories she told of the fires, massacres and fights through which she had passed shook the nerves of all.

Later in the morning Mathilde arrived, having made the journey from Montmartre after several failures; this too showed courage, for she was without escort for much of the way, and Verlaine, ashamed of himself, welcomed her warmly. He was worried, however, by the presence of Lepelletier and his friend and the prospect, looming ever closer, of a shooting squad for the three of them; and his relief was not veiled at all when the visitors having decided to leave, they had the good fortune to see Lepelletier's old Army regiment marching past. Lepelletier and his friend joined them and got away safely.

Two days later the Panthéon and Luxembourg had been taken and the Communards expelled from the Left Bank with a loss of fifteen thousand men, and within a week all fighting was over though the fires still burned and smoke covered Paris. The civil war ended as usual in a widespread witch hunt; of the leading Communards whom Verlaine knew, Rigault was shot, Louise Michel was transported to an overseas prison and the remainder escaped death only because they managed to make their way abroad, De Ricard to South America, most of them to London; even De Sivry who had done nothing more than act as registrar of births and deaths was imprisoned and treated brutally. Everywhere men were being denounced for working under the Commune; within a few months thirty-eight thousand people had been arrested, of whom a third were put into prison on the flimsiest of pretexts; executions were still going on two years later. Verlaine took fright not without reason. How could he who had refused to go to Versailles and was friendly with some of the Commune's leaders expect to be allowed to resume his work as though nothing had happened? He decided that the chance was not worth taking, and especially for a career that he was finding increasingly tedious. He stayed away.

At once he felt the pinch of his father's optimistic gambles on the stock exchange; the remnants of the comfortable little Verlaine fortune had shrunk after his mother had paid over the marriage dot of twenty thousand francs. This meant, since he was without a salary, that he must either get another job or live with one of the families until his poetry began to pay. Mathilde objected with reason to a further trial with her mother-in-law; she was also pregnant, a fact which clinched her arguments in favor of her parents' home. And to the rue Nicolet they returned.

Here there was almost immediate trouble. Monsieur Mauté had never liked his son-in-law; the stories told by Mathilde had raised this dislike to detestation. Verlaine, trying to control his craving for absinthe because of Mathilde's pregnancy, was in no mood to endure his father-in-law's pompous protests; there were arguments and undignified scenes day after day. Had it not been for Madame Mauté who liked Verlaine and had a sense of humor, the double ménage would have collapsed almost as soon as it began. As it was, Verlaine, experiencing for the first time an unadulterated potion of bourgeois life, seems for the first time to have faced the bourgeois in himself; the light-hearted satire on Monsieur Prudhomme bore a very different look when he actually lived with him.

In the summer he temporarily avoided further trouble by taking Mathilde on a round of family visits in the Pas-de-Calais, staying with Dujardin at Lécluse and his mother's relatives at Fampoux. For some months there was peace, the last he and Mathilde were to know together. Relieved from fear of arrest, relieved to be away from Monsieur Mauté, his optimism shot up, a natural optimism fortified by a generous supply of beer, absinthe being self-forbidden and, what was more to the point, difficult to obtain: all would be well, the countryside was the place for him, he would not worry about the future. Soon he was writing light-hearted notes to his friends in Paris, commenting to Blémont, for example, on the destruction of the Vendôme column by the Communards in the following fashion: "Our window looks out on a large courtyard in the center of which rises a Vendôme column which, less pretentious and more useful than the defunct, is content with the humble name of chimney. Beyond it are roofs pierced with a thousand pipes, each more bizarre than the other, then rats, more rats and yet more rats; and if you like treacle you will find it everywhere." And for himself "my cousin possesses a *very comfortable* garden. . . .

To smoke a couple of pipes here after a midday dinner, to have seven or eight drinks at the inn between four and five o'clock and to watch night fall in the woods while reading some tranquilizing book, this is my new life."

There was another side to this life, of course, and he could not fail to feel it. "Yes, it's charming, this existence here," he told Valade, "but absolutely devoid of the literary. All talk is restricted to war stories in which the words *treason* and *revenge* play a prominent part. . . . In short, all this gossip about the siege, MacMahon this, Bazaine that—no, my dear chap, I've had enough! These are the real horrors of war! When I can get into a corner with some good man who is kind enough to talk to me about beetroots . . . I'm happy . . . like a Coppée still drawing his salary."

The reference to Coppée is significant; Coppée had gone back to the War Office, Coppée's growing rectitude had begun to irritate the little *Vilains Bonshommes* group. Before the civil war broke it up, the group had decided to put together an album in which parody would play a large part, and the only stroke of work Verlaine did in the country was to write good but unkind parodies of Banville, Hérédia and "the abbé Coppée."

For the rest, such was his power of self-deception, which is a cold way of describing a natural bent for happiness, that after a few weeks of sitting in the open, walking, fishing, reading and talking to his hosts (all of whom made a great fuss of him) he persuaded himself without difficulty that the coming of a child would restore all the lost harmony between himself and Mathilde; a picture rose before him (disregarding the so recent past and the present lack of a home) of the fond father dandling the child on his knees, watching the growth of the infant poet and once again worshipping the woman who had brought this marvel into the world. The fact that he had abandoned the writing of serious poetry, the artist being a sounder judge of circumstance than the man, either escaped him or was put out of mind. Instead he sounded the depths of false contentment when he urged the newly engaged Blémont to "try to draw a good number" in the marriage lottery: "I can't complain of mine."

In this spirit he returned to the rue Nicolet early in September, for Mathilde's confinement was expected the following month. Before his contentment and good resolutions had time to collapse he found waiting for him in the passage Choiseul two letters which were to make an end of both. Yet Verlaine could not have suspected any threat to his specious security in the letters which had been written from the town of Charleville in the Ardennes a few miles below the Paliseul he knew so well; they were the kind of letter familiar to published writers, praising his work, complaining of the lack of opportunity in the provinces and begging him to read the poems enclosed. It is possible that Verlaine might have put the letters aside like many another author, the poems unread, possible but not probable because he was a kind man. But in this case his kindness was not put to the test, for there was a postscript to one of the letters by a man known to him, a Charles Bretagne who had once been customs officer at his uncle's sugar refinery at Fampoux, asking him to do what he could for the writer. This writer signed himself Arthur Rimbaud.

9.

RIMBAUD

1854-1871

Arthur Rimbaud was born in October, 1854 nearly ten years later than Verlaine. His parents bore a superficial resemblance to Verlaine's: his father was an Army man, had risen from the ranks and cut a fine figure in his regimentals; his mother was from the North and was of peasant stock. But in every important respect two couples could scarcely have differed more: Captain Rimbaud, a southerner, was a restless, wild and charming man; Madame Rimbaud remained the well-to-do peasant and had the peasant's virtues and failings to the point of caricature, deeply pious, inarticulate except in anger, dour, and close to a degree that makes carefulness appear frivolous.

Vitalie Cuif's surrender to the charm of Captain Rimbaud was the one weakness of her life; she accepted its penalties as a just punishment and as a lesson for the future. Their brief life together (he was usually away with the Army) was a disaster; his openhandedness, light behavior and unstable disposition offended all the peasant in his wife; they differed on every important point of conduct; violent scenes were frequent. By the time Arthur was a small boy the marriage had collapsed; Captain Rimbaud retired to Dijon and was never seen again.

If Madame Rimbaud needed further warning that her children's blood might be spiritually contaminated, she found it in the lives of her two brothers, both dissolute and worthless men, but the failure of her marriage was enough to raise all the Spartan in her character; she devoted herself with a grim passion to the upbringing of the children, determined that they should be everything that her husband and brothers were not, worthy and God-fearing citizens above all.

Arthur soon showed himself to be the most promising of her four living children. Indeed promising is hardly the word, for the boy was beautiful, clever and good; he had the noble forehead, wavy light-brown hair and startlingly clear blue eyes of his father, his disposition was sweet and it was obvious to all who had anything to do with him that he possessed a brain of exceptional brilliance. His mother's hopes inevitably centered themselves on him.

The parallel with Verlaine and his mother is plain but Madame Rimbaud expressed her pride and love in different fashion; the greater her hopes the stronger her fears, and she was if anything stricter with this model child than with the others. His physical likeness to his father was enough to put her on perpetual guard. Moreover, for she was far from stupid, she sensed the depth of Arthur's resentment at the restrictions she put on him—the ban on intercourse with other children, the refusals to give him a sou to spend, the homemade clothes which affronted his pride; and she realized that this child had a formidable strength of will which must be subdued for the good of his soul.

Nor did her iron regime relax after the boy had begun his sensational career at the College of Charleville; on the whole she was severer, afraid no doubt that his head would be turned. His triumphs would unquestionably have made an ordinary child insupportable. He was not popular, the boys at first envious, suspicious of his angelic expression and manner and making cruel but natural fun of his clothes. But eventually they took pride in the prodigy, a pride shared, with misgivings, by the masters. Not without reason; his reading was encyclopedic for a schoolboy, his memory prodigious, his vocabulary enormous, his facility on paper amazing. One day in his early teens, for instance, he wrote Latin verses on a set subject for every boy in his class, each series of verses differing in style so that the trick should not be observed—and this in the short intervals when the master was writing on the blackboard. At an examination held when he was just fourteen he wrote fifty-nine Latin hexameters in three hours.

By the age of fifteen the young Rimbaud had become the prize pupil and the pride of much of the town. He had to find satisfaction in this public approbation for he did not receive it at home. He searched for a "soulmate" and intellectual leader and found him unsurprisingly in a master at school. Georges Izambard joined the college at the beginning of 1870 and was much impressed as his predecessors by this remarkable pupil; but perhaps because he was more of an age with the boy—twenty-one to Rimbaud's fifteen—he understood something of the frustration beneath the shy and staid demeanor. He opened his library to the boy, talked to him, encouraged him to talk; they became close friends.

The immediate result of this friendship was the appearance of Rimbaud as poet. Before Izambard's arrival he had read as widely as he was able in French poetry, mostly Hugo, Baudelaire and one or two Parnassians, the moderns of the late sixties; he had even managed to publish a poem in a review taken, significantly, by his mother, a poem plainly yet individually based on Coppée's *Reliquaire*. Having the run of Izambard's books he swept at great speed through French literature, but always with the poets first at heart, and wrote poems showing first this influence, then that; yet almost always with a fresh and original method of approach. But the books of Izambard's that most fascinated him were the complete *Parnasse contemporain* of 1866 and several volumes of poetry by Parnassians, Banville and Leconte de Lisle particularly. He heard that a second *Parnasse contemporain* was being prepared and in May he wrote to Banville, his god of the moment, sending him three poems and begging him to insert at least one in the anthology.

The letter, an uneasy mixture of arrogance and humility, reminds one of Branwell Brontë's "condemn not unheard" letter to Blackwood, and though Banville replied with his usual courtesy he is unlikely to have reached the end of it or, if he did, would have been discouraged from reading the poems. This was a pity; the letter could have been written by a thousand boys infatuated with poetry—Banville must have received many such—but the poems could have been written by only one person in the world. They were as mature and original in everything but subject as the accompanying letter was juvenile. The poem mentioned particularly by Rimbaud, "*Credo in unam*," beat the Parnassians at their own game; it was an astonishingly successful evocation of ancient Greece, the spirit and the appearance.

Foiled for the moment, the boy of fifteen continued to read enormously, to win first prize after first prize at school and to write poems, one of which, the charming "*Première Soirée*," was

Nina de Callias

Mathilde Verlaine

printed in the satirical weekly *La Charge*. And it was apparently through this journal that he was first led to the work of Verlaine; at the end of July a note by the editor strongly recommended *La Bonne Chanson* by the well-known author of *Poèmes saturniens* and *Fêtes galantes*. Three weeks later Rimbaud was exclaiming to Izambard that these last were "most unusual, very strange and truly adorable!" and urging him to buy *La Bonne Chanson*. Rimbaud had not then read it but explained that "many journals have praised it."

He was not talking but writing to Izambard; term had ended, war had begun and Izambard was not going to return. The war completed the boy's unsettlement; it had been just possible for a would-be Parnassian to live in a cultureless Charleville with Izambard to encourage him. But Izambard gone and all the excitements of a war raging not many miles away abruptly snapped his patience. He would run away, he told his friend, a threat which he carried out late in August after his seventeen-year-old brother had led the way by secretly going off with a regiment on its way to the front. The escapade was a dismal failure; he managed to slip into a train bound for Paris but the moment he reached the terminus was arrested for traveling without a ticket. He was delivered from prison by Izambard and, after a short stay with his rescuer, returned reluctantly to a bewildered and furious mother. His one satisfaction was his temporary membership in the *Garde mobile* at Douai where Izambard lived.

He listened sullenly to his mother's reproaches, listened unmoved. A few days later he ran away again, this time walking to Brussels by way of the homes of school friends and ending again at Izambard's house at Douai. He was still writing poetry.

Once again he was returned to his mother, a mother convinced that she had to deal with the spit of her happy-go-lucky husband. His school had not reopened; Sedan, not far away, had fallen, Charleville was besieged and at the end of the year the Prussians entered the town. Rimbaud spent most of his time walking, talking and reading with one of his best school friends, Ernest Delahaye; they talked poetry, of course, and Rimbaud read and praised the Parnassians and Verlaine in particular; he was much struck by the hints (broad to him) in Verlaine's work of a new poetry, by his inversions, repetitions, his mastery of cadence, his humor, his musicality and modernity in choice and placing of words and, above all, by the signs of versification freed from classical forms. His own

poems showed something of Verlaine's gift for lyricism and he now
took the other hints, becoming as Verlainean as he had formerly
been Banvillean, but here too with a certain note of his own.

The two boys also discussed politics; faced with the Prussians
surrounding, then occupying their home town, with the shock of
the collapse of the much-vaunted French Army, with Paris under
siege for months and rumors of discord and treachery everywhere
freely repeated, no boy of spirit and intelligence could fail to react
vehemently. Both were, as might be expected, violently Republican,
and both echoed dark suspicions of the Government. But there they
parted company; Delahaye, at heart a prudent young man, would
criticize but saw nothing that he could usefully do other than walk
past the Prussian soldiers with a contemptuous expression on his
face and fit himself to teach young Frenchmen to make their
country truly great once more.

To Rimbaud this was weak-kneed, unthinkable. He panted for
action. "I've something in me, I don't know what, that wants to
soar," he had told Banville, and neither the nonappearance of his
poems in the *Parnasse contemporain* nor the failure of his two
breaks for freedom had daunted him, but merely determined him
to be off again as soon as possible. In vain his mother kept him
without money, in vain she insisted that he return to school when
the Prussians marched out and the College reopened; he had read
in the newspapers how the reported peace terms agreed to by the
newly elected government were stirring the *Garde mobile* to revolt;
was he to stay in Charleville, to go to school, to shelter under his
mother's skirts when history was being made in Paris? In February
of the new year, 1871, without a word he pawned his watch, bought
a ticket to Paris and walked late in the evening to the rue Lepic
studio of Gill whose work he had admired in *La Charge*. There was
no reply to his knock, but, Gill's door being unlocked as usual,
Rimbaud pushed it open and feeling tired and seeing a bed lay on
it and slept.

Gill returned from the cafés in the small hours, saw in astonishment a youth on his bed, shook the sleeper and asked what he was
doing there. Rimbaud, rubbing his eyes, complained that he had
been enjoying delightful dreams and would have preferred not to
be wakened—a typical remark which Gill received with a laugh,
being a good-tempered man, and a "I have delightful dreams also,
but in my own bed." Being kind, too, he questioned the "lugubrious

monster" as he afterwards described Rimbaud; and when the boy
explained that he was a poet and had come to Paris to make his
name, Gill advised him to go home and gave him all the money
he had in his pocket, some ten francs.

Rimbaud took the money but not the advice. He was still in the
city, living no one knows how, when an army of *Garde mobile* and
their women marched up the Champs Elysées in protest against the
peace treaty then being signed with the Prussians; was there three
days later when the Prussians marched in and when they left two
days afterwards. If he tried to join the *Garde mobile* he did not
succeed, nor did he manage to find Vermersch whom he knew to
be a power among the Communards. He spent most of his time
reading at the bookstalls on the quays as Verlaine had done before
him, reading Glatigny's second book, reading almost under Verlaine's
windows had he known it. Soon after the Prussians had left Paris
he followed suit, impatient perhaps because the long-promised
Commune had not come to pass, no doubt discouraged because he
had not met anyone of note except Gill, certainly forced to go by
shortage of food. Having no money he made the return journey of
one hundred fifty miles by the simple expedient of passing himself
off as a franc-tireur, successfully living off the country folk (applying
to the local mayor for food and lodging when the people turned
him away) and getting through the Prussian lines without detection.

By this time Rimbaud had shown himself as more than an infant
prodigy with exceptional physical appeal; this boy with the face of
a sulky angel and the brain of a brilliant student was also as cool,
daring and determined as the most adult of adventurers. He remained
nevertheless a boy of sixteen returning home again and again,
every hope frustrated. But he bided his time, taking his mother's
punishments and reproaches with outward sang-froid, and within
two months escaped to Paris again, stirred no doubt by the formation
of the Commune and the new siege of the city.

What happened to Rimbaud in Paris no one knows. There have
been many suggestions, none of them capable of proof. Of these, two
sound reasonable: that he suffered some unforgettable sexual experience, and that he reached the city only to find the *Versaillais* on
the point of recapturing it—a triumph of reaction which would em-
bitter the youthful revolutionary. At all events, the boy returned for
the fourth time in little more than six months to a mother who
must have been at her wits' end to know what to do with him.

He was now a problem child in every sense of the term. He reacted to the shock of his experience in Paris by presenting to his mother and to the town a new and unpleasant side of his nature, affecting the air of a cynical and depraved youth. He refused to return to school, refused to work, refused to wash, refused to cut his hair, and in general refused to conform to civilized life as Charleville understood it. The boy of the many prizes, quiet, well-behaved, neat to the point of excess, disappeared and in his place walked the streets of a shocked town a dirty, long-haired, foul-mouthed young man who hung about the school with a sneer on his face, wrote obscene poetry and sat for hours at low cafés reviling church, christianity, women, government, the bourgeoisie and any other institution he could think of, and with such a choice of vocabulary that his questionable audience would pay him in drink and tobacco for the pleasure of hearing a boy demean himself so artistically.

One of the most regular of this audience was Bretagne, a man of parts who not only had a nose for tax evasion but was a poet, musician, draftsman, and demonologist besides, with a small library of occult literature. He let Rimbaud loose in this library, curious no doubt to see what the brilliant boy would make of it. He must have been pleasantly surprised for within a few weeks Rimbaud was evolving rapidly a theory of poetry that had been hovering in his mind ever since he had first read Baudelaire. The poet, he told a friend of Izambard, must become a seer. Gautier, Leconte de Lisle and Banville were great seers but Baudelaire was a greater, "King of poets, *a very God!*" Yet even Baudelaire had failed to reach his goal, the infinity lying beyond reality; he lived in too artistic a milieu and the form of his work was paltry. New forms were needed, a new language and a new struggle to elevate oneself. This demanded "a long, immense and deliberate *derangement of all the senses,* the poet seeking every possible experience of love, pain and madness, tasting every poison, so that he can keep their quintessence." It also demanded superhuman fortitude and faith, for he would have to undergo "inexpressible torture" and would appear in the eyes of all men as "the great diseased, the great criminal, the great accused." Only then would he become "the supreme seer! For he arrives at the *unknown!*" The "unimaginable, unnamable things" he finds there might drive him frantic so that he no longer understands his visions, but no matter, "He has seen them!" and others will take over from him at the point where he collapses.

The theory is not original and could have been stated so only by a very young man and one who after the manner of Vincent van Gogh, though for other reasons, considered himself the despised and rejected. Psychoanalysts have a name for this state of mind and the grandiose compensatory dreams which accompany it. Its difference and its danger lay in the fact that it was set out as a plan of life by one who had no humility and in consequence failed to understand that the aim of the great *voyants* was self-abnegation not self-assertion. Nor did he realize that his hero Baudelaire's overriding sense of sin made quite another thing of the theory of self-assertion that he had taken over.

The remarkable part of this declaration by a sixteen-year-old provincial youth was not the ambition or the plan but his perception of the greatness of Baudelaire at a time when the work of Baudelaire was known only to the few and his genius scarcely recognized by any. And no less remarkable are the poems which he began to write. Charleville understandably presented lamentably few opportunities for deranging the senses in any but the most humdrum of fashions, and the frustrated Rimbaud could do nothing worse than drink too much if his patrons would sponsor him thus far, scrawl chalk slogans of "death to God" on church doors and seats in public gardens, draw savage caricatures of respectable Charleville citizens and talk filth in the lesser cafés. But there was nothing to prevent him from experimenting in the necessary poetic "new forms" and this he did. The first of these poems *"Ce qu'on dit au poète à propos de fleurs"* he sent to Banville in the middle of July with a letter different in tone from the one of the year before but still youthful: "Have I improved?" he asked.

Banville did not answer and one cannot be surprised; there was a limit to his tolerance. If he read the poem he must have appreciated the verbal dexterity but his pleasure would have been of the wry kind for the boy had made cruel fun of his *"cher maître"*; using a then fantastically wide and original vocabulary he destroyed with diabolical ingenuity the lilies, roses, violets, forget-me-nots spread so lavishly through the poems of Banville and of the Parnassians who followed him; the only flowers that he would put into his poetry, he said, were flowers never yet seen by man and existing only in the imagination. The "new form" consisted in the use of words and images then considered unpoetical; vulgarisms, colloquialisms, words from the sciences and from the gutter.

Rimbaud had begun to write his second "new form" poem and was worried by Banville's silence. But he had another hope up his sleeve. One could not call it second best, because he had already singled out two contemporary poets as the hope of the future— Mérat and Verlaine. He referred to them as the "seers" of the Parnassian school. And when toward the end of August his confidant Bretagne suggested an approach to Verlaine and offered to write a covering note, Rimbaud accepted eagerly and wrote straightway enclosing several poems; he was an admirer, he said, and a fellow poet incarcerated in a provincial town where his talent, his hopes, his ideals were all stifled.

Again he had no reply (Verlaine was then in the Pas-de-Calais) and in the first days of September he wrote once more. "I have a great poem under way and I don't want to work at Charleville. I can't come to Paris without resources. My mother is a widow and extremely devout. She only gives me ten centimes every Sunday to pay for a seat in church." He sent more poems.

Verlaine, back in rue Nicolet, read the poems. He was astounded: "You have a prodigious talent," he replied at once enthusiastically. But he was also disgusted with many of Rimbaud's vulgarisms: "Your lycanthropy makes me feel as if I'd caught a whiff from a sewer." And he was cautious, anxious not to encourage a young man to plunge into Paris without adequate backing: he must, he said, show the poems to other poets before helping him to leave Charleville.

He showed them to Cros and Valade. They too were impressed by the originality of the poems and Verlaine hesitated no longer; he wrote at once: "Come dear great soul, we summon you, we await you!" He invited Rimbaud to stay with him (Monsieur Mauté providentially still shooting in the country) and sent him the fare to Paris.

A day or two later, on September 10, Rimbaud arrived, bringing with him as luggage the manuscript of the "*Bateau ivre.*"

10.

RIMBE

1871-1872

[1]

Verlaine and Cros went to the station to meet him, waited at the wrong platform and returned to rue Nicolet to find Rimbaud with Madame Mauté and Mathilde in the salon. Mathilde hovered between amusement and disgust. Madame Mauté, like every *Parisienne* with pretensions to culture, had never lost hope of astonishing her world with a real live genius, but she had not reckoned on a genius at once dirty, surly and insolent, and by the time Verlaine arrived she had virtually written off Rimbaud as nothing but a nasty boy and her son-in-law's praise of his poems as yet another example of that too amiable, too trusting young man led astray.

Verlaine was flabbergasted by his first sight of the author of the poems he had praised so highly. He had expected to find a man in his twenties or thirties; he saw a disreputable youth sitting awkwardly and sullenly on the edge of his chair, a youth wearing a homemade suit of slate-blue serge out of which protruded in the manner of Glatigny a length of leg in coarse home-knitted blue cotton socks ending in heavy laborer's boots, bony wrists and large black-nailed red hands. His face was red and rough, a dirty string tie was tied loosely at the back of a dirty shirt, his hair had obviously not seen comb, brush or soap for weeks. His expression was ugly with the obstinate angry embarrassment of one who finds himself out of place.

But Verlaine was not only astonished, he was attracted. The others saw nothing but a dirty sullen peasant boy growing out of his clothes, he divined the charm and intelligence beyond the dirt and surly monosyllables. He remembered the extraordinary poems, and with the insight of physical attraction he understood something of what the visitor must be feeling. The others were kind but patronizing; he spoke to Rimbaud as to an equal and he spoke little where the rest rushed in with chatter intended to put the boy at his ease.

Rimbaud's feelings are not difficult to imagine; he felt his uncouthness, his lack of table manners, his inability to speak fluent nothings or move gracefully, he felt the incongruity of sitting in a daintily furnished drawing room or at a luxuriously appointed table—felt all and resented all. When the women spoke to him he sensed behind their polite façade of interest the curious, disgusted regard, Madame Mauté's secret fear that her silken cushions were being soiled, imagined Mathilde's bedroom comments at his provincial accent, and understood the perplexity of both at the invitation which had brought such a creature into their home. The fooling of De Sivry who joined them for dinner struck him, already rubbed the wrong way, as insulting and decadent. Even the serious inquiries of Cros could not mollify him; Cros wanted to know something of his poetical theories, how he had come to write, what his plans were. Rimbaud had plenty to say on this matter but would not say it in such company; Cros was "talking down" to him, he thought angrily, he was to be made an exhibit, the subject for their latest gossip.

He would not oblige. He was in a fury of hatred. That these people should dare to condescend to him, the genius who was to pierce the heart of the mystery, to be a god among men! His reaction was inevitable and he told himself he had the best of warrants for it; his king of poets had said a thousand times "épater le bourgeois." He had followed Baudelaire to the letter, as he thought, in Charleville. Was a smooth-speaking, well-clothed, addlepated group of Paris suburbanites to escape correction?

But he was perplexed and chagrined to find Verlaine in this bourgeois milieu. How reconcile the "seer," the great poet of the future and one of his guiding lights with such a setting? Evidently he decided to give him the benefit of the doubt; the difference in Verlaine's manner was impossible to avoid; the most touchy could not take offense at it. But to the rest he behaved abominably. He replied in monosyllables to every question; he listened with an insolent sneer while the others talked, and when in despair Madame Mauté rose for dinner, thinking perhaps that food might soften her difficult guest, he set himself to shock, eating noisily and, the moment he had done, resting both elbows on the table and lighting a pipe which he puffed over the plates of those who had not yet finished. He abandoned all pretense of listening to the conversation, moodily watching his hostesses' little dog running from chair to chair begging for scraps. "Les chiens, ce sont des libéraux," he said at last, the only remark Verlaine could remember during that unhappy evening. Then with a muttered "I'm tired" he took himself to bed.

That night Verlaine read the manuscript Rimbaud had brought from Charleville, and if he had had doubts of the boy after the fiasco of the evening he doubted no more. No admirer of Baudelaire could miss *"Le Voyage"* as the starting point of *"Le Bateau ivre,"* but the sweep of imagination, the verbal originality were Rimbaud's own.

The next day Verlaine took him off for a round of the cafés and introduced him proudly as the poetic prodigy of the age. His pride had to endure many shocks; Rimbaud, he discovered not without uneasiness, said exactly what he thought in the most pungent language to everybody's face, he respected nothing and nobody, would make no concessions, would endure no cant. But, the first shocks over, this was exhilarating and, to a man with a strong sense of humor, irresistible. Verlaine began to love the boy with a passion. With one or two intimates, the young Forain chiefly, Rimbaud displayed an uninhibited zest for life that warmed the heart. The sulky monosyllabic youth of rue Nicolet disappeared, the clothes, the gangling body, the awkwardness were of no account beside the winged words of a fiery, towheaded angel. Never had Verlaine heard such enthusiasm; beside it the talks at the Café du Gaz, at Lemerre's and at the prewar soirees paled to pettiness. And not merely enthusiasm; Rimbaud spoke with a fervor, a knowledge and a certainty of the triumph and glory to come; he would experience all things, dare all to write poetry of a kind undreamed of, the poetry of a man who had plumbed the depths and scaled the heights of sensation. And Verlaine, if he had the courage and the vision, could travel with him, could become a "son of the Sun," an immortal.

Listening by the hour Verlaine's doubts receded and something of his schoolboy faith returned. Who could doubt, hearing that eager voice with its northern burr, looking at the burning blue eyes?

Not Verlaine, and for a time not Verlaine's intimates. After a *Vilains Bonshommes* dinner at which Verlaine presented Rimbaud, Valade wrote to Blémont: "You missed a great deal by not being there. A most daring poet not yet eighteen was introduced by Paul Verlaine, his inventor, and in fact his John the Baptist. Big hands, big feet, a wholly babyish face like a child of thirteen, deep blue eyes! Such is this boy whose imagination combines great power with unheard of corruption and who has fascinated and terrified all our friends." One of them said, "Behold Jesus in the midst of the doctors." Another replied, "More likely Satan!" Valade thought, "We are witnessing the birth of a genius."

"His John the Baptist" was a fairly accurate description of Verlaine's role. His pride and amusement to see this brilliant youth demolish pretensions right and left rose to an ecstasy. What integrity, what an intellect and what charm! And when the winged words changed to obscenities, blasphemies and strange oaths, that too was a marvel of another kind coming from the sulky mouth of this youthful Lucifer. Everybody must see and hear. Verlaine took him to visit Hugo, who, if Lepelletier is accurate, promptly described him as the child Shakespeare. Another returned celebrity, Nina back from Switzerland, made a great fuss over the boy, and the writers' cafés generally were intrigued by the contrast of brief but devastating criticisms, claims of greatness and boasts of tasting every form of depravity, backed by foul language coming incongruously from this coltish, baby-faced youth with the candid blue eyes and charming smile who moved about like an unwashed and very badly dressed young god. Forain shrewdly sketched him with the chubby face of a two- or three-year-old child. Carjat took photographs of him, photographs which explain how irresistible he must have appeared.

Rimbaud was far from irresistible at the rue Nicolet. Verlaine, lightheartedly accepting the necessity expounded forcefully by his young friend of "a long and deliberate derangement of all the senses" as a good excuse for reverting to absinthe, began to arrive home much the worse for wear. By the women this was naturally put down to the influence of the rapscallion from Charleville, and Rimbaud's welcome wore thin. He accepted the hostility with a will and laid himself out to make sure that his hostess had good cause for it; his bed, for instance, was found to be crawling with lice and his favorite resting place on the few occasions when he showed himself seems to have been the graveled path in front of the house where Verlaine found him stretched at full length in the sun smoking his pipe.

The return of Monsieur Mauté before the birth of Verlaine's son brought matters to a head. The opinion he and Rimbaud had of each other is obvious and almost before he could demand the withdrawal of the viper from the love nest Rimbaud had taken himself away, no one knew where.

Verlaine searched for him and eventually ran into him in the street a week or two later, thin, pale and wretched, his efforts to support himself having sunk to peddling key rings. Overjoyed, he gave him a good meal, then put him into the hands of Cros and Gill while he looked around for a permanent shelter. Cros and Gill bore no ill will, nor did Banville when Verlaine begged him to look after his friend; he rented, and his mother with some trouble furnished, the attic of their apartment house in the rue de Buci for the destitute young poet, while Verlaine and his intimates clubbed together to give him three francs a day to live on.

[2]

Had Rimbaud been able to settle down on Banville's doorstep, so to speak, and had he allowed Madame Banville to mother him, his future would have been assured. But this, given Rimbaud as he was and the Parnassians as they were, remains a pleasant dream. On the very first evening of Rimbaud's arrival Banville heard a clamor in the courtyard and looking out saw the boy naked at the window throwing his clothes to the ground far below. Nothing can be hidden in Parisian apartment houses and the other tenants were soon in an uproar—one had already sent for the police thinking no doubt that Rimbaud was either mad or a sexual exhibitionist.

Banville ran upstairs. Rimbaud explained that he was not used to such a clean and tidy room and that he could not wear his clothes in it, full of fleas as they were. Banville hurriedly rigged him out with clothes of his own and invited him to dinner. But that too did not please the boy; the conversation bored, the condescension as he thought it angered him, and he began fingering a knife with an expression on his face that embarrassed and silenced everyone.

Mallarmé tells this story; he is a reliable witness and coming events were to confirm him. For this was the beginning of the end of Rimbaud as a figure of any moment in Parisian literary circles and, by corollary, of Verlaine also. He departed from Banville's, leaving the room filthy, and Verlaine found him a home with Cabaner in the Hôtel des Etrangers in the rue Racine. The dreamy Cabaner who had gone through both sieges of Paris under the vague impression that they were both by the Prussians was not easy to offend nor could he easily give offense, his life being disreputable enough to satisfy Rimbaud and his forbearance on the rare occasions when he noticed the outside world being almost without limit. There for a few weeks Rimbaud remained with his "Tronche," as he called the big hairy man with the mild eyes, writing poems, playing Cabaner's lute, drinking and talking with a crowd of literary men—the little set of the wartime soirees—and taking his first new step toward the derangement of the senses, the step consisting of the hashish praised so alarmingly by Baudelaire.

Delahaye, anxious about his friend, had come to Paris to look him up and, conducted by Verlaine, found him at the hôtel just coming out of a hashish trance, lying on a couch in a tattered overcoat much too large for him and with a shabby gray felt hat jammed on his head. He had grown rapidly in the few weeks since Delahaye had seen him, was emaciated and appallingly dirty, and was disgruntled by the failure of the hashish; rubbing his eyes he confessed with a grimace that he had seen nothing in his dreams but black and white moons chasing each other.

He was busy at odd moments compiling with his companions the *Album des Vilains Bonshommes* which Verlaine, Blémont, Valade, Mérat, Cabaner, Richepin, Carjat, Gill and Cros had been planning for their amusement during the siege. It was to consist, as Verlaine explained, of parodies after the manner of their elders and betters; having done Coppée and Hérédia he was at work on a *Joyeuseté galante* after Glatigny; and Rimbaud contributed, besides a sketch or two, parodies of Dierx, Coppée and De Ricard among others and a brilliant "new version" of a *Fêtes galantes* poem. The contributors also amused themselves, being Frenchmen, by trying to settle on a name for this circle, *Vilains Bonshommes* being too general for their liking and not a good rallying cry. Not that they sought adherents, the circle being rather exclusive. They therefore dispensed with even the element of program Mendès had followed in the early sixties; their one distinguishable aim seems to have been to differentiate themselves from the too respectable poets of the *Parnasse* though they would have been surprised to learn that their true distinction was to harbor two of the most famous poets of the century; for the rest, Cros' description of their function five years later holds good: "They are poets, musicians, writers, artists; nothing for use, all for pleasure." Even so a name appeared to them essential and provided a good excuse for fun over drinks; and Valade tells how he and other members, some known, some unknown, tried to find it, Rimbaud contributing his favorite monosyllable.

(MÉRAT) *Cinq sous! c'est ruineux! Me demander cinq sous?*
T'as d'insolents! . . . (PÉNOUTET) *Mon vieux! Je viens du Café Riche,*
J'ai vu Catulle. . . . (KECK) *Moi, je voudrais être riche.*
(VERLAINE) *Cabaner, de l'eau d'aff!* . . . (H. CROS) *Messieurs, vous êtes*
     saouls!
(VALADE) *Morbleu, pas tant de bruit! La femme d'en dessous ac-*
     couche . . .
(MÉRAT) *Avez-vous lu l'article sur l'Autriche*
Dans ma revue? . . . (MERCIER) *Horreur! Messieurs, Cabaner triche*
Sur la cantine! (CABANER) *Je* . . . *ne* . . . *pu* . . . *is répondre à tous!*
(GILLE) *Je ne bois rien, je paye! Allez cherchez à boire.*
Voilà dix sous! (ANTOINE CROS) *Si! Si! Mérat, veuillez m'en croire,*
Zutisme est le vrai nom du cercle! (CHARLES CROS) *En vérité,*
L'autorité c'est moi! C'est moi l'autorité.
(JACQUET) *Personne au piano! C'est fâcheux que l'on perde*
Son temps, Mercier, jouez Le Joyeux vio . . . (RIMBAUD) *Ah! merde!*

Rimbaud, it will be seen, was tiring even of the rackety set into which he had temporarily settled. He had already antagonized all the respectable, beginning with Lepelletier whom he addressed contemptuously as an "excreter of ink" and "saluter of the dead" because he had seen him raise his hat to a funeral. When Lepelletier told him to be quiet he grasped a knife from the table and threatened him. For this, Lepelletier, more than a little jealous, had his revenge when the Parnassians trooped to a first performance of a one-act play by Glatigny who, mortally ill, was still making spasmodic appearances in Paris without a sou to his name. Reviewing the play in a periodical, Lepelletier wrote under a pen name that among the bevy of writers was "the saturnine poet Paul Verlaine who gave his arm to a charming young person named Miss Rimbaud," thus beginning the gossip which was to end in Verlaine's ostracism.

Lepelletier was an obvious butt, too obvious perhaps to be worth Rimbaud's notice; but the boy was soon extending his field, stretching himself at full length on a seat in the poets' cafés, feigning sleep or grunting scornfully from time to time when he did not care for the poem someone was reciting. Such behavior from a mere child who would normally be expected to listen wide-eyed had the charm of novelty especially to those lacking the moral courage to express their true feelings, but as the number of victims increased the fun wore thin and Rimbaud's contemptuous attitude appeared first tedious, then unendurable. He began to be cold-shouldered.

The first open sign of disapproval came when Fantin-Latour proceeded with his projected "*Hommage à Baudelaire*" as a companion picture to his "*Hommage à Delacroix*." The composition suffered one setback after another. Verlaine insisted that Rimbaud should be included as a Baudelaire enthusiast and a poet who was successfully assuming the mantle of the master. Leconte de Lisle thereupon refused to sit. Then Banville withdrew, Rimbaud having upset even his equanimity. Finally Mérat, who found Valade's admiration for Rimbaud tiresome, retired; he took part in the opening sittings reluctantly but delivered an ultimatum after listening impatiently to Verlaine and Rimbaud who spent most of the time in verbal sparring, Rimbaud criticizing one thing after another in laconic tones which were too much like Mérat's own form of interjection to be bearable. Eventually Mérat declared that he would not sit with the young hooligan; Fantin-Latour must choose between him and the inseparables. The picture then lost its last remnant of purpose, to include "*Les Trois*," and became, according to the sitters, "*Dîner des Poètes*," according to their critics, "*Repas des Communards*." Eventually the name "*Coin de Table*" was agreed upon, Mérat's head being replaced by a pot of flowers.

By this time Rimbaud's attempts to exhaust the possibilities of alcohol were proving unhappy; he had not the head for it and felt sick and quarrelsome instead of god- or devil-like. In some such spasm of angry disappointment he broke with Cabaner on the grounds that he drank milk; and departed, having as a final gesture of disgust used the current milk bottle as a receptacle for urine.

His choice of homes narrowed as his reputation spread—and it was a small world he lived in—and contracted further when, after accepting Cros' offer of shelter, he tore up and used as toilet paper the pages of an expensive album particularly prized by his host. He also, if Mathilde is to be believed, doctored Cros' drink with sulfuric acid to express his displeasure at the criticism of his use of the album. But as the good-natured Cros merely asked him to leave and met him afterwards from time to time without recriminations it would seem that Mathilde allowed an understandable malevolence to lead her astray.

Verlaine was hard put to it to know where to place the boy. Before the coming of Rimbaud he had found himself treated coolly in certain quarters of the *Parnasse*. Leconte de Lisle's demand for the banishment of every Communard included Verlaine; indeed Verlaine was at the top of the list as being an intemperate drinker and far too good a poet to be left free in Paris. In the diminished circle at Boulevard des Invalides it would be difficult to say which name, Verlaine or Hugo, blurted out by an unthinking youngster, caused the lines to compress deeper at the side of the great man's austere but slightly flabby mouth; the irritating apparition of the returned Hugo, acclaimed Prince of Poets and receiving the despised plaudits of the crowd, could with an effort be dismissed with a shrug of the well-tailored shoulders and an expression which the few disciples would interpret as one of benevolent pity; the mention of Verlaine, possibly the greater danger (for Leconte de Lisle was not without acumen), brought out the judge on his bench, fingers tipped: this loose-living rascal would assuredly end on the scaffold; he had been given his chance but . . . And the master waved away with the graceful if rather pudgy right hand all further consideration of "this animal." Anatole France, Verlaine's one-time friend, had gone to Versailles when the Commune took control of the city and on his return proclaimed his detestation of those cads "the Communards," and France was then a power in the *Parnasse*, having diplomatically quarreled with Leconte de Lisle and ousted Mendès from the selection committee.

In short, "I have too many enemies—why, God knows!—at Lemerre's to go there any more," complained Verlaine pathetically. He was a little too fond of seeing enemies where they did not exist and he exaggerated here, but it was true enough that he had backed the wrong political horse, had written excessively un-Parnassian poetry (copies of *La Bonne Chanson*, officially published the next year, had found their way into disapproving quarters) and had been, openly, living an un-Parnassian life before his marriage. He now, by his association with Rimbaud, gave the envious and disapproving a handle which they used with relish.

By the end of the year, after going the rounds of the more long-suffering friends, Rimbaud had made sure that he and Verlaine were virtually isolated. The last dinner of the *Vilains Bonshommes* (the "*Zutistes*" of Cros not yet having found general favor) that year was held over a wine shop on the corner of the rue Bonaparte and the rue du Vieux-Colombier facing the Place St.-Sulpice. All went well until the meal was over and a poet, Jean Aicard according to most reports, began to read his latest work. Rimbaud who had as usual drunk more than he could master disliked the poem, as he disliked most of the poems he had heard read in Paris. He expressed his disapproval by an unmistakable "*merde*" every time Aicard came to the end of a line. At first the company tried not to notice him, listening with what must have been a comical overattention to the reciting poet. But Rimbaud was not to be silenced; his "*merdes*" grew louder and louder until the general pretense that he was silent, was not even there, collapsed. Carjat told him to be quiet. Rimbaud said loudly that he would stop for no one; he continued to punctuate the poem with his one-word comment. Carjat took hold of him, shook him and threatened to teach him his manners if he did not behave himself. At this Rimbaud leaped from the table, rushed to a corner of the room where Verlaine had leaned his sword stick, drew the sword and advanced menacingly on Carjat. Several men caught him by the arms but could not get a firm grip on him before he had wounded Carjat in the head. He was then carried bodily by a burly painter to his room and thrown on the bed where he at once slept.

Verlaine, meanwhile, was warned that the boy must be kept from all future gatherings; he would be welcome as usual, not Rimbaud. His reaction was an angry "both or none."

[3]

From this time their ostracism was almost complete. In the new year of 1872 Verlaine rented a room for "Rimbe," as he fondly called him on the rue Campagne-Première, and their society there and in the cafés was restricted virtually to the young Forain, "Gavroche" to them, Blémont, Richepin and Cros, if he happened to be present—that is to say he would not like most others go away or move his seat when they came into a café.

The view generally held of the disgraced couple was that, as Mérat had said, Rimbaud was an intolerable young hoodlum unfit for the society of decent men, who had bewitched Verlaine. This view was natural at the time—one would have had to be a most exceptional man to see beyond it—but it will not do now. Rimbaud behaved like a young "spiv" of today, but he was not a "spiv" and his behavior was due to something other than mere nastiness. He came to Paris to make a name as poet—a great name; he had good reason for his hopes, he believed rightly that his work was remarkable and he had been encouraged by Verlaine to expect a remarkable welcome. What he found was quite different; he was welcomed but not as the eighth wonder of the world, one who would revolutionize poetry; he was treated with affectionate curiosity as just another of the sensations which stirred parts of Paris from time to time, a Glatigny rhyming at the Alcazar, a rat with two heads, the novelty being all. One or two men excepted, no real interest was shown in his work, and his theory of elevating the poet to a seer through deliberate self-abandonment to every experience was received with tolerant smiles as a passing extravagance of youth.

Simultaneously, he discovered, with what emotions may be imagined, that these people who declined politely to take him seriously were not as he had imagined them from the intellectual desert of Charleville, that life in Paris at the very heart of the literary world was little more than an enlargement of that first dinner at rue Nicolet, that it consisted in the main of men talking cleverly, but without conviction, of some giant game that all were wittily engaged in. Banville revealed himself as a clown, a trickster, Leconte de Lisle as a sham, and almost all the men with whom Verlaine was surrounded appeared as pale shadows of one or the other. Their conversation infuriated the boy as a mess of gossip, insincerity and spite, their works as rubbish. For to deduce the work from the man was instinctive and it took only a matter of weeks for Rimbaud to reject the entire Parnassian theory and attitude. The Parnassians, he saw, lived in a world of cozy ideals, where all was beauty, order and reason, their poetry a bloodless abstraction.

Any talented boy with the strength of mind to resist the flattery of attention from older men might have gone as far. But at this point Rimbaud parts company with all, for to himself he was Rimbaud, the great "Rimbe," he was right, they were wrong, the entire literary world of Paris was wrong except one man whom he would save to be his companion in greatness. So thinking, with next to no sense of humor, with no head for liquor and an inexhaustible supply of moral courage, he began to show this world what he thought of it; he made himself impossible, as Vincent van Gogh was to make himself impossible—for these two men, outwardly so different, had much in common. His reaction to insult, as he saw it, took the form of an unparalleled rudeness. It was a youthful reaction—he was only seventeen in October—the reaction of a boy who became quarrelsome in his cups, who burned to parade his contempt for the world he had mistakenly envied, and whose arrogant belief in his greatness drove him to court this world's dislike as a necessary part of his suffering; the poet, he had said, must seek every possible experience of love, pain and madness, and what greater pain could he discover than ostracism by the gods of yesterday—was not this a form of "inexpressible torture"?

And the man he had picked out, wisely, as the one great contemporary poet, the man he had most unwisely "promised to restore to his primitive state of a son of the Sun," the "infatuated" Verlaine, what is to be said of him? Verlaine thought that Rimbaud was the most wonderful person he had ever met. Rightly: he was. Angel or devil? Verlaine was to ask himself that question for the rest of his life, answering first this, then that; but whichever he decided Rimbaud remained head and shoulders above other men as poet, in force of intellect, strength of character, beauty of looks and, when he chose, charm of manner. To Verlaine who was deficient in three of these qualities and too modest to claim the other two the boy seemed marvelous in almost all he did. Almost, for Verlaine was neither blind nor a fool. But one does not cease to love when the loved one behaves badly; the convivial Verlaine was embarrassed and unhappy when his friends were insulted by Rimbaud, but he understood something of the reasons for it and his chief feeling was irritation that they had not the perception to see the boy as the wonder he was. He knew; he had read, seen, heard; if they chose to see only a conceited young puppy so much the worse for them. For him, he chose to live fully for the first time in his life beside this extraordinary youth.

These bold thoughts did not harmonize with life in rue Nicolet and Verlaine made not the slightest attempt to reconcile the two. Sufficient for him was the good of the moment whether he was sitting in a café with Rimbaud or in the salon with Mathilde. But nobody else was willing to oblige him; Mathilde, Madame Mauté and Monsieur Mauté continued to protest in their different ways against the association with the young monster; Rimbaud, for his part, determined to save a great poet and companion in spiritual adventure from the living death of suburban domesticity, threw wrench after wrench in the works in the shape of caustic remarks whenever Verlaine said he would have to be going home. Verlaine, eternally hopeful of getting the best of both worlds, eternally self-deceptive, parried as best he could these attempts to force him into an unpleasant decision; why, he wondered, should he have to choose between a sensual love for Mathilde with a home to which he could retire at any moment, and a romantic love for Rimbaud with a glorious future as poet?

The birth of his son Georges at the end of October swung the balance heavily in Mathilde's direction; for a few weeks he became the model husband and father. But Rimbaud was not to be denied; and what Rimbaud had to say about a reconciliation by the good offices of baby fingers and a baby smile was too frightfully true to escape the proudest of parents.

He recommended "deranging his senses" which, hashish having so lamentably failed, boiled down to absinthe and plenty of it. Rimbaud had not a sou but Verlaine, generous to a fault, paid for everything, merely asking his mother whenever he ran short. In this manner the francs sped on their way and Verlaine returned home drunk many a night—and truculent too. Stung by the jibes of Rimbaud, he faced the shortcomings of his life with Mathilde; reproaches followed and sometimes blows before extinction came and he slept to wake without knowledge of what he had done and, when told, to apologize abjectly.

In January, a few days after the scene at the *Vilains Bonshommes* dinner and following a night of threats by a drunken Verlaine, Mathilde told her parents what had been going on in her portion of the house. They were appalled—a little surprising, this, since mother and daughter spent most of the day together. They acted immediately, sent Mathilde to the South, shut Verlaine out of the house and refused to give him her address.

But Verlaine did not accept the liberty freely offered him; three parts emotion, he was instantly struck to the heart, his conscience reproaching him for villainy; he could think of nothing but the happy times he and Mathilde had passed together, of the security of their home, the child lost to him. He besieged the house in a panic, demanding to know where his wife was. His letters would be forwarded, that was the only satisfaction he could get. He wrote, begging Mathilde to come back.

When Rimbaud had been sent away, Mathilde replied, she would return. And when Verlaine showed signs of resisting she threatened him with a legal separation. This so much alarmed him that he gave way; Rimbaud should go. By March Rimbaud was back in Charleville and the Verlaine household was set up again.

[5]

Mathilde had made the further stipulation that Verlaine and Rimbaud should not correspond. This promise, made under duress, Verlaine promptly broke; and although he had given way to his wife he privately held it against her and intended to right the matter as soon as possible. Meanwhile he extracted a certain pleasure from his dilemma, the mystery-loving side of him reveling in the situation. Thus he is found instructing Rimbaud to send his "*martyriques*" letters to the rue Lécluse so that the elder Madame Verlaine might the more readily part with money for his keep at Charleville and eventually support the idea of his return, while his letters "*touchant les revoir, prudences,* etc." should go to Forain's new studio on the Quai d'Anjou in the house where Baudelaire had lived. No doubt he enjoyed himself crossing Paris in search of secret missives; no doubt he persuaded himself that Mathilde would open the letters if sent to rue Nicolet; certainly he feared her discovery of their plans to meet again. But as he invariably carried all the letters back to rue Nicolet and left them where they could easily be read, his elaborate precautions disclose themselves for what they were, a game that might have been played by two rather silly schoolboys.

His letters are on a par with his behavior, peppered with "*merdes*" and talking with absurd gusto of the "joys, agonies, hypocrisies, cynicisms" they would share and of the "tigerish things" they would do to the villain-in-chief, Monsieur Mauté, whom Verlaine chose to see behind Mathilde's firm stand. Filled too with penny-paper mystery heroics: "*Certes, nous nous verrons! Quand? Attendre un peu! Nécessités dures! Opportunités roides! Soit! Et merde pour les unes comme merde pour les autres! Et comme merde pour moi!—et pour toi!*" He was having the time of his life and at the same moment—very cunning this, he prided himself—living, as he thought,

down to Rimbaud's determination that they should descend to the
depths before rising to the heights; doing his best to earn the title
of "*fils du Soleil.*" It scarcely convinces readers today and did not
convince the reader then. Yet the only scrap of Rimbaud's replies to
be known is on a similar level, distinguished by a row of nine
"*merdes*" in a few lines.

Rimbaud, however, was at least practical. Verlaine, finding money
hard to come by to send to Charleville, bent to the desperate expedient of taking a job in an insurance office and had the temerity to
suggest that his "Rimbe" might do likewise. Rimbaud was shocked
by this surrender to bourgeois influence the moment his back was
turned, hurt too by the implication that Verlaine was tired of sup-
porting him. He dismissed the blasphemy in a few words. "Work is
farther from me than my nail is from my eye," he said with a string
of "*merdes*": "When you see me reduced to the point of eating
merde you won't think any longer that I'm too expensive to feed."

To this there was for Verlaine, a Verlaine already finding domesticity decidedly dull without the alternative electric shocks of
Rimbaud, one answer only—surrender: "Love me, protect me, trust
me. Being very weak, I've much need of kindness." And he made
no more bones about getting Rimbaud back to Paris; he and Forain,
he assured his friend, had moved all the belongings from "rue
Campe" (Campagne-Première where he had last rented a room
for Rimbaud) and would put them safely in a room he was taking
in the Hôtel de Cluny of the rue Victor-Cousin.

By May, Rimbaud was back again and he and Verlaine took up
where they had left off, or so it seemed at first. They began to
speak and write, with rather too much dotting of *i*'s and crossing
of *t*'s, of mysterious goings-on in the Hôtel de Cluny as in Rimbaud's
earlier room. It is obvious, reading between the lines, that they were
hard driven to devise new methods of deranging the senses. Others
have found a similar difficulty—monotony will creep in. Hence the
need for mystification, to which Verlaine lent himself with a will.
"Ah, but it wasn't at all what you thought it!" he wrote at the end
of a sonnet brimful of horrid hints, and one can see the finger to
the upturned nose and the schoolboy gleam in those greenish eyes.

To hear Verlaine in this mood one might think that he and
Rimbaud spent their time in one long orgy; and if his listener or
reader were naïve enough to believe him he would be delighted.
But alongside this nonsense ran something very different. There

are poets who write, talk and live as dedicated men—Mallarmé
provides a good example—but Verlaine was not of this kind; he
did his work, his talking and thinking at the table of a noisy café,
walking crowded streets or perched on the bed of Rimbaud's
wretched room, and his behavior in public was chiefly that of a man
dedicated to drink and fooling. A less serious man would be hard
to find, one could reasonably assume, whose life since the coming
of Rimbaud seemed to have consisted mainly in drinking parties
and quarrels with his wife and father-in-law. Nevertheless, between
them he and Rimbaud were to change the face of French poetry and
not by accident; they worked for it but in their own way. The
compulsion came more often than not from Rimbaud, for he was a
serious young man. But Verlaine contributed the experience and the
prestige; he was, after all, the "seer" picked out by Rimbaud at
Charleville to be the leader of a new school.

So they talked over their drinks, talked in Rimbaud's room,
talked in Forain's apartment, talked in the cold, talked on empty
stomachs, talked, talked, talked sober and not so sober but almost
always to the purpose. An occasional listener who did not know
them well would be unable to recognize a purpose, he would distinguish only an apparently aimless bickering, but the purpose was
there, disguised as Verlaine loved to disguise the serious, and its
first results appeared before Rimbaud had long been back in Paris.

Their main problem lay in the long accepted laws of prosody,
laws so restrictive that French poetry had in the course of the
centuries fallen sufficiently behind the true life of the French
language to demand a pronunciation differing widely from contemporary prose, and that the similitude between poems of widely
separated ages appeared, according to individual reaction, either
laughable or lamentable since in effect the only substantial difference
between one poet and another was his subject matter. As a result
poetry came to be regarded in France as an artificial pleasure, not
to say hard work, and was relegated, except for the small "literary"
class, to the gorgeously bound, uncut volumes dustily placed behind
glass and mahogany. It bore no relation to life and, the French
saving their thoughts and energies for tangible rewards, its exponents
had their eyes on the Academy rather than on any possible poetical
immortality.

The Parnassians' two essays into adventurousness were the use
of a certain verbal dexterity and the placing of a great deal of

emphasis on the rhyme. To Verlaine and Rimbaud this emphasis which Banville had hoped would disguise the monotony of the line, in practice added to it, the weight being always in the same place, and went far to restrict the poet's message to the actual rhyming words which the reader would chiefly notice and remember. They set themselves there and then to break down the barrier between poet and reader by using French as it was then spoken, by throwing the emphasis where the sense lay and in general by breaking all the cherished centuries-old laws of prosody. Rimbaud, the obviously adventurous one, began to write *Illuminations*. Verlaine, because he could not help himself, took on the harder task, confined himself to the intimate, personal, homely note in which he excelled and wrote a number of poems in this genre. The account of an everyday happening or thought is always dangerous as Mérat, for example, proved; he was to become known incongruously as "gentle Mérat" because of his sweet and sentimental poetry. Verlaine, truly gentle, injected into his verses the saving grace of irony and humor and turned them away from the banal and the sentimental. But more than irony and humor was needed, and from this moment he began to display a dazzling technical mastery. Yet, so great a poet was he, the only people to be dazzled are the literary critics; the ordinary reader does not notice the skill in the pleasure of recognizing exactly what he too has felt at a similar moment. Take, for instance, the expression of a fear which has come to many people, parents particularly, when they look at the sleeping body of someone they love. Not only a fear but a wonder too, and all this Verlaine states simply, profoundly and beautifully in a few lines.

> *Ce soir je m'étais penché sur ton sommeil.*
> *Tout ton corps dormait chaste sur l'humble lit,*
> *Et j'ai vu, comme un qui s'applique et qui lit,*
> *Ah! j'ai vu que tout est vain sous le soleil!*

> *Qu'on vive, ô quelle délicate merveille,*
> *Tant notre appareil est une fleur qui plie!*
> *O pensée aboutissant à la folie!*
> *Va, pauvre, dors! moi, l'effroi pour toi m'éveille.*

> *Ah! misère de t'aimer, mon frêle amour*
> *Qui vas respirant comme on expire un jour!*
> *O regard fermé que la mort fera tel!*

O bouche qui ris en songe sur ma bouche,
En attendant l'autre rire plus farouche!
Vite, éveille-toi. Dis, l'âme est immortelle?

He was still experimenting but he anticipated his maturity in one poem after another in the early months of 1872. Here is one of the first examples of the manner in which he was to enfranchise French prosody with an original and elastic poetic diction, variety of stress according to meaning and supple flow of meter. Here too is the poet of suggestion and understatement of a sensation common to all sensitive people, securing attention and confidence by an apparently naïve confession and winning his reader partly by identification, partly by the mesmerism of an uncommon musicality.

Il pleure dans mon coeur
Comme il pleut sur la ville.
Quelle est cette langueur
Qui pénètre mon coeur?

O bruit doux de la pluie
Par terre et sur les toits!
Pour un coeur qui s'ennuie,
O le chant de la pluie!

Il pleure sans raison
Dans ce coeur qui s'écoeure.
Quoi! nulle trahison?
Ce deuil est sans raison.

C'est bien la pire peine
De ne savoir pourquoi,
Sans amour et sans haine,
Mon coeur a tant de peine.

*   *   *

Tears fall within mine heart,
As rain upon the town:
Whence does this languor start,
Possessing all mine heart?

O sweet fall of the rain
Upon the earth and roof,

Unto an heart in pain,
O music of the rain.

Tears that have no reason
Fall in my sorry heart:
What, there was no treason?
This grief hath no reason.

Nay, the more desolate,
Because, I know not why,
(Neither for love nor hate)
Mine heart is desolate.

And as if to show that he was capable of every variety of mood and expression, he wrote in the same season:

Le piano que baise une main frêle
Luit dans le soir rose et gris vaguement,
Tandis qu'avec un très léger bruit d'aile
Un air bien vieux, bien faible et bien charmant
Rôde discret, épeuré quasiment,
Par le boudoir longtemps parfumé d'Elle.

Qu'est-ce que c'est que ce berceau soudain
Qui lentement dorlote mon pauvre être?
Que voudrais-tu de moi, doux chant badin?
Qu'as-tu voulu, fin refrain incertain
Qui vas tantôt mourir vers la fenêtre
Ouverte un peu sur le petit jardin?

*   *   *

The keyboard, over which two slim hands float,
Shines vaguely in the twilight pink and gray,
Whilst with a sound like wings, note after note
Takes flight to form a pensive little lay
That strays, discreet and charming, faint, remote,
About the room where perfumes of Her stray.

What is this sudden quiet cradling me
To that dim ditty's dreamy rise and fall?
What do you want with me, pale melody?
What is it that you want, ghost musical
That fades toward the window waveringly
A little open on the garden small?

[6]

Their one steadfast companion during these months was Verlaine's
"little brown cat" Forain, two years older than Rimbaud. Although
unconcerned by the need to plumb every sensation Forain managed
to do so well for himself in this line that of the three he earned
the reputation of wildest. He and Rimbaud were much together,
and thirteen years later, when he was the most renowned caricaturist
of modern times, he remembered vividly "the days when we used
to wait for you, Rimbaud and I, in that little café in the rue Drouet
smoking our clay pipes and wetting our whistles with plenty of
bitter-curaçao."

Verlaine, in other words, remained so much the family and
business man, having somehow kept his job—Rimbaud acquiescing
lugubriously in this lip service to Mammon since one must eat and
still more drink—that his friends had often to cross the river to
collect him. There were occasional scenes at rue Nicolet but in
general Verlaine behaved well enough for Mathilde not to guess
that he had broken his promise. She said later that she did not
suspect Rimbaud's return to Paris—a confession which tells its tale
about Verlaine at home. The sober Verlaine disliked scenes, especially when he had scarcely a leg to stand on, and far from
entertaining a wish to break with Mathilde had a positive terror of
it; he simply wished to enjoy domesticity and Rimbaud in piquant
snatches and was pained when he struck obstacles. Moreover, there
were omens in the air that made him feel the need of an ally even
if the ally happened to be his wife. He was not without prescience,
could read in Rimbaud the signs of increasing impatience and
scented the coming of a crisis.

He was right enough; Rimbaud was becoming impatient and not
only with Paris. Signs of frailty in his companion were disturbingly
evident and had been ever since "love me, protect me, trust me."
These were scarcely the words of a superman and Rimbaud who did
not hoodwink himself, not at least in the obvious way, began from
time to time to look darkly at his innocently happy companion:
was he at heart just another empty, smooth-speaking Parnassian, lost
in the fleshpots; and why did he not leave the woman instead of
complaining about her—were some suburban ties still unbroken
there? At such times he loathed Verlaine, feeling that he had

owered himself to reveal his destiny to a weakling and was committing sacrilege by permitting this sensualist to dabble in higher
hings.

For Rimbaud was above all the son of his mother, an implacable
puritan, and it was agony to his soul, gulping down noxious liquors
which made him sick and quarrelsome but enduring all for the
cause of future spiritual glory, to see this impossible Verlaine
draining glass after glass with a disgusting relish as if he really liked
the revolting stuff, and not one thought of a desperate duty in his
featherbrained mind. What kind of soulmate was this! At times he
despaired. At other times he was savagely angry, for hell has no
fury like the fury of the earnest young man balked. His irritation
boiled over one night. He, Cros and Verlaine were sitting drinking.
He said suddenly to Verlaine, holding a knife over the table, "Hold
your hands out." To his disgust Verlaine was fool enough, as
Rimbaud saw trust, to obey. Furious, he dragged the blade across
the open wrists and when the hurt and startled Verlaine leaped
up and ran off, pursued him into the street and hacked his leg.

This was how Mathilde learned of Rimbaud's return; Verlaine
laughed off the limp and the bandaged wrists as fencing wounds but
the Cros brothers were visitors at rue Nicolet and Charles had been
horrified by Rimbaud's apparently senseless attack. He explained.
There was immediate trouble, trouble which ended in Mathilde
locking the bedroom door to her husband: he must choose, she
intimated.

But before Verlaine and Mathilde could come to a conclusion
Rimbaud had acted. Often enough he despised and almost hated
Verlaine, but who was there except this craven to keep him company?
With Verlaine he could at least have his way, for he had every
intention of being master; besides, a thrifty soul like his mother,
he needed his cash; and he also knew well enough in affectionate
moments that in Verlaine he had found a generous, loving and
obliging soul in a million. Above all, Verlaine was a great poet.

So Rimbaud swallowed the disadvantages of this excessively human
disciple and put him to the test. One day early in July Verlaine,
walking to the druggist to buy medicine for Mathilde who had
developed a sore throat, ran across his friend in the street. Rimbaud
was carrying a letter which he had intended to leave at the house
for Verlaine. It was to say that he was sick of Paris and intended to
leave it at once.

Shocked, Verlaine asked when he was going. That moment, replied Rimbaud. Was Verlaine coming too? Verlaine hesitated: "What about my wife?" he asked. "To hell with your wife," said Rimbaud contemptuously.

That tone had never failed to make Verlaine feel ashamed of himself. He threw his misgivings overboard, turned and went off with Rimbaud.

11.

FOOLISH VIRGIN

1872-1873

[1]

This was the end of Verlaine's marriage, even the shadow of it, yet none thought so at the time, he least of all. He did not consider that he had left his wife, told her so a little belatedly ("Don't grieve or cry. I'm in the middle of a bad dream. I'll come back one day.") and remained forever after aggrieved that such a thought could be attributed to him.

And curiously enough he meant what he said. He was a man of impulse but of what he would call calculation too; he went off with Rimbaud without a moment's notice yet not positively without thought; he had a habit of reasoning which possessed as its main supports an inveterate optimism and a firm bias toward his well-being. His mind had run something like this: that absence made the heart grow fonder; that any little rift between himself and Mathilde would close itself automatically when each learned the other's value; that she could not suffer hardship since she was in no way financially dependent on him at the moment; that her time was very much given to the child who would in a year or so be of real interest to him and would constitute a strong and necessary bond between them; that he, Verlaine, was a man who needed a home as rock, even if he did not happen to be living in it for a while, and would never dream of abandoning it—in thought anyway; that there had been rumors in Paris of a fresh drive against Communards still at large; and finally that with Rimbaud he would become the great poet—had not Rimbaud promised as much?— and this, with his consequent fame and fortune, would benefit all and all would be proud of him.

Mathilde, and still more her father, failed absolutely to follow this method of reasoning to Verlaine's everlasting chagrin ("you never understood me" he was to complain again and again); all they could see was a married man who without a word left his wife and child, to rollick off with a dissolute boy. To her the only other fact of moment was the unavoidable, almost unforgivable truth that his chief pleasure was no longer to be with her. For there was the small matter which even Verlaine could not blink, that he wanted to go with Rimbaud and expected to enjoy himself enormously playing the carefree truant. But to him this came under the heading of impulse.

Having taken the plunge, there was no feeling in him at first other than delight in a lark. He passed the mood on to Rimbaud who could be young enough on occasion and they shot off to Arras lightheartedly, Verlaine insisting that Rimbaud meet his aunt at Arras, his uncle at Fampoux, his cousins at Lécluse—a wish which suggests that he could see no harm in the friendship or the journey.

However, they got no farther than Arras police station. Arriving at the railway station in the early hours they waited in the lunchroom until they could call on Verlaine's aunt. But the spirit of the lark was still strongly in them and the sight and sound of the respectable men sitting at the tables set it soaring. Rimbaud began to speak in an audible sotto voce of crimes they had recently committed, and Verlaine went one better with a loudly whispered reference to their break from jail. They were soon rewarded by the sight of two gendarmes entering the lunchroom, summoned by an alarmed counter hand, and Verlaine, feigning not to have seen them, expressed great disappointment that they had failed to "pull that job" and assured Rimbaud that they would have another crack at it the next day.

This was enough for the gendarmes who took them in charge. At the magistrate's court the farce continued gaily, Rimbaud bursting into sobs and claiming protection from Verlaine who he declared had led him astray. And when Verlaine was asked what he was doing in Arras he took a high line, showing his papers and announcing that, having been born in Metz, then annexed to Germany, he had the right to choose between German and French nationality and—"upon my soul, after this illegal detention I doubt whether I shall continue to be a Frenchman."

By this time the magistrate had begun to scent a hoax and told

the gendarmes to escort the two friends to the next train for Paris.
But Verlaine, by then thoroughly in his part, protested that they
had been forcibly removed in the midst of their breakfast; he
demanded the right to finish it. The gendarmes escorted them back
to the restaurant, where they finished their breakfast gleefully, and
by evening they were back in Paris. They crossed at once to the
Gare de l'Est and took the first train for Charleville. There they
looked up Bretagne who provided a horse and cart that same evening
to take them across the frontier into Belgium. The next day they
were in Brussels.

For a time the light-hearted mood held. Tireless walkers both,
they explored a large area around the city. They did not care much
where they went or what they saw; movement was its own reward,
a movement paralleled by the activity of their minds. For they
were possessed by exhilaration, free to go where they pleased, free to
think and talk as they pleased. Verlaine felt as though he had been
born again, watching Rimbaud, who had shot up in the last months,
striding along like a young god; listening to the prophecies, surely
inspired, of words used as words had never been used before, of a
new literature fashioned by them. He was never to forget those
days on the roads of Belgium, he and Rimbaud "intoxicated to a
frenzy with art, talking and living art." He felt himself in the
presence of genius and for the first time felt the capacity for genius
in himself. He did not always go the whole way with his daring
companion but this too had its charm, the charm of defying one
principle after another with a catch of the breath. "Atrociously
delicious," he said long afterwards and one understands his feeling;
caught up by enthusiasm he would outdevil the boy and out-
prophesy him; he was eloquent on their future greatness; all was
possible when he felt the sun on his face, drew breath after breath
of country air, knew himself to be absolutely unrestricted and had
by his side the "devilishly seductive" boy leading him from one
glorious fantasy to another.

Practically, these rambles brought from him a small series of
poems on the Belgian countryside in which the mood of the
writer is reflected by the scene. Yet one of the most delightful
and technically one of the most brilliant poems he was ever to
write was inspired by the St.-Gilles Fair in Brussels itself where
Verlaine, strongly taken by the merry-go-rounds, came straight back
to their hotel to write:

Tournez, tournez, bons chevaux de bois,
Tournez cent tours, tournez mille tours,
Tournez souvent et tournez tojours,
Tournez, tournez au son des hautbois.

. . . .

C'est ravissant comme ça vous soûle,
D'aller ainsi dans ce cirque bête:
Bien dans le ventre et mal dans la tête,
Du mal en masse et du bien en foule.

. . . .

Tournez, tournez, sans qu'il soit besoin
D'user jamais de nuls éperons,
Pour commander à vos galops ronds:
Tournez, tournez, sans espoir de foin. . . .

But there were less happy moments. Rimbaud, not yet eighteen, could not always avoid being his age when for the first time in his life he wandered where he liked, expressed any thought that came into his head and could forget mothers, punishments and the question of where the next sou would come from. In these moods he was charming, irresistible. But he was a man of action too, a dedicated soul; all he did must further the grand design; all things, pleasures and pains, had their purpose. And when the taskmaster reminded him to examine his soul and the soul of his companion, trouble followed. Verlaine was obviously not a thoroughgoing *"fils du Soleil"* and perhaps would never be one. He talked largely on occasion but was not the truth less palatable, that he was just enjoying himself like any other clod and without taking real thought for the morrow? Worse still, it became plain that this man whom he had rescued from the spiritual death of domesticity had left Mathilde in body only, and that provisionally; the deluded creature was actually writing what he fondly hoped were secret messages to the woman. It became clear that Verlaine lacked the power to cut adrift from a hampering past; in some inexplicable fashion he continued to cherish it.

Deluded creature perhaps; but Rimbaud's opinion of his companion in his sterner moments was much less charitable; he was dealing with a traitor who would have to be led the hard way. He became angry, an anger fed by subconscious envy of Verlaine's uncomplicated enjoyment of this hateful world. And Verlaine suffered, one foot still on rue Nicolet, one on Rimbaud and the

Arthur Rimbaud
in Paris,
1871

"Le Coin de Table," 1872
(seated) Verlaine, Rimbaud, Valade, D'Hervilly and Pelletan
(standing) Bonnier, Blémont and Aicard

two drawing violently apart. Rimbaud could be unkind, none more
so. No need to slash wrists, there were other and sharper ways of
wounding. Verlaine's weaknesses were open to him and in exaspera-
tion he began to play on them. The man was a masochist as well as
all the rest, he discovered with a new contempt. Certainly he,
Rimbaud, intended to be leader, but where was the glory in dominating a man who asked nothing better than to be dominated?
The defrauded idealist—and there is none so implacable—set himself to frighten Verlaine out of his wits by practical jokes.

Verlaine spent wretched hours; all he asked were love, companionship, drink and time to write his poems, happy ones by preference.
But the poems became mournful, sometimes querulous.

> O triste, triste était mon âme
> A cause, à cause d'une femme.
>
> Je ne me suis pas consolé
> Bien que mon coeur s'en soit allé,
>
> Bien que mon coeur, bien que mon âme
> Eussent fui loin de cette femme.
>
> Je ne me suis pas consolé,
> Bien que mon coeur s'en soit allé.
>
> Et mon coeur, mon coeur trop sensible
> Dit à mon âme: Est-il possible,
>
> Est-il possible,—le fût-il,—
> Ce fier exil, ce triste exil?
>
> Mon âme dit à mon coeur: Sais-je
> Moi-même, que nous veut ce piège
>
> D'être présents bien qu'exilés,
> Encore que loin en allés?

> * * *

> Oh, heavy, heavy my despair,
> Because, because of One so fair.
>
> My misery knows no allay,
> Although my heart has come away.

Although my heart, although my soul,
Have fled the fatal One's control.

My misery knows no allay,
Although my heart has come away.

My heart, the too, too feeling one,
Says to my soul, "Can it be done,

"Can it be done, too feeling heart,
That we from her shall live apart?"

My soul says to my heart, "Know I
What this strange pitfall should imply,

"That we, though far from her, are near,
Yea, present, though in exile here?"

Another matter was causing him misgiving. He sent this and other
poems to Blémont, the man who had printed earlier poems in the
journal he had founded, *La Renaissance littéraire*; the man who
had been the first to assure him after the collapse of the Commune
that he thought none the worse of him. Now nothing happened;
Blémont admired the new poems, would have been proud to print
them, but . . . The very marrow began to desert Verlaine's bones;
he forgot the trails of mystery laid so industriously by Rimbaud
and himself, he forgot Rimbaud's behavior in Paris, he saw only an
innocent man trying to reach infinity and write deathless poetry
by the side of a loved friend or, in another mood, a man on a
harmless spree, whichever sounded better. But innocent. And in
his absence, while his back was turned, this horror! His imagination
rushed to the most disagreeable conclusion; he was being cut by
his friends, his career as poet was broken; Paris, wife, child, home
were all barred to him. And he could not discuss his fears with
Rimbaud; Rimbaud had a short way with those who indulged in
despondent imaginings. He had to keep an anguished silence.

Then, suddenly, came a note from Mathilde; she had followed
him to Brussels with her mother, she was in the hotel from which
he had first written to her.

At that moment Verlaine was perhaps feeling one of his revulsions
against life with Rimbaud; he was certainly suffering severely from

lack of sex; and when, entering the hotel bedroom, he saw Mathilde stretched invitingly on the bed he joined her without thought, without any sensation but joyful relief.

Mathilde had come to take him from Rimbaud but the method she used made absolutely certain that he would not go. When they at last got up from the bed Verlaine made the motions of surrender but with a sinking heart and a growing sense of shame. And when Mathilde was fully dressed and he saw before him not a beautiful body but a pert and rather silly young *Parisienne* his guilt stared him in the face.

He agreed to meet the triumphant Mathilde and her mother on the train for Paris in a few hours and he went out to find and tell Rimbaud. Until the train was due he and Rimbaud sat together drinking, then he joined the train and traveled in silence with the two women as far as the frontier. There they had to change coaches. When Mathilde and her mother had found their new seats there was no sign of Verlaine. He did not appear until the train began to move, and then only on the platform. Madame Mauté leaned out of the window and urged him to jump in. He simply shook his head and the train steamed off without him.

It has been said that Rimbaud was in another compartment of the train from Brussels to the frontier. The practical joke that is not really funny certainly bears all the marks of Rimbaud, as does Verlaine's shamefaced silence in the train. But Verlaine's note to Mathilde suggests that he is rejoining Rimbaud in Brussels and it is possible to imagine without strain a contemptuous last command from Rimbaud at the café after the manner of "Oh, go off with your precious woman—she's all you're fit for!" which would send Verlaine to the train but would effectually prevent him from reaching Paris.

Before leaving the station for Brussels Verlaine sent off what for him was a savage note to his wife: *"Miserable fée carotte, princesse souris, punaise qu'attendent les deux doigts et le pot. Vous m'avez fait tout; vous avez peut-être tué le coeur de mon ami. Je rejoins Rimbaud, s'il veut encore de moi après cette trahison que vous m'avez fait faire."*

Later when the affair had mellowed in his mind, he wrote it out as usual in *"Birds in the Night,"* one of the most beautiful poems he was ever to compose.

[2]

The effect of this interlude was to bind Verlaine more firmly to Rimbaud. For some time to come when Rimbaud was difficult or disagreeable Verlaine could tell himself that he had the right to be all that and more. He attributed his own feelings to Rimbaud though it is doubtful whether the boy would have suffered as Verlaine imagined except in lack of funds.

Not that Verlaine had abandoned Mathilde; it was not long before he was proposing enthusiastically that she join him and Rimbaud in Brussels in a *ménage à trois*. Rimbaud, he assured her, was doing very well there—a fact scarcely calculated to move her. Actually she was leaving his letters unopened, a chilly procedure unknown to Verlaine who wrote on outlining his plans.

Rimbaud might have been doing well in Brussels, though there is no sign of it, but Verlaine unquestionably was not. He could find no work and his mother, though taking his side in the dispute, was not being very forthcoming with the cash. Early in September therefore they moved to London, Verlaine believing that he could find work there, knowing that he would find Communard friends in exile there and, having heard much about London from Blémont, curious to see it. Moreover his extensive reading in English literature had made him something of an Anglophile; he had not failed to see part of himself in the English lyrical poets.

Rimbaud's reasons for agreeing to the move—and one cannot doubt that he had the major say—remain uncertain. But he was anxious to master as many languages as possible so that he could write a universal poetry, and Verlaine, who liked to flourish his knowledge of English by incorrect phrases in his letters, had whetted his appetite. In any case he was restless and yearned for fresh worlds to conquer. Brussels seemed even less conquerable—or worth conquering—than Paris. And, as one can despise and feel the lack of a thing at the same moment, the social oblivion in Brussels would contrast unpleasantly with the attention he had first received in Paris. He may have expected better things from London. It may even be that he hoped to find there new methods of deranging the senses; he was young enough and innocent enough for that.

They crossed from Ostend on a Saturday, a rough crossing which did not disturb them, slept at Dover and were up early walking through the town and along the cliffs. About eight o'clock, feeling hungry, they looked for breakfast and found most places closed, the others turning them away with looks of suspicion. Only when they ran across a French interpreter did they get served and then only by declaring themselves bona fide travelers. That, says Verlaine, "was my first experience of an English Sunday."

In London they found a room in Soho, then called on Régamey who had a studio on Langham Street. Régamey remembered the *Vilains Bonshommes* dinners vividly and gave Verlaine a hearty welcome. He thought that the manner of the unexpected visitor was charming "and although most scantily provided for in the linen department he didn't show the slightest sign of embarrassment." Rimbaud also "didn't exactly sparkle with elegance" which was a kind way of saying that both looked like tramps, as a sketch of Régamey was to show, a sketch of them walking the streets, a policeman pointedly ignoring their existence.

Verlaine was in high spirits; he fancied his English, quite without cause; he was delighted to be in the country of the poets he admired so much; and in general vague terms he hoped much from the change. It was true that his poetry appealed more directly to the English than to his own countrymen, that the light ironical note was an English form of humor and that his forte of suggestion and avoidance of heavy emotion was an English trait also; but for the moment England, as represented by the London police, barmaids and dispensers of jobs, cast a chilly eye on the seedy man who proclaimed himself by his exuberant gestures and by his friends as yet another political refugee given unenthusiastic shelter.

He worked off some of his good spirits at Régamey's with a couple of satirical sketches to which, with Rimbaud's help, he attached clever but unkind parodies of Coppée who, having won another success in the Paris theatre, was testing the generosity of his friends to a breaking point. Régamey told them that Vermersch was about to get married—"insane" commented Verlaine with greater accuracy than he knew—and that they could probably take over his room on Howland Street. And within a few days they were living a few steps from Fitzroy Square, a district then fashionable, and Verlaine was heading his letters 34-35 Howland

Street with mock complaints that the street numbers "instead of going by odds and evens fluttered about scandalously with every breath of wind."

Free to look about them, they sightsaw with thoroughness, walking vast distances through and about the city. In the first few weeks they made the usual rounds of the tourist with the difference that they did all on foot and that Rimbaud strode the streets with a shiny top hat on his head which contrasted oddly with the shabby clothes below. They made themselves at home in the West End and City, examined the docks at Woolwich, walked through the Tower subway and the Thames tunnel, went over the Tower and Madame Tussaud's, stared at the children with blackened faces and strange outfits collecting farthings for Guy Fawkes Day, watched the changing of the Guard and the Lord Mayor's procession, listened to the orators in Hyde Park, visited the National Gallery and Wallace Collection, and one of the exhibitions at the French Gallery where to their astonishment they saw themselves on the wall in *"Coin de Table"* which hung with the Impressionists. "Fantin forever!" exclaimed Verlaine vaunting his mounting vocabulary, the improvement of which, however, had reduced itself chiefly to memorizing unprintable English words. They became regular theatregoers, listening to Offenbach at the Alhambra, Hervé, Shakespeare at the Queen's and Princess's, Sheridan at the Vaudeville and French players at the Royalty. And they were delighted with the minstrel shows then popular, one of which especially pleased Verlaine because the clowns in a skit on the Jesuits "all looked like Leconte de Lisle!"

At first Verlaine was disappointed not to say horrified by the look of London "as flat as a blackboard" and the Londoners, noisy, quarrelsome and unwashed—"the reek of humanity in the theatres!"; by the atrocious climate, thick gray skies, fog and "rain, rain, rain!"; and by the disgustingly hypocritical life in the city "black as a crow, noisy as a duck, prudish *in the face of every kind of flaunting vice,* forever drunken in spite of ridiculous tracts against insobriety." He realized quickly that the Sunday at Dover had been a dream of freedom compared with the shattering austerity of London: "passers-by dressed up in their Sunday best like savages, few cabs, *no carriages, not one! . . . Everything* closed. No trade. The letter boxes closed too . . . No theatres open, naturally . . . Oh! Very dull!" With stupefaction he heard a policeman threaten the bootblack who dared to ply his trade on the Sabbath, saw policemen "watch in hand timing the opening and closing" of the few pubs and dining rooms permitted to open from one until three and six until eleven.

And what meals they served in these eating houses! "So-called oxtail soup" an abomination; "coffee PLAIN per cup" a ghastly mixture of milk and dried chickory; fish "horrible . . . all looking like octopus, soft, sticky and *slippery*"; Gin "concentrated sewage water"; and, final insult to the man with a palate, "warm beer!" Nor was he less shocked by the places in which men and women were expected to enjoy their food and drink: the public houses with their slatternly, blowsy barmaids and taciturn barmen, the customers tippling furtively, jammed against one another at a bar and breathing fetid air, or, tiresomely loquacious, being thrust outside unceremoniously. And outside he looked with disgust at the dirt lying thickly everywhere, the garbage blowing about, the drunks reeling along the narrow pavements, the incessant brawls, the rags and beggars side by side with elegance and wealth. Even their tobacco was dirty, their cigars unfit to touch, and their matches . . . ! On English matches he became lyrical; they never lit, "*never*, you understand, *never*." He predicted a fortune for the first enterprising man to import French matches. He longed for the sparkle, the cleanliness, the good meals, the beauty of Paris and, above all, for the cafés where one could sit indefinitely over a drink and hear intelligent talk.

But within a week or two he began to change his mind. He was a perceptive man; the poet in him responded eventually to the charm of London, so much less obvious than the beauty of Paris. He was or would be a domestic man clinging to security the farther removed he found himself from it; the cozy, homelike atmosphere of London which he rightly saw as "a collection of small towns," an atmosphere in which the dirt played its part, soothed him with its suggestion of safety in permanence. He was a man with a strong sense of humor; he found this echoed in the frequent exchanges between Londoners. He was a friendly man; the English, he thought, though less good than his own people, were kind beneath an unpromising façade of manner as the French were not. And, to see the matter from another angle, he was a man unaccustomed to plain speech until he met Rimbaud; he admired "the very great candor" of the English.

His first stay in England, Verlaine confessed later, "was of a rather frivolous nature, to use no stronger expression." But he was writing for a special audience toward whom he adopted the manner of the reformed rake, as being what was expected of him. The truth was less exciting: he and Rimbaud drank a fair amount but not the unobtainable absinthe; their language was deliberately foul; they seem to have sampled opium in Limehouse following their reading of Baudelaire's translation of De Quincey, and if so, this was their solitary success in the search for fresh experience of evil. If Verlaine tried it the effects are unnoticeable in his life or work; he got more experience, no doubt, from patronizing the prostitutes who to his amazement solicited openly in the main streets. In general, the lives of the two young men were harmless enough; if Verlaine failed to get work it was not only for want of trying but because of his connection with the Communards, the competition among the many refugees, the indifference of his English and his dilapidated appearance, which Rimbaud's top hat (Rimbaud accompanying him everywhere) merely emphasized.

From Verlaine, writing briskly to Lepelletier and Blémont, came one optimistic announcement after another: he was working hard, he was no lazy blackguard to live on women, he assured them. Positively, he proposed to write for two "serious" French newspapers being launched in London and for American newspapers there— "they pay well"; he also hoped to become a businessman in spare moments, "employing myself in French correspondence" for a friend "at the head of a big business"; finally he had written some "extremely curious notes" on Belgium and was writing his travel sketches *Croquis Londiniens* which he pressed his Paris friends to print in their journals, both being editors.

Little came of all this. Blémont and Lepelletier showed no eagerness to print anything of his and their apologetic evasions led to anxious inquiries, "Who is for me and who against me?," which his friends in Paris avoided as best they could; led also to sarcastic references to "the *nice* little poets who write *nice* little books on their *nice* little companions-in-exile"—this chiefly because Richepin had attacked Jules Vallès whom Verlaine had met in the Communist circle in London; led finally to particular irony at the expense of Mérat, the once best friend whose withdrawal from *"Coin de Table"* still rankled; Mérat, who was not to be fully forgiven for another year until Verlaine heard the rumor that he had tried to hang himself in the forest of Fontainebleau.

No money from Paris and no money from big business either. He did in fact know a businessman; a relative, a Monsieur Istace, owned the Baccarat Crystal Glass Company of Hatton Garden, but Monsieur Istace evidently decided that Verlaine would not make a good man of business, a decision with which none but Verlaine would quarrel. The matter rested. The newspapers also proved broken reeds; no dollars found their way into the optimistic man's pocket; one of the French newspapers never reached publication stage and the other, though serious enough in its way, turned out to be Vermersch's *L'Avenir,* a Communist journal which did not survive the winter.

It is unlikely that these failures to earn a living—or, to be precise, a single sou—weighed on Verlaine for more than an hour or two at a time. He could tell himself with a clear conscience that he had done his best and could then, at the side of Rimbaud, turn light-heartedly to enjoyment of the biggest city in the world at the expense of his ever-obliging mother. They saw a good deal of Régamey, Andrieu and Vermersch, joined their revolutionary and literary club, attended a meeting on the first floor of a saloon on Old Compton Street to honor the memory of the lately dead Gautier and, less harmlessly, listened to a fiery speech on the "martyrs" of 1832 which inspired Verlaine to offer "Des Morts" to *L'Avenir*— a poem which did him no good on either side of the channel since it convinced certain quarters in Paris that he was a dyed-in-the-wool Communist and made doubly sure that the London police would report him to their confreres in Paris as one of the exiled plotters against the Republic. His call on the French Consul-General to choose French nationality (the first of October being the final date for those born in the lost departments) was, the Paris authorities might well have thought, a dubious compliment.

Verlaine spoke hopefully of a meeting with Swinburne, one of the advanced poets in French eyes, but this seems never to have taken place. He also spoke of meeting another "astonishing" poet, almost certainly the prodigy son of Ford Madox Brown who was tutored by Andrieu and lived on Fitzroy Square. Whether he met any English writer of moment seems most doubtful; that he enjoyed himself is clear; he liked London more and more, liked the company he was keeping, he even found a café, the Café de la Sablonnière et de Provence, in which he could write his letters and poems and from which he looked out on the life of Leicester Square, giving occasional horrified exclamations of "what drunkards!"

Leicester Square was his center, for there were grouped the French cafés and "tolerable" eating houses; a dreary center with its border of "dirty trees in the middle of which is a zinc horse painted red, its rider—George IV, I think—fallen to the ground." For the rest, he and Rimbaud drank with their friends, talked with them, heard the hand organs trundle out the serenade from Coppée's *Passant*, patronized the theatres and music halls, listened to concerts and walked, walked indefatigably.

Verlaine said at the time, "My life is entirely intellectual. I devote myself to poetry, to intellectual pursuits and to serious artistic conversations in a small group of artists and literary men"; and although this sounds unlikely in the light of the activities dealt with so far, it was, though no more exact than the later apology for his "rather frivolous" existence in London, a good deal nearer the truth. In the midst of their apparently aimless life in Paris he and Rimbaud had talked poetry and written poetry. In London they did likewise, Rimbaud pressing insistently toward a poetry that should be absolutely modern. This he produced in his London sections of *Illuminations*. Verlaine too described his own work as being "more and more *modernistic*." And so, in its way, it was. In these months before the end of the year he wrote much of what was later to be published as *Romance sans Paroles*, an echo of the vogue for Mendelssohn in the London of those years; he wrote most of the poem about Mathilde which he first intended to call "*La Mauvaise Chanson*," a better title than the eventual "Birds in the Night" which he took from Sullivan; one day he sat in a bar at the corner of Greek Street and Old Compton Street after watching the fair in Soho Square and wrote the now famous "*Dansons la gigue!*" known under the title of "Streets"; and he composed the little masterpiece which was to be made popular by the settings of Debussy and Fauré:

> *Voici des fruits, des fleurs, des feuilles et des branches,*
> *Et puis voici mon coeur, qui ne bat que pour vous.*
> *Ne le déchirez pas avec vos deux mains blanches*
> *Et qu'à vos yeux si beaux l'humble présent soit doux.*

J'arrive tout couvert encore de rosée
Que le vent du matin vient glacer à mon front.
Souffrez que ma fatigue, à vos pieds reposée,
Rêve des chers instants qui la délasseront.

Sur votre jeune sein laissez rouler ma tête
Toute sonore encor de vos derniers baisers;
Laissez-la s'apaiser de la bonne tempête
Et que je dorme un peu puisque vous reposez.

*   *   *

See, blossoms, branches, fruit, leaves I have brought,
    And then my heart that for you only sighs;
With those white hands of yours, oh, tear it not,
    But let the poor gift prosper in your eyes.

The dew upon my hair is still undried,—
    The morning wind strikes chilly where it fell.
Suffer my weariness here at your side
    To dream the hour that shall it quite dispel.

Allow my head, that rings and echoes still
    With your last kiss, to lie upon your breast,
Till it recover from the stormy thrill,—
    And let me sleep a little, since you rest.

[3]

Verlaine's contentment with life in London was marred by two
things. First and least by Rimbaud's behavior from time to time.
Verlaine's letters are spattered with "*geindres*," a sure sign that
Rimbaud had been whining, about him, about his friends, about
shortage of money, about anything. The boy's usual way of speaking
except in moments of enthusiasm was a cross between drawl and
whine, lips barely opened, an exaggerated version of the manner of
the *Ardennais*. In his good humored moments this formed part of
his charm—one has only to remember the vogue of the "sulky"
film star to understand how fascinating the quick and sharp-speaking
Parisians found his slow, reluctant, blurred speech. But when
Rimbaud was displeased—and he found much wrong with the
world—the sulk lost its charm and degenerated into the whinings
of an indulged prig. This pained Verlaine who alternated between

fears that he could never live up to his spiritually strait-laced companion and annoyance that he, his friends and especially the amount of money provided by his mother should be criticized.

But far more disturbing was the bad news from rue Nicolet. When he heard from Lepelletier in November that Mathilde was taking steps to obtain a legal separation Verlaine was shattered or made a convincing show of it. He ought not to have been surprised, though he did not know that his letters remained unopened, but he was undoubtedly shocked and his indignation was genuine enough, being merely the customary reaction to shock. So he is found protesting with all the conviction of injured virtue; and when Lepelletier told him that one of the grounds for the separation was to be the relations of the two friends he exploded in fury and alarm. He was writing a full statement of the case "in which I reduce the foul accusation to pulp," he declared; a statement which he believed would constitute a landmark in medical, psychological and legal studies. He would defend the case and call witnesses. He challenged any doctor to examine Rimbaud and himself and find them guilty of unnatural practices. As for his feeling for Rimbaud, his statement would show clearly and soberly "my very real, very profound and *very persevering* friendship for Rimbaud—I don't need to add *very pure.*"

Agitated letters flew to Lepelletier who had read in law. He was not too optimistic but dropped hints that a rapprochement with Mathilde might not prove impossible if Verlaine would return to Paris. This Verlaine refused to do, though whether he most feared the police, snubs by former friends or a rebuff at rue Nicolet, perhaps even he did not know. Instead he begged his mother to intervene and incidentally to bring away from rue Nicolet his papers and clothes and a manuscript of what he described as Rimbaud's greatest poem. Madame Verlaine obeyed but the interview was not pleasant, Monsieur Mauté, who had taken on with some relish the job of putting an end to the connection with Verlaine, refusing all requests. Verlaine then appealed to *La Mère des Gracchi* as he had nicknamed Madame Rimbaud, a strange appeal on the face of it; but his instinct was right. Yet she too failed to move Monsieur Mauté.

The one tangible effect of these interventions proved distasteful to Verlaine; Monsieur Mauté's attitude convinced both mothers that Verlaine and Rimbaud must separate if there was to be any hope of a reconciliation between husband and wife; and Verlaine, after protesting that this would merely provide Monsieur Mauté with precisely the tacit admission of guilt he sought, gave way—gave way, it appears, in the belief that his mother would replace Rimbaud and set up a home in London where they could live "respectably."

By the beginning of December Rimbaud was back in Charleville. Madame Verlaine, however, was not to be persuaded to abandon France and by Christmas her son had begun to languish in solitude. Christmas in London was "like Sunday, only worse, and practically as hypocritical," he complained on Boxing Day, "which is almost as bad." He was not too unhappy to comment in passing that "the goose is delicious" and, though missing Rimbaud, enjoyed himself well enough until he caught influenza. This was an illness unknown to him and he at once decided that he was dying. An element of calculation entered into this solemn moment; urgent messages sped to Rimbaud and his friends and telegrams to his mother and, with a deathbed reconciliation in mind, to Mathilde. To Rimbaud he enclosed notes for Blémont, Forain and, it seems, Delahaye: "I am *dying* of grief, of illness, of boredom, of loneliness," he said. "Excuse this brevity from one who is very ill. Good-bye, perhaps for ever."

The result of this barrage of farewells fell some way short of expectations. "*Only* my mother has come!" he was soon crying; for Madame Verlaine accompanied by a niece had hurried to London. She found the corpse very much alive but wretched and, unable to deny him anything, sent fare to Rimbaud who was horribly bored in Charleville and only too glad to leave it. He diagnosed his friend's condition, with what mixture of weariness, contempt and affection can be imagined: "Verlaine is like a child left in a room without a light, sobbing with fear. If I come back to him the talks and long walks will cure the body quickly because they'll cheer the mind."

It was so; after a week or two Verlaine was recovering and by February his mother left London happy to see her son on his feet again but worried by the intimacy she had reëstablished. For his part Verlaine showed a natural reluctance to admit to those who had so recently received his dying farewells that he had in fact escaped death: "I'm feeling better but I'm afraid that my health is likely to remain precarious. In fact I fear—shall I say fear or hope?— that I shan't live very long. My life has been wrecked by a thousand gross and treacherous injuries." He was left, it is true, with a heavy cold and the after-influenza depression which persisted long enough for him to tell Blémont, "You will soon be receiving my little book, perhaps a posthumous one."

The little book was *Romances sans Paroles* which he had failed to get published by the printers of *L'Avenir* and he was now urging upon Blémont and Lepelletier. Then no more complaints are heard; he and Rimbaud resumed their explorations of London, visiting Hampton Court, the Crystal Palace, Kew Gardens and, in general, "We know the whole of London," Verlaine claimed. "Drury Lane, Whitechapel, Pimlico, Angel, the City, Hyde Park, etc. have no more mystery for us." He believed himself to be quite the Englishman, enjoying his glass of beer, his seat in the gallery, his Sunday perambulations of Hyde Park, accepting dirt, smell, noise and even fog with what he hoped was English passivity. He and Rimbaud were reading hard at home and in the British Museum, and writing; quarreling too, however. Verlaine's frailties had grown no fewer; he would follow Rimbaud in attempts at dissipation and follow him as far as he could in poetic theory—"I'm soon hoping to write poems after a system which will be very musical without the puerilities of Poe," he was to announce. But he was intellectually lazy, he was decidedly taken with pretty girls, commenting frequently how much better-looking the English women were than the French; and most depressing and infuriating of all, he was still worrying about Mathilde.

This led to scenes. Rimbaud regarded him as a brand plucked from the burning—"Remember what you were before you met me," was one of his favorite maxims when Verlaine showed retrograde motions—but Verlaine obstinately continued to smoulder. How was it possible to advance, thought Rimbaud, with this dead weight who seemed at times absolutely riveted to his body, gluttonous and liking it? Irritated by his financial dependence—for he could not even leave him—Rimbaud worked off his irritation in characteristic fashion.

Then, abruptly, in the midst of work, pleasures, quarrels, they left London at the beginning of April.

[4]

It is not known why they left so quickly or even why they left at all. But some facts are known which suggest reasonable assumptions. Madame Verlaine, Lepelletier and Blémont had all continued to press Verlaine to return to Paris; and Madame Verlaine directly and Lepelletier by implication had urged him in any event to separate from Rimbaud, at least for a period, if he wished to stand any chance of preventing Mathilde's application for a separation. Verlaine had resisted this flow of advice but it had not left him unaffected. As in Belgium, whenever Rimbaud showed his unpleasant side his friend thought longingly of his wife. He went so far as to tell Blémont that although "the recent arrests demand prudence" he would come to Paris if *Romances sans Paroles* was published. The book was not published, neither Blémont nor Lepelletier being able to find a publisher. Robbed of a dignified reason for capitulation Verlaine decided at the beginning of April to capitulate without giving any reason. Whether Rimbaud was to come with him, to stay in London or to return home does not appear; but as Verlaine was coming around to a short separation as a diplomatic gesture and a means of allowing some of his companion's spleen to subside, it seems probable that he proposed to go alone.

He did not get farther than Newhaven, or to be precise, the ship in harbor. There, he said, he overheard a conversation which convinced him that he was being watched by police agents. He hurriedly left the ship and returned to London.

This story, which may have had some romantic touches thrown in, was nevertheless substantially true; Verlaine, like all refugees regarded as political, was being watched by police agents; his visits to Victoria Station to ask about trains and buy his ticket were noted and reported to Paris; he was on his way there, a police report said later. But this was an error; Verlaine, badly frightened, had quickly changed his destination; for the moment he was almost as scared of London as of Paris and returned only to leave it again the next day for Dover and Ostend.

Rimbaud went with him and the friends disappeared for more than a week. Verlaine is next heard of ten days later with his aunt at Jehonville near the Paliseul of his grandfather a few miles from the French frontier; he explained inadequately that the missing days had been spent mostly at Namur where he had suffered "a kind of brain fever." This fever remains a mystery for he settled down with his aunt and no more is heard of it. Rimbaud was already at the family farm at Roche where he appeared on Good Friday, April 11.

Separated from Rimbaud for a time Verlaine at once approached

Mathilde and renewed his requests to all and sundry, Hugo included, to bring her to reason.

This done he amused himself by the making of more literary plans, including a prose drama, the completion of the lyrics for the operetta begun with De Sivry years earlier, a novel to be written "very crisply," a series of sonnets and a book of poems from which mankind was to be "banished completely." He had the titles, all that remained was for the poems to be written, but this, like all that went before, seemed unlikely: "Perhaps it's a foolish idea after all," he admitted. He was enjoying a prolonged discussion with Lepelletier who approved the *Romances sans Paroles* with reservations about the "heresies of versification" and the proposed dedication to Rimbaud —done as a protest against vile rumors, said Verlaine, and in gratitude because Rimbaud had urged him to write the poems. Verlaine gave way on the dedication but held firm to the heresies; he was aiming, he explained, at Glatigny's facility without his banality, a remark which shows that he had traveled far from the *Parnasse*.

For the rest, the holiday (for that is what it was) slipped by pleasantly with self-taught lessons in English, with hour after hour of trout-fishing and in the evenings a round of friends and relations anxious to honor this Parisian poet of a nephew and cousin. For a few weeks the peace, the friendliness and the favors soothed one who had come to look on Paris as a nest of enemies. Eventually, however, boredom set in; better than most Verlaine could make himself at home with all kinds of men but he was too intelligent not to wish for intellectual companionship and the sense of progress, too intelligent and by that time too much dependent on Rimbaud as mental stimulator to endure life without him. Then he had a letter from Mathilde, a short note asking him not to bother her further, and the last reason, if it could be called a reason, for him to stay on disappeared. He decided that it was time to return to London and, forgetting all the recent quarrels, summoned Rimbaud and Delahaye (then teaching at Charleville) to meet him on the frontier at Bouillon. Rimbaud was a little difficult to move from his retreat, not surprisingly when the nature of his work at Roche is known, but he was penniless, drinkless and bored. "What a horror this French countryside is," he wrote from Roche. He gave way to Verlaine's importunities and by the end of May they were back in London, this time in a room on Great College Street in Camden Town.

[5]

This new settlement in England lasted barely six weeks and ended in disaster. It was a hopeless enterprise from the beginning, yet from the emotional Verlaine's short-sighted point of view there was reason to hope for good things in London. He had come to like England and the English, he believed the same of Rimbaud; he had visions, optimistic but not impossible, of earning a living there in a manner not entirely distasteful to him; he felt that responsibility for the break with his wife had been put firmly onto her shoulders and he had temporarily persuaded himself that, this being so, he could rest easy. In any case he wanted to be with Rimbaud, and when Verlaine wanted something difficulties melted; no man was more adept at persuading himself that the desired object was the right object, and no man was less able to maintain the fiction.

And as far as his few friends in Paris heard of it, this second attempt to get a foothold in London was altogether more successful than the first. He was, Verlaine said, delighted with his new home in a "gay" and picturesque district, near Vermersch and within striking distance of the hills and woods of Hampstead and Highgate. He and Rimbaud walked there often, they were often at the theatre, they saw all the sights including the Shah of Persia during his state visit, they sailed again on the Thames, they read enormously in the British Museum, they wrote poems and they even began to earn some money.

This last was perhaps a doubtful satisfaction but was forced on them. Madame Verlaine indefatigably traveled once more to London, to see her darling well settled in, no doubt, but more important to warn him that the drain on the small remaining family capital must stop; he had spent thirty thousand francs since meeting Rimbaud, she complained. Verlaine was occasionally aware that he and Rimbaud could not live on his mother indefinitely, hence the plans and vast prospects lurking largely in his letters to Paris. He now used some of the money his mother gave him, before she returned home, to advertise for pupils. Before long he and presumably Rimbaud too were actually giving an occasional French lesson; sometimes accepting English lessons in return. Verlaine even reached the point of an interview for a post as assistant master in a school, a post which he thought he might take if the head "wasn't too much of a Dickensian type"—for Dickens was included in his bouts of reading. Possibly he was not given the chance to decide; nothing came of it; but the idea stuck.

The lessons seem to have been no more than moderately successful. "Perfection, finesse" he claimed in his advertisement. It may have been so, but in hard cash "it isn't a gold mine but it pays for the room and my tobacco." And it is clear from the tone of his letters that he felt a certain pride in acting the practical man, boring though the lessons often were and interrupting all his pleasures.

Rimbaud felt no pride, only disgust. But then Rimbaud was disgusted with virtually everything, himself not least, Verlaine most of all; he could not forgive himself for the weakness of the return to London, he could not forgive Verlaine for tempting him to return. For the king of men to accept a bribe is an ugly thought but in effect that is what he had done; he had no money at Roche, he would have money in London, and for that he rejoined a man he despised, a man he was about to satirize savagely in his latest poem. He was fond of Verlaine too—even a would-be god felt the attraction—but this he saw as yet another betrayal of his principles; to be moved by Verlaine's affection or kindness or generosity or trust was to compromise with the world and the flesh, it was a weakness that must be stamped out.

Brave thoughts; meanwhile he remained a dependent boy; he literally could not move without begging the fare home. He did not blink at the facts, that was not his way; he faced them, accepted them and began to try to write them out of his system. Verlaine watched him writing and sketched him as he wrote, bowler-hatted, long pipe smoking, in a public house. "How he wrote *Saison en Enfer*" he scribbled under the sketch. Did he read what Rimbaud was writing? The answer is not of much moment for soon after their return he lived it. Rimbaud could not write the bitterness out of himself, what he wrote merely inflamed it. Rimbaud, plunged in *Faust*, the book and the opera, felt the need of behaving devilishly; to write devilishly was child's play. At his side, never leaving him, was the man who had made him sin against his convictions. It was not a temptation, it was a duty to give this creature a taste of hell.

This was what Rimbaud was writing, from the life:

"Pitiful brother! What a lot of atrocious night watches I owe to him! 'I wasn't taking this enterprise seriously. I made fun of his weakness. We should go back into exile, slavery, and it would be my fault.' . . . And almost every night the moment he had gone to sleep the poor brother got up, his mouth putrid, his eyes torn out—so he dreamed—and dragged me into the room howling his dream of idiotic grief."

Again, regarding "The Infernal Bridegroom" through the eyes of "The Foolish Virgin" he wrote:

"Hear the confession of a companion in hell:

" 'O heavenly Bridegroom, my Lord, do not deny the confession of the most unhappy of thy servants. I am lost. I am drunken. I am unclean. What a life!

" 'Forgive me, heavenly Lord, forgive me! Ah! forgive me! What a lot of tears! And even more tears later on, I hope!

" 'Later on I shall know the heavenly Bridegroom! I was born subject to Him. The other can beat me now!

" 'At present I am at the bottom of the world, O my friends! . . . I am the slave of the infernal Bridegroom, the one who ruined the foolish virgins . . . I am a widow . . . I used to be a widow . . . why, yes, I was perfectly respectable at one time. . . . He was almost a child . . . His mysterious delicacy seduced me. I forgot all human duties to follow him. What a life! Real life is absent. We are no longer in the world. I go where he goes, I must. And often he grows furious with me, *me, poor soul.* The Demon! He is a demon, you know, *he is not a man.*

" 'I listen to him making a glory of infamy, a charm of cruelty . . . On several nights, his demon seizing me, we used to fight, I wrestled with him! Often at night, drunk, he stations himself in streets or houses to frighten me to death. "I shall have my throat cut; it will be disgusting." Oh! those days when he wants to walk about with a criminal air! . . . How many hours of the night I have stayed awake beside his dear sleeping body trying to understand why he wanted so much to escape from reality. Never did man have such a desire as that. I recognized—without being afraid of him—that he might be a serious danger to society. Perhaps he has secrets for *changing life.* No, I told myself, he is only looking for them. Finally, his kindness is enchanted and I am its prisoner. No other soul would have the strength—the strength of despair!—to endure it . . .

" 'Oh! the life of adventure which exists in children's books, to reward me, I've suffered so much, will you give it to me? He cannot.

I don't know what his ideal is. He has told me that he has regrets, hopes: that should not concern me. Does he talk to God? Perhaps I ought to appeal to God. I am at the very bottom of the abyss and no longer know how to pray.

"'If he were to explain his sorrows to me, should I understand them better than his mockeries? He attacks me, spends hours in making me ashamed of all that has touched me in the world and becomes indignant if I weep.'"

Under the satisfactions of Verlaine's letters to Paris, then, letters in which Rimbaud is rarely mentioned, and always happily, ran this other nightmarish life of dependence on a boy who played the devil; not the kind of deviltry Verlaine understood but a satanic impulse ranging from schoolboy tricks to a merciless malevolence. Rimbaud would wait for him in hiding, pounce on him and laugh at the shock he had caused. He revealed a genius for mockery; he mocked Verlaine for his cowardice, for his looks, for his position as a mélange of hanger-on and toady, for his beliefs; every good feeling of Verlaine was dragged into the open and made to appear despicable and weak. He even reproached him for unsociability and meanness. So preposterous was this last that the mild Verlaine, too easily convinced of guilt, reacted angrily.

Naturally there were breaks in the torture; Rimbaud was not the fiend he tried to ape but a self-disgusted and exceedingly critical young man reënacting a play with an eagle eye for spotting weaknesses. But for every sign of affection that he permitted himself there were several attacks verging from the pinprick to the savage wound, and matters between them soon reached a crisis. No matter what Verlaine persuaded himself in daring or drunken moments, his thoughts returned to Mathilde whenever Rimbaud scathingly pictured his degraded and hopeless state. It was true, he told himself, he had become an outcast not only from rue Nicolet but the entire world of Paris in which he had moved so lightheartedly. Even more dreadful, not to be thought of except in the most harrowed moments, he had been led not only to deny his God for a human god but taught to blaspheme Him and spit on Him. He did not believe in God? Small comfort at such moments; for a Verlaine, unbelief was practically impossible at heart; he could talk, bluster, blaspheme, outshout his mentor; no matter, the childhood teaching would come back, the adult need for protection rise up. And was he damned, then, eternally, irrevocably damned? And when he and Rimbaud quarreled—and they were almost always on the verge—he saw himself lost and cheated, having, for nothing, thrown up all that he cared for—in this world and the next.

Not even thrown up; and this was perhaps the bitterest reflection. He had never intended to leave Mathilde finally, witness the letters he had written to her, but somehow what he saw as a harmless spree had been turned into a possibly unbridgeable separation. And by whom? Peace, security, a calm conscience, all driven off. And by whom? By his own weakness, certainly, but who had taken advantage of it? He became frantic with fear and self-loathing and he looked at the mocking, japing boy with a horror sometimes not far from hatred. And it was he, not the disgusted Rimbaud, who finally made the break.

It came, as these things do, after the mildest of spurs, the jeers of Rimbaud at Verlaine's appearance as he came home with the food one day early in July, a herring in one hand, a bottle of olive oil in the other. That was all but it was enough; Verlaine took the next ship leaving for Antwerp.

Evidently he left a note or Rimbaud guessed that he had really done what he had so often threatened to do. He followed him but by the time he reached the docks the gangway had been raised and Verlaine, standing on the deck, shook his head against all the frantic signs to him to come back.

The ship sailed and Rimbaud returned to Great College Street feeling respect for Verlaine for the first time since their meeting. Before this solitary act of firmness the boy collapsed, sitting down the next day to write a letter ludicrously out of character:

"Come back, come back, dear friend, only friend, come back. I swear to you that I'll be good. If I was unpleasant to you it was only a joke I obstinately persisted in; I'm more sorry than I can say. Come back and all will be forgotten. What a pity you took the joke to heart. I haven't stopped crying for two days. Come back. Be brave, dear friend. Nothing is lost. You have only to make the journey again. We will live here again bravely, patiently. Ah, I beg you. It's for your own good too. Come back, you'll find all your things here. I hope you've realized by this time that our argument was meaningless. Frightful moment! But when I signaled you to leave the ship, why didn't you come? Fancy living together for two years only to end up like this! What are you going to do? If you don't want to come back here, do you want me to join you?

"Yes, I was in the wrong.

"Oh say you won't forget me.

"No, you can't forget me.

"As for me, I think of you always.

"Speak, reply to your friend, aren't we to live together any more?

"Be brave. Reply to me quickly.

"I can't stay here much longer.

"Listen only to your good feelings.

"Quick, tell me if I'm to join you.

"Yours for life."

He added a postscript in the same uncharacteristic manner, show-ing as he was to show more seriously a few days later that a shock to his confidence could reduce him to his true age, without courage, pride, dignity and with no more trace in him than Verlaine of a *"fils du Soleil."*

"Quick, reply; I can't stay here later than Monday evening. I haven't a penny; I can't even post this. I've given Vermersch your books and papers.

"If I am not to see you again I shall enlist in the Marines or the Army. O come back, I cry for you all the time. Tell me where I can find you and I'll come. Tell me, wire me. I must leave Monday evening. Where are you going? What are you going to do?"

Verlaine, however, threw away his one chance of asserting himself; before Rimbaud could post the letter, before he had been on the ship more than an hour or two, the enormity of his conduct struck him. He remembered, not the last sordid quarrelsome weeks, but the days of wandering in Belgium, godlike, carefree, happy. All that he owed to Rimbaud. Was he mad, to leave the boy and leave him without a penny? Conscience-stricken, he tried to justify himself with heroics:

"I want to tell you that you must *at heart* understand *at last* that it was absolutely necessary for me to leave, that this life of violence and *scenes* with no better excuse than your whim couldn't go on any longer. As I have loved you tremendously (*honi soit qui mal y pense!*), I also want you to know that if I'm not reconciled in full amity with my wife in three days I shall blow out my brains! My last thought, my friend, will be for you, for you who were calling to me from the pier recently and who I didn't want to rejoin *because it was necessary for me to make an end of myself*—AT LAST! Will you accept my dying embrace?"

At this and more Rimbaud came to his senses; he metaphorically tore up his letter and wrote another. "As for dying," he commented, "I know you! And while you're waiting for your wife and your death you'll be going all over the place in a great state and boring everyone you meet."

Having dismissed the suicide, he tried to bring Verlaine back to realities as he saw them. But he had his own weaknesses to grapple with; by this time he could neither bear to have Verlaine with him nor away from him; the first sign that Verlaine hankered after his wife was enough for him, all past experience going for nothing, to try to recall the backslider to his duty and the glorious future:

"Do you really believe you would be happier with others than with me? *Think!* Of course you wouldn't! You can only be free with me, and since I've sworn to be very kind in future, since I'm sorry for all the wrong I've done, since I've at last got my mind clear and since I love you very much, if you don't want to come back or me to rejoin you, you are committing a crime *for which you'll* suffer MANY LONG YEARS *by the loss of all freedom and by miseries more atrocious* perhaps than those you've already endured. After all, remember what you were before you knew me!"

This letter discovered Verlaine at an embarrassing moment. As soon as he had reached Brussels three days earlier he had sent letters and telegrams in all directions—three to his wife, one to his mother, one to Madame Rimbaud and to sundry others, including Hugo once more—announcing his imminent decease at his own hands if Mathilde did not join him within three days, outlining his manifold miseries, saying a fairly elaborate farewell and giving directions for the disposal of his literary remains. As usual his mother was the only one to respond immediately; she hurried to Brussels where she spent her time trying to dissuade him from putting an end to himself, a not unagreeable pastime for Verlaine whose first and last suicidal impulse had sunk on board ship long ago. He found it desirable to retire publicly from this resolution by degrees, a desirability all will understand, solemnly telling Lepelletier that "my mother is trying to weaken my resolve but I don't think she'll succeed." Knowing privately how well she would succeed, his rancor fastened itself once more on Mathilde who had once again failed to respond to an appeal, and such an appeal. Nor had his dying words to his friends done the trick; no one hastened to Mathilde as he had hoped and begged her to save his life. He was left to save it himself.

Bogged in this dilemma he had a reply from Madame Rimbaud

which pointed to an honorable way out. This letter took him more seriously than he deserved, Madame Rimbaud not being the kind of woman who could imagine a man threatening to take his life without the slightest intention of doing so. But she did understand that he was wretched and her letter dealt nobly with that situation.

"I hope that by this time your mind has become calm and thoughtful. To commit suicide just because one is stricken by misfortune is *despicable;* to kill oneself when one possesses a godly and loving mother who would give her life for you and whom your death will kill, and when one is the father of a little being who is stretching his arms toward you now, who will smile at you tomorrow and who one day will need your guidance and support—to kill oneself in such circumstances is *infamous:* the world condemns those who die by their own hand and God himself can't pardon so great a crime and casts the sinner from his bosom.

"Monsieur, I know nothing about your quarrels with Arthur but I have always foreseen that your relationship would end unhappily. You will ask me why. Because whatever has not been authorized and approved by good and upright parents cannot bring happiness to the children. . . .

"You complain of your unhappy life, poor child! How do you know what the morrow had in store? Hope then! What do you understand of happiness on earth? You are too sensible to think that happiness consists in the success of a plan or the satisfaction of a whim, a fancy: No, anyone who had all his wishes granted, all his desires satisfied, certainly would not be happy; for the moment that the heart ceases to feel aspirations no more emotion is possible and so no more happiness. Therefore, as the heart must beat let it beat at the thought of good—good that one has done or wants to do.

"I too have been most unhappy. I have suffered much, wept much, and I have been able to turn all my afflictions to my advantage. God has given me a stout heart full of energy and courage. I have fought against every kind of adversity; then I have reflected, I have looked about me and I am sure, absolutely sure that each one of us has a wound more or less deep in our hearts. To me my wound seemed much deeper than those of others; that is natural enough; I could feel my own injury but not those of others. Then I said to myself— and I see every day that I am right—that true happiness consists in doing one's duties however painful they may be.

"Do as I do, dear sir; be strong and courageous in the face of every affliction; drive all bad thoughts from your heart. Fight, fight without ceasing against what is called the injustice of fate and you will find that misfortune will stop pursuing you and you will become happy once more. It is necessary to work hard and give one's life an aim to follow; no doubt you will still have plenty of unhappy days, but however wicked men may be never despair of God's help. Believe me, he alone can console and heal."

Verlaine never commented on this letter; it is unlikely to have touched him deeply then although he was soon to understand its truth; for the moment it chiefly offered him the sanction he needed to withdraw from the foolish position he had put himself in. He forthwith abandoned even the pretense of suicide.

But he remained unhappy, he could not follow Madame Rimbaud into stoicism, and uncertain what to do, whether to return to London as Rimbaud was urging him to do (though with a sadistic "what will Andrieu and company think?" to punish him) or to take his courage in both hands and go to Paris. An intermediate choice was badly needed, and this he thought he had found when, meeting an acquaintance and unloading his woes, he was advised to volunteer for the Carlist Army.

Anyone less of the soldier, the mess table excepted, would be hard to find; yet at first the unmilitary Verlaine saw in this desperate and uncongenial act the one answer to his dilemma: if he died fighting he would at least die in a good cause. Besides, would not his friends, would not even the flint-hearted Mathilde, relent when they heard of his gesture—relent, forgive and love again?

Nevertheless to die was a thought and would obviously ruin everything; in fact death must on no account be thought of. But death is not so easily disposed of, not by a man like Verlaine. It haunted him. He feared that he would go mad. Solitude (for his mother had lost the power to comfort him) became intolerable. In sudden terror he telegraphed to Rimbaud.

Rimbaud was still at Great College Street. Verlaine had long since written to Matuszewicz, one of their London circle, to look after him; and as Rimbaud had promptly sold most of his friend's clothes for ready cash he was in no great hurry to move. He believed that Verlaine could not do without him and would return to London.

Then he received the telegram: "Volunteering Spain. Come here, Hotel Liégeois. Laundry, manuscripts if possible." He left at once and was in Brussels that evening, July 8.

[6]

Rimbaud found Verlaine a civilian still, the Carlists refusing to
accept foreign volunteers. He was annoyed; he had been inveigled to
Brussels for nothing. He became angry as the next day dragged on
without decision. They sat at the cafés drinking and arguing. Verlaine
wanted to return to London but Rimbaud would not hear of it; they
would look ridiculous in the eyes of their friends, he said. This from
Rimbaud was unconvincing, preposterous. He had begged him more
than once to come back, Verlaine objected, and had written "it
would be a mark of courage" to do so.

Verlaine could not move him; he wanted to go to Paris, he said,
and demanded the fare.

As the evening wore on Verlaine became terrified; Rimbaud was
tired of him, wanted to leave him—was it not obvious? But if he
showed fear Rimbaud would certainly go; that was a sure way to
lose him. To gain courage he drank more and the more he drank the
more confused he grew. Should he go to Paris with the boy, risk
trouble with the authorities? But where would they live and how?
And how could he face the cut direct? For Blémont had not left
him in much doubt about the Parnassian view of the flight from
Mathilde. And Mathilde? If he went to Paris . . .

The thoughts jostled one another, there was no end to them.
What to do for the best? Rimbaud, watching him and contemptu-
ously parrying one suggestion after another, seemed to the wretched
Verlaine to be icy with scorn, immovable.

The next morning the one-sided argument was still going on; they
had moved to the hotel, nothing else had changed. To every entreaty
Rimbaud, leaning against the communicating door between the bedrooms of Verlaine and his mother, replied with a monotonous chant
of "Money, money" holding out a hand.

At last Verlaine ran out of the hotel, drank himself stupid at the
nearest café, returned and showed Rimbaud a revolver. He would
shoot the lot of them, he swore. He sat on the end of the bed and
begged the boy to stay.

He was never to forget the next few minutes; for the rest of his
life he saw Rimbaud standing near the door to the corridor "his
arms folded, defiance in every line of his body, the cruel light of a

damned archangel in his eyes." He felt absolute despair, knowing that nothing he could say would move him.

Madame Verlaine, realizing that her son was beside himself, put a hand on his shoulder fearing that he would leap up and attack Rimbaud. For several minutes there was silence, Verlaine and Rimbaud staring at each other. Neither moved.

Then Rimbaud turned away. "I'm off," he said. He went out. Verlaine could hear the wooden boards creak as he rushed down the stairs.

Verlaine "saw red." He felt that Rimbaud was "carrying away his brain and his heart." When the sound of the boy's footsteps could no longer be heard he got up as if in a trance and hurried to the door determined to bring him back and lock him in the bedroom. His mother tried to bar the way. "You're mad, Paul!" she cried. "Come to your senses. Think of yourself."

Verlaine, carried away by anger, flung her aside with such force that she was thrown against the window frame on the far side of the room. He ran downstairs and out of the front door. Ahead of him was Rimbaud walking slowly "and with an indecisive air" on the street leading to the Boulevard Botanique. He caught up with him. "You'd better come back or there'll be trouble," he said.

"Let me alone," said Rimbaud without looking at him. But he went back.

Once they were in the bedroom again Verlaine locked the door, placed a chair against it, sat down, drew his revolver and aimed it at Rimbaud. "Go, will you?" he shouted.

The boy lolled against the wall mockingly. He said only the same maddening refrain, "Money, money," hand held out.

Verlaine fired. The first shot hit Rimbaud just above the left wrist, the second missed him and buried itself in the wall.

Stupefied by what he had done, Verlaine, suddenly sober, sat staring at Rimbaud. Then he burst into his mother's room and flung himself on the bed sobbing. After a moment Rimbaud followed him, watched by the petrified Madame Verlaine. Seeing him, Verlaine raised himself on the bed, handed him the revolver and begged him to shoot. Rimbaud waved the weapon away and told his friend not to be a fool.

For a time Verlaine was inconsolable. Then his mother, recovering her wits, said that Rimbaud's wound must be properly treated. She bound it and all three walked off to the hospital. No one in the hotel seemed to have heard the shots.

At the hospital the wound was dressed but the bullet could not be extracted that day. They returned to the hotel where argument broke out again. Verlaine begged Rimbaud to change his mind. Madame Verlaine advised him to stay and let them look after him or at least to wait until he had been to the hospital the next day. Rimbaud refused to change his mind, refused to stay the night, refused to wait until the bullet could be taken out. He declared that he was going to Charleville that afternoon. Once more he held out a hand with his chanted "Money, money."

Madame Verlaine opposed him no further and gave him twenty francs to buy his ticket. In the early evening the three walked out together again, toward the station. They had not gone far, they were crossing the Place Rouppe, when Verlaine, who had not ceased to beg Rimbaud vehemently to stay in Brussels for the moment, ran ahead a few paces, turned and faced him.

At this point the accounts of Verlaine and Rimbaud differ. Rimbaud declared, though with decreasing emphasis in successive statements, that Verlaine threatened to shoot him if he did not abandon his intention of leaving. Verlaine declared that he threatened to blow out his own brains if Rimbaud persisted in taking the train.

The truth is not difficult to come by. The time was seven in the evening; Verlaine had drunk nothing since early morning and Verlaine sober was incapable of hurting a fly. But he had eaten nothing, he had been in continuous emotional excitement for days, he was light-headed and desperate. The idea that having shot Rimbaud when drunk he could repeat the shooting when sober is fantastic; few men could do such a thing twice on the same day whatever their state, and certainly not Verlaine. But he had bought the revolver with the purpose of shooting himself and he could threaten once more to do it—that, he would reckon, would cost nothing and might gain his point.

He did not draw the revolver; even Rimbaud in his first fright never suggested it. But he put his hand in his pocket and Rimbaud was taking no chances. And having appealed to a policeman Rimbaud was obliged to make some sort of charge; hence his account. If he thought at all in those few seconds it was with the idea of putting Verlaine out of the way until he could reach Charleville; the whole question could be discussed by letter when heads had cooled. He did not think that Verlaine would be detained for more than a day or two; not even a man versed in the law could have foreseen what was to happen. So Verlaine put a hand in his pocket, Rimbaud cried for help, ran to a policeman and demanded protection. The policeman arrested Verlaine. Depositions were taken from all three at the police station, Verlaine was put in the lockup for the night, charged with attempted murder, and the other two were told not to leave the city.

Verlaine was searched and the next morning taken to the Petits-Carmes prison where he was interrogated by an inspector. It was then that the affair changed its character. The offense, an unpremeditated attack, was not serious; but when Verlaine declared that the cause of the shooting, which he did when he was not himself, was the intention of Rimbaud to go back to France "which threw me into despair," the inspector at once suspected that he was dealing with a homosexual who must be rigorously punished—not for the shooting but the homosexuality.

Why, he asked, was Verlaine thrown into despair by the departure of a male friend? Were the relations between them other than friendship?

"No," replied Verlaine, "that is a calumny invented by my wife and her family to injure me." It was, he believed, one of the means being used to obtain a separation.

The denial was useless. From that moment Verlaine's fate was decided; all further questioning, and there was much of it, was directed to the one end; the original offense was pushed into the background.

The next day Rimbaud, in the hospital waiting for the bullet to be taken out, was interviewed by the same man. He repeated the story told at the police station and extended the details of their life together. Two of his statements were curious: that one cause of their quarrel in London was his complaints of Verlaine's "idleness"; and that when he came to Brussels he wanted to take up their life together again "because there was no reason why we should separate." The first comes strangely from him; the second made nonsense of his wish to go to France. But the inspector was interested only in their relationship: had Verlaine's wife ever complained about his intimacy with her husband? "Yes," said Rimbaud, "she has accused us of having immoral relations but I shan't give myself the trouble of denying such calumnies."

Neither this frankness nor the contemptuous denial—a most significant reply from one with the moral courage of Rimbaud—made the slightest effect on the inspector. He had established that Rimbaud was kept by Verlaine, that Verlaine shot him when he threatened to leave, and that Verlaine's wife believed them to be homosexuals: to him this meant one thing only.

The police doctors then got to work; instructed to try to discover traces of homosexual practices, they examined Verlaine and stated that the traces *"ne sont pas tellement marqués qu'il y ait lieu de suspecter des* habitudes invétérées et anciennes, *mais des pratiques plus ou moins récentes"*—a statement which they had no medical warrant for making and which is in fact meaningless. To the police inspector, however, the report was excellent. To it he could add various letters and poems found on Verlaine which could without difficulty be interpreted as indecent and—another useful tidbit— some evidence that the company he had kept in London was not only immoral but politically undesirable.

It was a strong case even though it had no bearing on the charge and one made stronger by the arrival in Brussels of Mathilde's lawyer who worked hand in hand with the police to secure Verlaine's con- demnation; a Verlaine shut away for a substantial prison term could not defend the separation case in Paris and his sentence would without doubt make judgment in the wife's favor certain.

After this all else, collection of evidence, further examinations of Verlaine, Rimbaud and Madame Verlaine were formalities. To Verlaine, herded with common criminals in the prison under dis- gusting conditions and trying to save sanity by composing poetry, the whole thing was a nightmare out of which he tried to believe that he must soon be delivered. To Rimbaud, the more obviously realistic of the two, the portents were ominous; lying in his hospital bed after the third examination and considering the direction of the questions put by the police inspector, he regretted the moment of panic and the appeal to the policeman in the Place Rouppe. He began to see that Verlaine was likely to be used as a scapegoat. The next morning, July 19, released from the hospital he went straight to the law courts and insisted on making a final statement. Verlaine, he declared, was so drunk in the hotel bedroom that he did not know what he was doing, that he had no premeditated or hostile thought in his mind, and that the cause of his drunkenness was trouble with his wife. He withdrew all claim to compensation and said that he did not wish to bring any charge against Verlaine.

Having done what he could to repair the damage he had uninten-
tionally caused, Rimbaud went off to Charleville. His final gesture
was useless; he was regarded as a fellow sinner with Verlaine and
nothing that he could say had any weight.

Verlaine's sufferings in prison soon afterwards came to a welcome
end. His mother, horrified by his forced company and labor had
petitioned the prosecutor for him to be treated more leniently. Her
appeal was unexpectedly strengthened by a letter which arrived for
Verlaine and was opened by the police. The letter was from Hugo,
a belated reply to Verlaine's "suicide" letter, promising to intercede
with his wife. Hugo was held in honor in Brussels and Verlaine was
promptly transferred to a detention ward where he could have some
privacy and buy food.

The respite was short-lived, was in fact an added misfortune since
the ebullient Verlaine, treated with a certain respect for the first
time, at once jumped to the conclusion that he would be fined and
allowed to go free. And on August 8 when he was brought to trial he
entered the courtroom comparatively light-hearted.

His complacence collapsed in the first few minutes and was succeeded by incredulous horror. The prosecutor at once attacked him
and Rimbaud as sexual perverts of whom the prisoner, as the elder,
was the chief culprit. Verlaine's counsel protested in vain that this
was irrelevant and inadmissible evidence; the judge permitted the
prosecutor to continue and from that moment Verlaine was a lost
man, used by the police as an example to deter the homosexuals of
Brussels. Rimbaud's final statement was passed over on the grounds
that he was a biassed witness—thus disregarding the fact that the
whole case against Verlaine depended on him. In any event, a jury
of those days had only to hear that a man was suspected of unnatural
practices to condemn him outright on any charge. They found Verlaine guilty and he was sentenced to two years' hard labor and a fine
of two hundred francs. An analysis of this sentence abundantly proves
bias: Verlaine was given the maximum term of six months for
criminal assault; the maximum term of one year for premeditated
assault; and a further six months for incapacitating Rimbaud from
work. Of these only the first could be described as justifiable and in
view of the evidence would be considered severe in any court of law.
The second—premeditation—was plainly untrue. And the third was
not only ridiculous but directly conflicted with the whole purpose of

the prosecution—to prove that Rimbaud had been deliberately kep
by Verlaine for immoral purposes.

Shattered by the sentence Verlaine broke down after he had beer
taken out of court, but he pulled himself together when the warder
explained sympathetically that he could appeal. He did so. The
prosecution retaliated by demanding a longer sentence.

Verlaine's misfortunes continued. The Brussels police applied to
Paris for his dossier. A few days earlier, on July 4, Matuszewicz had
decided to return to France to try to trace his mistress who had been
missing since the defeat of the Commune. He had no sooner reached
Paris than he was caught, arrested and condemned to death. On him
was found Verlaine's letter asking him to help Rimbaud. This led the
Paris police to trace Verlaine's record which, when finally sent to
Brussels on August 21, was damning, though, like the accusation of
homosexuality, absolutely irrelevant: Verlaine was described as an
intimate friend of Vermersch and Andrieu, influential Communards
his action in working under the Commune was condemned and his
private life, after he had conceived his *"passion honteuse"* for Rim
baud, was dismissed as one long gratification of the *"goûts dépravés"*
he had formed with that youth.

Six days later, on August 27, the appeal was dismissed with costs

12.

P R I S O N

1873-1874

[1]

Considering the lives of men, it is difficult not to believe in a providence of a kind watching over them; not of course in the obvious form of leading them where they would go but by providing inescapable opportunities for development of whatever in them contributes to the general good. Or it may simply be that this thing in men, the immortal, communicable part of them possesses a will to grasp from every circumstance that which it needs to thrive. The savage sentence of the Brussels court, intended to crush Verlaine, proved the making of him.

Before the shooting he remained at twenty-seven years of age a rudderless adolescent drifting from mood to mood, taking pleasure where he found it, his one constant background the sea of his affection. During his two years with Rimbaud he was regarded by his friends as completely bewitched. They forgot his sense of humor. To a point he was alarmingly dependent on Rimbaud and could be swayed by him and hurt by him with ease, at his mercy as the warm-hearted are always at the mercy of the cold. But there was another side to their relationship; Verlaine understood the boy well in some respects, loving him through his faults; he laughed at him, mocked his peculiarities, recognized his weaknesses. And as always he expressed this knowledge in poetry. Here, for instance, is one of his brilliant take-offs of the countrified Rimbaud with his coarse provincial burr that mangled the French language, his peasant meannesses, his complaints of this, that and the other. The inimitable *"Dargnières Nouvelles,"* written throughout in the lazy, sulky *Ardennaise* of Rimbaud, and employing the argot, the crudities and the 'secret' language of abbreviations and association used by them together, exposed the boy with a devastatingly humorous and penetrating irony. Here is Rimbaud, as he spoke, lived and thought; not only the Rimbaud of past and present but the Rimbaud of the future.

C'est pas injuss' de s'voir dans un' pareill' situate! . . .
Et pas la queu' d'un pauv' keretzer sous la patte! . . .
J'arrive à Vienne avec les meyeurs intentions,
—Sans compter que j'compt' sur des brevets d'inventions—
En arrêvant je m'coll' quéq' Fanta comm' de jusse,
Bon! V'là qu'un cocher d'fiac' m'vol' tout! . . . *C'est pas injusse?* . . .
Voui, m'fait tout jusqu'à ma limace et mon grimpant
Et m'plant'là dans la strass par un froid. Pas foutant?
Non! vrai, pour le début en v'là-t-y un triomphe:
Ah! la sal' bête! Encor plus pir' que la daromphe.

* * *

Je renonce à Satan, à ses pomp', à ses oeuffs!
Je vous gobe, ô profonds mugissements des boeufs.
J'fonde eun' nouvelle école, et sans coll', j'agricole.
Coll'-toi ça dans l'fusil, mond' frivole, et racole-
Z-en d'autres. Désormais j'dis merd' a les Gatti,
A les Russ', à les Vienne et aux Scaferlati
D'contrebande, et j'vas faire un très chouett' mariache.
Je m'cramponne à toi, Roche, et j'défends qu'on m'arrache
Eud'toi . . . *Viv' le lard dans la soupe—et soillions*
Sérillieux,—et qu'nout'sueur alle abreuff' nos sillions!

Nevertheless the relationship had had its day. Each had influenced the other for good as well as bad. Rimbaud had saved Verlaine from that worst of fates, from living as so many of his Parnassian friends lived, playing at poetry from the shelter of a safe job or an adoring parent; he had forced him to balance artistic integrity against all that he loved so well—comfortable home, friends, respectability and license neatly mixed, good feeling everywhere—and to come down on the side of the first; and he more than any other man had made Verlaine the poet.

But that lesson had long been taught and, with some backslidings, learned. Rimbaud had had more than enough of everything to do with Verlaine except his money. Verlaine would not recognize that their friendship was at an end. He characteristically bore no ill will

for his deliverance into the hands of the police—he never made
a single complaint against Rimbaud but blamed himself steadily—
and if he ever suspected the truth he closed his eyes to it at once
in sheer terror of loneliness and lovelessness. He had, it seemed,
lost his wife, lost his friends in Paris, lost his freedom; the thought
of losing the person for whom he had thrown these overboard was
unbearable.

Perhaps a prison sentence was the least painful way of cutting
the knot, and although Verlaine could not know it, the successor
to Rimbaud was already at work in him. Intellectually Rimbaud
had emancipated him as poet; humanly something else was needed.
In prison his poetry at once took on a new heart. Consider, for
instance, the poem he composed during his first night in prison
when, sleepless and stupefied with horror and fright, he watched
mice running over the floor of the cell crossing the stripes of
moonlight thrown through the barred window. A line of La Fontaine
came into his mind, *"Mais attendons la fin,"* and he wrote *"Impression Fausse."*

> *Dame souris trotte,*
> *Noire dans le gris du soir,*
> *Dame souris trotte,*
> *Grise dans le noir.*
>
> *On sonne la cloche:*
> *Dormez, les bons prisonniers,*
> *On sonne la cloche:*
> *Faut que vous dormiez.*
>
> *Pas de mauvais rêve,*
> *Ne pensez qu'à vos amours,*
> *Pas de mauvais rêve:*
> *Les belles toujours!*
>
> *Le grand clair de lune!*
> *On ronfle ferme à côté.*
> *Le grand clair de lune*
> *En réalité!*
>
> *Un nuage passe,*
> *Il fait noir comme en un four,*
> *Un nuage passe.*
> *Tiens, le petit jour!*

Dame souris trotte,
Rose dans les rayons bleus,
Dame souris trotte:
Debout, paresseux!

*   *   *

Little lady mouse,
Black upon the grey of light;
Little lady mouse,
Grey upon the night.

Now they ring the bell,
All good prisoners slumber deep;
Now they ring the bell,
Nothing now but sleep.

Only pleasant dreams,
Love's enough for thinking of;
Only pleasant dreams,
Long live love!

Moonlight over all,
Someone snoring heavily;
Moonlight over all,
In reality.

Now there comes a cloud,
It is dark as midnight here;
Now there comes a cloud,
Dawn begins to peer.

Little lady mouse,
Rosy in a ray of blue,
Little lady mouse,
Up now, all of you!

"*Impression Fausse,*" with its overtone of Verlainean humor, its undertone of sorrow, was the work of a poet who had gained in artistry but to whom artistry was no longer the chief consideration, a man who like the Russians wrote under the eye of death, in a manner distinctly English but with a delicacy of touch wholly French. And no sooner had the court passed sentence than he wrote a second and even greater poem. "*La Chanson de Gaspard Hauser,*"

as he called it, dealt ostensibly with a boy whose mysterious career
had long attracted the Parnassians, Villiers in particular. Found in
a dungeon at the age of seventeen, he blinked at light and refused
the finest food, preferring crusts of bread. Verlaine now, like Villiers,
identified himself with the unhappy Gaspard Hauser who claimed
noble birth, but, unlike Villiers, he was concerned with the unhappiness and not the nobility and, again unlike Villiers, with
marvelous tenderness crystallized the feelings of the world's misfits.

> *Je suis venu, calme orphelin*
> *Riche de mes seuls yeux tranquilles,*
> *Vers les hommes des grandes villes:*
> *Ils ne m'ont pas trouvé malin.*
>
> *A vingt ans un trouble nouveau*
> *Sous le nom d'amoureuses flammes,*
> *M'a fait trouver belles les femmes*
> *Elles ne m'ont pas trouvé beau.*
>
> *Bien que sans patrie et sans roi*
> *Et très brave ne l'étant guère,*
> *J'ai voulu mourir à la guerre:*
> *La mort n'a pas voulu de moi.*
>
> *Suis-je né trop tôt ou trop tard?*
> *Qu'est-ce que je fais en ce monde?*
> *O vous tous, ma peine est profond:*
> *Priez pour le pauvre Gaspard!*

* * *

So here I come, an orphan calm,
　　Rich only in mine eyes so still,
Before the folk of these great towns,
　　Who naught in me have found of ill.

At twenty, a unique disease,
　　Of which love's fire is eke the name,
Has made me find all women fair;
　　Alas! they've not found me the same.

Though lacking country, lacking king,
　　With no great store of bravery,

I would on battle-fields have died;
   Alas! death would have none of me.

Am I not born too soon, or late?
   In all this world what can I do?
And so profound my pain's become:
   Pray for Gaspard, all of you!

[2]

Verlaine, naturally enough, did not view his imprisonment as providential. He was not normally a reflective man but a servant to every emotion and impression; that these latest verses showed a new depth was not his concern, he was preoccupied by his role as man of sorrows, for once with apparent good reason. Many men, perhaps most, would have given way to despair when so harshly sentenced; how much more the gregarious Verlaine, hating and fearing loneliness? He imagined himself a bitter, broken man, but optimism and an inborn sweetness of temperament would bubble up. Moreover he was poet before man, or perhaps one should say above man; anything and everything served him as poetic material and a prison provided him with novelty. The reader has seen what he could do with the apparently slender motive of mice scampering across the floor of a cell. And when there was absolutely no incident—and for a man sentenced to solitary confinement incident does not abound—he had his thoughts and feelings.

> Le ciel est, par-dessus le toit,
>   Si bleu, si calme!
> Un arbre, par-dessus le toit,
>   Berce sa palme.
>
> La cloche, dans le ciel qu'on voit,
>   Doucement tinte.
> Un oiseau sur l'arbre qu'on voit
>   Chante sa plainte.
>
> Mon Dieu, mon Dieu, la vie est là,
>   Simple et tranquille.
> Cette paisible rumeur-là
>   Vient de la ville.

—*Qu'as-tu fait, ô toi que voilà*
Pleurant sans cesse,
Dis, qu'as-tu fait, toi que voilà,
De ta jeunesse?

*   *   *

The sky is up above the roof
　So blue, so soft.
A tree there, up above the roof,
　Swayeth aloft.

A bell within that sky we see,
　Chimes low and faint;
A bird upon that tree we see,
　Maketh complaint.

Dear God, is not the life up there
　Simple and sweet?
How peacefully are borne up there
　Sounds of the street.

What hast thou done, who comest here,
　To weep alway?
Where hast thou laid, who comest here,
　Thy youth away?

So this would-be man of sorrows passed his days and weeks at the Petits-Carmes in a prevailing mood of peaceful detachment which would appear incredible were it not that prison routine, like the routine of an army, conveys in the midst of its unpleasantness a certain sense of security. Yet even granted this aid to sanity, the sang-froid of the so-called weakling amazes. Unquestionably he was a coward in the popular sense of the word: he would quiver at the sound of a popgun, he hated the sight of blood, he was far from easy when left alone in the dark. He has also been voted a moral coward but perhaps laziness is the mot juste; if he could find someone to deal with his problems he never hesitated to hand them over with relief. In prison there was no one to lean on and there was an abrupt separation from the all-obliterating absinthe. Doctors have told us in no uncertain terms what that means. We wait, therefore, for the sobs, the collapses, the piteous screeds, the appeals to warders, governors, anyone within reach by this coward who, deprived at one blow of companions, drink, comfort, hope for two solid years, could not possibly sustain existence. But we wait in vain. And even when, caged like a wild beast, he was transferred to the prison at Mons in October and was locked away by himself day and night except for one hour each day, and that hour forbidden to look at his fellow prisoners, his main reaction was a pleased comment on how much nicer a building the pink stone prison was than the Petits-Carmes—and much cleaner. All of which suggests that he was not the absinthe addict his critics claimed and that somewhere in that apparently will-less human being was an unexpected source of strength.

He did of course suffer, no feeling man could do otherwise, and one of his most powerful poems tersely communicates this suffering.

> *Un grand sommeil noir*
> *Tombe sur ma vie:*
> *Dormez, tout espoir,*
> *Dormez, toute envie!*
>
> *Je ne vois plus rien,*
> *Je perds la mémoire*
> *Du mal et du bien . . .*
> *O la triste histoire!*
>
> *Je suis un berceau*
> *Qu'une main balance*
> *Au creux d'un caveau:*
> *Silence, silence!*

> *   *   *

> Sleep, darksome, deep,
>   Doth on me fall:
> Vain hopes all, sleep,
>   Sleep, yearnings all!
>
> Lo, I grow blind!
>   Lo, right and wrong
> Fade to my mind. . . .
>   Oh sorry song!
>
> A cradle, I,
>   Rocked in a grave:

Speak low, pass by,
Silence I crave!

But in general, during the next six months, until April 1874, his only serious complaint was of boredom: he could do nothing, not even write, he said. But he deceived himself; he could and did write masterly poems in this vacuum. One of them he wrote, typically, in a moment of disgust with "poetical" poetry; wrote it and thought no more of it than that it was another step toward another volume that would surely make his fame and fortune. This jeu d'esprit was to become a gospel of the new generation of poets.

De la musique avant toute chose,
Et pour cela préfère l'Impair
Plus vague et plus soluble dans l'air,
Sans rien en lui qui pèse ou qui pose.

Il faut aussi que tu n'ailles point
Choisir tes mots sans quelque méprise:
Rien de plus cher que la chanson grise
Où l'Indécis au Précis se joint.

* * *

Prends l'éloquence et tords-lui son cou!
Tu feras bien, en train d'énergie,
De rendre un peu la Rime assagie.
Si l'on n'y veille, elle ira jusqu'où?

* * *

De la musique encore et toujours!
Que ton vers soit la chose envolée
Qu'on sent qui fuit d'une âme en allée
Vers d'autres cieux à d'autres amours.

Que ton vers soit la bonne aventure
Éparse au vent crispé du matin
Qui va fleurant la menthe et le thym . . .
Et tout le reste est littérature.

* * *

Music first and foremost of all!
Choose your measure of odd not even,

Let it melt in the air of heaven,
Pose not, poise not, but rise and fall.

Choose your words, but think not whether
Each to other of old belong:
What so dear as the dim gray song
Where clear and vague are joined together?

* * *

Take Eloquence, and wring the neck of him!
You had better, by force, from time to time,
Put a little sense in the head of Rhyme:
If you watch him not, you will be at the back of him.

* * *

Music always and music still!
Let your verse by the wandering thing
That flutters in the light from a soul on the wing
Towards other skies at a new whim's will.

Let your verse by the luck of the lure
Afloat on the winds that at morning hint
Of the odors of thyme and the savor of mint . . .
And all the rest is literature.

[3]

Here, then, was Verlaine, in his "chateau" as he described it, clothed in a coarse green serge uniform, heavy clogs on his feet and on his shaven head a leather cap with linen face flap which he was forced to lower whenever he met another prisoner. His cell measured ten feet by six, its only furniture an upright chair and a board which served as bed by night and table by day. He was forbidden to speak to anyone but the warder and, since the warder took an instant dislike to him, this meant that he spent every day in silence except when he tried to answer the man's daily reprimands for untidiness. His food was barley soup, bread and water every weekday, pea soup on Sundays. He had no books, no newspapers, nothing to distract his mind from the day-long task of grinding coffee. His one amenity was the pipe of tobacco permitted to every prisoner during the silent midday break. He composed poetry because he could not help it, writing on odd scraps of paper, and that kept him sane. He saw his mother twice and each time she had to tell him that there was no hope of a reprieve, the French Ambassador in Brussels refusing to intercede for a former Communard. No one else attempted to visit him; Rimbaud had returned temporarily to Brussels to arrange for the printing of his *Une Saison en Enfer* but did not come near him. He seemed a dead man.

The strain of such an existence—ignored by his friends and treated like a machine in the prison—on such a man as Verlaine does not need emphasizing. His poetry saved him but can scarcely account for the exemplary behavior which in a few weeks and despite the dislike of the warder led to a certain relaxation of the austerity of his life; for this one must look to the man. He was plainly of a different type from most of the prisoners and was fortunate to have a perceptive chaplain and governor.

Late in November he was moved to the detention ward as in the Brussels prison. He was given a bed, slightly more palatable food and, saving grace, was allowed books to read and the free use of paper for composition and letter-writing. At once he sprang into activity, reading hard, mostly in Shakespeare, trying to improve his English, and elaborating a host of Verlainean plans: to write plays, to make translations from the English, to fit himself for a lucrative post in England, to turn publisher and, choicest delusion, to resume his job at the Hôtel de Ville—all this over and above the poems he was writing and the preparation of his next book, *Romances sans Paroles*, for the press.

This last appeared a lost labor but Verlaine, to whom the book meant Rimbaud, persevered against every indication. The little collection had met one obstacle after another ever since Vermersch, editor of the Communard journal *L'Avenir* in London, failed to publish it. In Paris one publisher after another refused it. Lemerre, the first to see it, spoke for every Parnassian when he gave as reason not the shortcomings of the poems but of their author. Literary judgment was not to be found there nor, it seemed, anywhere in Paris. Lepelletier, entrusted by Verlaine with the task of placing the manuscript, did not speak as plainly as he might—a tactful gesture which did him credit—and Verlaine either did not or would not realize how thoroughly he had damned himself in the eyes of the contemporaries with whom he had mixed in apparent good fellowship so short a time before. Friendship in the arts is a transitory thing at the best of times but Verlaine, having little of the cynic in him, did not understand just how transitory. There was the matter of Rimbaud, certainly, but Rimbaud had gone and his companion was in prison. He felt something of the apprehensions of the small boy locked in his bedroom for committing a petty crime, but he had like the small boy a belief, without which he could scarcely have continued to live, that the punishment was too bad to be true and must surely absolve him.

He deceived himself; the prison sentence, bad though it was, was limited, the other sentence was for life. As far as most of the men were concerned with whom he had disported himself in the Paris cafés, at Nina's, at Mendès' and the rest of the gatherings, he was beyond the pale; the mere suspicion of unnatural practices frightened the most licentious. And when to this suspicion was added another, that this reprobate was also a dangerously good poet, no hope existed that he would obtain a hearing or, if he somehow obtained it, that his work would be judged on its merits. A few, Valade and Blémont chief among them, were more charitable than most but had not the courage to defend him. De Sivry missed a lively companion and was always ready with an "Oh come now, he's a good sort" but De Sivry had no say in Parnassian or any other poetic circles; nor had Cabaner, Forain, Carjat or the erratic Richepin, the minor bohemians of their time. Neither Banville nor Coppée wished to impair their comfortable positions, Banville's assured, Coppée's more and more flourishing. For the rest, Mendès' comments were lewd, Leconte de Lisle's libelous and their followers acted as followers do; Glatigny was dead, Nina's mind beginning to give way, Villiers grown too remote from reality to take a stand, Cros siding ingloriously against the grain with the Mauté family.

Yet from his prison cell, lovably or laughably ignoring reality, Verlaine was exhorting Lepelletier to get the poems printed and, anticipating his friend's success, was making lists of the men he had talked and drunk and fooled with, each of whom was to receive a complimentary copy. He varied his inscriptions with an absurdly naïve calculation—Hugo and Banville remaining his "dear master," Leconte de Lisle receiving only his "duty," others being given his "respects," others again his "cordial friendship" and so on—but he might have saved himself the trouble. The book did indeed see the light of day thanks to Lepelletier's admirable efforts; puzzling efforts too until one remembers what Lepelletier goes out of his way to belittle, the irresistible charm of his friend. There is no more convincing evidence of it than the lifelong loyalty of Edmond Lepelletier.

Lepelletier, denied by every Paris publisher, eventually placed the manuscript outside the city. His own political journal *Le Peuple Souverain*, the title explaining its outlook, was banned by the authorities and he moved it to Sens, south of Paris and outside the city boundaries. And he persuaded the printer at Sens to print *Romances sans Paroles*.

The optimist in his detention ward at Mons began happily to correct proofs between spells of coffee-grinding and the weaving of dreams. Lepelletier, he said, must be sure to send him every review. He began to calculate how many copies he would sell and what he could do with the money when his sentence had ended.

All in vain. The dedication to Rimbaud had been removed but Lepelletier's caution and Verlaine's regrets were both wasted. One review—by Blémont—appeared. Not one copy was sold.

Too much indignation has been spread on this silence. The recognition of genius has almost always been left to the next generation. Great poems are to be found in most of the volumes written by Verlaine; there were great poems in *Romances sans Paroles*, some of which have already been quoted; but its chief distinction as a book is that the poems show for the first time Verlaine emancipated by the proselytizing Rimbaud: too much under Rimbaud's influence when his preoccupation with forms leads him to an overdone simplicity; but in general there is found here a rhythm and a directness of speech long lost to French poetry and a freedom from rhetoric and disregard of rules which no Frenchman since Villon had dared to put before the public. Yet Verlaine was far from the usual self-conscious rebel: "*L'Art, mes enfants,*" he was to say, "*c'est d'être absolument soi-même*"; that was to be his sole rule. *Romances sans Paroles* is mainly composed of experiments but such was Verlaine's taste and sincerity as poet that very few of them read like experiments and the book marks a notable advance toward "being absolutely oneself."

But there it was: one review, not one sale. And before Verlaine could recover from this underlining of his isolation a blow fell that drove from his mind every thought of failure as poet. The book was published early in March, 1874. Two weeks later the governor came to his cell and explained as gently as he could that Mathilde had

just been awarded a separation by the court in Paris, Verlaine to
pay the costs and alimony of one hundred francs a month; this on
the grounds of habitual drunkenness and physical ill-treatment of
his wife.

[4]

During his months of imprisonment Verlaine had thought and
written much about Mathilde, veering between abuse of a wife who
had betrayed him and a longing for reconciliation. The latter attitude
predominated. "I don't feel any bitterness toward her," he told
Lepelletier. "God is my witness that *even today* I would forgive her
everything." And again: "It's astonishing the way I grieve for her
with all my heart when I think of what is going on, knowing her to
be in a milieu unworthy of her and separated from the only person
who really understands her—I mean *myself*." He regarded the
lawsuit at one moment as a chimera, at another as a vile plot
fostered by Monsieur Mauté, which must be defended to the last;
though how he was to fight it from prison did not appear.

It is easy, too easy, to dismiss Verlaine as a hypocrite; he was
a blend of the naïve, the cunning and the self-deceiver and in his
way loved Mathilde, not the Mathilde of fact but the shy poet-adorer
of their first meeting and the willing bed companion of the early
months of marriage, the beautiful body and the receptive mind.
He deceived himself but, being what he was, the deception was
essential. Rimbaud silent, his whereabouts, thoughts and plans
all unknown, Verlaine was thrown back on his second string. So
he loved the Mathilde of fiction, dreamed of a reconciliation and
a firm base on which to rest his life and affections. He had never
once abandoned her in mind. If at times he suspected that he could
not be content with Mathilde and would seek distraction elsewhere,
he dared not face these moments of clear-sightedness; he had an
unhappily strong sense of what the world expected from him, a relic
of his bourgeois upbringing, and a desperate desire for security.
Hence the whipped-up tirades against Monsieur Mauté, the pose
of the injured man, the pretense that Mathilde, left to him, would
be ideally happy, the dismissal of their differences with a light-
hearted reference to an occasional drunken spree.

And hence the overwhelming shock when he heard the governor's
news; every prop struck from under his feet at one blow. It is

useless for the onlooker to protest that the props did not exist; he believed them to exist and that is the only thing that matters.

When the governor pityingly handed over the copy of the court's judgment Verlaine collapsed. A short time afterwards he sent for the chaplain and said that he wished to be received back into the Church. He was given devotional books. Some days later he told the chaplain that he had recovered his faith. The chaplain, impressed but cautious, imposed a further delay before confession and a yet longer one before absolution, but Verlaine remained steadfast and ardent. He amazed all who had to do with him, the governor, chaplain, warders in the prison, his mother and even the skeptical Lepelletier who visited him; he was a changed man, mild, contented and at times even radiantly happy and eager to do good to others. There was little scope for this last in prison but he managed to give French lessons to one of the Flemish warders. Like all converts he rushed to extremes, declaring that he would abandon the writing of verse and the reading of secular books; fortunately for him the chaplain, a sensible man, advised him to put his gifts to good use rather than to bury them. Verlaine happily began to write religious poems; the kind of poems one would expect from him, dialogues between himself and God, descriptions of his state of mind simply and ardently set down. He had a new love and this was his theme.

Looked at in a certain light Verlaine's conversion is both comic and insincere. But there are other lights. The basis of the skeptical attitude is that he sank into the comforts of religion only when denied earthly comfort, an attitude analogous to the popular sneer at the taking up of religion by spinsters. The fallacy lies in the assumption that an act loses validity because it appears forced. Verlaine could neither live without love nor exist without moral support; the Church offered both; he flew to it. His conversion was as simple as that. How sincere he was in the moment of decision, who shall say? The proof of belief, then or later, is shown in deeds. Verlaine was not made into a new man, all the old Adam remained, but he managed to live cheerfully for years without love and to live soberly—this from a highly sexual man who had been the near-slave of absinthe for the past ten years. The reader can draw his own conclusion.

As for his poetical expression of this new element in his life, *Sagesse* was to be the eventual title of the collection of poems and

Verlaine tells how the book was born, tells it in a letter showing that he had lost neither sense of proportion nor sense of humor. "One night in June of 1874 at Mons," he said, "after having thought for week after week—yes and fought and struggled too!—I prostrated myself before a distinctly vulgar image—but what did that matter!—of the *Sacré-Coeur* and remained there in tears until the bell sounded for the morning rising and the cleaning out of the cells. From that moment *Sagesse* was conceived." Like most poets, when Verlaine tries too hard he fails, and like most converts he often protests too much; some of his religious poetry is self-conscious argument which reads insincerely and therefore embarrassingly. But at times he wrote from the heart; then he is convincing, as in this sonnet from the sequence *"Mon Dieu m'a dit."*

> —*Seigneur, c'est trop! Vraiment je n'ose. Aimer qui? Vous*
> *O! non! Je tremble et n'ose. O vous aimer, je n'ose,*
> *Je ne veux pas! Je suis indigne. Vous, la Rose*
> *Immense des purs vents de l'amour, ô Vous, tous*
>
> *Les coeurs des Saints, ô Vous qui fûtes le Jaloux*
> *D'Israël, Vous, la chaste abeille qui se pose*
> *Sur la seule fleur d'une innocence mi-close,*
> *Quoi, moi, moi, pouvoir Vous aimer. Etes-vous fous,*[1]
>
> *Père, Fils, Esprit? Moi, ce pécheur-ci, ce lâche,*
> *Ce superbe, qui fait le mal comme sa tâche*
> *Et n'a dans tous les sens, odorat, toucher, goût,*
> *Vue, ouïe, et dans tout son être—hélas! dans tout*
> *Son espoir et dans tout son remords, que l'extase*
> *D'une caresse où le seul vieil Adam s'embrase?*

* * *

> Lord, 'tis too much! I dare not. What? Love whom?
> Thee! Nay, I shake, I dare not! Courage goes!
> I would not, I unworthy,—thou the Rose,
> The great Rose of the winds of Love, the sum
>
> Of all Saint-hearts, yet once in jealous gloom
> The King of Jews,—thou chaste Bee which doth pose

---

[1] *Saint-Augustin*

On the sole innocent flower with petals close;
What—I have strength to love thee? Sure, there's room

For brains in Father, Spirit, Son? This base
Arch-criminal, who sins as 'twere his place,
Possessing in each sense, smell, touch, the ear,
Taste, eyesight, yea, whole soul,—even, I fear,
In hope, remorse,—caresses' ecstasy,
Which none save the old Adam fire with joy?"

13.

NOUVEAU

1875

[1]

On the morning of January 16, 1875, he was released from prison having earned the full remission for good conduct. He went off with his mother to Fampoux in a state of apprehensive exaltation. Not for him the wild unthinking breath of freedom; he was leaving not only a prison but a protection. How would his vows, his new leaf survive in the midst of worldly temptation? In a year and a half he had changed physically. He was thinner and as his hair reappeared his head took on the outline by which he is best known; bald from forehead to crown, the hair growing bushily at the sides and back. The thick eyebrows remained as compensation shielding the long slits of eyes, and a mustache drooped over the wide mouth and covered much of the deep upper lip. He gave the impression at one and the same time of benevolence and of a kind of faunish humor. He looked much older than his age, yet when he smiled, as he often did, the veneer of venerability dissolved into a childlike promise of mischief.

In manner he had changed too; always affable, he was then sweetness itself, like his uncle Dehée's sugar refinery which he dutifully visited; regular at meals, drinking only an occasional beer, walking vast distances over the flat fields, anxious to help his mother and her family, a model companion around the table and fireside, punctilious in his churchgoing, a man whose weekly confessions were so wholehearted, so thorough as to become not far removed from orgies.

However, since man does not change but only promotes one aspect of himself above another, the unregenerate stirred lustily in the background. Verlaine was after all not yet thirty-one, strong, healthy, eating and sleeping well in the brisk air of the North. In such a mood as he then was, there could be no working off his sexual energy with the girls of the village but some form of release was imperative. The poet came to the rescue. Had not the chaplain expressly counseled him not to avoid the profane? Possibly their interpretations of the word differed, although even this is uncertain, the Catholic Church's view of venial sins being profoundly sensible, but before he left prison Verlaine had returned to his Shakespeare and all that Shakespeare implied and had dropped into the habit of paralleling (this being the word he was later to use) his religious poems with poems frankly and at times startlingly profane; his argument being, the first untenable ecstasy over, that man is a spiritual and physical being and that ideally for moral health both sides should be fully expressed. In fact, he could do no other than express the physical side but justification is man's privilege and he freely availed himself of it; and if there was at times a twinkle in his eye as he wrote these poems one does not like him the less for it.

But another thought was agitating him in those first weeks at Fampoux. As a man who had seen the light he was filled with love for all, burned to wipe away all stains from his past, yearned to forgive and to be forgiven. He and Mathilde were legally separated, but what of it? In the eyes of God they remained man and wife, sinners both. The thought, together with the blessed prospect of relief from alimony, was no sooner in his head than he wrote straightaway to Mathilde and commanded Lepelletier to make a démarche at rue Nicolet.

Rue Nicolet maintained a contemptuous silence and repulsed Lepelletier's attempt to intercede. The collapse of Verlaine's dreams cut cruelly into the calm he had imposed on himself. In a twinkling he was back in the first days of his conversion; he had held out a hand to the world and the world had rejected him. Very well: he would withdraw himself from the world. He had heard of a Trappist monastery at Chimay a few miles inside Belgium and although forbidden to reënter that country he crossed the frontier secretly (the many paths had been known to him since youth), presented himself at the monastery and announced that a new monk stood before them. The father, accustomed to statements of this kind, imposed a week's trial of fasting and silence. Within a few days Verlaine was reminded unpleasantly of his first months in prison, and the flesh nagged at him after hours of meditation on an empty stomach. Nothing would put it down. Poems not of the godliest or chastest sort thrust themselves unbidden into his brain and onto his lips. By the end of the week he was wondering whether zeal had not carried him too far. The father mercifully thought likewise and the novice retired from the lists and sought the world again at Fampoux.

By no means satisfied, however, he lusted after converts. And Mathilde obdurate, what greater prize than the one whom he had helped to lead astray? Far from bearing ill will toward Rimbaud he had come to feel responsibility as the elder; and being Verlaine he could no more discard love than stop breathing. He wrote to Delahaye, then master in a college at Rethel, enclosing a letter for Rimbaud. The letter was in pious vein, begging Rimbaud to follow the writer's example: "Let us love one another in Jesus" it ended and, as argument, pointed out that the conversion was no hurried matter lightly undertaken: "I have meditated on the subject for these last six months."

The tone of the letter came as no surprise to Rimbaud; some religious poems smuggled out of prison had been used by him as toilet paper at Roche. He replied to Delahaye with a string of blasphemies and a contemptuous permission for "Loyola" to visit him. "A pretty thin piece of meditation," he said acidly, foreshadowing the reception Verlaine was to get.

During Verlaine's prison sentence Rimbaud had finished *Illuminations* and *Une Saison en Enfer*, had printed the latter and taken copies to Paris where he and his work were pointedly ignored. He had not yet reached the point at which he would see these writings as extraordinarily clever examples of preciosity leading, if anywhere, straight to the madhouse. But his aims were already changing; the vast literary aspirations had given way to a wish to make money and with this money to conquer fresh fields. When Verlaine's proselytizing letter reached him he was living as tutor with a family in Stuttgart so that he could learn German—this being the first stage in a campaign to master as many foreign languages as possible.

The idea of his old disciple in evil panting to convert him was a joke after his own taste, an excellent opportunity of power-demonstration and unveiling of hypocrisy; he would show Verlaine exactly how much his new-found consolation was worth.

A few days later, at the beginning of March, in a letter partly occupied by drawings of a fantastic creature spitting all the way down the left-hand margin, he was writing delightedly to Delahaye: "Verlaine arrived here the other day with a rosary between his claws. . . . Three hours later he had denied his God and had made the ninety-eight wounds of our Saviour bleed afresh."

Up to a point the meeting had followed its expected course, Verlaine arguing, Rimbaud leading him from bar to bar until he was tipsy, ashamed and angry. The day ended in a walk by the Neckar, the discussion still incoherently raging, and a fight on the bank of the river. The older man, not yet recovered from his prison austerities, was no match for Rimbaud; he was finally knocked insensible. Rimbaud left him lying there and walked back to the city. Some peasants discovered Verlaine, carried him to their hut for the night, washed his wounds and sent him off the next day shaken and bruised.

It would be fitting and even romantic to record that this was the last meeting of the two men but it seems clear that they not only met again but met in amity, a fact which will surprise no one who imagines Verlaine's guilt feelings and remembers his inextinguishable fondness for Rimbaud. On the triumphant Rimbaud's side there may have been some trace of compunction; certainly, Verlaine's vows satisfactorily broken, Rimbaud would bear in mind his ever-present need of money, not only for the learning of languages but also for the conquest of music, yet another realm that he meditated.

They met in amity, then, and Rimbaud handed Verlaine a group of poems which he hoped might be published after the fashion of *Romances sans Paroles*; he also counseled him or agreed with him— one cannot be sure which—to seek a teaching job in England after the visit to Paris on which Verlaine was then determined. It seems probable and in character that Rimbaud would recount, in preparation for the story of his adventures in London while Verlaine was in prison, his one triumph in Paris: how, sitting alone at one of the poets' cafés, he had been approached by the young Midi poet, Germain Nouveau, daring the disapproval of the men at neighboring tables to express his admiration of Rimbaud's work; and how, when Rimbaud announced that, disgusted with Paris, he intended to leave at once for London, Nouveau had gone with him without money, as he stood, and carrying with him, forgotten, the key to the room he never even troubled to revisit.

If Verlaine heard this story at Stuttgart he must have thought, and with what emotion, of Nouveau's forerunner a very few years past. Yet though Rimbaud remained in essence the young man who had exercised that peculiar fascination and though Verlaine had succumbed to it once more only a few hours earlier, he had changed more than his young friend, changed to the extent that Rimbaud had influenced him for the last time. Verlaine is unlikely to have imagined any such thing after the collapse of his vows at the first time of asking, but he had the sense to leave Stuttgart. If he tried to persuade Rimbaud to join him in London, which is doubtful, he was not successful. So he went off to Paris and to a succession of failures: failure to meet Mathilde, failure to obtain a reduction of the alimony, failure to convert Lepelletier (learning no lesson he embarked enthusiastically on this formidable task), failure to place or publish Rimbaud's poems, failure to ingratiate himself with his former companions. Not that he tried this last very hard, he was too timid, too fearful of public snubs; but in Paris one could tell without difficulty how the wind was blowing and clearly it was not blowing his way; he met a preoccupied harassed Villiers, shabby and prematurely gray about the head; he was received by a Blémont genuinely impressed by his latest poetry; and that was all, the full extent of his attempt to take up his old life.

For other reasons he feared Paris, though longing for the life there. The final executions of Communards were only two years past and many men and women remained in prison. Feelings still ran bitter. He could not feel absolutely safe; he remembered the police agents with a shudder. Another fear and a more serious one was that the bars and cafés would tempt him beyond his strength. Once again he limited himself to an occasional glass of wine or beer but Rimbaud had exposed his weaknesses and he longed to be gone. To long was to do; two days later, toward the end of March, he was in London.

[2]

England with or without Rimbaud's recommendation was an obvious choice for a man who had so recently endured the disgrace of a prison sentence and the shock of realizing that his conversion did not necessarily protect him from a relapse into alcoholism. In England his prison record would be unknown, he would not be encouraged to drink by ever-open cafés or convivial friends, and

even if watched by police agents he could not be arrested or imprisoned for his part in the Commune. Besides, the agents, if they
troubled to follow his movements, would discover nothing to his
disadvantage; he had done with revolutionary politics as he had
done with drink and prisons. From now on he would tread the
straight and narrow path; not quite so straight and narrow as the
Trappist regime—there was such a thing as overdoing virtue—but
far from the primrose path. His natural impulses must be fettered
but the fetters must not chafe, and the English were past masters
at this kind of thing.

For once his calculations were correct and he was fortunate too;
having registered with a scholastic agency and waited in London for
a few days seeing friends and reading in the British Museum, he
was told that a William Andrews of Stickney in Lincolnshire would
engage him as French and drawing master in exchange for board,
lodging and laundry; and he found himself by chance whisked as
far from temptation as he could wish and living amid as nice a
set of people as he could have imagined. At Sibsey, the station
nearest to Stickney, he was met by a pony cart driven by a groom
and accompanied by a chubby-faced boy of twelve. The pony, Taffy,
the Andrews' main link with civilization, took to Verlaine at once.
As they rode along sedately through the twilit lanes Verlaine looked
with contentment on this first rural scene he had known in England,
a scene which had something in common with his mother's Pas-de-
Calais, and the experience was embodied as usual in verse.

Opposite Stickney church on the village street they turned into
the yard of a large thatched Tudor cottage with lattice windows.
Whether Andrews was there to greet him seems uncertain, but he
soon appeared, a man of about Verlaine's age, with a large mustache
and enormous whiskers. A short dialogue followed, each man doing
his best with the other man's language:

"Welcome, *moussou*."

"Excuse me, I have got plenty of dust."

"*Veux-tu laver?*"

"Yes."

They went into the kitchen, where Verlaine washed his hands,
and then into the parlor. To the astonishment of the visitor, unused
to the vagaries of English cottage architecture, every room appeared
to have been built on a different level; there were "steps everywhere"
and, another English peculiarity, every chair flaunted its lace anti-

macassar. In the parlor Mrs. Andrews bent wearily over a cradle in which lay a little girl apparently dying. Formality, which could never live long with Verlaine, at once collapsed. Moved by the mother's distress he burst into sympathetic tears. He tried to express his sympathy but since Mrs. Andrews had no French, her husband only a word or two, and Verlaine's English broke down under the strain, he was driven to gestures. But his tears were sympathy enough; Mrs. Andrews wept too and from that moment all three became good friends.

This story, like so many of Verlaine's, should not be taken as exact truth; he was not a stickler for accuracy when his imagination ran away with him, and he wrote his reminiscences of Stickney twenty years later. In her old age Mrs. Andrews could not remember the incident; the "dying" is pure Verlaine; enough for him to see a child in a cradle and a mother in tears. But the essential point, shown in this way or another, is Verlaine's immediate sympathy; it was practically impossible, living with him, to remain on anything but intimate terms, and the Andrews took to him at once; he was strange, certainly, with his black clothes, premature baldness, restless deep-set eyes, eloquent hands perpetually waving and his absurd attempts at English, but he quickly showed himself kind, considerate and wonderfully good fun; as far as his sense of humor was concerned he might have been born an Englishman.

Next morning he was up as usual soon after dawn and went for an exploratory ramble. The macadam playground rather shocked him—"too much like French courtyards"—but he reveled in a bowling green enclosed by hedges and poplars of a greenness rarely to be seen in France. Strolling here and making a sketch of the poem already written, in the notebook he always carried, he was greeted by an old whitebearded man who introduced himself as Canon Coltman, rector of Stickney for the past forty years. The Canon delighted Verlaine by speaking a tolerable French and still more by revealing that he had been a neighbor and admirer of Tennyson who was born in the same county. The Canon modestly confessed himself an author, though of a different kind, having published five years earlier his *Flowers from Fatherland Transplanted into English Soil*—for he was a traveled man. They got on famously, discussing literature, art and theology under a slowly rising sun. Verlaine was nothing if not accommodating and could and did attend service at the village church just as he could talk about comparative religion without trace of acrimony. In church he sat in bliss through Handel voluntaries—"what soul-stirring music!"—and was pleasantly surprised by the poetry of the hymns, and out of church he fell into a friendship with the old rector, dining with him frequently, and saying of him, "I am sure if there be a God, and this God is Catholic, he must be saved; he was so charitable in addition to all his other virtues."

On this first morning, after visiting Taffy in his stall, a pig and chickens, in proper English fashion he breakfasted with the Andrews at eight o'clock and was then introduced to the mixed class of boys and girls, which was addressed by Andrews after he had obtained silence "with difficulty" and had said prayers, as "Monsieur Verlaine, who is a B.A. of the University of Paris. . . . He knows English as well as an Englishman but of course he cannot pronounce it quite well"—a statement which Verlaine accepted complacently. "I am convinced," continued Mr. Andrews, "that you will like and respect this gentleman. But should any of you take advantage of his foreign accent to show him the least want of respect I shall lose no time in correcting the error."

The correction seems to have been unnecessary. Verlaine as teacher depended on his gift for drawing and his sense of humor rather than on the knowledge he could communicate: "I teach in English—and what English!" he told Lepelletier with a grin. But he found his pupils "well-bred and industrious" which was another way of saying that the boys and girls, intrigued from the beginning by his comic feats on the blackboards, accepted him and even came to be fond of him. And since he was quickly on excellent terms with the family and pets, a great favorite of George the boy and Lily the little girl, of Nero the fat poodle, of Taffy and even the "funny black kitten," his post at the grammar school was assured. And this meant that he was received—and soon gladly welcomed—by the gentry as a gentleman and excellent company. To bring in a little pocket money, he began to give private lessons to a pupil of the Vicar of Sibsey, to the four daughters of a Sibsey doctor and to the three daughters and son of the local Colonel—dining from time to time at these houses and with another cleric, a former curate of Stickney, who had a living in the next village. He also made a pact with Mr. Andrews, to teach him the elements of the classics in return for lessons in English.

In no time he had become a recognized village character,

punctiliously attending church Sunday after Sunday, walking daily
with the children, even taking part in their games. Every Saturday
he walked, when he could not get a lift, the eight miles into Boston
to attend Mass at the Catholic church, and this too pleased every
body but the most rabid Protestants; Frenchmen were Frenchmen
after all, knowing no better, and regularity was regularity even though
it led to papistry. Vastly encouraged, he began to plan a future
for himself in England, a hazy but enthusiastic one, when he had
perfected his English; he liked the people, loved their poetry and
could see himself and his mother settled in some picturesque cottage
happy, honored and respectable. Happy days and industrious too.
He read largely in English, notably Tennyson, spurred by the
Canon's enthusiasm which he quickly reciprocated to the point of
a wish to translate, Milton, Browning, Goldsmith and Bunyan, and
he made some progress in Dante and *Don Quixote* in the original.
He wrote poetry, walking the garden daily, notebook open, pencil
busy—Mrs. Andrews used to watch him with puzzled affection—
his plans heavy with greatness: an epic poem on Joan of Arc, a set
of up-to-date Verlainean Psalms, a "huge" sacred poem that would
"turn on the Virgin . . . span from Adam and Eve to the present
day, include all civilizations, all legends" a poem of which he had,
he assured Delahaye, the "framework nearly ready." Fortunately
what he actually wrote, or finished, in that notebook were some
religious poems later to appear in *Sagesse*, in which hymns, ancient
and modern played their part, and some fleshly poems which he
began to speak of publishing as *Cellulairement*.

Mrs. Andrews would no doubt have been surprised, possibly
scandalized, had she read some of the poems that the strange but
eminently respectable foreign gentleman was writing in his little
book; but she would have been wrong, for what Verlaine was doing
was not indulging his lust but working it off harmlessly or at least
keeping it at bay. To live those happy days was not always the
simple matter it appeared. Verlaine the potential drunkard, potential
wencher, remained very much alive under the black clothes and
amiable talk, and Verlaine the Parisian lived under the surface of
that admirer of the Lincolnshire countryside. The country was well
enough, gave one pleasant thoughts and built up self-respect, but
from time to time he felt nostalgic for the brightly lit bars, the
brisk exchange of ideas in the cafés, the piles of newspapers, the
scent of caporal. No, it was not easy. "I'm fighting to put down

hat old Me of Brussels and of London, 1872-3, fighting with a kind
f ferocity," he told Delahaye. He claimed no credit. Unaided, he
onfessed, he would have fallen and the English idyl would have
ollapsed, but he was not unaided and he did not fall. He remained—
haste, sober and, in the main, contented.

One homely item played its part; Mrs. Andrews was an excellent
ook. Verlaine had never before known English home cooking and
e was ravished, his letters ecstatic with descriptions of puddings
nd other dishes strange to him. He ate as he did everything with
usto; longings, regrets, ambitions were all smothered by the
oporific weight of those huge meals.

Happy days; and one can imagine the shock of receiving through
)elahaye a letter from Rimbaud demanding money for pianoforte
essons and to support him while he worked for the *baccalauréat*
nd hinting that if no money was forthcoming the prison past of
he "B.A. from the University of Paris" would be revealed in the
ight quarters. The letter was a shock but scarcely a surprise; Verlaine
vas accustomed to Rimbaud's monetary demands and to threats of
ne kind or another; the one serious, the other usually playacting,
nd he was accustomed to think of these demands as justified by
Rimbaud's precocious brilliance. The habit was difficult to discard,
articularly when a fondness remained; one did not leave a Rimbaud
r even be left by him without backward thoughts: what would he
lo with that talent and assurance, where would he go? Greatness
urely awaited him. However Verlaine had no money and Rimbaud
night just possibly do what he threatened. So he was reduced to
he delightfully conspiratorial device of concealing his address
vhich he did with uninhibited glee, and of swapping military
necdotes with the Colonel, anecdotes so heavily embroidered that
is fellow *Gardes nationales* would not have recognized him as one
f the modest heroes of the siege. Even then, he explained, he was
arassed, not to say in peril, not daring to return to Paris and
ollowed to the very haven of Stickney by horrid threats. And he
eplied at length to Rimbaud—"I explained in detail my arithmetical
easons for not sending him money." He also took the opportunity,
emonstrating as never before his unconquerable optimism, of
ttempting Rimbaud's conversion once more, by argument and by
he example of further religious poems. " 'Loyola's' latest vulgarities,"
hared the fate of the first batch: "I've no more time or energy to
vaste on him," commented Rimbaud incorrectly, for he was soon

feeling the pinch again and, irritated by this unexpected firmness
in Verlaine, was writing further pseudo-blackmail demands, this time
to Arras where he had heard that Madame Verlaine had taken
a small house.

[3]

Verlaine came back to this house for his summer holidays after
a first meeting with Nouveau at King's Cross, which produced one
of the *Dédicaces* in which, with the *Invectives*, poems are to be
found addressed to everybody Verlaine had ever known, as well
as to some he had never met, poems including at least one of the
finest of this genre ever written. This, however, was not the poem
to Nouveau which, sobered in tone no doubt by their meeting
place, tells how they repaired to one of the "attractive bars" where
they were served with bitter ale by "tall misses whiter than ermine"—
a picture which demonstrates Verlaine's Anglophilism at its height.
Or perhaps the after-friendship with Nouveau colored recollection
for the men took to each other at once.

Nouveau was seven years younger than Verlaine. He had been
born in the rock town of Pourrières under the shadow of Cézanne's
Mont St. Victoire and had been persuaded by Richepin to try his
luck in Paris, a luck so inconspicuous that unlike Verlaine he had
gone off with Rimbaud without the slightest harm to his reputation.
He and Rimbaud had worked together and separately in London
had parted after a typically Rimbaudian stroke, and Nouveau
bearing no malice, had ranged through Belgium, Holland and
northern France, writing poems and painting pictures (for he was
then more painter than writer) as he might in the snatches between
earning sufficient bread and beer to keep strength in himself. Some
of these methods of earning a livelihood made good stories: such
as the love lyrics sold to a wealthy Russian to hand to the Belgian
actress he was courting until Nouveau, allowing his imagination
too much leeway, wrote one that earned the Russian a box on the
ears. Verlaine had sent him the poems handed over by Rimbaud
at Stuttgart, for having won the liking of Charles Cros among
others, Nouveau seemed to have a better chance of placing them.
There followed a short exchange of letters which impressed Verlaine
sufficiently for him to make an appointment in London. They compared notes, with what emotion on the part of the susceptible

Verlaine can be imagined. The words *"fils du Soleil"* were repeated by Nouveau; so Rimbaud had tried again! They also compared impressions of those extraordinary English amid whose silence, broken only by the shouted order, the occasional dirty joke whispered in a corner, the drunken laugh rising above a glass- and cup-littered table, they drank and talked. "Undocile, incurious, calm, never amused"—so Nouveau saw them. "In France," he said, "one goes out to live; in England one goes in . . . a disgusting life for the unmarried."

But if Verlaine had been moved primarily by curiosity to see his successor for "Thing," one of his names for Rimbaud, he had other reasons for the journey from Stickney, planned originally to meet his mother and bring her back to Lincolnshire. He thirsted for news of Paris as well as of Rimbaud, for talk of poetry, of the Parnassians—in a word, for intellectual discussion. He quickly rated Nouveau as a "lover of learning" and honored him, in a scribble at the bottom of a letter, by admission as junior member to the group of "seekers," Rimbaud—Delahaye—Verlaine. Nor was this the end or even the major part of Nouveau's attraction; he was, Verlaine discovered, violently impressionable and wonderful material for a man hankering after converts; Rimbaud, Delahaye, Lepelletier had all rejected Verlaine's good offices, but Nouveau though calling himself atheist was made of different stuff with a strong religious background and a nature which, like Verlaine's, demanded a strong hand. Verlaine got to work in the short time allowed him, not without success. He did not convert Nouveau but his warnings against the temptations of London and the stultifying effect of a small school had immediate effect; Nouveau withdrew hurriedly from London where he had intended to spend many months, and from the country school where he had acted as assistant master for two days; returning to Paris and then to Pourrières with a thankful "I should have been properly caught if God hadn't been waiting for me there." For God in this instance one reads "Verlaine," who returned to Stickney with the glow of well doing, leaving Nouveau with an agreement that they would meet at Arras as soon as possible.

At Arras that summer Verlaine was sweetness and light; Delahaye, influenced by the cynical jokes of Rimbaud, came over from Rethel with a friend expecting to unmask a hypocrite, but he could find no trace of insincerity, no excess of religious emotionalism; Verlaine took his long walks because he liked them, avoided the cafés because

he had made up his mind to keep sober, talked and joked free
with the air of a man of good conscience, worked hard at his Englis
and in spurts at his poetry. Only one incident marred the harmony
Verlaine at his mother's request showed Delahaye the inevitabl
book of photographs. As he turned to the page on which a photo
graph of Mathilde was fixed, another photograph slipped to th
ground. Madame Verlaine picked it up with an exclamation. "Ye
it's my bane, *Mossieu* Rimbaud," said Verlaine, mimicking Rin
baud's uncouth accent. He held out a hand and despite his mother
protest fitted the photo of Rimbaud on the page opposite the phot
of Mathilde and slammed the book shut "with a mischievous grin.
"There!" he said. "I've united the two creatures who have caused m
the most suffering."

If proof were needed of Verlaine's humility the chance was offere
this same holiday. The rump of the Parnassians was preparing fc
a third and, as everyone else realized, a last *Parnasse contemporair*
The Parnassian movement was dead though not unexpectedly non
of the survivors would confess to this. Leconte de Lisle indeed ha
never been more master of all he surveyed, which was not now ver
much. Banville continued charmingly witty about less and less, an
the rotundity and hairlessness of the middle fifties made his boyis
fun seem a little, ever so little, absurd; he had to face increasin
danger that he would be laughed at for himself instead of for wha
he said. Mendès had become the laughing stock of Paris; the agein
Hugo had made a cuckold of him, had ravished his young an
beautiful wife under his very eyes, so to speak. Already displaced fror
all influence in the *Parnasse*, Mendès blustered his way out of th
new reverse by a display of riotous living which offended the sobe
members. And the *Comité des Grâces* of Banville, Coppée an
France not only privately criticized each other (Coppée was marke
for early extinction as altogether too popular) but together, led b
France who was no Parnassian and no poet, resolved to throw ove
board all that could be spared which in practice reduced itself to a
unwelcome to them. The jettisoning was considerable; of thos
known to the reader, Mérat and Valade went, Sully Prudhomm
("He is not of this house," Leconte de Lisle ruled), De Ricard ("H
poems need cleaning," France said), Charles Cros who had becom
persona non grata at Leconte de Lisle's apartment ("I resign if h
goes in," threatened France) and even Mallarmé, both Coppée an
France rejecting him—"He is making a mock of us," the latter de

clared. Mallarmé's rejected poem was "*L'Après-Midi d'un Faune.*"

Then in blundered the ever-hopeful Verlaine. Surely, he reasoned, he would be taken back into the fold now that he had paid for his transgressions, had seen the light and could offer work demonstrating his advance as poet. He submitted a number of recent and near-recent poems, including "*Beauté des femmes,*" which was in a world of inspiration and artistry far from the accepted Parnassian contributions. His entry caused an embarrassed sensation. Banville and Coppée refused to vote one way or another. The decision was left to France who settled his place in literary criticism by writing "No. The author is unworthy and his lines are some of the worst I've ever read."

Verlaine's overtures to this passé remnant will seem comical to the most cursory reader of French literary history, yet from his point of view he had good reason. As a young man he had tried to be a good Parnassian because he hated the thought of being a poet (or anything else for that matter) in isolation; his friends were or wanted to be Parnassians—that was argument enough. And the argument held good for him in 1875 as in 1861; to be received into the third *Parnasse contemporain* would have meant reconciliation with his old companions of the sixties, the lifting of the moral ban, the prospect of walking the familiar streets or sitting at the familiar cafés without being obliged to avert his eyes every five minutes. That was the purpose of his application, the purpose of his whole life one could say. "*L'amour, voyez-vous, croyez-m'en plutôt que de m'en blâmer d'avance, c'est sinon le tout, ah! du moins le presque tout, le mobile quasiment unique de toutes les actions dignes de ce nom, et ne me parlez pas d'autre chose, ambition, lucre, gloire! tout au plus peut-être de l'Art. Et encore, et encore, l'Art, tout seul . . . ?*" That was Verlaine.

He reacted well to Anatole France's display of ignorance and bigotry, to the cowardice of Coppée and Banville; his first remark was "this is laughable, this proscription of Lemerre's; it began with the Commune, don't you think? Ever since then Leconte de Lisle has regarded me as an ogre." He did well to point to Leconte de Lisle who has been a pig to me after most friendly relations" for he remained what power there was behind the movement and he had dismissed Verlaine with a "people with more merit than this animal have been shot on sight." But after the first shock Verlaine followed the true Christian tradition, turned the other cheek and offered, when

the anthology appeared, to try to sell it in England. This too wa
refused, and he returned to Stickney to make the best of school
mastering in England.

He had not long been back when Rimbaud began to pester hin
again. Verlaine protested to Delahaye who remained their inter
mediary. Delahaye, one of Rimbaud's greatest admirers, was shocked
by the decline of his god. Rimbaud, he reported, was declaring tha
he would write no more, that he despised literature. "What inso
lence!" Rimbaud was impious and sneered at religion. "Unhapp
wretch!" Rimbaud would stoop to the meanest deceit to eke a littl
money out of his few friends in Charleville. Was he going mad
Delahaye thought that this was the most charitable conclusion; h
would surely end in Charenton.

Verlaine knew Rimbaud better; no madness there; but he was hurt

"First he [Rimbaud] replied with impertinences garnished witl
vague threats of blackmail, then with ridiculous calculations by whicl
he demonstrates that it would be good business for me to lend hin
the money. Not to mention a letter written in a kind of drunke
gibberish amid which I made out the statement that future letter
would include the demand that I 'fork out' or else—*zut!*

"In a word he is still banking on my old foolishness, on my wicked
stupidity not so long past, of wanting to live only through him an
by him. Add the intolerable rudeness of a child whom I spoiled
and who repays me—the logic, the justice of it!—with criminal in
gratitude. Hasn't he in fact killed the goose who laid the golde
eggs?"

He could not see Rimbaud in an institution like Charenton bu
he believed that a young man who thought that to be insolent wa
to be strong and that to swindle one's friends was a sign of clever
ness was no better than a dirty cad who would become at thirty ;
very nasty customer. In a real sense this exceedingly brilliant youtl
was behaving unintelligently. Verlaine's admiration was perhap
built on sand, but all the same if Rimbaud would only show a sign o
change of heart his affection and friendship was "Christianly avail
able, that goes without saying."

This letter passed on by Delahaye silenced Rimbaud. But Verlain
who was nothing if not contrary or, to put the matter more charitably
who longed to share his blessings, was not easy in mind. He feared
for the blasphemer and grieved over the lost poet who had writter

such masterly verses at Charleville. His conscience worried him. Look at Rimbaud now! How much was he responsible?

Such thoughts clouded some of the autumn and early winter days at Stickney, days of a calm and delightful monotony otherwise, days which began with the morning ramble—Verlaine light-heartedly leaping stiles, continued with the little morning service before school ("But what a sad cult, this, and absolutely without reason," he told Delahaye) and was enlivened by huge helpings of Mrs. Andrews' masterpieces, gooseberry fool and seed cake. At length, before leaving for Arras to spend the Christmas holidays, Verlaine's anxiety broke out in a final appeal:

"Despite my promise (if I remember rightly) I haven't written to you earlier because I was waiting for a satisfactory letter from you. Nothing received, nothing answered. Today, however, I break my long silence to confirm all that I wrote you some two months ago.

"I remain the same always. Strictly religious because this is the only good and intelligent thing to be. Everything else is trickery, wickedness, stupidity. The Church has made modern civilization, science, literature: she has made France, particularly, and France is dying because she has broken with her. That's clear enough. And the Church makes men too, *creates* them. I'm astonished you don't see this, it's so strikingly obvious. I had plenty of spare time during these eighteen months to think again and again on these things and I assure you that I cling to it as my only plank. And seven months spent among Protestants has confirmed me in my Catholicism, my legitimism, my resigned courage.

" 'Resigned' for the good reason that I see and feel myself as justly punished, justly humiliated, and know that the severer the lesson the greater the pardon and the obligation to respond to it.

"How can you think that this is a pose or a pretext on my part? Why do you write to me of—I can't remember the exact words—*'modifications of the same sensitive individual, rubbish, tommy-rot,'*—all bunkum and a medley of nonsense unworthy of a Pelletan and other assistant-Vacqueries.

"So I'm always the same. The same affection (modified) for you. I greatly wish I could see you enlightened, reflective. It's a great grief to me to see you following such idiotic paths, you so intelligent, so ready to see the light (however much this may surprise you!). I appeal to your own disgust with everything and everybody, your perpetual anger against all things—just enough at bottom, this anger, though you don't know *why*.

"As for this matter of money, you can't really fail to recognize that I am *generosity itself*: this is one of my very rare virtues—or one of my very many faults, as you please. But, this granted, and the need to repair, by little economies, the enormous breaches made in my tiny capital by *our* absurd and shameful life three years ago—and bearing my son in mind also, and also my new and firm principles, you must understand perfectly well that I can't support you. In any case, where would my money go? On drinks and pub owners! Piano lessons? What *humbug!* If you really wanted them your mother would pay, wouldn't she?

"In April you wrote me letters so revelatory of your base and wicked plans that I can't risk giving you my address—although any attempts to harm me would be ridiculous and powerless from the beginning and besides I warn you that they would be answered *legally*, with evidence. But I pass over this odious hypothesis. It's some fugitive *caprice* of yours I'm sure, some unhappy brainstorm which a little reflection will drive away. However, prudence is the mother of safety, so I won't give you my address until I'm certain of you. . . .

"Come, confound it all, show a good impulse, a little heart, some consideration and feeling for one who remains always, as you know, your very cordial P. V.

"P.S. I'll explain my plans—very simple!—and the counsels I should like to see you follow, religion apart, though this would be my great, great, great counsel, when you have replied *properly* via Delahaye."

Rimbaud did not reply and communication between him and Verlaine ended.

14.

TOWARD DOMESTICITY

1876-1879

[1]

Verlaine had intended the Christmas term at Stickney to be his last. He believed, a shade optimistically, that his English was good enough for him to strike out on his own and earn some money and he planned to establish himself at Boston where he had made friends. But the Andrews' were reluctant to let him go, a fact which says much for him as master or more probably as enlivening companion —it is, after all, not every day that an English village is given the honor of a Verlaine—and he was offered a small salary and some lessons in German if he would stay on. He agreed to remain for the spring term.

"L'arrrgent *avant tout, vous savez,*" he told Blémont, mocking the pronunciation and abiding weakness of Rimbaud, but his plan to move was not made solely for money. Stickney and its people were as near perfection as Verlaine was likely to reach, they had given him almost everything he had dreamed of in prison: safety, respectability, affection, good living. But he discovered that there were other things; for an intelligent Parisian in his early thirties an English village showed itself after a few months as not far distant from death, a pleasant death but death all the same; and he realized that he would prefer less perfection and more life. Boston was a town, it had life of a kind, and if Verlaine had his way it would have more. It was not his intention to set up in Boston on his own; he hoped to persuade Nouveau to join him, either as French master in his place at Stickney or at Boston helping in the decoration of the Catholic church.

He had been thinking a great deal about Nouveau; in him he had found, it seemed, a substitute for Rimbaud and a more amenable if less exciting one, master and pupil changing places. Nouveau was flatteringly conscious of Verlaine's status as poet and responded eagerly to his encouragement, writing and sending him poems for criticism. A correspondence was soon in full swing, Verlaine presenting his "Nouve" as he quickly became with a photograph of himself taken in Boston and Nouveau trying to persuade his new leader to return to Paris. Why bother about the Parnassians? he asked; the *Parnasse* was "a detestable milieu and generally sickening. I shall arrange in the future to have nothing more to do with *them.*" Nina, to whom he had put the question, said roundly, "If I were Verlaine I should definitely come back to Paris and get along very nicely without going to the Voltaire or seeing my former comrades (not very amusing anyway) and in face of success (journal or theatre) they'd come around all right—if I still wanted them."

Verlaine, however, was not Nina and after he had spent a few days of his Christmas holidays in Paris Nouveau recognized his objections as just and eventually came around with a "Knowing you so much changed, I ask myself whether you don't do well to go to Boston." Yes, he had changed but this did not mean that he was resigned to a lifetime of exile, not merely physical exile but mental and emotional too; he still had a heart and a tongue and was less than half a man with both virtually out of action. If Paris was undesirable on several counts, perhaps a snatch of Paris could be brought to him. Rimbaud's obduracy had left a gap, not in his affections which were inexhaustible but in his opportunities for tangible expression of them. But if God took with one hand He gave with the other. "Nouve" had a look of "Rimbe" if one was not too hairsplitting; he too was eccentric, and with an eye that held the attention, he was willful, he dressed as weirdly, he was just as dirty. He had not Rimbaud's ambitions which was perhaps as well, he was often timid and nervous where Rimbaud was bold and assured, he showed no sign of Rimbaud's extraordinary intelligence. This too was perhaps a mercy. And he had great potentialities—Rimbaud, after all, had taken him up as a possible *fils du Soleil*—and a temperament which Rimbaud was without. One could call it madness—it was to be called that—but to Verlaine the flashes of excessive emotion, the queer flights of imagination appeared chiefly as an intimation that in Nouveau he had found pupil, convert, companion and stimulator all in one. There was besides a kind of poetic justice in the event; Rimbaud gone, his chosen lieutenant takes his place.

And not Nouveau only; Nouveau had a sister who admired Verlaine's poetry, who wrote poetry herself—"not bad," said her brother, who even had a look of Verlaine in the oriental setting of her eyes, who was "very loving" and whom Nouveau "would much like to see married." Marriage was not in Verlaine's cards but all else was possible. So let them both come, and in the Lincolnshire wilds let them found a little Paris in which love, art and religion would go hand in hand!

But the new year of 1876 had not ended its first month before these hopes were dashed in a manner well known to Verlaine: "her poverty as well as mine," reported Nouveau, prevented them from raising even the fare. And the move to Boston at once took on a new and less promising aspect.

He summoned his mother; having gone so far, having spoken to Andrews more than once about his wish to leave, he would try to establish that respectable little English home which had been hovering in his mind for years. If his hopes were realized he might after all be able to pay for Nouveau and his sister to join them.

Madame Verlaine arrived late in February or the beginning of March. She knew only one word of English but at once made a good impression; what struck everybody was the deep affection between mother and son, an affection shown possibly rather too openly for English tastes (their morning embrace, for instance, was almost loverlike in its fervency) but which nevertheless went to the heart. Verlaine, who had already added to his popularity by a display of virtuosity on the ice—the winter was a hard one—won golden opinions by his touching attentions to the ageing mother then in her sixty-eighth year.

Madame Verlaine amused the village by her talkativeness and vivacity—she did not get older with the years—and quickly made herself at home. She lodged with the tailor, the man who made such queer noises in the choir every Sunday, but took her meals with the Andrews'. She had the gift which her son displayed in even greater degree, of getting on good terms with the most varied of people; the children took to her and she went the round of the pets with Verlaine, feeding Taffy and in short displaying the kind heart and streak of sentimentality beloved of the English. She was asked out to dinner with her son and finally crowned her popularity by responding to a village disaster, a small fire, with unmistakable gestures of sympathy and by the gift to the unfortunates of a sovereign, she having no more sense of the value of her money than the son who had spent it so regally during the previous years.

When she and Verlaine left for Boston at the end of the month they were seen off by a little crowd truly sorry to see them go. For perhaps the first time in his life Verlaine left no mixed feelings behind him; he had shown in that year at Stickney all the best side of his nature and not one serious weakness, which says much for Stickney and its people and more for his so recent resolution. It was unfortunate for him perhaps that he could not stay there; but if he could have brought himself to do so he would not have been the man of his life and poems; he did good work at Stickney because he was inspired by the novel life there; the moment the novelty wore thin the poet was doomed; and whether he knew it or not the man was motivated by the poet, which expressed all of him and not just the fair but slightly unreal face of a half-man.

Stickney had been a lucky chance; Boston was a mistake. Verlaine perhaps counted on a paid post at the grammar school there; this seems to explain his reference to finding "a more lucrative position at Boston" and his daily hopes of a letter about it. But the good news never arrived and he set off with his mother into the blue with nothing more encouraging ahead of him than his friendships with an Italian photographer (the one who had taken the portrait sent to Nouveau and others), an Irish customs officer and the Catholic priest, the German Père Sabela; there were no more free meals, lodging and laundry; everything had to be paid for.

He and his mother put up at an inn and Verlaine advertised two or three times for pupils in French, Latin and elementary drawing. The result was disappointing; at the end of two months he could muster only three pupils, one of them Père Sabela's brother who was decorating the little church—the work in which Verlaine had hoped Nouveau might join.

He called regularly at the Sabela house for tea and taught French as best he could in English, their one common tongue. The best was not very good but for a few weeks he and his mother lived happily enough, visiting the Sabelas and attending Mass at the chapel. Canon Coltman, an open-minded man, had contributed to the decoration of the little building, the Haydn and Mozart played there pleased Verlaine, the congregation made up of foreigners, Irish and one or two of the old English Catholic families, interested him. For the rest, Verlaine spent much of his time in a museum in the form of a grotto which belonged to the inn. Except in one particular museum the exhibits were unremarkable—queer shells, pebbles, old weapons and armor—but the complete skeleton of a whale fascinated Verlaine; he loved to sit inside with his friend the Italian, smoking his pipe and drinking a glass of beer as a modern Jonah.

By the beginning of June he abandoned hope of earning a living on his own. And, because his mother feared for the remnant of her small capital he went back with her to Arras, leaving his name once more with the 'agency in London. He was soon engaged as French and Latin master in a school at Bournemouth ("Bournemouse" to him) and took up the post in September.

Although he was paid sixty pounds a year, all found except laundry, in this new post it proved to be far from another Stickney. The principal, Frederick Remington, a Protestant clergyman converted to Catholicism, was a big bearded man with pince-nez, reserved and severe. His school, St. Aloysius College as it was impressively named, was one of the many catering to boys whose parents considered their health too "delicate" for a public school, which was a delicate way of attracting the snob, the stupid and the misfit. Verlaine found no more than a dozen or so pupils to be taught, but the dozen included some "absolute devils" of Irish boys, one of whom was to throw a snowball weighted by a stone which knocked the master unconscious. Unlike Stickney, the classes were all male and the average age of the boys at Bournemouth was higher; there was no more amusing of children by comic blackboard sketches, and Verlaine's disciplinary weaknesses must have been rudely exposed.

He managed nevertheless to earn Remington's approval, though this may have been more by charming the principal than disciplining the boys; and it was not so much the classes which worried him as his obligation to "superintend the pupils generally." Ominous words, which in practice meant daily walks and monitorial duties beyond classroom hours. As long as the warmth lasted the walks were tolerable since they ended in sea bathing for all, but in winter, with conversation practically at a standstill, they became an almost unmitigated bore and the overseeing duties even more so.

As consolation he enjoyed his Sunday services at the church attached to a picturesque *Jesuitière*, services sweetened by good music;

and when he was free to walk out alone, the miles of sea with its foreground of gorse-covered cliffs awoke all the poet. As at Stickney grandiose plans abounded but the poems actually written remained genuine impressions and not a moral hotchpotch conceived in duty.

But though he could write poetry, worship Shakespeare and adulate Tennyson—promising himself to translate *"In Memoriam,"* though he could enjoy the soothing English somnolence of thought and action, the quiet voices, the soft country and seascapes, hard facts would intrude; he was bored, he had no outlet for his affections. His mind turned once more, as always, to Paris. News from there was politically reassuring; the *Comité des Grâces* had at last finished its work, most of the people arrested for complicity with the Commune had been freed from prison, there was even talk of a general amnesty. Surely he would be safe. And he would again be within reach of Mathilde and his son Georges.

For he had not given up hope of Mathilde. The erratic "Nouve" rushing aimlessly from the Midi to Paris, Paris to Belgium and back again; the steady Delahaye, the upright Lepelletier, Rimbaud careering over Europe and beyond—none of these offered a warm and stable hold on life. He had God, true; but at times he had to confess that the comfort was cold: *"Parfums, couleurs, systèmes, lois,"* he groaned to himself in such moods.

And why not Mathilde? What was a separation, as legal as man could make it? When he thought of her he loved no part of Catholicism quite so much as the decree that man and wife once joined are inseparable in the eyes of God. He had consulted Delahaye among others, had even meditated proposing, had his Boston venture succeeded, that Mathilde should join him there. The best thing, Delahaye had advised "would be perhaps to convey to the young person *alone*—carefully avoiding contact with the *papa*—some frank and simple words in which you would categorically propose to her that she come to join you in England. Who knows if this little coup d'état wouldn't tear aside the spiders' webs?"

Verlaine did not forget his friend's advice. Boston had failed, he had not made a home for himself in England, but the advice still applied. Moreover, he had thought up a new tactic, one which had the merit of unambiguous feeling: he would recover Mathilde by way of the fatherless child.

Georges was then almost six years old. Verlaine had not seen him out of swaddling clothes. Georges would love his father; why should he not enjoy a father's love? Verlaine lashed himself into a passion and the thing, in imagination, was done: childish arms around his neck and the rest would follow.

He was enormously encouraged by a chance remark of Hugo. He sent some poems to the old man with the customary assurance that such merit as they might possess had come from the master's example. "Your poems," replied Hugo, "are simply superb. I am proud to have inspired them; you should be not less so to have written them. . . . Give my compliments to your charming wife." So Hugo believed that husband and wife were happily reunited! If he believed it, a reunion must be possible, reasonable, not just an optimistic delusion of the husband. Verlaine's reply to the ancient Don Juan's attempt to add another pretty woman to his collection of scalps has unfortunately been lost, but the encouragement was plain.

But to be with Mathilde and his son he would have to regain Paris and earn a living there if only to appease Monsieur Mauté. Lessons in English in a French school: that was the obvious answer. Hugo's letter reached him at Christmas when he and his mother were on a visit to Paris. He at once consulted Lepelletier. Testimonials from your English schools, answered Lepelletier; anything less than a year's residence might sound a little thin.

Verlaine soared back to Bournemouth, dreams gloriously weaving; he would earn the second of his testimonials and then—"for the capital of the world 'where one has a good laugh' as the poet says!" But for himself, he assured Lepelletier, "I shall lead a more monastic life than ever, my only pleasure an occasional sight of my little boy."

The year dragged itself out. The snowball fight was a grand incident in a life of futile agitations, of tedious hours with the boys, of pipes smoked slowly over Remington's fire in the winter evenings, of long spring walks across the heath to Poole, the pocketbook busy. At last *Sagesse* was ready, blend of the boring and the inexpressibly beautiful, with that one line shouting Verlaine across time:

Vous voilà, vous voilà, pauvres bonnes pensées!

Again he called on the help of Lepelletier: a religious publisher this time, he urged; but even that kind seemed wary; nothing happened. Evidently he ought to place the book himself; another and final argument in favor of a return to Paris.

Another and very different matter worried the militant Catholic he had become in the company he was keeping. It seemed to him at times that England was almost entirely composed of Protestants turned Catholic; there was Remington, in the *Jesuitière* were two more converted parsons—one of them a nephew of Manning, at Boston there had been English strong in the Faith, even the Canon had contributed toward the decorations of the church on the canal bank. Manning's nephew, Anderton, had given a series of talks at Bournemouth on the Catholic Church and its doctrines; heard, read or repeated, they were timely to influence the impressionable Verlaine; everywhere the tide was turning, yet he, a brand snatched from the burning if ever there were one, a magnificent example of what the Church could do for the least of wretches, remained without a scalp to his name, he was taking no part in the great movement that was sweeping England and that must regenerate France.

The fact was, though happily Verlaine was unaware of it, that his face would not satisfactorily absorb a pious expression. In religious mood he looked the hypocrite; the piety dissolved into a Tartuffian smugness which clearly though incorrectly cloaked some unworthy design—the Mephistophelean eyebrows declared it as did the half-closed, deep-set laughing (or was it sneering?) eyes.

This he did not know; he felt that at least if the world would not hear his poetry it might be made the better for his presence. So he yearned in proselytizing moments to bring others into the fold and yearned vainly until, in the summer of 1877, having completed his year at Bournemouth by, it seems, "superintending" through the holidays, he went back to Arras with a testimonial from Remington in his pocket. He was joined there by Nouveau and lo, the miracle!

Hitherto Nouveau had repulsed all attempts at conversion with what he regarded as jocularity. Not that he was fundamentally unsympathetic insofar as he could be said to have any guiding light in him at all; two of his family were in a convent in Pourrières; but he remained in essence a disciple of Rimbaud, wrote weak and incomprehensible poetry, painted lascivious pictures, disported himself when in Paris at the rue des Moines where Nina was rapidly going downhill, and in brief followed every whim and said whatever came into his head, being governed only by the need to earn a living. This in 1877 had brought him to Charleville as *"surveillant"* in a mental institution. Perhaps this experience led him to Arras in thoughtful mood; he may well have noticed a certain resemblance between the patients and their keeper; whatever the occasion or the cause he lent an ear to the voluble Verlaine and to his mentor's joy announced himself a reclaimed Catholic.

Followed a few days of spiritual revelry as the lost lamb was welcomed home. Then perplexity reared its head as Nouveau made clear that the revelry was to remain strictly spiritual. Nouveau was a young man who did not comprehend the meaning of half-measures. He never let up. His religious ardor became frightening, almost indecent in its ferocity, and the piety of his converter was exposed as having the consistency of water. There were long and, to one of the party, slightly wearisome discussion on the nature of faith, the precise duties of the true Catholic; dogma seemed to hound all their conversations. "Nouveau is charming, isn't he; but what a Jansenist!" wrote Verlaine uneasily. "Verlaine," wrote Nouveau firmly, "is a child who needs to be led. Sometimes I am very fierce with him; but without this one would achieve nothing." "Here I'm living more and more like a hermit," wrote the child with a decidedly mutinous pout. "I've given up the 'Sanpeur' café or at the most go there on Saturday afternoons to look at the illustrated papers." For there had been trouble over the Christianly glass of beer at the Arras cafés. One, perhaps; two at a pinch; but when Verlaine made motions to order a third Nouveau's thick eyebrows would contract and his eyes flash remonstrance. At home Madame Verlaine, bewildered, watched the unedifying struggle between the two sons of the Church. Opposition merely whetted Verlaine's appetite. Came the day when he and Nouveau faced each other across a café table close to hatred. Verlaine, unexpectedly obstinate, had managed to persuade eight glasses of beer to slip down the throat of the sultry convert; he was about to order the ninth round, a light not recently seen illuminating his eye, when Nouveau rose and took an angry leave of Verlaine, the café and Arras.

Verlaine wrote to him apologetically, prostrating himself. Nouveau would not answer. Verlaine played his last card: meet me, he begged, "at High Mass at Saint-Sulpice" on such and such a day. In Paris, an agitated Verlaine attended the Mass; no Nouveau.

It was about this time that Delahaye gave him news of Rimbaud. Verlaine and Rimbaud were not to meet again or to correspond, but one at least did not forget the other. Verlaine heard then of Rimbaud's wanderings through Italy, his enlistment at Marseilles as would-be Carlist volunteer, enlistment in Holland in the Dutch colonial army, voyage to Batavia, desertion and escape to France, journey to Vienna, to Hamburg as interpreter in a circus, to Sweden, to Denmark, learning Spanish, Arabic, Italian, Dutch and modern Greek as he went—a flight from himself that aroused loving bitterness in the heart of the one man who truly cared for him. How well he knew the boy and how futile he knew this odyssey of the modern Wandering Jew to be! He expressed himself as usual in a poem, the *"Dargnières Nouvelles!"*

Nouveau gone, he turned to his own flesh and blood; if all the world rejected him there remained his son. In Paris again, he sent a peremptory note demanding that Georges be allowed to spend some days with him. Georges did not appear.

Lepelletier could not cheer him: no one would publish *Sagesse*; no one wished to engage him as English master. That the baffled Verlaine, a step from the Paris cafés and their absinthe, somehow shunned the sorceress said much for the faith that Nouveau had found so weak. Then, as reward came light, which came casually as Verlaine, wise in his butterfly ways perhaps, loved it to come. He had made up his mind to apply for another post at an English school when he ran into Delahaye. They adjourned to a café. Delahaye explained that he was on his way to Orléans where he had found a new and better post. Verlaine raised his eyebrows at this and Delahaye explained why he had left the college at Rethel. Verlaine was a good and sympathetic listener—Delahaye, like many others, comments on his ability, so rare, to hear the other man out and really listen, not merely to wait with patience for his own turn to speak. And as usual he had the reward of a good listener; Delahaye went on too long, his complaints amounting to nothing more serious than that the atmosphere at Rethel was a little too religious for his liking.

At this Verlaine leaned back with a dreamy laugh: "What you give up so cheerfully would be paradise to me. To live in the midst of good priests . . . myself as a Christian profiting from all . . . if I had had this happiness, this half-monastic life without the rigidity —too much for me—of vows and total renunciation . . . !"

Delahaye, however, did not see the college at Rethel in this light; the conversation moved to other things, including Verlaine's imminent departure for London and the scholastic agency. They dined together, drank a beer or two at the cafés, Verlaine laughed and joked as always in company he liked; apparently he had not a care in the world, certainly he had nothing more to say about Rethel.

One week later Delahaye received a letter which opened "Dear

Predecessor." The morning after their evening together Verlaine, precipitately abandoning England, had taken the train to Rethel, sought out the man in charge of lay teachers, introduced himself as a friend of Delahaye and offered his services as English master. The man was impressed by Verlaine's testimonials from Stickney and Bournemouth and by his appearance and behavior, for Verlaine was at this time a fine figure of a man, tall, straight, slender, and his bearing when he chose to employ the fingertips technique could be momentarily impressive—grave, reverend, judicious, the very soul of propriety. He was engaged.

[2]

Verlaine's instinct had served him rightly and was to give him two of the happiest years of his life. The college of Notre-Dame at Rethel was an institution after his heart at that particular time, offering peace, security, company, occupation, all within the framework of organized religion. It even provided a familiar and well-liked background, for Rethel stood in the Southern Ardennes a few miles below Charleville, and the countryside was reminiscent of Bouillon and Paliseul where he had spent so many months of boyhood and of which he had only happy memories.

The college, though a Church institution primarily interested in preparing boys for the priesthood, was open to all and offered a general education for those wishing to lead a secular life. And though, like all of its kind throughout France, it was staffed mainly by priests, the atmosphere differed little from any ordinary secondary school; the religious background was not obtrusive. In fact, if Verlaine at first felt out of his depth it was because his exaggerated assumption of all the Christian virtues set him apart from the human and quite jolly staff; he declined their modest daily glass of wine with a scarcely concealed gesture of horror, he regarded the smoking briar with apparent disgust, stood aloof when after-dinner tales circulated, and was in every respect too good to be true.

But as we have remarked before, Verlaine's piety appeared suspiciously close to hypocrisy. Far from being thought, as he had fondly imagined, a model master, he was shunned as—of all things!—a *pudeur* employed secretly by the college patron, the Archbishop of Rheims. Happily this object lesson in misguided hypocrisy ended abruptly one day when Verlaine's sense of humor, tickled beyond control, came out in a great burst of jovial laughter. This unexpected sound from the college Malvolio staggered and relieved everyone; no spy could laugh so. He was offered and accepted a glass of wine, he lit up the hungry pipe, he told a fairly decorous story or two and was suddenly found to be a very good fellow.

From then onwards his path was smooth. He may not have been a good teacher but he was certainly a most unusual one. His method of teaching English was to persuade his pupils to pronounce French with an English accent; the lesson began each day as Verlaine entered the room with the class on its feet chorusing *"Baoun-jaur, maossiun Voeulaine!"* Nor does the following dialogue suggest that he was the ideal teacher of history although it does show how far he had moved from the politics of Parnassian days:

"Who were the Girondins?"

"The Girondins sir—the Girondins—were—the deputies from the Gironde."

"Well?"

"Sir?"

"Their views, the role they played?"

"Sir?"

"You don't know. Right! Then who does know?"

"I do, sir."

"Well?"

"They were—the moderates."

"They were not the moderates. Someone else—yes, you."

"Sir, they wanted to end the revolution."

"Not on your life!"

"Sir, it says so in our history book."

"Never mind what your book says. The Girondins were the maddest, the most dangerous fools in the whole frightful revolutionary crew, do you understand?"

His sense of discipline, once the mask of unimpeachable righteousness had slipped awry, was slight to the point of nonexistence. But he was popular with the boys, masters and servants (especially with the servants), and every evening made coffee in his room for a little crowd of callers. He accepted gratefully the small bottle of wine supplied with lunch and the liqueur after dinner and showed not the slightest disposition to augment them. He had ample leisure to write his poems but not too much to tempt him elsewhere. He had privacy when he wanted it after classes were over, and if he preferred company that too was open to him. The daily prayers, the public readings from the Scriptures, the prolonged Sunday devotions all wove a comfortable web of good-thinking about him. "This is a kind of paradise to me," he told Lepelletier, "where I have peace and calm and freedom." He wrote in similar sense to Mallarmé, who was also teaching English, and to Delahaye. All that he had to teach, including history, literature and geography, was "amusing and distracting." Delahaye, witnessing this enthusiasm with a smile, hoped that he would settle down and not show himself "a hideous Anglophile" incapable of appreciating his own country. And so it seemed. His behavior remained exemplary and the legend (not begun by him) that he was a pious gentleman in reduced circumstances seemed, if action is the criterion, more truthful than the facts with which naturally enough he had not troubled the headmaster.

A year went by. He astonished all in Paris and in Arras where he had spent his holidays by presenting a front resolutely Christian and by resisting without apparent effort the many temptations of the Exhibition then filling the capital. And when the Archbishop of Rheims made his annual visit to the college he was more than a little surprised to discover that one of his teachers was an ex-convict, Communard, drunkard and estranged husband, Verlaine seizing this opportunity to release his conscience of its burden in confession. Absolution followed and with it the job remained safe—for life, the exhilarated Verlaine began to hope.

Yet it was not to be for life and perhaps none but Verlaine would even have thought so. The security and the guidance appealed powerfully to him but he had a body healthy as never before because of the English years, strong and with strong needs which could not be balked indefinitely; he was only thirty-four despite the misleading bald pate and by no means ready for a semimonastic life if ever such a man could be. The question was, in the long run, whether his physical needs were to be satisfied in respectability or not; would Mathilde accept him again. And there was another question. At Rethel he endured—the word is not too strong—chastity, respectability and mental decorum—endured them mainly in the hope of winning Mathilde back. The last of the three was not the least agonizing to a man with a remarkable if erratic intellect. How long could he bear the musty common room conversation, the very graveyard of intellectual liberty?

In Paris that Exhibition summer he had got in touch with De

Sivry. That happy-go-lucky individual was free from moral judgments and welcomed him enthusiastically. In no time they had agreed to go into parnership again, De Sivry agreeing to write the music for an opera on the Temptation of Saint Anthony, Verlaine's libretto to follow Flaubert. This was slightly off the beaten track for the musical director of the Chat Noir but De Sivry would agree to anything for the sake of a good huddle over a drink. Not that Verlaine drank much but De Sivry could always drink enough for two.

Verlaine having salved his conscience with Saint Anthony used De Sivry as ambassador at rue Nicolet; he was to present a beautifully written copy of *Sagesse* to Mathilde with the author's compliments and with special verses written in honor of her and of little Georges; he was also to comment in passing on the astonishing moral reformation of the author and of his fitness for a second bout of married life.

This the "most brotherly" De Sivry did without visible effect. But by this time Verlaine had obtained an entrée; his son fell ill, he begged to be allowed to see him and was permitted. Twice he came, the second time finding himself alone with Madame Mauté. He seized the opportunity to speak of his changed character and his unchanged hopes. Madame Mauté, always well disposed toward him, did not rule out a reconciliation in time, perhaps a long time. Back at Rethel Verlaine began to correspond with her, sending gifts for Georges, reports on his own progress and stressing his unalterable devotion to Mathilde and her child.

Months passed and the new year of 1879 came and went with no more than cordial messages from the mother-in-law to keep the fire burning in the would-be husband and father. Verlaine was not the most patient of men and his plans were expected to mature with tropical rapidity. Madame Mauté's "years" might as well be centuries for all the use they were to him. But he could not believe her, or rather thought that he was cleverer than she. Would she ever have thought, for instance, of sending Delahaye as formal emissary, Delahaye, the correct, the most obviously respectable of his friends short of a priest? For that is what the by then feverishly impatient Verlaine did.

Delahaye was received courteously by Monsieur Mauté and explained his errand as tactfully as he could, painting the new Verlaine in bright colors and offering as tempting background the view of the rebuilt Hôtel de Ville in which a sober hard-working official not unknown to rue Nicolet sat at his desk from nine to five, rein-statement as civil servant being the latest of Verlaine's designs. But when Delahaye at last spoke of a possible reunion between husband and wife Monsieur Mauté turned the conversation.

Delahaye reported failure. Verlaine would not accept it; there had been no direct refusal. Go again, he begged. Delahaye went again and listened to muted praise for Verlaine's regeneration and a polite inability to see in what way it could concern Monsieur Mauté and his family. Again, demanded Verlaine. This third time the some-what weary Delahaye came straight to the point and was answered to the point: Mathilde would never live with Verlaine again, never.

For the moment he accepted the refusal but not the reasons for it, and for the rest of his life was to name her as the chief architect of his misfortunes. But his slide from grace was not as one might ex-pect rapid and calamitous; the power of religion and habit were still strong in him and before either could collapse absolutely he had found another reason and a more compelling one for sobriety and hope; yet not until his colleagues at the college had witnessed with astonishment and pain a change in the habits of the "pious gentle-man." He had long since made friends in the town; visiting them in the evenings he was invited to take a nightcap before leaving and, when he assented, to take a second. This he had invariably refused. Now he no longer refused. He began to sit on, arriving back at the college slightly fuddled. He also found the customary half-pint of wine insufficient for the day and augmented it, carrying from the town almost every day a bottle or two unskillfully concealed about his person. And these failing to quench the mounting thirst he began to slip out after lunch to a nearby café for a beer or two or three. Sometimes his afternoon class had to be dismissed, the master feeling "indisposed." Apart from the evening liqueur, he still drank nothing stronger than wine or beer, but the deterioration could not be hidden from so self-contained a community. Following the change in habits came change in manner, geniality often giving way to depression and even moroseness. The evening visits for coffee and a talk dropped away, he was avoided and before the summer term ended he was in-formed that the English course would be discontinued from the open-ing of the autumn term. This gentle method of dismissal meant that from August he was an unemployed man. At the end of that month he left Rethel for England. Not alone, however; there traveled with him one of the pupils, Lucien Létinois.

15.

LUCIEN

1879-1883

[1]

Lucien was then eighteen. He was the son of a peasant proprietor of Coulommes near Rethel who had sent his boy to the college in the hope that he would raise himself to the priesthood or into the teaching profession. Up to a point Lucien had fulfilled the hopes; his speech had lost its coarseness, he showed a fair intelligence, he had become moderately ambitious, and in person seemed far removed from the peasant, wearing a collar as though he had been born to it, eating delicately and talking with a certain eloquence.

He first held Verlaine's attention not by his virtues but because of a certain impudence in his tone that at once revived the memory of another boy. And color apart—for Lucien's eyes and hair were dark brown—there was resemblance to Rimbaud in this tall and slender youth who spoke with the slow *Ardennaise* burr, who looked his master straight in the eyes and answered him with a directness bordering on insolence. Lucien had not Rimbaud's dazzling good looks but he had a pleasant face, rounded and childlike, which like Rimbaud's contrasted violently with his manner and speech.

Later Verlaine spoke and wrote of him as his adopted son to replace the son he was forbidden to see. This was misleading. If Delahaye has dated his letters correctly he met Monsieur Mauté at least once that year and the old man asked why Verlaine had not been to visit Georges—a question which Verlaine, then in England, would find distinctly awkward to answer. It was true, however, that all hope of living with his real son had long since gone; true too that he came to regard Lucien as a son; but the first attraction was not chiefly to a man cut off from his kin but to a man who must love someone and love him at hand; that Verlaine should stress the point merely shows how bad a name the dog had been given.

The likeness to Rimbaud was decisive. Rimbaud was lost, Nouveau had soared into regions too rare for sinful men to follow; but here, Verlaine had no difficulty in persuading himself, was yet another Rimbaud to be trained, and a Rimbaud with principle, a Rimbaud who would not wreck either his life or the life of his patron-father but ennoble them. For Lucien in his rather sulky and argumentative fashion was a good boy to the point of priggishness. No Rimbaud here, for those frank brown eyes were alight with the faith of the Church. Of Rimbaud's extraordinary intelligence he had no trace and he had none of the gifts of Nouveau, but this did not worry Verlaine who on the whole must have felt relieved that for once he could more than hold his own. In fact, when Lucien first forced himself on the notice of a Verlaine benevolently expecting good behavior from all, he was not only impudent but on the lazy side and Verlaine was soon giving much of his spare time to coaching the boy for the *baccalauréat*.

What Lucien thought of Verlaine is difficult to determine. That he responded in some degree to the warm affection is certain; he would have been less than human had he not. That he was flattered by Verlaine's attentions is clear. For the rest, one has to judge by his actions and his later complaint that Verlaine, though extremely good to him, fussed too much and did harm to himself and his family. He also criticized the weaknesses which by that time had become obvious. But granted the weaknesses and the tiresomeness of the adulation heaped on a young man who preferred young company and preferably of the other sex, the remarks leave an unpleasant taste in the mouth and suggest that at heart Lucien was another Rimbaud; and this is what one would expect, opposites attracting each other once again. That he had not cast off the peasant mentality is plain, for when in spite of all Verlaine's not very skillful efforts he failed in his *baccalauréat*, he and his parents acceded gladly to everything that optimist suggested for his betterment and took all that the open-handed man had to offer.

Lucien's failure coincided with Verlaine's failure at rue Nicolet and subsequent dismissal from the college. Verlaine's regrets for this last were therefore less poignant than they might have been. As it happened he had already received news which made him regard the disasters with positive light-heartedness. The "hideous Anglophile" was tenacious in his friendships and since leaving England had corresponded with the Andrews' at Stickney, the friends at Boston and Remington at Bournemouth. He had just heard that his successor at Stickney was to leave at the end of the term and at once pictured Lucien in his place perfecting his English, gaining valuable teaching experience and enjoying the pleasantnesses of life with an English family in the English countryside. He put the matter to Lucien and his parents, glowingly no doubt, and carried off the boy in triumph to Boston.

For himself he had no fears, registering again with the London agency; and sure enough, by the beginning of the autumn term Lucien was installed as French master and tutor at Stickney and he had obtained a post in a school at Lymington.

This post was a little more profitable than his others, the Solent Collegiate School having some thirty pupils, and for a short time Verlaine was a truly happy man. He liked the little port with its view of the Isle of Wight where his god Tennyson lived; he liked his walks in that part of the New Forest which runs down to the outskirts of the town, seeing in it the equivalent of the Arden which had inspired his beloved Shakespeare; smoking long black cigars over the fire he passed congenial evenings discussing everything under the sun "until unheard-of hours" with his Scottish headmaster, William Murdock, and the football and cricket-playing Irish priest, Patrick O'Connell, and he enjoyed the Catholic services at the church up the road. Everything was delightfully old and delightfully English and he reveled in the belief that he was making himself a part of it. Even Murdock's sister, "a strict Presbyterian," accepted the foreign Catholic in her good-natured moments. Above all he loved Lucien's weekly letters.

Knowing Verlaine one can imagine his optimistic thoughts as he strolled through the forest or sat up in bed reading these letters; eternal child that he was, he had forgotten the ennui at Stickney, the boredoms of Bournemouth; he could see only Lucien well placed and protected, himself well liked and mildly prospering, a lifetime of steadily improving scholastic posts ahead of them in this calm, quiet country with its glorious literary tradition stirring his own muse, the temptress Paris relegated safety to strictly limited holiday visits.

[2]

The dream collapsed with horrid rapidity, collapsed too, a pleasant novelty, through no fault of the faulty Verlaine but through the weaknesses of the upright Lucien. His later letters of the year began to hint that all was not well at Stickney and he did not exaggerate: he was not happy in England, his English was poor, he was an indifferent teacher, he could not keep order and, not being liked (one suspects a lack of humor), was made wretched in class. Furthermore, like so many prim young men, he had an eye for girls and had committed the unforgivable sin of becoming involved, with whom and to what extent has never been discovered, with a local girl.

Just before Christmas the blow fell on a Verlaine already become uneasy; Lucien had not been reëngaged for the spring term, he was leaving for London on Christmas Day. Verlaine announced sadly to a puzzled Murdock that he would have to give up his post because of his mother's poor health; his one wish then and always was to protect Lucien's reputation. On Christmas morning he left what had probably been his happiest berth in England and left, one gathers, to the regret of all.

Of all days Christmas Day is the most wretched for the traveler in England; and as if to emphasize the cloud on Verlaine's spirits this particular day arrived at the height of a foggy spell. He reached London after a long drawn out journey of interminable stops on the line, a journey shrouded in Stygian gloom. London was in the grip of a pea-souper, rank in the nostrils, clutching at the throat, fouling all it touched, a blanket of murk through which street flares glimmered inadequately at the crossings.

Beset by anxiety Verlaine crawled in a cab to King's Cross. There he had to wait, every moment increasing his uneasiness, for the long delayed train to arrive. By the time Lucien stepped off the train he was in panic. He had known another Christmas Day in London seven years earlier and the forsaken feeling it implants in the foreigner. But then at least he could see the sky above him, had been in a home of sorts, had been invited to the Christmas meal, had been given an illusion of belonging. Now he and Lucien might have been on another planet for all the likeness London showed to its normal dingy self. They had nowhere to go, no friends, nothing, Verlaine having abjured Communism. About them everywhere, in every house families and friends were merrily eating and drinking; they had only the station bar. And there they had it out, an unhappy series of exchanges in keeping with the day, for they could not even take pleasure in each other. Lucien did not like England, never wished to see it again; that was the first blow. Worse, his confidence in his ability to teach, never very strong, had disappeared; some other future had to be foreseen for him. His tactlessness in the affair with the girl was likely to affect Verlaine's much prized friendships at Stickney. And Verlaine, unused to facing, let alone making decisions, had now to do both, with a heart filled with foreboding. In addition to his grief and embarrassment at the failure of Lucien he was distraught by personal fears. For he assumed that Lucien's fate was his fate. Every plan for the future had collapsed and a new life had to be made. He had to say good-bye to the safety of England where absinthe was unknown, where drinking of all kinds was made so difficult, where the very atmosphere of the country threw a protective mantle of respectability over one's every act, where the "not done" was a godsend to a Verlaine anxious to hold to his prison vows. He would be forced back on France, a France he loved but with reservations. Dreadful premonitions of ruin, of the collapse of his life haunted him.

He was not to forget that day; he was to remember everything, details which with the ordinary man would have been crowded out by emotion. But with that extraordinary response of the artist to every nuance of life, even in the midst of concern for others, the poet Verlaine was unconsciously noting the scene, his and Lucien's feelings along with the most trifling incidents, which he was to embody in the often misinterpreted O *l'odieuse obscurité*.

> *O l'odieuse obscurité*
> *Du jour le plus gai de l'année*
> *Dans la monstrueuse cité*
> *Où se fit notre destinée!*
>
> *Au lieu du bonheur attendu,*
> *Quel deuil profond, quelles ténèbres!*
> *J'en étais comme un mort, et tu*
> *Flottais en des pensers funèbres.*
>
> *La nuit croissait avec le jour*
> *Sur notre vitre et sur notre âme,*

Tel un pur, un sublime amour
Qu'eût étreint la luxure infâme;

Et l'affreux brouillard refluait
Jusqu'en la chambre où la bougie
Semblait un reproche muet
Pour quelque lendemain d'orgie.

Un remords de péché mortel
Serrait notre coeur solitaire . . .
Puis notre désespoir fut tel
Que nous oubliâmes la terre,

Et que, pensant au seul Jésus
Né rien que pour nous ce jour même,
Notre foi prenant le dessus
Nous éclaira du jour suprême.

—Bonne tristesse qu'aima Dieu!
Brume dont se voilait la Grâce,
Crainte que l'éclat de son feu
Ne fatiguât notre âme lasse.

Délicates attentions
D'une Providence attendrie! . . .
O parfois encore soyons
Ainsi tristes, âme chérie!

But what did Lucien wish to do? In a few months he would be
called up for military service and, unless steps were taken to prevent
it, would be due to serve for five years. The answer seemed to
lie first in farming as the one job that could be carried on by others
in his absence; and after some weeks of discussion in the little house
at Coulommes he decided that he would be a farmer. Verlaine, recalling idyllically his holidays in the Pas-de-Calais and the Ardennes,
and ready to try anything to soothe the boy's wounded vanity,
promptly declared that he too would like nothing better.

The parents' farm at Coulommes was small and in the eyes of
Lucien and Verlaine unworthy of the scholar of Rethel College.
Verlaine had just received a legacy from a paternal aunt at Bouillon;
with the help of his mother he bought a large farm at Juniville ten

miles away, bought it in the name of Lucien's father and installed the
parents in it. Madame Verlaine completed the family when she
could get away from Arras.

There remained the shadow of the five years' military service. A
payment of fifteen hundred francs and the passing of a not too
difficult examination would reduce the term to one year. Verlaine
borrowed the money from his mother and gave Lucien the necessary
tuition in the evenings.

The farm was not a success. Verlaine's efforts to play the farmer,
wearing his battered top hat and raincoat of English days, led to the
neighbors' contemptuous comments that he was an English gentleman
amusing himself with a serious job. He liked the animals and, with
sentimental memories of Taffy and his sugar lumps, spoiled them
hopelessly. He took enormous pride in watching the tall straight
figure of Lucien behind a plough, wielding a scythe, threshing, cutting and binding faggots, work in which he lent a hand occasionally
but without conspicuous success. He bought a dogcart in which he
and Lucien inspected the farm, paid visits or merely went for a spin.
For the rest, he enjoyed the few obvious pleasures, the harvesting
par excellence, and the mugs of beer that ended the day. Farming,
he discovered, gave one a thirst; he began to drink more. When rain
fell or the fields were damp his rheumatism, legacy of the siege, reappeared and he sat at home reading and writing.

That summer Nouveau visited the farm. In Paris a few weeks
earlier Verlaine, still trying to find a publisher for *Sagesse*, had paused
by a kiosk for a little cheap reading—a weakness of his, this—when his
shoulder was slapped and the familiar husky voice cried, "Here's the
man who can never resist reading the newspapers! This light man
fascinated by useless, worldly things!" The quarrel was done with, as
though it had never been, and Nouveau had to inspect the new
venture, make his home there if he wished. Come! At once! The
Ministry of Public Education, where he then worked side by side with
Izambard, Rimbaud's old master, and the young De Maupassant,
put unreasonable obstacles before this ideal grouping of good friends
and Catholics; holidays were holidays, however, and Nouveau arrived
only to be tormented by toothache. This kept him from the fields
but not from his crayons; to everybody's delight he announced his
intention of making a pastel of Lucien. The pastel done, the Létinois
father and mother gazed uncomprehendingly at the auburn hair, the
royal beaked nose: "But his hair is brown, his nose straight!"

Nouveau reproached them brusquely: these peasants and their craze for outward signs! "You are wrong to want him brown," he said severely: the soul of Lucien, that was what he conveyed. And he had, strangely enough, caught the expression of the eyes, the straight frank look. Verlaine was to revere this pastel; for the moment it remained, Nouveau apart, something of a joke. As was the farm that lively summer, reduced in Verlaine's eyes to a pleasant background for visitors; in the future when Lucien, the bogey of the Army removed, would give it his full attention, the farm would become a profitable venture.

Old Létinois, the one man who might have handled the farm with advantage, remained overawed by its size and the need to employ labor; he had made the change too late from his own compact *campagne*. The boy, too grand perhaps for farming, too much preoccupied by the threat of the Army, or succumbing too often to the lure of trips in the dogcart, seemed never to get a grip on the work. Then he took and passed his examination and late in the summer of 1880 was posted to the Artillery at Rheims.

His departure was the virtual end of the farm though his father struggled on at a task beyond his strength or experience. Verlaine soon lost the last remnants of a never more than amiable acquiescence in a pastime and followed Lucien to Rheims. There he got himself some sort of work in a school in order to see what he could of Lucien, to see and admire, and eventually to write, somewhat fatuously, proud-fatherly panegyrics on the handsome erect soldier sitting his steed and wearing his uniform with such inimitable aplomb.

Lucien accepted the compliments but was far from returning them wholeheartedly. Criticisms had begun at the farm. Lucien had the usual self-righteous intolerance of youth for the frailties of his elders; he chided the venerable-looking Verlaine with his great ivory dome supported by thin clusters of side hairs: why did he sit about so much before a mug of beer? it was neither wise nor dignified. And at Rheims there was Verlaine waiting at the café for him to come off duty, a Verlaine sometimes slightly thick in speech. He had had to wait so long; that was no excuse; Lucien was grateful for all that Verlaine had done for him and was doing, but . . . "But my boy!" A stiff forgiveness would come, Verlaine promising amendment over and over again, at Rheims and, later, at Châlons-sur-Marne whence Lucien was moved and which Verlaine visited whenever he was able.

[3]

When Lucien was in the Army, in the autumn of 1881, *Sagesse* was at last published, Verlaine's first book of verse to get into print for six years. The text had been completed in the summer of the previous year by the fine "*Vous reviendrez bientôt,*" which Verlaine dashed off indignantly after the expulsion of the Jesuits from France at the end of June, and by the pathetic "*Et j'ai revu,*" written after a further visit to Georges which he had made as soon as he could get down to Paris. The tone of this poem suggests a prevision that the glimpse of his son might be the last, as it was; the visit and even more the two poems in *Sagesse* pleading strongly for Mathilde's forgiveness—"*Faites le geste qui pardonne!*" one ended—showed that he continued to hope for reconciliation with his wife. They showed too that he did not place too much store on the permanence of the relationship with Lucien though he would face such a thought only in poetry.

When in Paris, acting probably on the hint of Lepelletier who was becoming an editor of some importance, he showed the poems to Victor Palme, the publisher of Catholic books. Palme accepted them, but only on payment of six hundred francs, so that in this matter Verlaine at thirty-seven, with a body of imperishable poetry behind him, was back where he had begun at twenty-two. He paid, of course, and when he had received the proofs announced the forthcoming publication to his old friend Valade who responded; a correspondence which had been broken since Verlaine left Paris with Rimbaud was taken up afresh.

Verlaine affixed a preface to the book breathing the overconfidence of a man who has seen the light; an unfortunate tone when he was on the verge of returning to error and one that failed to appease those who had blackballed his earlier work because of his association with Rimbaud. His moral critics now dubbed him hypocrite. Some of his few friends regretted his change of tone: Mallarmé, a staunch admirer, said that he was disappointed not to read another *Fêtes galantes*—a compliment to this work but not truly perceptive since Verlaine, most subjective of poets, could not be expected to repeat an objective tour de force. Others, Lepelletier

nd Blémont for example, did their best but it was not enough.
His enemies either ignored the new book or made rude remarks
bout its author. "What, isn't the fellow dead yet?" exclaimed
Leconte de Lisle. Most reviewers passed it over. A despairing effort
by Verlaine to print his own review of "this remarkable book" was
disqualified at the starting post. Sales were negligible.

One scarcely needs to repeat that the failure, as it then seemed,
was undeserved, this being true of every book Verlaine had published,
he first only excepted; *Sagesse* is an uneven book but it contains
one or two of the finest poems he was ever to write. But reviewing
then was concerned more than now with the standing of the author
and Verlaine had no standing, almost all his old friends gone, his
visits to Paris few and fugitive, and no store of capital to make a
how when he did return. Nina might have helped him—he had
called on her occasionally in the last few years—but Nina was no
longer a power in the literary world, only a mental wreck who,
believing herself dead, played extraordinary music on the pianoforte.
He had no way of getting back to notice and favor beyond the
publishing of a book—and this in Paris as in London was not enough.

Disappointed but not dismayed, Verlaine turned to another form
of literature. Although the bulk of the poems in *Sagesse* had been
written years earlier he had not the material to make another book
of a kind that he considered publishable. He had the name of a
new book—*Amour*—but not enough poems. As far as poetry was
concerned, the period at Rethel had been two years taken out of
his life; he wrote nothing of value there. He therefore wrote his
first prose work, *Voyage en France par un Français*.

This could not find a publisher and one cannot wonder. Verlaine
was capable of writing a pleasant witty prose but to do this he had
to have a subject in keeping with the real man; the moment insincerity or effort creeps in he and his reader are lost. They were both
lost here; the *Voyage* was in tone rather like the unfortunate preface
to *Sagesse*, and in manner the most prosy of documents. Nothing
less edifying has ever existed than Verlaine deliberately being edifying, and in this book he excelled himself; it reads like the work of an
excessively hypocritical Colonel Blimp lecturing the youth of France
on the way it should think and behave.

Turning with a slight shudder from this book one asks how
a great poet came to labor over it. Its raison d'être is found in
Lucien's pained reproaches; it was to be proof at once to Lucien

and to himself that he knew, no man better, the rules of the good
life even if very occasionally and by hazard he chanced to break
one of them. It was also a further, and futile, effort to impress the
world with the picture of a reformed spirit who asked no more
than that an appreciative public buy his wares; but this, since the
book did not appear, they could not do. Of its effect on Lucien
who no doubt read the manuscript, we can judge only by aftereffects
which seem to have been absolutely nil. He was prig enough with
out this invitation to priggishness.

[4]

By the time Lucien returned to Juniville from the Army the farm
was as good as gone. For some months well into 1882 the hopeless
struggle was carried on; then the Létinois, father, mother and son,
moved out hurriedly and into nearby Belgium, apparently but
unnecessarily alarmed by mounting debts. Verlaine put the farm
up for sale (eventually getting back about half the purchase price
which he returned to his mother—the one example on record of
Madame Verlaine receiving money paid out) and took rooms in
Paris in the rue de la Roquette. From there, his first regular
Parisian address for eleven years, he made efforts to help Lucien
and himself; he applied through Lepelletier to be readmitted to
the Hôtel de Ville, and through Delahaye for a school post for
Lucien.

This was in October. The first application, though promising
well for a week or two, was hopeless; the Communards and their
sympathizers might by then be regarded indulgently by a government feeling itself secure, but this did not mean that renegades
were to regain official positions; this final effort to return to the
life respectable was denied him; his application was refused.

He had better luck with Delahaye, and a somewhat reluctant
Lucien was placed as master in the semimilitary institution Esnault
at Boulogne-sur-Seine and his parents were established in the suburb
of Ivry close by. Verlaine, retaining his rooms in Paris for the use
of himself and his mother (who had gone back to her little house
in Arras), took a room near the school in a hotel in the rue du
Parchamp. Almost every evening he met Lucien, gave him dinner
and, when the weather was obliging, walked with him in the Bois
de Boulogne, listening to the recital of daily events in the school,

ympathizing with the young man's ambitions (which did not
est at school), discussing the marriage he foresaw as inevitable
hough quite unable to visualize a girl good enough for the peerless
reature, and even venturing into philosophical discussions which
ιe and Lucien must have found difficult at times to sustain. Their
ιne strong link was religious belief but even in this it seems im-
ιrobable that the critical and modern Lucien could listen without
ιward reservations to the childlike faith of Verlaine who believed
vithout so much as a quiver of incredulity that his still infant soul
vas being guarded by the Holy Mother, Father and Son—a belief
hat he was to express with touching beauty in his poem "*Prière du
Matin.*"

Lucien no doubt wondered, as a severe and rather stupid young
nan would wonder, how Verlaine reconciled such a faith with the
ailings of his everyday life. For inevitably the talk sometimes dwelt
ιn the use to which Verlaine was putting his spare time; what did
ιe do with himself while he waited for Lucien? Was there not
omething feeble in the thought of a man hanging about day by day
'or the sake of a few hours' conversation at night? Lucien's feelings
oward Verlaine had become cooler since the failure of the farm
ιnd the uprooting of his parents: "Better if we had never met him,"
ιe said privately to Delahaye. But he was a conscientious boy aware
ιf Verlaine's goodness; grateful too, no doubt; greedy, it may be;
ιe continued to see his patron regularly, to talk freely, to be affection-
ιte—one could not dislike Verlaine whatever resentment one felt.
3ut critical he certainly was.

And it was true that Verlaine seemed to be slipping; he took no
:are of himself, looked seedy in his old raincoat and battered hat,
ιnd he was drinking. He continued to keep clear of absinthe but the
ιeers followed each other down his throat with alarming ease.

He was not helped in this by his one regular outing every week;
ιn Friday evening he took the horsecar from Auteuil to Saint-Sulpice
ιnd walked to the Café Voltaire when he found one or two old
:ompanions who would drink and talk with him. There was Valade
ιnd, thanks to Valade, there was Verlaine's "Great Albert" shaking
ιis hand again, all ill-feeling gone. There too were Blémont, Dierx
ιnd Mendès, a tarnished Apollo nearing forty but tossing golden
ιair in the manner of the sixties, talking as glibly and with a finger
ιn every pie except that of the *Parnasse* which he was now busily
ιenying to have been a movement. He did not object to Verlaine,

he could scarcely afford to in face of his own life, but he missed
the poet then as he had missed him in Parnassian days.

Looking about the Voltaire one almost received the impression
of time standing still: Mérat—Rimbaud gone, to Cyprus, to Aden
to Abyssinia the vague reports comfortingly said—had his head in
air as ever, cigar-puffing, stick-tapping, flinging provocative remark
into every silence as if he had just climbed the corkscrew stairs a
Lemerre's; Valade, black beard a little fuller, but his old benign
self, as shy as if he were hesitating on the threshold of a De Ricard
soiree; Mendès, flashily and aggressively youthful as if he were
presiding at one of his teas in the rue Douai; Dierx, gentle, pensive
and quiet as he had been in Nina's garden night after night; the
fair, plumpish Blémont as smooth and comfortable as on that first
meeting at Banville's. Only when the eye fell on Verlaine did time
rush on; crazily, for Verlaine looked as far beyond his years as the
others looked below them, shining bald head as venerable as the
slits of eyes were youthful. Gone the monocle, the smart stick, the
frock coat and dainty cravat; in their place moved a shabby old
ruin not yet forty years of age.

He contrasted so oddly with the company that a stranger would
have been puzzled to explain his presence. It was not entirely
not mainly because old friends had relented; they remained conscious
of the years between and what had happened in those years; their
attitude to the reformed reprobate was not far from condescension
But there were others present at the Voltaire on these Friday
evenings; there was a young Greek with a dead white face and
great black mustaches, Jean Moréas his adopted name; there was a
provincial youth, Charles Morice, dark and handsome too but in
more conventional style, dressed always in worn but correct and ever
dandified frock coat and striped trousers; and there was a sprinkling
of young men who broadly followed the lead of these two. These
youthful poets were unconcerned with the morals or the past
behavior of this seedy character; they questioned him, read their
poems to him, they were not far from deferential; but not the
deference of youth for age—this was given, amusingly enough, to
the ever-young ex-Parnassian friends of Verlaine. For as Mendès,
whose presence showed him to be on the scent of novelty again,
had looked back twenty years earlier to Banville, Leconte de Lisle,
Hugo and Baudelaire, so Moréas and Morice were fumblingly

experimenting with a new theory based on the work of their elders. The theory had not arrived but it was in the air and their attitude and words made clear that it would be based not on the Parnassians, not on the work of Mérat, Valade or Dierx, not even on the perseveringly youthful and friendly Mendès, but on the two men who in their very different ways had been found wanting by their contemporaries—Mallarmé and Verlaine.

For *Sagesse*, flat though it had fallen, had been noticed by one or two youthful eyes, and Verlaine in the closing stages at Juniville, in the rue de la Roquette and in the hotel bedroom at Boulogne-sur-Seine had done more than swill beer and look fondly on Lucien, he had been writing poetry and this poetry was beginning to appear in print. In June, to celebrate the resumption of relations with Mérat, he wrote one of his most sparkling sonnets, sparkling like a movement from Mozart with its wit and profundity.

> *Et nous voilà très doux à la bêtise humaine,*
> *Lui pardonnant vraiment et même un peu touchés*
> *De sa candeur extrême et des torts très légers,*
> *Dans le fond, qu'elle assume et du train qu'elle mène.*
>
> *Pauvres gens que les gens! Mourir pour Célimène.*
> *Epouser Angélique ou venir de nuit chez*
> *Agnès et la briser, et tous les sots péchés,*
> *Tel est l'Amour encor plus faible que la Haine!*
>
> *L'Ambition, l'Orgueil, des tours dont vous tombez,*
> *Le Vin, qui vous imbibe et vous tord imbibés,*
> *L'Argent, le Jeu, le Crime, un tas de pauvres crimes!*
>
> *C'est pourquoi, mon très cher Mérat, Mérat et moi,*
> *Nous étant dépouillés de tout banal émoi,*
> *Vivons dans un dandysme épris des seules Rimes!*

The following month was a landmark; for the first time in ten years his work was printed in a Paris periodical. That bare statement does not convey the full magnitude of the landmark, and it is unlikely that Verlaine, used to the vagaries and bankruptcies of publishers and the fleeting appearance of literary journals, could have guessed what was in store for him. Yet this unpropitious

moment was to show itself as the turning point of his literary
fortunes. For the owner of this new periodical was not in the
ordinary run of publishers; Léon Vanier, an unprepossessing little
man of thirty-six, was a tradesman trying his hand at publishing
a realist but, strange to say, a man of literary discernment too. He
had read one of the few circulating copies of *Sagesse*, he had then
read everything of Verlaine's he could find, and he at once opened
his periodical to him. He did more, he offered to publish Verlaine'
poetry in book form and to pay for it.

Good fortune when it comes, comes in good measure. In Novem
ber the same journal *Paris Moderne* printed more of Verlaine'
poems, this time including the *Art poétique* he had written in prison
at Mons. At first Morice at least protested. *Art poétique*, he
complained in a letter written under a pen name to *La Nouvelle Rive
gauche*, preached a rigidity of poetic form and a contempt for rhyme
that was deplorable coming from an established poet. Verlaine
replying, explained, "We're really of the same mind in essentials
that's why I continue the discussion: we both want impeccable
rhymes, correct French and above all good poetry no matter what
the trimmings are." The discussion continued further; the critical
Morice gave way and more than gave way, he became one of
Verlaine's first disciples. Verlaine was invited to contribute to the
journal in which the battle had been fought, and *Art poétique* was
accepted as a battle cry by the young men dissatisfied with past and
present poetry; the news of it circulated slowly but with effect
And the bewildered Verlaine, who had merely thrown off the poem
as the expression of a particular mood, found that he began once
more to have entree to the avant-garde journals—his poems appeared
the next year in *La Nouvelle Rive gauche*, *Le Chat Noir* and
Lutèce—and that he was received at the Voltaire with a certain
flattering interest as if a moldering scarecrow had suddenly put
forth a flower. There was, of course, little money in all this but
there was gratification for a friendly soul as well as amusement for
one who regarded "movements" with a secret grimace and rude
aside; the thought of any poem of his providing an anthem for
a new school was an excellent joke.

However, there he was, a man with a publisher, at the Voltaire
and in company and very glad of it, a man who put all his hopes
not in this swing of the pendulum but in the young man he met,
walked with and talked with almost every evening, whose brilliant

future was always in his mind. His own poetry, yes, fine; but Lucien, that was another thing!

But if Verlaine's heart sent his sense of proportion toppling, his good angel had other plans. He did not enjoy the Voltaire for long; after two months at school Lucien, who had been looking around for something that suited him better, found a job with good prospects in a factory at La Chapelle. He began work at once and Verlaine took his place at the school until the end of the term.

The evening meetings continued whenever Verlaine could leave the school; he would wait at the foot of the stairs at Auteuil Station for Lucien to arrive in the train from La Chapelle:

> *Ame, te souvient-il, au fond du paradis,*
> *De la gare d'Auteuil et des trains de jadis*
> *T'amenant chaque jour, venus de La Chapelle?*
> *Jadis déjà! Combien pourtant je me rappelle*
> *Mes stations au bas du rapide escalier*
> *Dans l'attente de toi, sans pouvoir oublier*
> *Ta grâce en descendant les marches, mince et leste*
> *Comme un ange le long de l'échelle céleste,*
> *Ton sourire amical ensemble et filial,*
> *Ton serrement de main cordial et loyal,*
> *Ni tes yeux d'innocent, doux mais vifs, clairs et sombres,*
> *Qui m'allaient droit au coeur et pénétraient mes ombres.*
> *Après les premiers mots de bonjour et d'accueil,*
> *Mon vieux bras dans le tien, nous quittions cet Auteuil,*
> *Et sous les arbres pleins d'une gente musique,*
> *Notre entretien était souvent métaphysique.*
> *O tes forts arguments, ta foi du charbonnier!*
> *Non sans quelque tendance, ô si franche! à nier,*
> *Mais si vite quittée au premier pas du doute!*
> *Et puis nous rentrions, plus que lents, par la route*
> *Un peu des écoliers, chez moi, chez nous plutôt,*
> *Y déjeuner de rien, fumailler vite et tôt,*
> *Et dépêcher longtemps une vague besogne.*

> *Mon pauvre enfant, ta voix dans le Bois de Boulogne!*

"Mon pauvre enfant," he said in the poem; for this pleasure too, this breath of life one could say, was to be short-lived. The school term ended and Verlaine went back to his hotel, his beers, his poetry, his Fridays at the Voltaire. Then toward the end of March of the new year, 1883, Lucien fell ill and was taken to the Hôpital de la Pitié at Ivry. He had caught typhoid fever. Verlaine never left his bedside, unable, refusing to believe the inevitable. On April 7 Lucien died.

16.

COLLAPSE

1883-1885

[1]

The death of Lucien led directly though not immediately to the collapse of Verlaine's remaining hopes of leading a respectable life and to the production of one of his greatest series of poems. The elegy *"Lucien Létinois"* was written over the years that followed, ending in 1888. It consisted of twenty-four poems. A late addition, and by no means the least masterly, was written to the memory of Elisa; the rest covered the time, less than four years, that Verlaine had known Lucien.

The elegy was based, in theory, on "In Memoriam"; in fact, there is only the slightest resemblance, and that technical, between the two. Verlaine claimed in 1888 that "this series, sorrowful and I dare to believe moving, is in any event unique in our literature." The claim was correct; *"Lucien Létinois"* expresses a passion of love and of loss that one scarcely expects from Verlaine (regard, for instance, the poems recalling the dreadful days in the hospital as the helpless Verlaine watched the boy slowly die) but does so in a manner unmistakably Verlainean; it is restrained, unpretentious and simple and—perhaps the most marked of all its virtues—although a few of the poems tend to the trivial—there is throughout the whole series not one obviously "heart-rending" word put in after obvious searching by the poet.

With Verlaine, examples are always more effective than argument. One or two of the poems have already been quoted. The poem below is the most passionate; the reader can decide for himself how much is artistry consciously sought and feeling unavoidably felt:

J'ai la fureur d'aimer. Mon coeur si faible est fou.
N'importe quand, n'importe quel et n'importe où,
Qu'un éclair de beauté, de vertu, de vaillance
Luise, il s'y précipite, il y vole, il s'y lance,
Et, le temps d'une étreinte, il embrasse cent fois
L'être ou l'objet qu'il a poursuivi de son choix;
Puis, quand l'illusion a replié son aile,
Il revient triste et seul bien souvent, mais fidèle,
Et laissant aux ingrats quelque chose de lui,
Sang ou chair. Mais, sans plus mourir dans son ennui,
Il embarque aussitôt pour l'île des Chimères
Et n'en apporte rien que des larmes amères
Qu'il savoure, et d'affreux désespoirs d'un instant,
Puis rembarque.

If the reader is able to detach himself from the feeling and the expression of that feeling he may protest that these great and moving poems are built on sand since Lucien was not the heroic figure he appeared in Verlaine's agonized recollection. For the purpose of the poems, however, Lucien as he appeared to Verlaine is the criterion and not Lucien as he was. But in view of Verlaine's future it is necessary to be clear about what it was in Lucien that really attracted him and which resulted in this movingly controlled outpouring of grief. The superficial resemblance to Rimbaud was nothing but bait; the real attraction of Lucien was his monumental ordinariness. Handsome, yes; high-minded, yes; but the heart of his appeal was the ordinary, the safe, which every look, every word of that young man proclaimed. Verlaine could scarcely sustain the loss of anybody he loved, as his collapse after the death of Elisa demonstrated. But he had been young and hopeful when Elisa died, with friends, money, ambitions; the death of Lucien left him with the feeling that he had been finally deserted by the norm he yearned after so intensely and hopelessly all his life. His last example and stay was gone. Mathilde, hearing that he had begun to drink again and was without regular employment, and in any event disapproving of the intimacy with Lucien, had on the insistence of Monsieur Mauté refused to let him see Georges again. After his fight of eight years, resisting every natural inclination, he was left entirely outside the respectable—no job at the Hôtel de Ville, no wife, no child, no Lucien and with no one whom he could at once love and lean on.

Collapse after that could not long be delayed. One is only surprised that it did not follow at once. He had not lost his faith, however; he was never to lose it, and he cried again and again for strength in poignant verse:

> *Et puis, bon pasteur, paissez mon coeur:*
> *Il est seul désormais sur la terre,*
> *Et l'horreur de rester solitaire*
> *Le distrait en l'étrange langueur*
> *D'un espoir qui ne veut pas se taire,*
> *Et l'appelle aux prés qu'il ne faut pas.*
> *Donnez-lui de n'aller qu'en vos pas.*

He had not lost his faith but he had lost what was more necessary to a sense of proportion, his sense of humor, and the company he kept did not help him to regain it. After Lucien's funeral at Ivry he went back to his rooms in the rue de la Roquette where he was joined by his mother. She had never been good for him and she was not so then. She was over seventy and although she remained active her mind, which had never been normal, was obviously failing. She was embarrassingly skittish with the men who called to see Verlaine, insisting playfully, for instance, in the midst of one of Moréas' dramatic declamations of Baudelaire, that he "shut his eyes and open his mouth" into which she immediately plunged a stick of barley sugar "for his sore throat." The barley sugar had become a symbol of her approval as had also, to the earnest young visitors' distress, her invitations to join in a game of ball.

Verlaine's main prop in these unhappy days—a self-constituted prop—was Nouveau. But Nouveau was no longer the gay and charming companion, Nouveau had gone from vision to vision and was by that time a rabid Catholic, the man who a few years later was to dash from a drawing class, jump into a fiacre, get out in the center of the city, stop the traffic, sink onto his knees in the middle of the street and kiss the paving blocks. The police then took him off to a mental home, but in 1883 he roamed freely about Paris when not in his office or not in the mood for an office; not mad in the committable sense but distinctly unbalanced. One delusion was that his mission in life was to rescue Verlaine from alcohol, a worthy aim no doubt if carried out with tact but defeating its object when pressed home with the kind of ferocious wild-eyed insistence that he called sincerity. He was scarcely a good advertisement for sobriety. Verlaine, obliging to the last and indeed grateful for Nouveau's

particular brand of affection, countered by limiting himself to one
glass in the evangelist's company with no more than an upward
crease of the forked eyebrows; Nouveau gone or his attention distracted by a flighty Madame Verlaine anxious to dispense sweetmeats
or play ball with her favorite visitor, Verlaine would be off and
around the corner in a twinkling to make up for lost time. He
still confined himself to beer; after enough of it he found that his
shattering sense of loss subsided in a kind of warm mist, his bowel-
weakening fear of lovelessness blurred into a general affection for
all who stood at the bar or sat before their glasses at the round
tables.

But always the effect wore off, and there was his mother, there
was Nouveau, there were frightening thoughts beating at his brain.
One couldn't drink all the time; not only Nouveau's stern and
watchful eye but the shade of a sad, reproving Lucien forbade it.
The few visitors reminded him that he was not altogether forgotten,
the magazines were slowly opening their pages to him, the poems
would be written, nothing could stop that self-explanatory flow; but
his main reaction to these hints of a more promising future was to
see them as mockery rather than comfort.

Paris suddenly became unbearable. Then came the thought, how
obvious, that he could be with Lucien as nowhere else in the house
in which the boy had been born and reared. Moreover, to buy the
house, which old Létinois still owned, would be to recompense the
parents for the dislocation of their life: Lucien would approve. The
thought was scarcely in his head than it became a devouring necessity. His mother—was ever mother of a famous man so unfailingly
unfortunate in her advice and encouragement?—enthusiastically
seconded the plan; her son, no longer a pariah, had the freedom of
the cafés again; to sit and talk was to drink; at Coulommes, com-
panionless and untempted, he would work soberly all day long. So
she reasoned if reasoned is the word.

By July the house was theirs and they had put Paris aside. For
some months—until the end of the year—the unpromising gamble
seemed to have succeeded; Verlaine drank his luncheon and dinner
beer with conscious rectitude, with measured face he walked top-
hatted about the countryside, he wrote and revised poems for *Jadis
et Naguère* as he had decided to name his next book, he dreamed
nostalgically about the dead Lucien and his life under that roof:

here he had been born, here learned his lessons, here eaten his frugal meals, here slept and prayed.

Holy ground indeed; and Verlaine, incurable idealist in emotional moments, may well have thought that God had answered his prayer, that the miracle had happened and that, breathed over by Lucien's pure spirit, he would end his days in peace and useful labor. But Verlaine could never be satisfied by a spirit; fleshly he was and fleshly would remain. The explanation of these quiet and fruitful months is found, the charm of novelty apart, in a fresh hope which had entered that unpractical heart. For, incredible though it may seem, he still could not take his mind from the possibility of a reunion with Mathilde. There is a parallel here with the persistent efforts which Paul Gauguin was then making to persuade his wife to rejoin him. Both men were unrealistic, they would not admit incompatibility, but both tried again and again for years to renew a marriage broken on the surface by themselves.

But Gauguin was a strong man; Verlaine, though not the weakling he sometimes appears, was at the mercy of his feelings as Gauguin was not. So, Lucien dead and the isolation of Coulommes beginning to prey on a companionable spirit, his mind turned once more to rue Nicolet. Mathilde had objected to further meetings between Georges and his father, a cruel ban yet perhaps not utterly without a gleam of reason. But what mother could object to her son associating with a father who led an honorable and diligent country life in his own house in his native Ardennes? And, one thought following another with what the bodily starved Verlaine regarded as logic, what wife could or ought to resist a rapprochement with a husband so solidly placed, a man moreover who now had his own publisher, a following and a future?

The correspondence with Madame Mauté was resumed; she remained kind and guardedly hopeful, she alone of the family having some notion of the man her daughter had married and some pride in the poet. He began to imagine wife and child established contentedly in the house at Coulommes. And had he set eyes on her as she then was, the poor man would never have spent an easy night, for Mathilde had not become less desirable physically; the "hint of plumpness" marked by Verlaine's expert eye at that first interview had come to pass. A brief glimpse of her is seen at this time at one of the first gatherings of Zutistes which Cros, making use of the old name, had formed with the comprehensive aim of "nothing for use, everything for pleasure." One Thursday evening Mathilde, a formidable young woman patronizing the "poets, musicians, writers, artists" gathered under the wing of *"le premier des monologuistes"* as their president styled himself, walked with assurance into the "maison de bois" in the rue de Rennes, "a piquant brunette, well covered, with superb shoulders, large eyes missing nothing and her nose in the air," to sing the songs of De Sivry.

It is impossible to say how Mathilde's mind would have run if she had been left to make her own decisions. Had she been able to see into the not so distant future, a matter of five or six years only, her view of taking up life with Verlaine again might have been much changed. As it was she obeyed her father, how willingly will never be known. And since Monsieur Mauté was the power in the home, only the presence of her mother preserved a slight element of uncertainty. Early in the new year of 1884 the last element of doubt disappeared. Madame Mauté had a stroke. Paralyzed, she lay on rue Nicolet slowly dying.

The news shattered the unnatural calm in which Verlaine had been living for months. He no doubt, being poet before man if they can ever be distinguished from each other, meditated at once the elegy he was to complete on the tenth anniversary of Madame Mauté's death:

> *Vous fûtes bonne et douce en nos tristes tempêtes.*
> *—L'Esprit et la Raison parmi nos fureurs bêtes,—*
> *Et si l'on vous eût crue au temps qu'il le fallait*
> *On se fût épargné que de chagrin plus laid,*
> *Encor que douloureux! Puis, lorsque sonna l'heure*
> *Définitive où d'espérer n'était qu'un leurre*
> *Dorénavant, du moins vous fîtes pour le mieux*
> *Quant à tel modus vivendi moins odieux*
> *Que cette guerre sourde ou cette paix armée*
> *Qui succéda l'affreux conflit.*
> > *Soyez aimée*
> *Et vénérée, ô morte inopportunément!* . . .

A beautiful poem; but the *"morte inopportunément"* insofar as Verlaine applied it to himself was unreal. He did not dare to think so, however, and, temporarily freed from despair and the bout of drinking in which he had drowned it, busied himself with the

enlistment of new allies. He first begged Cros' wife, a good-humored
Scandinavian who liked him, to plead his cause. She fared no better
than Delahaye four years earlier. Then he asked his disciple Moréas
to intervene, a strange and unlikely choice which would have
occurred to none other than Verlaine. The reception given to this
excessively proud young man rebounded onto his hero, admiration
thereafter being mingled with contempt.

The immediate result of these rebuffs, which seemed final enough,
was absolute collapse of the flimsy structure of the country life.
Verlaine had never been accepted at Coulommes, appearing to his
neighbors as at Juniville as a man living "out of his class"; what had
he to do with farms and fields, with solitude, when terror gripped
him, when he saw himself loveless and unwanted? Yet there he was,
master of a house he did not want, looked at askance by the people,
his every movement known, his prayers unheard. God had forsaken
him: he rushed to that conclusion; he was unworthy of Lucien;
home, child, wife, the bourgeois boons of the weekly pay envelope,
a bus to the door every evening, the courteously lifted hat, all forever
denied him.

Desperate for company he consorted with the only people who
would grant him more than a frigid word, the riffraff of Coulommes;
desperate for forgetfulness he drank with them, spreading his money
freely abroad until he reached home penniless but beyond reach of
self-criticism. There followed black looks from neighbors, protesta-
tions from a frightened mother, more drink, more forgetfulness. The
round was broken by fits of repentance, by a visit to Paris and by
composition, the muse as usual flourishing in wretchedness.

It is faintly possible that, helped by his writing and his conscience,
he might have pulled himself together, but two events in the
summer demoralized him still further. In June Valade died suddenly.
He was only forty-three, one of Verlaine's oldest friends and one
of the few who had stuck to him in trouble.

Verlaine, shattered, sought his usual consolation and the next
month, before he could get back to an approximation of normality,
Nina died insane in a mental home. He had not seen much of her
recently—her mind had been unhinged for some time before she
died—but he remembered her soirees nostalgically. And she, like
Valade, had defended him through the years of isolation.

He came down to her funeral. There he met Hector de Callias,
faultlessly dressed and sober for the first time in many years. The

effort exhausted De Callias and, the ceremony over, he trailed through the bars of Paris accompanied by Verlaine discussing wives, discovering belatedly the perfection of Nina and, by contrast, the vileness of Mathilde. Verlaine, meeting sympathy, lashed himself into a factitious hatred. It was then, it appears, that he first broke the vow made in the prison at Mons ten years earlier and drank absinthe.

Once admitted, the sorceress did not lose her grasp a second time. At Coulommes, Verlaine moved from one drinking bout to another until he became a byword. His violence alarmed Madame Verlaine so much that in the new year of 1885 she took shelter with the next-door neighbors, a grocer and his wife, who had many times counseled her to discipline Verlaine by withholding money and, that failing, had urged her to leave him.

The drink and the violence were the result of a crowning blow. At the end of 1884 the disestablishment of the Church of France, so long and so bitterly debated, became a fact; and on the first day of the new year divorce was legalized. Mathilde was one of the earliest applicants and was one of the first to receive the decree. On February 9 the divorce was pronounced and Verlaine was ordered to pay a *"pension alimentaire"* of twelve-hundred francs.

As a Catholic Verlaine did not recognize divorce; but morally and spiritually sound though he might feel this attitude to be (and he was to make great play of it in future years), from a practical view even he could sense an absolute end to hope. The affair was finished. Wife and child were gone forever. When the news reached him he hurried down to Paris and put up for the night at an English hotel. He had never before stayed there and the hotel and district were both outside his customary haunts in Montmartre, Montparnasse and the students' quarter. Possibly a hope stirred in his muddled brain that an English atmosphere would restore sanity as England had done before. If so his hope failed as did the notion which had caused the plunge into Paris, of a wild appeal to justice, a dramatic facing of Mathilde, a snatching away of the child, anything but inaction; he sought calm and strength of purpose at the English bar and lost the most rudimentary command of himself. The next morning he rushed back to Coulommes dangerously drunk. There he found that the grocer had forced a way into the house and removed Madame Verlaine's clothes and personal belongings.

This discovery snapped what restraint he still possessed. He stormed into the grocer's house and made a scene the details of which remain uncertain to this day since Verlaine, his mother and the grocer all told different stories. The upshot was that Verlaine found himself in court once more, charged with violence and threats to kill his mother. He protested that on the contrary he had threatened to kill himself if she did not come back to him. This statement, which was almost certainly true and has an interesting psychological parallel in Vincent van Gogh's behavior at Arles three years later, was not discounted as it had been discounted in Brussels twelve years earlier. The magistrate, in view of the conflicting evidence and Verlaine's wholehearted repentance, imposed the reasonable sentence of one month's imprisonment and a fine of five hundred francs. Verlaine made no appeal; he sold his house, paid the fine and in the second week of April entered the prison at Vouziers.

If the sentence was reasonable the conditions in prison were lax to the point of farce. As the sole educated man he read evening prayers with an air that captivated all, and as a born convivialist, charmed his warders so thoroughly that the daily tasks were either excused or, when hurriedly and ineffectually done, overlooked. He wrote his poems undisturbed and made friends wholesale, his chief companion being the prostitute Lily—the *Vouzinoise* as he called her—whom he was to see much of in Paris later. He may well have paid for her to go and to live there, for he continued to splash his money about, giving, for example, fifteen hundred francs to a passing drinking companion to buy a merry-go-round almost as soon as he had come out of prison.

His movements after leaving prison in May remain obscure. He went down to Paris for a few days where he seems to have rented the room in the Hôtel du Midi, 6 cour Saint-François off the rue Moreau, which he was later to inhabit. But he did not stay there then; he felt restless and he had money to collect, from the sale of the house at Coulommes and from Juniville where the last part of the purchase price of the farm had only just reached the lawyer.

For Verlaine to possess money in his mood of that time was to invite confusion; he had not yet found anything or anybody to replace Lucien or the shades of Georges and Mathilde. To forget was everything. Money therefore melted, and before he reached Juniville he was begging his way, a not unhappy tramp.

He was rescued from drift by the Church. Above Juniville was the retreat of Corbion and in charge was the Abbé Dewez whom Verlaine had known as a child. He called because he was sociable and would not pass an acquaintance without a word; he found perhaps not altogether with surprise, a bed, food and discipline. There he stayed until September, outstaying his welcome one suspects, for the hopes of Rethel were no longer in him; he was forever escaping, to collect money here or there, to sprinkle it in Paris on Bastille Day and, in short, to fit himself for renewed repentance at Corbion.

There are limits to clerical patience; in September came a rather strained farewell, an erratic progress back to Paris, and there, the next month, a belated settling in the cour Saint-François. His wanderings were over.

[2]

No reader could be blamed for imagining that these years between the death of Lucien and the final settlement in Paris were years of excess, disgrace and waste. Nevertheless the cold facts tell us that while morally and physically Verlaine seemed to be going from bad to worse he was working hard and was winning in absence a reputation in Paris that present and sober he had never been able to obtain. One has only to think of the rise of the genius of Vincent van Gogh under the influence of drink to realize that the ordinary standards of morality do not apply to the great artist.

As has been seen, the publication of "Art poétique" at the end of 1882 was to lead gradually to its adoption as a kind of "theme song" by the young Symbolists led by Moréas and Morice. In June of the next year Le Chat Noir published, among other poems of Verlaine, his "Langueur."

> Je suis l'Empire à la fin de la décadence,
> Qui regarde passer les grands Barbares blancs
> En composant des acrostiches indolents
> D'un style d'or où la langueur du soleil danse.
>
> L'âme seulette a mal au coeur d'un ennui dense.
> Là-bas on dit qu'il est de longs combats sanglants.
> O n'y pouvoir, étant si faible aux voeux si lents,
> O n'y vouloir fleurir un peu cette existence!

O n'y vouloir, ô n'y pouvoir mourir un peu!
Ah! tout est bu! Bathylle, as-tu fini de rire?
Ah! tout est bu, tout est mangé! Plus rien à dire!

Seul, un poème un peu niais qu'on jette au feu,
Seul, un esclave un peu coureur qui vous néglige,
Seul, un ennui d'on ne sait quoi qui vous afflige!

* * *

I am the Empire in the last of its decline,
That sees the tall, fair-haired Barbarians pass,—the while
Composing indolent acrostics, in a style
Of gold, with languid sunshine dancing in each line.

The solitary soul is heart-sick with a vile
Ennui. Down yon, they say, War's torches bloody shine.
Alas, to be so faint of will, one must resign
The chance of brave adventure in the splendid file,—

Of death, perchance! Alas, so lagging in desire!
Ah, all is drunk! Bathyllus, hast done laughing, pray?
Ah, all is drunk,—all eaten! Nothing more to say!

Alone, a vapid verse one tosses in the fire;
Alone, a somewhat thievish slave neglecting one;
Alone, a vague disgust of all beneath the sun!

This was hailed as a perfect expression of their aims by another group of young poets then forming in Paris, the Decadents as they were to name themselves or, rather, as Verlaine inadvertently named them. Soon after the publication of *"Langueur"* he was asked by these young poets to support a new periodical, *La Décade*; to which he returned a blunt "The whole bunch of you will be told to go to the devil, you'll be called the Decadents"—a warning which the leader, Anatole Baju, eventually converted into a challenge by christening the group periodical *Le Décadent*.

The rights and wrongs of the matter can be left to the literary critics; the essential point in Verlaine's life at that moment was not whether he was or not the founder or inspirer of these groups but the fact that he was increasingly regarded as such by a few young men who were to form the literary judgment of the near future. Nor was this all. Illuminating those years of gloom and restlessness with gleams of cheerful promise was a star which, had Verlaine been more practical or even more himself, would have appeared as a saving grace; a reply to his petitions, though as such replies usually do, it did not take an anticipated form. A curious star indeed, the unromantic Léon Vanier with the fat cheeks and gross leer; but there it was, Verlaine had not only found a publisher but a man who actually welcomed whatever he was given. The relationship was some way from the ideal but Vanier saw the joke and the genius. The joke was to prove too much for him from time to time but his faith in the genius persisted. And if one asks how it was that a fat little purveyor of fishing tackle with a hankering for publishing could discern genius—and profitable genius—when the poets and critics had been blind to it for a decade or more, the answer must remain a mystery. On Verlaine's side he saw Vanier as a milch cow miraculously lowered from the skies, a delightful fellow slightly crazed or with more money than he knew what to do with, who was prepared to pay cash for, apparently, anything that Verlaine would write or, better still for a congenitally lazy man, could extract from the precious bundles of manuscripts stuffed into every pocket. Never had he destroyed a line he had written and how right he had been!

So Verlaine obliged. In these years he wrote much of the Lucien elegy and some of the other poems which were to make up the volume later known as *Amour*, he wrote many occasional poems for the three journals then printing him, he completed his *Jadis et Naguère* and, prose seeming to be as acceptable to Vanier as verse, relieved his mind of some of its spleen toward Mathilde by writing, after the divorce, an account of life with the Mautés which was eventually to appear in his *Mémoires d'un Veuf*. Of the occasional verse, mostly excellent, one was outstanding even in such company: "*La Dernière Fête galante*" published in *Lutèce* in December, 1884 is a brilliantly amusing attack on his own book.

> *Pour une bonne fois, séparons-nous,*
> *Très chers messieurs et si belles mesdames.*
> *Assez comme cela d'épithalames,*
> *Et puis là, nos plaisirs furent trop doux.*

> *Nul remords, nul regret vrai, nul désastre!*
> *C'est effrayant ce que nous nous sentons*

D'affinités avecque les moutons
Enrubannés du pire poétastre.

Nous fûmes trop ridicules un peu
Avec nos airs de n'y toucher qu'à peine.
Le Dieu d'amour veut qu'on ait de l'haleine,
Il a raison! Et c'est un jeune Dieu.

Séparons-nous, je vous le dis encore.
O que nos coeurs qui furent trop bêlants,
Dès ce jourd'hui réclament, trop hurlants,
L'embarquement pour Sodome et Gomorrhe!

*   *   *

Let us be separated and eternally,
Dear damsels and dear knights after your fashions
Enough of all the tragedy of our passions.
Of our comic pleasures passed infernally.

Let there be no regret and no disaster!
It is so awful to feel our own affinity
With wicked little elves' divinity
Ridiculous as this ridiculous poetaster.

Let us be separated, who knew not what the dark meant.
O that our hearts that for our sins were yearning
After sad Sodom cry for Gomorrah burning
As Sodom did and for our last embarkment!

Jadis et Naguère has often been called a hotchpotch and it is true that the presence of the one-act comedy *Les Uns et les Autres*, a not ineffectual extension of *Fêtes galantes* to the stage, and the *Vers jeunes* put in simply because Verlaine could not bear to waste a line he had written, have given the book a bad name. But a volume which contains the sonnet to Mérat, "*Art Poétique*," "*Luxures*" and "*Vers pour être calomnie*" should not be underrated. Nor are these poems, as fine in their way as anything he had written, the whole of the good things; every poem in the two main sections, *Jadis* and *Naguère*, is first rate, such as the early sonnet "*Circon-spection*" in which expression, feeling and atmosphere are blended with a subtlety worthy of the master Verlaine had become.

Donne ta main, retiens ton souffle, asseyons-nous
Sous cet arbre géant où vient mourir la brise
En soupirs inégaux sous la ramure grise
Que caresse le clair de lune blême et doux.

Immobiles, baissons nos yeux vers nos genoux.
Ne pensons pas, rêvons. Laissons faire à leur guise
Le bonheur qui s'enfuit et l'amour qui s'épuise,
Et nos cheveux frôlés par l'aile des hiboux.

Oublions d'espérer. Discrète et contenue,
Que l'âme de chacun de nous deux continue
Ce calme et cette mort sereine du soleil.

Restons silencieux parmi la paix nocturne:
Il n'est pas bon d'aller troubler dans son sommeil
La nature, ce dieu féroce et taciturne.

For the first time the merits of a Verlaine book of poems were not thrown away; his work was at last being watched; and when *Jadis et Naguère* appeared on the last day of November, 1884, it immediately increased his growing reputation. A sign of the times, as noteworthy in its way as the cordiality of Mendès at the Voltaire, was the breaking of Banville's long and tactful silence. Perhaps regretting the cowardice which had prevented him from voting for Verlaine's inclusion in the third *Parnasse contemporain*, certainly carried out of caution by admiration, Banville came into the open with a letter of congratulation. He had his reservations: "At times you skirt the cliffs of poetry so closely that you risk falling into music"; but he chose wisely to waive them with a "Well, you may be right."

But it was neither *Jadis et Naguère* nor his occasional poems which had the decisive effect on Verlaine's standing. This came curiously but with poetic justice, through Rimbaud. Amid Verlaine's work in 1884 not yet mentioned was what appeared as an easy task, a pot-boiler: to write introductions and make selections of poetry for a series under the title *Les Poètes maudits*. The series appeared first in *Lutèce*; then, in April, Vanier published it as separate small books. The work was not particularly well done, Verlaine being too kind-hearted for true criticism, but it was perfectly timed. Verlaine chose as his poets Rimbaud, Mallarmé and a Breton, Tristan

Corbière, who had published a book of poems *Les Amours jaunes* exactly ten years earlier, when Verlaine was in London. The poems were scarcely noticed and Corbière died the next year at the age of thirty, an unknown man. He had something in common with Verlaine and even more with the young Symbolists then struggling for a hearing; Verlaine's book made a hit among the young poets and Corbière was read, studied and elevated to a niche in the Symbolist temple.

The effect of the next book, on Mallarmé, was even more remarkable. Mallarmé had by that time escaped from the provinces and was teaching English with indifferent success in the Collège Rollin, but he was a choosy man as to companions, no lover of the cafés, and the move to Paris had done little for his reputation. Then *Les Poètes maudits* appeared and Mallarmé became almost overnight one of the gods of the Symbolists; Moréas, Morice and their followers read and worshipped; from that moment Mallarmé and Verlaine stood as twin pillars of the movement. To Verlaine the little book was intended as an agreeable memento of the mutual admiration subsisting between himself and Mallarmé—one can scarcely call it friendship since in their wisdom the men, differing so markedly in their pleasures outside poetry, took care to avoid all but an occasional meeting. In any event, he found himself hailed as the man who, not only a fine poet, had brought Corbière and Mallarmé to life.

The little book on Rimbaud made even more of a sensation. By then Rimbaud although still only twenty-nine years old had become a legendary figure in Paris. He was remembered when at all as a rather nasty youth who had made a meteoric and unpleasant descent on Paris, had seduced Verlaine from his friends and family and had then gone off no one seemed to know where and few cared. Delahaye, who heard something of him from time to time, was a provincial schoolmaster rarely seen and as little listened to, his one-time familiar Forain was uncommunicative, Nouveau his last companion was scarcely sane, and Verlaine was little wiser than the café crowds. The young poets knew nothing of his work and no more than rumors of his life.

Then came Verlaine's book. The avant-garde poets read with astonishment "*Le Bateau Ivre*" and the vowel sonnet, read and marveled. In the Latin Quarter cafés one could hear little but talk about this mysterious man who had written highly original poetry, thrown up literature in his teens and vanished. A Rimbaud cult began which would lead in time to yet another school of poetry. But for the moment attention and esteem fell almost equally on Verlaine; Verlaine who had brought him to life, who knew him as no other man, who had suffered because of him. Verlaine, almost as unfindable for the time as Rimbaud himself, shared in the glamour.

Then came *Jadis et Naguère*, Banville's compliment and following Banville—the disapproving Leconte de Lisle and Hérédia excepted—the rest of the old guard, of whom only Dierx, Mallarmé, Valade, Lepelletier and Blémont had remained more or less faithful at a respectable distance. Middle-aged approval; youthful enthusiasm and imitation: here was change indeed, somewhat ironical when one remembers that at this time the respected author was serving his month in prison for assault and afterwards wandering on drunken sprees about the Ardennes countryside. But the respect of Banville and company was, all understood, intellectual merely; the days of Parnassian or any other kind of soirees were, as far as Verlaine was concerned, gone for good; he was to be praised at a safe distance. It was to the young and to the few unrespectable faithful of his old companions that he had to look. But if he paused to consider his position during these three years of moral collapse he must, despite that most uncharacteristic lapse of humor, have felt intimations that if he had to lose for the moment he would gain in the long run. And, intimations or not, this was the truth. The last and in many ways best period of his life was about to begin.

17.

PARADISE BROUSSAIS

1885-1888

[1]

The Hôtel du Midi was one of the least prepossessing of the scruffy lodging houses in which Paris specializes. It sat dismally in the apology for a street called the cour Saint-François, a noisome cul-de-sac behind the Place de la Bastille, was rat- and bug-ridden like every other house in the neighborhood, and was practically without the light of day, huddled under the arches of the railway to Vincennes and quivering from head to foot every time a train rumbled overhead. When its inhabitants were not shaken and deafened by the busy railway, their nerves were torn by the day-long scream of a saw—for next door was a timber warehouse piled high with enormous logs.

Verlaine's room in this palace with the high-sounding name was rather worse than the imagination bargained for; after stumbling down the foul-smelling street with its open drains, even after sighting the hotel through the gloom, most of his visitors recoiled in disgusted horror from the den that he described as his home. Occupying most of the ground floor of the hotel was a wine shop; visitors had to walk through this shop to reach Verlaine's room—"small, sordid and sinister like the cut-throat place at the bottom of which it squatted. There was no floor, not even flagstones; one trod on the bare earth which was damp and muddy. . . . A tiny cupboard served as Verlaine's library; it was crammed with books and manuscripts. A narrow table and two wicker chairs completed the furniture."

To Lepelletier who wrote this description, Verlaine, obliging as ever, said what Lepelletier expected to hear: all the doing of that unspeakable Mathilde *"horrible, horrible, horrible femme!"* and the old . . . her father. Lepelletier would nod sympathetically, a little shocked by the abuse but familiar with the routine? And now? What an outlook! He wanted to earn his living by the pen, but . . . If Lepelletier could give him a few more introductions . . . And so on, until Lepelletier having done his duty and heroically concealed his distaste hurried away with a shudder.

Most people repeated Lepelletier's shudder but there was another point of view. The budding young symbolist poet, Gustave Kahn, a sharp youngster with an eye for weaknesses in his elders and betters, came to persuade Verlaine to give some poems to the opening number of a new periodical, came squelching through the same slush, dodging the same balks of timber, pushing through the same shoddy crowd of prostitutes, pickpockets and down-at-heel laborers in the wine shop. He noted that the great man had chosen to live in a "*picturesque quartier.*" He found Verlaine wrapped in an ancient blue overcoat, a bottle and glass before him on the table. The bottle was not full. He broached his mission but Verlaine, disliking brevity, went off on a tangent. With "an exaggerated friendliness" which reminded the critical visitor of Banville, he spoke of Kahn's growing reputation and, just to prove that there was no deception, quoted some verses of his with an admiration that the young man felt to be excessive.

Kahn came from Metz; Verlaine knew that too and went off into a rhapsody about the beauty of the Esplanade and his happy child walks there, his first love affair. Kahn repeated his request; some poems please. Verlaine replied that he felt the honor deeply; it was "a recompense for living at the beginning of an infirm old age to hear the young man say that he had written good things." Changing the subject again, he spoke lyrically of Mallarmé whom Kahn particularly admired and recited his poetry "with curiously grandiloquent intonations." This done, he asked after Kahn's latest work.

Kahn reverted again to his purpose: was not Verlaine writing further *Poètes maudits* and was there any chance of the new periodical printing them? Ah, the *Poètes maudits*! Now Desbordes-Valmore, what a poetess: so simple, so direct, so sad, a northerner like himself! Taking up a book and assuming a formidable and heavily blurred pair of spectacles, Verlaine raised his head and, apparently glancing beneath the glassess, read several poems, the tears running down his cheeks.

Reduced to melancholy he put down the book at last, drained his glass and began to tell his visitor of his return to Paris, of his many sorrows, of his false wife, his imminent poverty, his failing health. Fresh tears fell. Another glass was emptied.

But there were compensations, suggested Kahn; growing fame, respect from the young poets, a good publisher, a body of superb poetry behind him and even greater to come. And to live in the heart of the working quarter of Paris, this too . . .

Verlaine, who had cheered up, agreed enthusiastically; he would not miss the morning walk, clip-clopping to the Place de la Bastille in search of newspapers. Even to take part in that futile maneuver, to try to insinuate oneself onto the omnibus of the faubourg Saint-Antoine black with workers reeking of garlic, even that was, well it was Paris and one loved every wasted moment of it, the abuse that meant nothing, the smell, the incredible noise.

He abruptly fell back a decade and with great éclat told stories of his days at the fortifications with the *Garde nationale* which made even the purposeful Kahn laugh. Ridiculous wasn't it, he a soldier, a Communard?

The anecdotes flowed, the bottle was done, the boy from the wine shop replaced it, the glasses were filled and emptied, the tireless Verlaine talked on. Kahn repeated his requst. Poems? Of course. And Verlaine, scrabbling in the little cupboard, handed his guest a sheaf of papers covered with the beautiful writing.

After a moment's hesitation he produced another paper. "I suppose you couldn't use this? A powerful piece of work." Kahn looked at it; it was a scurrilous attack on Mathilde. "No, I'm afraid not." "Oh, well"; and the paper went back into the cupboard.

But there was one more point. The periodical, Kahn explained reluctantly from the doorway, clutching the manuscripts, was new, uncertain of its future, and in short the rates of payment were not high, in fact they were low, practically nothing to be exact.

Verlaine spread wide arms from the midst of his squalor. "I had never given it a thought," he assured Kahn with the air of a man beyond money; and Kahn escaped gratefully with his precious papers which would insure the sale of the first number. To him, as has been seen, the slum was picturesque.

But most people shuddered like Lepelletier. And if the reader asks why Verlaine, who was not entirely without money at the time, had chosen to plant himself there, the explanation is simple: the wine merchant was his friend; he liked wine and he liked friends and would rather be miserably uncomfortable in company than in comfort and alone.

Miserably uncomfortable but not miserable. Most visitors thought and most readers would naturally assume that he must be both. But it was not so, as his letters clearly show. "I am filled with joy," he told Vanier, now become his chief correspondent. "Found heaps of things, prose and verse, I thought I had lost. Seen Izambard who has lent me early Rimbaud poems. Plan definitely fixed for *Madame Aubin* which will be one act only. In labor with two long chapters for *Mémoires d'un Veuf*. Have written verses for serious, paying periodicals (Prudence and Chastity) which do pay. Some very daring biographical verses are just going to be published by *Lutèce*. Confound it, I'm burning my boats. Chatter and publicity."

That is a sample of Verlaine's state of mind for the greater part of the next two and a half years. He was busy, hopeful and had at his back a publisher who could generally be persuaded to fork out an advance of five francs or so when funds were low. He was having enormous fun chasing the periodicals that sprang up like mushrooms, writing this for that, that for this; he was enjoying the conversion of every experience into reading matter for the insatiable Vanier to put into print.

But to have plenty of work, to feel that it is good work and that it is usually to be paid for, to know that one's reputation is rising, does not compensate for detestable physical discomfort. Knowing Verlaine's happy-go-lucky disregard of fame, knowing him to be a sensuous animal loving comfort as much as any Frenchman, and brought up from his early years in what most of his countrymen would describe as luxury, one has to look elsewhere for the answer. He had at last come to terms with himself. In future, life was to do what it liked with him and he accepted everything, good and bad, with no more than the famous satyrish grimace and commonly with a joke, rude if possible. Nothing, fame, money, poverty, pain, flattery, malice, could disturb his fundamental balance. As a result the last years, the years of city vagabondage, years of discomfort, homelessness, poverty (self-imposed most of it)—everything that he had struggled against—nevertheless form the most admirable period of his life. He was contented if not happy; to him, whose conscience remained lively, the past was recalled as a time of many errors and downright sins and his present life, as a direct result of them, appeared a second best; but even this he no longer regretted; and his humility and good-humored resignation are better worthy of comment than the physical excesses. His life from 1885 onwards is not commonly put forward as an example of the good life, but it may well be that the general judgment is at fault; it would not be for the first time.

Moreover, he wore the sign at times incongruous but always unmistakable of the man who is himself from morning to night, believes in himself and is not forever finding himself in a false position. With Mathilde, Rimbaud, Nouveau, Lucien he had played a part; often with the best intentions but a part nevertheless; and in consequence he had invited criticism and mixed feelings. Now he had dignity. Dignity was not the characteristic one would expect to find in a man who had "sunk low" as the expression goes, whose tastes were dubious and whose life was to be passed in cafés, miserable bed-sitting rooms and hospitals, yet that was the first and last impression of every perceptive witness. One will suffice, a young man later to become well-known who happened to be sitting in the corner of a café when Verlaine came in, sat down and put his game leg on the chair opposite. He was quickly "surrounded by young people, some disciples, some merely curious. He sat silent. He was offered a drink. Finally he accepted it but with a dignity not less admirable than he had previously shown in refusing it. He had the air of one completely at home with himself." And the witness, who was to see him often, adds, "Not one of the pharisees who criticized him as a disgrace could rival in dignity the Verlaine of the 'undignified' life."

In one important way he was helped to throw off restlessness and idealism. It was no mighty effort of will, of which he was incapable; it was no miracle; it was simply that he became all at once unable to do more than potter about city streets and that he accepted with a grace remarkable in a strong man of forty-two a life conditioned by an incurable disability. He had been settled into his room for only a few weeks when his left leg began to swell. The pain became so great that he called in a doctor who diagnosed water on the knee. The knee was put into plaster. His mother came down from Arras to which she had retreated after the court case early in the year and took the room above him.

By December he was up and out, explaining Kahn's "clip-clopping," for he then took the form in public by which he was to become and has remained famous: the black slouch hat, shabby cape, the heavy stick in the right hand and the deep limp. He could not be missed and was not, first because of his height, secondly because of his clothes which grew fantastically worn with the passing years, lastly because of his manner, affable, hail-fellow-well-met with all, yet not to be dismissed as another bum, crank or down-at-heel clerk. He would be heard murmuring as he limped along; not talking to himself as the passer-by might imagine—he had no need of that lonely man's compensation, not being lonely—but sounding out the possibilities of words. He was forever striving after the perfect word; subjects met him wherever his eyes turned, and when they turned inwards there too was the subject, inexhaustible, of the mystery of man. Superficially there is something paradoxical in this seedy scare-crow dealing in delicacies, but the poet in man bears no more relation to social values than do clothes to the man himself; his province is bounded only by the range of his feelings and the fineness of his reaction to the most everyday occurrence. And never was poet born with a more quivering, antennalike sensibility than that of this tall, disreputable, shambling creature with the quenchless thirst and the humorous eye.

So Verlaine limped heavily to the Place de la Bastille every morning, mouthing words meticulously, pausing to make a note, limping on, stick tap, tap, tap, keen eyes darting in every direction, missing nothing from the stir of a leaf in the dirty gutter to the flutter of a handkerchief from some high and uninviting window, comical flat nose registering every scent, caporal, garlic, coffee, croissants newly baked, faunlike ears distinguishing every small sound hiding behind the din of crowded streets.

Arrived at the Place he made a tour of the kiosks, lingering until the owner objected to prolonged free reading, moving on until the round accomplished, he sat down at a café overlooking the great square, a bundle of newspapers under his arm if in funds; if not, summoning the waiter to bring him what papers the café possessed. Followed a quick but thorough perusal, the lighting of a foul-smelling pipe, more drinks, conversation with any likely neighbor or the making of more notes. Plans innumerable ran through his head: what he would write and where he would send it; should he stand immovable, rocklike outside Mallarmé's school where Georges was then studying and insist on seeing the boy whom Mathilde was keeping from him; Mathilde—this thought called for another drink with furrowed, angry face; Vanier—how much could he eke out of him, five francs, ten, even fifteen? On and on the thoughts chased, one drink took the place of another, the morning was gone, lunch had to be sought if there was money for lunch, otherwise a friend or admirer must be found to stand him one. That was not difficult on most days for he was a character whose conversation repaid hospitality, adapting himself readily to the tone of his companion.

Toward the end of a day he was not always affable, the absinthes having their effect. He did not drink as heavily as in youth and the after passions had gone, but he could be irritable, quarrelsome. And one evening, differing from the waiter about the reckoning, he went so far as to call a gendarme, a rash step which ended in a night in a prison cell. This, the penultimate "imprisonment" which he noted in the amusing "*Mes Prisons*" he was to write for Vanier, was a turning point in his relations with the police. The time was not far distant when they were to take a pride in preserving him, not simply from a prison cell but from the curious and impertinent bystander, he having won the freedom of a city peculiarly responsive to the arts.

For the moment, however, his drinking resulted in more trouble with his leg. And in January 1886, when he was bedbound again, his mother caught a chill and died; died without him, since he was too heavy and too tall to be carried up the narrow steps to her room. So ended, to the sound of Verlaine's passionate regrets, a relationship which for all the exceptional feeling on both sides can only be regarded as a disaster. The last twenty years of Madame Verlaine's life were sadly harassed, that is to state the obvious; less obvious but equally true were the many satisfactions which only another Madame Verlaine would fully understand. One thing can be appreciated by all, however; that Madame Verlaine, abnormal though she was and wickedly though she spoiled her son, was in the rights of it when she gloried in his loving disposition; he caused her endless trouble but she weighed the good against the ill and considered that the one amply compensated for the other.

Practically, his mother's death meant that Verlaine once again had money to spread abroad. It was not a great deal and of what there was Mathilde to his fury demanded and was awarded half; but it was enough to bring his health to a crisis; and in July, all money gone and both legs covered with sores, he was admitted to the Tenon Hospital.

[2]

From this time until May, 1888—that is, for the best part of two years—he moved, with short and penurious intervals, from one hospital to another; from the Tenon to the Broussais, from the Broussais to the Cochin, from the Cochin to the Convalescent Asylum of Saint Maurice at Vincennes, back again to the Tenon and so on, doing the rounds but with a growing and decided preference for the Broussais.

Any attempt to take this hospital period seriously is defeated by the patient himself who in many of his letters and in his *Mes Hôpitaux* (hurriedly turned out later on to earn an advance from Vanier) makes high comedy of his efforts to stay put or, having been dislodged from one hospital, to seek shelter in another and, successfully installed, of his life there as undisputed master of the ward. In reality it was not always the joke he pretended, but all efforts to discover when exactly he went into the hospital because his health demanded it and when he tried to go there because he was penniless end in confusion. But it is of no great moment and one accepts the comedy gladly, mentally noting that he was a sick man for much of this time and that his sufferings must have been considerable.

Even the exact nature of his ailments remains uncertain. He began with water on the knee, then sores on his legs, then complete rigidity of the limb; he also had acute rheumatic pains. The diagnoses differed as did the treatments but there seems little doubt but that some part of the trouble was syphilitic; Verlaine at any rate freely blamed the prostitutes of Paris and London. Alcohol was the worst possible thing he could take but he took plenty, with the result that, out of the hospitals, he at once began to undo the cure by over-liberal doses of the green sorceress. Scarcely less harmful was his attempt to bite the hair of the dog by indulging too often in women, including his friend Lily, whom he picked up. In this instance homeopathy did not work; when not reinfected he was exhausted and wide open to any microbe which happened to be on the spot. Back then he went in a week or two, the treatments beginning all over again. And when, as sometimes happened despite his best endeavors, he remained on his feet with empty pockets he would besiege one hospital after another manufacturing a pain or two if nothing "curable" showed itself at that moment.

At first sight this passion for hospitals appears strange. Granted the boons of regular and free food, clean clothes and skilled attention to a man who could never save a penny, be sure of a roof over his head or the next meal, the disadvantages of perpetual discipline, loss of freedom and friends would seem to outweigh them. But Verlaine had the habit of bending everything to his comfort, even a hospital. There were times when he was really ill and treated like every other patient. There were times, too, when he felt himself to be badly done by and expressed his feelings in delightfully Coleridgean manner: "But all the same it is hard after a life of work set off, I admit, by accidents in which I have had a large share, catastrophes perhaps vaguely premeditated—it is hard, I say, at forty-seven years of age, in full possession of the reputation (of the *success*, to use the frightful current phrase) to which my highest ambitions could aspire—hard, hard, hard indeed, worse than hard, to find myself—good God!—to find myself *on the streets* and to have nowhere to lay my head and support an ageing body save the pillows and the *menus* of a public charity, even now uncertain and which might at any moment be withdrawn—God forbid!—without, apparently, it being the fault of anyone—oh! not even, and above all, not mine!" But this excursion into the pathetic was written for a public, with tongue well in cheek, humor not absent (see the *menus*), and the operative words are the opening "But all the same." Out of hospitals he did not dwell on these moments, but thought with absolute longing of the days and the weeks when treatment had reduced itself to medicines, which he could often slip overboard untasted, and to massage, which when the masseuse was pretty or plump he by no means abhorred. And thinking so he could not wait to get back to "that paradise, the Broussais" where he was uncrowned king. For rules disintegrated before his blarney and cheerful courage, visiting hours elongated themselves almost round the clock, and his ward became workroom, salon and even bar.

So for much of the time he really did enjoy himself enormously, not so much because he felt well as because it was in his nature to find the good in everything rather than to concentrate on the bad. He suffered a lot from his legs, the doctors did devilish things to them occasionally, that was a bore, an unbearable outrage; he would shout

it, then forget it. He was being looked after like a child, he had absolutely no responsibility, that was wonderful and he reveled in it. He
was confined to his bed but that was about all he was confined to;
sitting up on his pillows, hospital nightcap (his "halo") jauntily
askew, he wrote his way through reams of hospital paper, pouring
out poems, prose, letters innumerable, presided in state over all the
affairs of the ward, dispensed advice, cheer (by much mimicry, quite
well done, of visitors, doctors, nurses and men of the day) and,
when he judged it necessary, medicines unprescribed by the doctors
which he drew cautiously from underneath his bed. Every afternoon
he received callers: the successful Coppée, an Academician since
1884, a thought-provoking example of what prosperity does to a man
of letters, looking no longer a mild Napoleon but a third-rate actor
who had come into money, who when leaving slipped fifty francs
into a not unwilling hand; the fat Vanier weaving plan after plan for
their joint profit; the youthful Morice and his crowd who after
listening rapturously to recitations of Verlaine's latest work and to
his comments on the poems they recited would withdraw reluctantly,
carefully depositing under the inverted chamber pot a bottle of
brandy or a flask of absinthe, some cigars or a packet of the invalid's
favorite tobacco.

The doctors and nurses soon came to take pride in this glorious
eccentric. He was incorrigible, he would not be permanently cured,
that was much clear. But what good company, what a flow of rakish
speech, what bonhomie and, even in melancholy moments, what
style! And with a shrug of the shoulders and a wink of the eye almost
all let him do as he pleased. An occasional reproof, a short repentance, this was the beginning and end of discipline.

The hospital years, therefore, blossom into high comedy, then
into downright farce. He is forever scheming to get back before he
has even been discharged: "I *must* leave on Friday, the first of July,
so that I can return in a few days' time. It's compulsory—a bore, but
compulsory"; and, to Vanier, "I beg you to send by return a *mandat*
or note for fifty francs. Without it I'm liable to be discharged any
day. See what a spot you've put me in! I absolutely dared not go out
yesterday." Again, to the same correspondent from the Broussais
after a short absence: "Received back here like the prodigal son.
Mild reproaches, that's all. And arrived in very good shape in spite of
all the absinthes."

His letters to Vanier became a travesty of the popular idea of author to publisher. Every week, every few days he dashes off a note to the long-suffering man on the Quai St. Michel. The requests veer from the piteous cry to the peremptory demand, having in common only their inevitability; scarcely a letter was without the money element; most of them had no other purpose. Always there were promises, as much to himself as to Vanier who was utterly un-concerned with his author's morals or morale, promises of amend-ment, promises grandiose, promises descending to the farcical. "It is pitiful to live so. I assure you that my heart weeps as I write all this. But I shall do nothing that is not dignified and straightforward. *Potius mori quam foedari:* that is truly my motto. That, and to die a Christian death worthy of my parents and an example to my son . . . Yours very cordially and very sadly but determined to be strong."

But the cry for money was the great thing. He did not waste space: "Great need of cash. It's true, no kidding. Quick. Quick. Great need of cash"; "Be so good as to send me fifty francs at once." And not only for money as such; the theme was varied. Vanier inevitably assumed more and more the shape of a universal provider: "Don't need money but . . . chocolate, stamps, a small carafe of wine from time to time, etc. (the etceteras aren't numerous or alarming!). In short, please send me a *mandat* for fifteen francs"; "If you aren't a bread-and-butter publisher . . . you'll recognize and recompense my activity, my zeal, my punctuality, my patience and all my virtues by COMING WITH ALL MANUSCRIPTS AND STAMPED PAPER."

Vanier must also buy clothes: "I hope to get back into the hos-pital . . . but I must look a bit respectable. A pair of shoes at any rate and a reasonably decent hat to liven up this old carcass . . . in short, bring or send me (send by *mandat*) all you can spare as soon as possible. This business of petty debts, of thinking what is due, etc., bores me without counting the frightful fatigue of keeping up appearances"; "Now if it turns out to be impossible to prolong my 'rest cure' here and to get into another hospital right away (what a life I lead, my dear chap!) . . . I must eat and I shall need one of those hats at three francs, sixty, not to mention a shirt and some shoes . . . and a nice little sum in my pocket. So, send these . . . so that I can leave here for the 'Great World' well armed for the 'struggle for life' in the depths. And may heaven bless you"; "Will you—and this is very serious—get me a pair of summer trousers, gray, the same kind that I bought for three francs last summer?"

Vanier must repay the few loans which, to Verlaine's horror, the lender seemed to expect to be settled, and Vanier must settle the restaurant bills Verlaine had signed during his few days or weeks between one hospital and another. "Now be a good fellow and don't forget Monsieur Allemoz"—this being the owner of his then favorite restaurant in the rue Moreau; and again, "Have you paid good mother Allemoz?"

But Vanier did not always pay. Then, Verlaine having sent Delahaye, Morice, Carjat or some other familiar in vain to the Quai St. Michel to collect what he had come to consider his due, a haughty letter was dispatched to "Monsieur Vanier" ending with the formal "Agréez, Monsieur, mes civilités." "I'm on very distant terms with Vanier," he explained to Lepelletier, "and for a very good reason"—failing, however, to give the reason.

But he was too good-tempered—and too often completely broke—to keep up a tone so widely out of character. He had to be friends; all had to be loved except Mathilde, who had committed the final crime by remarrying—this time to a building contractor, the Monsieur Delporte who was later to divorce her—her father and the incorrigible Leconte de Lisle. These apart the world was all love to Verlaine when it was not despair. He and Vanier were quickly reconciled and Vanier usually paid up in the end.

Vanier, however, must not be romanticized. That Verlaine did more than amuse him is unlikely; he had no time for sentiment in business; and if he seems absurdly generous to this indigent author it was because he knew that he had discovered a good thing. All honor to him for that; he was the first man to realize Verlaine's potentialities. But his advances, numerous though they were, were always very small; Verlaine, who could never keep in his head the idea of his growing importance, continued to ask and be grateful for the five odd francs that a beginner would have had a right to. In sum they did not amount to as much as he could have demanded legitimately had he possessed the slightest head for business.

In one way only did Vanier take a risk; it was necessary that Verlaine should not merely write about the many works he had in view but should actually produce them. And here he was fortunate; for although Verlaine gives every appearance in his letters of being the cadger to outdo all cadgers and a hopeless weaver of impossible plans, he was in action one of the most prolific writers of his time. "I'm writing very much," he tells Vanier, the "very much" in

English; "I work en masse and I have great hopes for the future"; "I'm worked to death"; "I continue courageously with my literary work so as to provide if possible for my old age"; "I write verse and lots of prose between a couple of sighs and some ghostly groans when I'm treated with sulphate of copper—not very aphrodisiac, this regime of mine!" So the messages went, wan, rude, humorous, dignified as the case might be; but the burden of them all was work. And astonishingly the work was done.

[3]

It has become a truism that Verlaine never wrote anything really good in his last years, but even truisms need looking into from time to time. It is certainly true that Vanier was a menace as well as a godsend. Put a man like Verlaine, put any man with vigorous appetites and inexhaustible generosity into the position where he has only to write to be paid, or even worse to be paid before he writes, and he will write too much. Verlaine was never one to labor overmuch; he would find the right word for his poems but he would do it en passant as it were, while he walked, before he went off to sleep. For the rest he was an instinctive poet, writing as naturally as he breathed. He was not a born writer of prose, however; he could write well but he could also write badly and he did not take enough trouble; indeed it is a question whether he took any trouble at all.

And there is the basis for the popular belief; there and in his habit, now that ready-money Vanier had come onto the scene, of rescuing from his only too well preserved archives every line he had ever written and of palming off on publisher and public youthful follies, failures put aside years earlier, anything and everything that would fetch a franc or two.

Let us examine the work written and published in these years to the middle of 1888. In prose Verlaine's principle was the journalistic one of converting into cash any and every *rencontre*, memory, experience that could be fashioned into an article or a book: hence his confessions, his reminiscences of hospitals and prisons. But these, although begun or already in mind at this period, were crowded out by other and more pressing tasks; for his confessions could end only with his life, he could not be sure that he had experienced his last prison and he was quite certain that there were more hospitals to come. In 1886 Vanier published his *Louise Leclerq*, a book of three long short stories including *"Le Poteau"* and the supposedly auto-biographical *"Pierre Duchâtelet"*—a book of no more than moderate merit. This was followed by another short play *Madame Aubin* and by the *Mémoires d'un Veuf* to which he had been making additions over the years, including a good account of the formation of the *Parnasse* (a counterblast to Mendès' much criticized account two years earlier) and a slightly shocking but salutory "reëstimate" of the enhaloed Hugo who had died just after Mathilde's remarriage.

The reception given to the *Poètes maudits* and especially to the volume on Rimbaud had encouraged Vanier to advise Verlaine to prepare for a reprint and an enlargement of the series. Three more were added, one on Desbordes-Valmore, one on Villiers and, Verlaine seeing no reason why the inventor should not benefit from his invention, one on a mysterious *"Pauvre Lélian"* which turned out, not to the great surprise of anyone, to be an anagram of Verlaine himself; an exceedingly clever anagram which went the rounds of Paris so thoroughly as almost to rechristen Verlaine for the rest of his life. He was working on all of these during the hospital years and, thinking this to be a pretty easy way of earning money and a reputation, began to write for another series, *Hommes d'aujourd'hui*, in which he would if given the chance have included every man of any moment he had known, going as far down the scale of fame as De Ricard, then back in France in his rightful place as editor of a newspaper at Montpellier.

Of this last series only the little volume on Rimbaud need be noticed here. Verlaine on Rimbaud reminds one immediately of Charlotte Brontë's introduction to the work of Emily; the same strong, simple prose, the same profound admiration, the same puzzlement and almost awe before wayward, self-willed genius: *"Le tout simple comme une forêt vierge et beau comme un tigre."* Verlaine had already begun to search for the manuscripts of Rimbaud, who was still in Abyssinia, so that he might print and introduce them all. In this period he introduced an edition, the first to be printed, of *Les Illuminations* put out by *La Vogue*, the periodical in whose interests the young editor Kahn had called at the noisome chamber behind the wine shop.

Important though his work on Rimbaud was to prove and staggering in its effect on contemporary writers, his own poetry remained his raison d'être. In the hospital years he wrote poem after poem,

Verlaine at the Broussais, 1890

Verlaine and Rimbaud
in London, 1872

Verlaine, 1890

many of them appearing in the Left Bank periodicals; poems which ranged from the fragment of the Temptation of Saint Anthony libretto, Verlaine wasting nothing, to the decidedly free *"Lombes,"* from the heart-rending Lucien sonnets to the delightfully witty *"Ballade en faveur des dénommés Décadents et Symbolistes"* dedicated tactfully to Vanier who had made himself publisher-in-chief of the movement or movements—one cannot say the one or the other with certainty because the participants were never able to agree on the matter.

Quelques-uns dans tout ce Paris,
Nous vivons d'orgueil et de dèche.
D'alcool encore qu'épris,
Nous buvons surtout de l'eau fraîche
En cassant la croûte un peu sèche.
A d'autres fins mets et grands vins,
Et la beauté jamais revêche!
Nous sommes les bons écrivains.

Phoebé, quand tous les chats sont gris,
Effile d'une pointe rêche
Nos corps par la gloire nourris,
Dont l'enfer, au guet, se pourlèche,
Et Phoebus nous lance sa flèche.
La nuit nous berce en songes vains
Sur des lits de noyaux de pêche.
Nous sommes les bons écrivains.

Beaucoup de beaux esprits ont pris
L'enseigne de l'Homme qui bêche,
Et Lemerre tient les paris,
Plus d'un encore se dépêche
Et tâche d'entrer par la brèche;
Mais Vanier à la fin des fins
Seul eut de la chance à la pêche.
Nous sommes les bons écrivains.

ENVOI

Bien que la bourse chez nous pèche,
Princes, rions, doux et divins.
Quoi que l'on dise ou que l'on prêche,
Nous sommes les bons écrivains.

To turn from the absurd to the sublime, by the first month of 1888 Verlaine had completed the poems for his next volume *Amour* and almost half the poems for the volume to follow it—completed with a typical letter to Vanier: "To the rescue, infamous publisher! You are a rotter for never turning up. I've waited ages for you! To punish you, here 'herewith' is the TRULY LAST piece for *Amour* which I hope will soon be coming out. It's now or never, I think."

Amour appeared toward the end of March. It is a pity that those who wish to form an opinion of Verlaine's religious verse do not read this book as well as the more famous because first printed *Sagesse*. The Lucien and Elisa elegies, great as they are, tend to divert attention from the remainder of the poems in *Amour*; but many of these also are exquisitely phrased and deeply moving, and beyond this they provide, as the elegies often do not, an exact picture of Verlaine's faith. When he wrote *Sagesse* he was still in the state of exaltation which follows conversion; poetic genius apart, the substance and mood of the religious poems might have been those of any other recent convert—the tendency to hysteria, the divorce from the world, the horror at all he had been; certainly they did not express the true faith of the writer. Later, in the years now reached, Verlaine had begun to explain far and wide, "*Moi*, I am a Catholic of the Middle Ages." This was near the mark; he was, naturally, being compared with "*pauvre Villon*," and took pleasure in the comparison which was just if not precise. In the *Amour* poems we see this modern Villon, this Catholic of the Middle Ages, no mystic but a child often bad, often repenting, again bad, again repenting ad infinitum but always with the touching belief that his sins would truly be forgiven him by a merciful and loving Father—no awful, unapproachable figure, this, but *un vrai Père*. This belief he demonstrates best in "*Un Conte*" which first appeared in Moréas' and Kahn's short-lived *Le Symbolist*:

> *Simplement, comme on verse un parfum sur une flamme*
> *Et comme un soldat répand son sang pour la patrie,*
> *Je voudrais pouvoir mettre mon coeur avec mon âme*
> *Dans un beau cantique à la sainte Vierge Marie.*

> *Mais je suis, hélas! un pauvre pécheur trop indigne,*
> *Ma voix hurlerait parmi le choeur des voix des justes:*
> *Ivre encor du vin amer de la terrestre vigne,*
> *Elle pourrait offenser des oreilles augustes.*

Il faut un coeur pur comme l'eau qui jaillit des roches,
Il faut qu'un enfant vêtu de lin soit notre emblème,
Qu'un agneau bêlant n'éveille en nous aucuns reproches,
Que l'innocence nous ceigne un brûlant diadème,

Il faut tout cela pour oser dire vos louanges,
O vous, Vierge Mère, ô vous, Marie Immaculée,
Vous blanche à travers les battements d'ailes des anges,
Qui posez vos pieds sur notre terre consolée.

Du moins je ferai savoir à qui voudra l'entendre
Comment il advint qu'une âme des plus égarées,
Grâce à ces regards cléments de votre gloire tendre,
Revint au bercail des Innocences ignorées.

Innocence, ô belle après l'Ignorance inouïe,
Eau claire du coeur après le feu vierge de l'âme,
Paupière de grâce sur la prunelle éblouie,
Désaltèrement du cerf rompu d'amour qui brame!

18.

PRINCE OF POETS

1888-1894

[1]

In May, 1888, he took rooms at the Hôtel de Lisbonne, 4 rue Vaugirard, and from this date it is possible to say that he enjoyed some semblance of a home of his own. Not that he had done with hospitals, but in the future he was to go back to them chiefly when he was too unwell to stay away; he no longer had to hang on there or to reinsinuate himself at the earliest possible moment in order to insure a square meal and a change of clothing.

"Rooms" be it noted, the move coinciding with improved health and a conglomeration of payments which even Verlaine, lashing out with a will, could not manage to dissipate in a few days or even weeks: he had at last received the final payment on the farm at Juniville, nine hundred francs; the repayment from a friend of the family at Arras of an old loan from Madame Verlaine, a thousand francs; and perhaps more surprising the repayment under some pressure of fifteen hundred francs which he had lent in mysterious circumstances (some say as conscience money on the insistence of the fanatical Nouveau) to the Abbé Salard, at the time a curate of Saint-Gervais—"a hard nut to crack, a curate of Saint-Gervais," he told Lepelletier gleefully, "but fifteen hundred francs is a juicy morsel"; and to this total windfall of three thousand four-hundred francs, a small fortune for him to scatter abroad, was added at much the same time a sum not far removed from this in royalties, advances on books and contributions to periodicals. *Amour* was selling well, the first of his books to pass a sale of one hundred copies, and Vanier was busy with new editions of *Poèmes saturniens, La Bonne Chanson* and *Sagesse*—that is to say, he was wherever possible rescuing unsold

stock from the cellars of other publishers to reissue under his imprint
—and with the next volumes of poems, giving advances on all.

This was not Verlaine's first return to the Left Bank. After his
first stay in the hospital, in July, 1886, he had abandoned the
Hôtel du Midi and the Right Bank. Afterwards whenever unsympathetic doctors obliged him to find and pay for lodgings he would
cross the river and camp out in one of the rooms near the Sorbonne
favored by impoverished students. The discomfort there does not have
to be imagined; it can be experienced today in, for instance, any of
the mean streets favored by Verlaine on each side of the Boulevard
St. Michel. It need only be said that, fresh from a hospital and with
memories of armchairs and generous heating and floor coverings, he
lived wretchedly enough not to rest until he had persuaded some
hospital that his state demanded immediate treatment.

Needless to say, with such as he, compensations offered themselves
even in the midst of squalor and physical discomfort. Some, the
women, the drinks, the cafés, are obvious; others less so. There was, for
example, the *rencontre* with Leconte de Lisle. The two men met at
the counter of a tobacconist. Leconte de Lisle, portly, dandified,
hair long, thin and white, legs a little unsteady, dignity Olympian
(he had assumed the mantle of Hugo as Prince of Poets and grand
old man of French literature and had followed—a sad grievance, the
"followed"—Coppée to the Academy), stared through his square
monocle, then bowed frigidly to the seedy Verlaine who looked
vaguely like something from a hayfield. Verlaine returned the bow
and motioned Leconte de Lisle to the counter. After some mutual
protestation Leconte de Lisle was served first and with due delibera-
tion bought a box of Corona-Corona. He paused to extract one, cut
and light it, pointedly unaware of Verlaine's continued presence.
Verlaine who had gone with the intention of buying a pinch of
caporal took from his pocket all the money he possessed (a few sous)
and planked it on the counter with a grand gesture: "Give me the
biggest cigar you've got." The cigar handed over, big, cheap and nasty,
he copied the motions of Leconte de Lisle and, turning, inhaled
deeply, blew a cloud of rank smoke into the face of the great man,
bowed and limped from the shop. Such was their last meeting and
such Verlaine's impromptu revenge for the calumnies of the "old
ass."

The other notable satisfaction of the hospital period was of a
purer nature, a visit to a Mallarmé soiree. By the time Verlaine visited

him, *"les mardis"* of Mallarmé had become the most exclusive literary soirees in Paris. The Stalwarts were Villiers and the Catholic writers J. K. Huysmans and Léon Bloy, but the bulk of the visitors were young Symbolist poets headed by Kahn. The atmosphere in the rue de Rome every Tuesday evening from nine until midnight was one of ordered and domestic calm. Madame Mallarmé sat next to her husband, her head bent over embroidery; Mademoiselle Mallarmé sat next to her mother prepared to open the door to the disciples who, seated solemnly around the room, helped themselves to tobacco from a Chinese jar on the center table and listened with devout attention to what was practically a monologue from the master. No sound marred the smooth flow; a thick carpet muffled all footsteps, the door was draped with thick velvet, the windows were tightly shut and Japanese curtains closely drawn before them. The fireplace was sacrosanct; there Mallarmé stood by the small, hot stove or propelled himself softly up and down in the rocking chair close to the stove. Protecting his feet from draught were thick carpet slippers, over his shoulders rested a large plaid shawl. His urbane voice quietly filled the room, the neatly pointed beard moved up and down, through the long mustaches filtered the smoke from the eternal cigarette, the calmly shining eyes veiled by long lashes were fixed on the ground or, in more fervent moments, on the tastefully decorated ceiling. He discussed the theory of poetry and, disliking self-assertion and direct assertion, never permitted himself a plain statement; everything was put in the form of questions. A pause for reflection preceded every question.

Into this exquisite Symbolist paradise limped one evening the disreputable Verlaine. Next to nothing unhappily is known about this visit but Mallarmé's feelings are not difficult to recover, liking for Verlaine and admiration for his work struggling with horrid fears: would he be intoxicated as was only too likely, would he make rude jokes as was equally probable, would he even mock Symbolism itself, a proceeding that he was fully capable of? Even Verlaine's motive for appearing is lost—he usually and tactfully continued the friendship by letter—but it can be confidently surmised: he was either too drunk to know what he was doing or, more probably, having spent his last sou and having nowhere to lay his head for the night, he called to collect an immediate loan, the soiree evening being preferable because there was a good chance of securing a handout.

It is just possible Verlaine's visit coincided with the historic eruption of Hérédia, a graying Hérédia, stouter, louder, and even more opulent in his evening dress, who had left the Opéra after the first act, who crashed into the quiet room with a huge "Hm. Stuffy here, isn't it? Hot, eh?" and marched heavily over to the rocking chair, sat himself down with a thud and proceeded to lecture the guests for the remainder of the evening.

The unhappy host, teetering between stove and table like a lost soul, said nothing because he was too polite and too much appalled by the solid vision with the massive expanse of shirt front and cuff brightly studded with over-obvious pearls; the disciples remained quiet because Hérédia was a man with a reputation, a man freely named as Prince of Poets after the ageing Leconte de Lisle.

If Verlaine's visit coincided with that of the mighty Hérédia who gave him a condescending nod in the streets, keeping well clear of physical contact, he would have sat quietly enough and would not have failed to collect an extra five or ten francs from the great one. In any event, Verlaine's reception from the disciples would be an inimitable blend of intense respect and uncontrollable laughter. For he was a great man too, even though he resolutely and comically refused to act the part. Of those present at the Mallarmé soiree, Bloy, Huysmans and Villiers of the older generation all admired him, the first two particularly for his Catholic poems, and the young Felix Fenéon, Edouard Dujardin the Wagnerian, Laurent Tailhade and Maurice Barrès of the disciples were notable for their persistent imitation of Verlaine's as of Mallarmé's verse; Barrès was soon to prove his devotion practically by paying the rent at the rue Vaugirard when the master's money ran out.

Nor was he set up simply by those who admired and imitated; even more significantly he was marked out by the opponents of "modern verse" as the begetter-in-chief of the horror. As far back as 1885 "*Il pleure dans mon coeur*" was quoted in Paul Bourde's famous attack —the attack which put the modern movement on its feet—on the "*horrible décadents*" as embodying all the typical vices of this "*maladive et bizarre*" school. In his reply and in his "Symbolist manifesto" published a year later, Moréas proudly claimed Verlaine as one of the chief inspirations of the Symbolist theory, following Poe, "that the beautiful is the only legitimate domain of poetry," that the poet "should use suggestion and music as the basis of his work" and should be the implacable enemy of "didacticism, of the objectively descriptive and of the insincerely sensitive." This was fol-

lowed by the flat statement by Baju in *Le Décadent* that Verlaine
was the greatest poet of the nineteenth century. And just before
Verlaine moved to the rue Vaugirard, another and better known
periodical, the *Revue Bleue*, published an article by Jules Lemaître,
one of the most influential critics of the day, in which he confirmed
Baju's statement. Morice was writing a critical study of Verlaine's
poetry, the young Debussy and Fauré were setting his poems to music
and there was even talk of a *Selected Verse*.

This last peak of popularity, or even talk of it, indicates Verlaine's
stature. He was not nor would ever be a rival of, say, Coppée who
had become the poet of the people, easy, optimistic, sentimental and
respectable. The growing fame of Verlaine was of quite another kind;
he remained little known to the man in the street, his contemporaries
respected and envied his work but avoided him—keep him at a
distance with an occasional loan was their motto—and the youth of
the Left Bank proclaimed him a neglected genius.

Insofar as he was winning fame through association with the
Symbolists and Decadents Verlaine pooh-poohed the idea, though, a
latter-day Figaro, willing enough to pocket the rewards: "I'll take
anything you have to give" was his attitude. But he could be scathing
enough when pushed too hard. "Symbolism?" he exclaimed one
day. "Don't understand it. Must be a German word, eh? Anyway I
couldn't care less. When I suffer, when I enjoy, when I weep I know
quite well that it's not a question of symbols. That epithet [*Décadent*]
was thrown out as an insult. I picked it up as a war cry. But fundamentally it doesn't mean anything at all."

Plain speaking; understandable from a man who had thrown off
in a humorous moment the skit which the Decadents persisted in
seeing as their gospel; and it was true enough that he was not the
innovator that some of his disciples claimed; Moréas looked back,
correctly, to Poe, and the general worship of Wagner by the Symbolists and Decadents (with which Verlaine associated himself)
showed that they knew their origins. But it was also true that at a
crucial moment the young poets discovered in his verse the essence
of Symbolism. There is always a time lag in the development of
literary modes and it is possible to see a similarity between the
coördinating work of Mendès in the sixties and of Moréas, Morice,
Kahn, Baju and the rest twenty years later; Mendès had gone far to
form the *Parnasse* on the work of Leconte de Lisle who expressed
ideas formed earlier by other men; and in a greater way Verlaine

expressed the mode of the future already present in the work of earlier artists in words and music. The difference was that Verlaine expressed these things unconsciously and that what he expressed was, unlike the *Parnasse*, a true forward movement which was to spread through the arts, to Debussy, Gauguin and the other great creators. But unconscious it was; his poetry is musical, intimate and filled with suggestions of thoughts and feelings—symbols in fact—but in Verlaine this is not an intellectual striving but merely the man talking aloud and writing as and what he felt. No wonder that he chuckled secretly when the young men claimed him as one of their gods. Let them worship and pay up!

Another mood is expressed in his inquiry to Vanier: "How goes Fame—that is, how go the sales?" If he had vanity it kept out of sight while he collected and spent the gains. This was all that fame meant to him now, this and drinks, more drinks, friendliness on all sides, talk, gross talk, fine talk, and still more drinks until the hero would lurch home, the gendarme explaining proudly to the inquiring stranger when a crowd gathered: "That's the poet, Monsieur Verlaine. He has to be in that condition to write his poetry."

Yet another mood led him to the room in the rue Vaugirard overlooking the Luxembourg Gardens and within a stone's throw of the Voltaire, the François Premier, the Procope, the Soleil d'Or, at all of which he was to have his special seat for the rest of his life. For at last he could show his face freely again. No more fear of snubs. Salutations everywhere. If this was fame he liked it; crowds of youngsters around him at the François Premier firing questions, manuscripts and drinks at him. No need to put one's hand into that emptying pocket, the young men insisted on paying all. They would help one home too. They were not always respectful—their worship was modern—but who wanted adulation? Not Verlaine, or not for long, a moment or two enthroned in a hospital bed, perhaps; no, give him young men interested, cheeky, talkative, alive.

In the autumn of 1888 and the spring and summer of the next year he first became the great sight of the Boulevard St.-Michel. There's Verlaine! Here's Verlaine! And the men would collect, the news passing quicker than the large shambling figure in his black hat and thick stick tapping solidly with every step. He was game for everything, to recite a poem, deliver a judgment, empty so many glasses in a given time, tell an unmentionable anecdote, even to unroll a bandaged leg to show a threatened ulcer. He could be silent too, listening with grave attention, one finger tapping the marble table, head lowered. When he lifted his head his eyes fascinated everyone: "Gray or green, I could never be sure, they looked like sloes. Soft and sharp, weary and lively, at times almost spiteful then mistily veiled as though they had been inwardly drowned in tears, giving themselves up to internal sobbing, to the dream of an unfathomable sadness. Those eyes begged; arrogant, hurt, angry, they were heavy with supplication." So wrote André Suarès.

The young men laughed with him and at him but they loved and respected him too and went home to write imitation after imitation of the magical lines written by this drunken sot, this buffoon, this soft-hearted, not-so-old rascal who would weep at a tale of misadventure, share his all, confess sins that neither he nor any other man had committed and in the midst of all retain that curious but unmistakable dignity.

Another reason for the settlement, if one dare use such a word of this bohemian who protested in and out of season that he was nothing of the kind, was the arrival in his life of—one can't say a disciple—a boon companion, biographer and portraitist in the person of F.-A. Cazals. In the mirror of his room, when he had one, Verlaine stuck the portraits, grubby through long life in his pockets, of Lucien and of his son Georges soon to be removed by his mother to Algiers, out of harm's way. Rimbaud he was honoring (and profiting from) by printing the poetry as he discovered it. Cazals, the last of the tribe, was quite another kettle of fish. A dandy who reminds one of the photographer Carjat, this humorous, perky, happily married young rake with the flair with the pencil and crayon had constituted himself a kind of unofficial guardian to Verlaine, looking after him when ill but not ill enough to need a hospital and toning down occasionally some of the more fanciful extravagances. But he was in no sense a moral guardian, originating as well as playing a leading part in many of the "sprees" with which the ancient-looking (he was forty-five) but lively Verlaine, his legs excepted, indulged himself. It was just that, being more French than Verlaine in this, an economical streak occasionally uncovered itself in him and he pulled up with a temporary jolt that kept a little money unexpectedly in his companion's purse.

As for the "sprees" it is not known what part Cazals played in the arrival of the delegate from the advanced poets of the South, come to pay homage, who found two naked women reclining on Verlaine's

bed. Verlaine, not at all put out, welcomed the young man, introduced him with courtly gestures to the two ladies and improved the
occasion by exclaiming, "How fortunate! Now you can tell all your
friends that you've actually seen proof that I'm not the homosexual
my enemies have whispered." And although one feels that just one
woman on the bed would have been even more convincing, the
young man from the Midi, though he blinked an eyelid, rallied
quickly and returned home with a glowing report of the master's
liberality.

Cazals certainly had a large hand in the soirees that Verlaine was
able to hold for the first and last time; his Wednesdays of 1888 and
1889 became famous throughout the Latin Quarter. The company
jammed into the room every Wednesday evening was a mixed bag;
Forain was there, Carjat too, but of all the men who had gathered
with Verlaine at De Ricard's, Mendès', Nina's and Lemerre's only
one remained. Glatigny, Valade, Nina were dead and, the year that
Verlaine set up at the rue Vaugirard, Charles Cros also; another kind
of death explained the absence of Coppée, Mendès and the rest of
the band: Verlaine was no longer respectable. In the *Parnasse* circle
it had been consistent with respectability to drink too much, to fool
to excess, to womanize, but Verlaine had committed the sin of sins;
not the sin, as it was seen at the time, of his association with Rimbaud—that had been overlooked—but of failing to keep up appearances; he had "let himself go."

The exception (the good-willed Mallarmé, Dierx and Blémont
shunning the racket not the man, Lepelletier despising the company
he kept) was Villiers, a subdued, embittered Villiers, beard and
mustache turning gray, hat reddened with age, frock coat thread-
bare, trousers frayed, face prematurely old. He had outlined the
plots of his stories too often; friends so-called had purloined them,
written them up and when Villiers at last put them into shape and
sent them to the magazines his manuscripts were returned with
accusations of plagiarism. That was sobering even to a volatile spirit.
He had almost immediately destroyed the reputation and money his
Contes Cruels brought him, beggaring himself and making himself
a laughing stock by writing to the papers demanding that the Porte-
Saint-Martin theatre withdraw a play in which a De l'Isle-Adam of
the fourteenth century was shown as a traitor. The author of the play
was long since dead—it was first staged in 1834—but nothing would
mollify Villiers. The only effect of the letter was to fill the theatre

night after night. Villiers brought an action against the theatre, prosecuting his suit with a fury that would never have been wasted on a true ancestor. He lost the case and his money. The cafés ridiculed his pretensions and the rumor spread that he was the son of a grocer.

Poor Villiers never lived down the fiasco; within a few months of his appearance at the Verlaine soirees he was dead. By that time, in the late summer of 1889, Verlaine, again in trouble with his legs, had been sent to Aix-les-Bains to take the waters. There he heard of his friend's final humiliation, the deathbed marriage with his mistress "to preserve the title" and the discovery when she came to sign the documents that she could only make a cross. Verlaine had little in common with Villiers except an inability to keep money, but Villiers had not shunned him and that was enough to make him rate the friendship higher than it deserved. He wrote on the spot one of his best *Dédicaces,* as the collection was named the following year.

This poem, lively letters to Cazals and the delightful verses on the statue of Ganymede in the public gardens were the only good things to come out of Aix-les-Bains. Verlaine had never been south of Paris since he was a child and he never went south again. He was first refused admittance to his pension, the owner mistaking him for a drunken beggar or thief and, when he did get settled in, he didn't care for it: "an evangelist asylum, English spoken, water closets, fixed price, all right," or for the town: "a kind of Bournemouth with less sea and more mountains . . . fewer cafés than in Paris and dearer." The one really favorable item was the massage after his daily hot baths, "very pleasant, almost voluptuous," but this was more than canceled by the sunshine and strong light: "As a man from the North I have little liking or admiration for the sun, it makes me feel sick, giddy, it BLINDS me, and like my dear great Mallarmé I much prefer *lucid winter.*" So he was soon writing the rounds to raise his fare back to Paris, arranging to enter the Broussais for a short season and exhorting Cazals to help him to lead a more careful life so that hospitals and begging letters could be put in their proper place. He went regularly to Mass in Aix, and to this, to his detestation of loneliness and to the spa atmosphere his new resolutions were due: he would give lessons in English, he declared, write stories with Cazals, make more poems more often; he would not end like Villiers, dying in the charity of a monastic retreat.

The resolutions did not long survive the sight of Paris. After a short stay at the Broussais, he undid the good that Aix had done by launching himself into short-lived cohabitations with Lily from Vouziers, the notorious Princess Roukine of the poem, and with a new friend Caroline Teisen whose birthplace of Metz first won his attention; into café-crawls, brothels, night clubs including, across the river, the Chat Noir where De Sivry still provided the music and the Mirilton where he heard the roars of applause that greeted Aristide Bruant's argot songs, heard with a smile remembering the night at Nina's when he had recited his own amusing little poem, forerunner of all:

J'crach' pas sur Paris, c'est rien chouett'!
Mais comm' j'ai une âm' de poèt',
Tous les dimanch's j'sors de ma boît'
Et j'm'en vais avec ma compagne
   A la campagne.

Nous prenons un train de banlieu'
Qui nous brouette à quèques lieu's
Dans le vrai pays du p'tit bleu,
Car on n'boit pas toujours d'champagne
   A la campagne.

Ell' met sa rob' de la Rein' Blanch'
Moi, j'emport' ma pip' la plus blanch';
J'ai pas d'chemis', mais j'mets des manch's,
Car il faut bien qu'l'éléganc' regne
   A la campègne.

Nous arrivons, vrai, c'est très batt'!
Des écaill's d'huîtr's comm' chez Baratt'
Et des cocott's qui vont à patt's,
Car on est tout comme chez soi
   A la camp—quoi!

Mais j'vois qu'ma machin' vous em . . . terre,
Fait's-moi signe et j'vous obtempère,
D'autant qu'j'demand' pas mieux qu'de m'taire . . .
Faut pas se gêner plus qu'au bagne,
   A la campagne.

[2]

There succeeded a confused period of hospitals and mean lodging houses until the middle of 1894 when he at last regained the rue Vaugirard. But this period of four and a half years differed from the "hospitals period" of the late eighties; he now went to a hospital because he had precipitated his "ageing body" too often into beds not his own or had overdone the absinthes too many days and weeks in succession; he ran out of money—and he was always running out —because he spent everything on friends, drink and women. He was never well off in the sense that Coppée was well off but his earnings increased steadily. He helped himself as before by begging loans— Mendès, Coppée, Blémont and a new admirer Robert de Montes-quiou, the rich dilettante immortalized by Proust, being four of the most heavily "tapped" sources—and by a new device, composing sonnets in praise of all and sundry, sending one copy to a periodical for publication and the other to the honored subject; he then waited hopefully for a tangible expression of gratitude. When he had written sufficient to form a book he persuaded Léon Deschamps, editor of the latest Symbolist periodical *La Plume*, to publish it.

The Saturday soirees of *La Plume* were reminiscent of the gather-ings at Lemerre's twenty years earlier; almost suffocated by heat and tobacco smoke and stunned by noise, the newcomer fought his way down to the basement of the Café de l'Avenir where two hundred poets were sandwiched into a room built for forty. Here poetry was read and discussed and here Verlaine, not only an honored guest but one of the liveliest men there, recited his poems amid acclamation. Régamey, long back from London, sketched him at the age of fifty at the *La Plume* banquet when he was proclaimed president by Mal-larmé; physically he looked far older than his years but the expression of his face was youthful as ever. Saturday after Saturday his neatly ironical wit set the room in a roar, he drank innumerable free drinks and pocketed a few loans before being assisted out in the small hours. And, more to the point in the early years, he collected advances for *Dédicaces*, collected them to such a pitch that even the easygoing Deschamps was shocked; from the book, he told a friend, "Verlaine is drawing more than from all his previous books. The author of *Sagesse* has been on a frightful binge. I've given him six hundred francs in one week. He got through it all. I'm going to put the brake on."

He put the brake on; but the six hundred francs in a week demonstrates not only Verlaine's powers of spending but also his powers of drawing. No longer was he the great obscure; from all sides public protests arose that one of the foremost French poets should be allowed to live in squalor; journalists, discovering wonderful "copy" in this ragged king of the Left Bank cafés, returned with snapshots and inimitable dialogue with the "neglected genius" who, leaning back in his "reserved" seat, clouded glass on the table before him, eye lazily twinkling, gave the man what he expected, exposing his legs and telling hair-raising tales of starvation, freezing rooms, cold hand hopelessly tracing one poem after another on toilet paper. Not much exaggerated, these stories, all that was withheld being the way in which he spent his money; and if he ran out of anecdotes one of the admirers crowding around would chime in with some horror capping all that had gone before.

But the field was not left to the journalists; the young poets entered the lists with letters to the daily papers complaining that their master was denied his due. Baju openly accused Verlaine's Parnassian friends of sitting back in luxury while their old companion starved. Even Lepelletier joined in with a dignified complaint of the virtual ostracism of Verlaine by old friends and lesser poets who had turned respectable. This troubled the conscience of Lemerre to the extent of offering Verlaine a hundred francs for a preface to a novel he was just about to publish by Vermersch who had died insane in an English asylum twelve years earlier; and it stung Mendès into a public reply; he would contribute, he said, to a fund from which Verlaine could draw regular sums.

Verlaine's reaction to this blast of public appeal and reproof varied comically between gratitude and resentment; declarations that he owed his privations "to a series of legal and other 'accidents,'" protests that he did not wish to be classed with "consumptive and 'interesting' poets" and a grandiose finale rejecting "what might resemble an insinuation prejudicial to his honor" and claiming "he has little left to him except his poverty but he insists that this at least shall be respected."

The wave of assistance came to a would-be grand climax in May 1891 with a gala performance at the Theatre Vaudeville for the joint benefit of Verlaine and Gauguin. The men had much in common, above all the fact that both were great artists at odds with society. Both had known years of near starvation, both had been isolated from their fellow artists, both possessed large sexual appetites, and both retained for the greater part of their lives a hopelessly impracticable regard for their wives. Both also shared a distaste for marching under the banner of a movement even when their name was inscribed prominently on the flag; they met occasionally, introduced by Morice the admirer of both, at the Voltaire where every Monday the Symbolists sat down to dinner, Gauguin having been chosen as the painter-representative of Symbolism, an honor he just managed to swallow with the substantial free meal. Next to nothing, unhappily, is known of their conversation, but Gauguin chuckled appreciatively at Verlaine's "Bah! These cymbalists!" in the midst of some particularly Symbolist speech from the head of the table. They became friendly enough for Verlaine to visit Gauguin's soirees a year or two later.

Gauguin, holding an unexpectedly favorable auction at the Drouot, was lucky enough to get off to Tahiti before the benefit performance. There he waited hopefully for his estimated share of not less than fifteen hundred francs. Verlaine appeared in person. The foyer of the theatre was hung with Gauguin canvases, "*Les Uns et Les Autres*" was played, together with a sketch by Mendès, and poems by Verlaine and others were declaimed from the stage. Unfortunately the organizers had been overlavish with the extras; almost all the receipts were eaten by expenses. The profits worked out at two hundred francs to be shared by the two men. Verlaine, hearing the news during the performance, retired to the bar to drown his disappointment: "*Benefice!*" he cried when the "magnificent sum" was handed to him. "*Malefice* they mean!"

[3]

A few months later, after the death and magnificent funeral of Banville, a train left Paris on August 23 carrying Rimbaud to a hospital at Marseilles. He had traveled down from Roche. Had he stopped in Paris he would have found himself the greatest sensation the city had known for many years. But he was desperately ill and he despised the poetry about which the cafés were excitedly talking. He passed straight through; no one knew that he was there; all he saw of Paris was the wet streets between the Gare de l'Est and

the Gare de Lyon. In the first week of December the news reached
Paris that he had died in Marseilles on the 10th of the previous
month; he was thirty-seven years old, the age reached by Van Gogh,
Toulouse-Lautrec, Burns, Pushkin, Mozart.

Twice at least false reports of his death in Abyssinia had been
circulated in Paris, and each time Verlaine had written a poem to
his memory. When he heard of his death at Marseilles Verlaine
was busy with a new edition of *Illuminations* to which he had added
Une Saison en Enfer, having discovered the manuscript; on the 7th
he wrote a postcard to Vanier from the Broussais: "Come then!
Or write. What about the preface for the Rimbaud? (dead, I hear)"
And the next day: "Have received confirmation . . . of the death
of Rimbaud and burial at Charleville." And that was all, to Vanier,
except that in the weeks following he pressed him to hurry on with
the new edition of *Illuminations* so that it would "cash in" on the
publicity following Rimbaud's death. That was the journalist.
Another Verlaine sat down to write.

> *Toi mort, mort, mort! Mais mort du moins tel que tu veux,*
> *En nègre blanc, en sauvage splendidement*
> *Civilisé, civilisant négligemment . . .*
> *Ah, mort! Vivant plutôt en moi de mille feux*
>
> *D'admiration sainte et de souvenirs feux*
> *Mieux que tous les aspects vivants même comment*
> *Grandioses! de mille feux brûlant vraiment*
> *De bonne foi dans l'amour chaste aux fiers aveux.*
>
> *Poète qui mourus comme tu le voulais,*
> *En dehors de ces Paris-Londres moins que laids,*
> *Je t'admire en ces traits naïfs de ce croquis,*
>
> *Don précieux à l'ultime postérité*
> *Par une main dont l'art naïf nous est acquis,*
> *Rimbaud! pax tecum sit, Dominus sit cum te!*

His periods in the hospitals reflected the change in his status; they
had always been pleasant; now, although the treatments were
severer, they formed one triumph after another. His visiting hours
magnified themselves into crowded receptions, his bedside was
besieged by callers, from De Montesquiou to the wealthy American

woman "seeing the sights of Paris" who thrust orchids at the preternaturally geniuslike Verlaine, from the young poet who plumped on his knees by the bed with a "Master! Dear Master!" to the head doctor, by this time a firm friend and admirer, conducting the grand tour, who would stop by the bed with a flourish and a "Gentlemen, the greatest Catholic poet of the century!" His bedside table was heaped with flowers, bowls of fruit, a pile of visiting cards, manuscripts of youthful poets awaiting his verdict and the paraphernalia of the invalid; all contrasting oddly with the great man at his ease after the receptions, pipe belching, "taking off" his visitors and recounting the latest dirty story with a wealth of telling gesture to a ward rollicking with laughter.

After the news of Rimbaud's death the flow of visitors no longer amused him; he became moody, abstracted, melancholy until one of his young Symbolist visitors, Adolphe Retté, a protégé of Kahn, called with an article he had written on Rimbaud. Since Rimbaud's death there had been a burst of publicity, Delahaye, Isabelle Rimbaud and Paterne Berrichon, who was to marry her, all beginning to write accounts of the dead man, and many young men like Retté discussing his work. Retté asked Verlaine to read the article before sending it to the periodical. He found him in a small ward with four beds, sitting near the window looking like a Doge of Venice with white wool cap and long blue dressing gown and brandishing his cane like a scepter. He read Retté's article, then sat silent, looking unhappy. Retté got up to go but Verlaine took his arm: "Let's take a turn in the garden, it's stifling here." They strolled and smoked in the garden—although January, two months after Rimbaud's death, the weather was autumnal—until Verlaine stopped: "I'd like to walk off black thoughts but my leg won't stand it." Could he help? Retté asked. Verlaine shook his head with a melancholy smile: "It's not money this time. My dreams worry me. Since the news of Rimbaud's death I've seen him every night, he dies again and again." He fixed Retté with eyes like black diamonds and said in a harsh voice, "I can't accept his death. It's many years since we saw each other but Rimbaud's face still shines before me, his genius still stirs me to the depths of my soul."

Retté, touched by his misery, urged him to unburden himself and Verlaine related the history of the shooting in Brussels: he had forgotten nothing. Then he sighed: "There was a devilish seductiveness in that boy. Hordes of memories of the days we spent wandering along the roads come back to me charged with atrociously delicious perfumes. I've known true happiness twice in my life. First through my wife, the only person I've ever loved deeply; a happiness which would have made another man of me if I'd been master of my senses. Then I tasted the painful joys of living intensely, to the very top of my being, in the company of Rimbaud. I've never been able to console myself for the loss of either."

He tapped Rette's manuscript: "You write that Rimbaud is a legend. From the literary point of view you are no doubt right. But to me Rimbaud is always a living reality, an inextinguishable sun flaming on me. That's why I dream of him every night." And lifting his hand in the familiar gesture he recited the two last stanzas of the poem he had written four years earlier when Rimbaud's death in Abyssinia was first reported:

> Mort, tout ce triomphe inouï
> Retentissant sans frein ni fin
> Sur l'air jamais évanoui
> Que bat mon coeur qui fut divin!
>
> Quoi, le miraculeux poème
> Et la toute-philosophie,
> Et ma patrie et ma bohème
> Morts? Allons donc! tu vis ma vie!

[4]

Rette had found Verlaine with a temperature chart in one hand; he had been writing a poem on the back of it. And had Rette called another day he would have seen much the same; a temperature chart, a prescription form, the back of an envelope, anything would do. For Verlaine was almost always writing; letters and poems poured from hospitals, lodging houses, cafés; he would snatch the nearest scrap of paper or rummage in his pockets and, head bent, lips mouthing words, would cover the crumpled, torn, dirty sheet with his neat, legible writing. The mere list of published books since Amour, excluding reprints and the long roll of insertions in periodicals, gives some idea of his industry. In 1889, the year after Amour, came Parallèlement; in 1890 Dédicaces; in 1891 no fewer than five books, Bonheur, Mes Hôpitaux, Chansons pour Elle, Femmes and Choix de Poésies; in 1892 Liturgies Intimes; in 1893

Odes en son Honneur, Élégies and *Mes Prisons*; in 1894 *Quinze Jours en Hollande, Dans les Limbes* and *Épigrammes*; in 1895 *Confessions*; and after his death *Hombres, Chair, Invectives, Biblio-Sonnets, Oeuvres Oubliées* in two volumes and *Oeuvres Posthumes* in three, not to speak of the many poems discovered later and printed in periodicals.

Industry: that is the word; and when one deducts earlier poems which he had preserved against a rainy day, he still wrote too much, for the time had come, especially after the appearance of *Choix de Poésies* which made him really popular, when he could sell every line he chose to write. This wholesale writing only partly explains the fall in standard. He was a contented man and the contented man rarely produces works of great art. He was hard pressed for cash and this too does not encourage good writing.

The two remaining books of religious verse, *Bonheur* and *Liturgies Intimes,* are inferior to the two earlier ones; the faith has lost its fire, lost the appeal of simplicity and become merely naïve. There is more than a suspicion of the hand organ in the last of the four, and no wonder, for it was manufactured to order.

The three "fleshly" books, *Chansons pour Elle, Odes en son Honneur* and *Chair* contain better things and one critic has even compared the first with Villon's *"Ballade des Femmes de Paris,"* a comparison which would have pleased Verlaine. Nevertheless, if Verlaine bores rarely, he can be too simple and, as in some of the love poems to Mathilde, too coy. One misses the humor and the flight of imagination. The books were written to please and with a few exceptions they show it.

Not so with the two books published *"sous le manteau," Femmes* and *Hombres.* The same subject as before but written for pleasure. Both are rated as pornography, and as a section of every community discovers provocation in the most natural events this is no doubt inevitable, but pornography they are not if by pornography is meant a deliberate excitation of sexual appetites. What Verlaine does is to relive past and present sexual joys, to praise the human body and to get out of his system what most people harbor secretly all their lives. There is much of the schoolboy in these poems, a good deal of the poet too; one of the best describes the various feminine odors and is, if the subject be admitted, beautifully written, full-blooded, taut, expressive and with a wealth of exact and original imagery.

Dédicaces, consisting in the main of unblushing "puffs" in the hope of a loan or favorable review, makes poor reading but even here one lights on good things, for instance the poems in memory of Villiers and Cladel, and once or twice on the superb as in this sonnet to Rimbaud:

> *Mortel, ange ET démon, autant dire Rimbaud,*
> *Tu mérites la prime place en ce mien livre,*
> *Bien que tel sot grimaud t'ait traité de ribaud*
> *Imberbe et de monstre en herbe et de potache ivre.*
>
> *Les spirales d'encens et les accords de luth*
> *Signalent ton entrée au temple de mémoire*
> *Et ton nom radieux chantera dans la gloire,*
> *Parce que tu m'aimais ainsi qu'il le fallut.*
>
> *Les femmes te verront, grand jeune homme très fort,*
> *Très beau d'une beauté paysanne et rusée,*
> *Très désirable d'une indolence qu'osée!*
>
> *L'histoire t'a sculpté triomphant de la mort*
> *Et jusqu'aux purs excès jouissant de la vie,*
> *Tes pieds blancs posés sur la tête de l'Envie!*

Invectives, "owing more to Martial than to Juvenal," has been described as not poetry; this depends on the point of view; what is clear is that Verlaine wielded a sharp knife on occasion and that his surgery can be of the first class. Witness this to a sadist doctor of the Broussais:

> *Tu fus inhumain*
> *De sorte cruelle.*
> *Tu fus inhumain*
> *De façon mortelle.*
> *Tu fus inhumain*
> *Sans rien de romain.*
>
> *Tu n'as d'un Romain . . .*
> *De la décadence,*
> *Tu n'as d'un Romain*
> *Que ta grosse panse.*
> *Tu n'as de romain*
> *Que d'être inhumain.*

Tu fus dur et sec
Comme un coup de trique.
Tu fus dur et sec
Comme une bourrique
Qui ruerait avec
Un rein dur et sec.

Le pauvre à ta voix
Tremblait comme feuille,
Le pauvre—à ta voix!
Qu'épuise et qu'endeuille
La faim, à la fois,
La soif—et ces froids!

Et maudit sois-tu,
Selon tes mérites!
Donc maudit sois-tu,
Vil bourreau dodu!
Oui, maudit sois-tu
Suivant ta vertu!

In *Parallèlement* we are on a different plane. He described the book many times, perhaps the most Verlainean effort being in his preface to the religious *Liturgies Intimes.* "This quite small book," he wrote, "is intended for a quite small and select public, and is indeed the complement—dare I say, the crown?—of a work of considerable extent which the author believes to be in accord with the Faith. This work is in four volumes: *Sagesse*, the conversion; *Amour*, the perseverance; a backsliding deliberately confessed, *Parallèlement*; and *Bonheur*, conclusion sorrowfully calm in the supreme consolation."

Anyone less sorrowfully calm than Verlaine would be hard to find, and anyone less methodical. In his religious books queerly unreligious poems are to be found, and in his professedly carnal books the spiritual element will obtrude. The "backsliding" which led to *Parallèlement* had a long history; it began in the prison at Mons when the chaplain advised the impassioned convert not to confine his poems to religious subjects but to express the other, parallel, side of himself. No doubt Verlaine would have done so in any event as his fervor declined but he preferred sanction to unleash the earthy man. The book was originally to be called *Cellulairement* but as so

many of the poems were written out of the cell Verlaine happily
changed it. The eventual title indicated the physical running alongside the spiritual; it also stood for one of his major influences,
Rimbaud, moving parallel to the influence of Mathilde, first one
then the other taking possession of his muse.

The poems range from the Lesbian sonnets of 1867 through the
"Laeti et Errabundi" of 1887 to the savage *"Les Morts que l'on fait
saigner"* written in the year of publication. There is not one bad
poem in the book, many superb ones and at least two masterpieces;
of all the books by Verlaine this best expresses his nature and genius
in maturity; he is himself all the time in every kind of mood; the
moving *"Impression Fausse"* and the brilliant *"La Dernière Fête
galante,"* already quoted, rest side by side with the charming *"Pierrot
Gamin"* written to the clown Willette beloved of Verlaine as of
Toulouse-Lautrec and half Paris:

> Ce n'est pas Pierrot en herbe
> Non plus que Pierrot en gerbe.
> C'est Pierrot, Pierrot, Pierrot.
> Pierrot gamin, Pierrot gosse,
> Le cerneau hors de la cosse,
> C'est Pierrot, Pierrot, Pierrot!
>
> Bien qu'un rien plus haut qu'un mètre,
> Le mignon drôle sait mettre
> Dans ses yeux l'éclair d'acier
> Qui sied au subtil génie
> De sa malice finie
> De poète-grimacier.
>
> Lèvres rouge-de-blessure
> Où sommeille la luxure,
> Face pâle aux rictus fins,
> Longue, très accentuée,
> Qu'on dirait habituée,
> A contempler toutes fins,
>
> Corps fluet et non pas maigre,
> Voix de fille et non pas aigre,
> Corps d'éphèbe en tout petit,
> Voix de tête, corps en fête,
> Créature toujours prête
> A soûler chaque appétit.

Va, frère, va camarade,
Fais le diable, bats l'estrade
Dans ton rêve et sur Paris
Et par le monde, et sois l'âme
Vile, haute, noble, infâme
De nos innocents esprits!

Grandis, car c'est la coutume,
Cube ta riche amertume,
Exagère ta gaieté,
Caricature, auréole,
La grimace et le symbole
De notre simplicité!

* * *

It is not Pierrot in the grasses,
Nor Pierrot when the wild wind passes,
It is Pierrot, Pierrot, Pierrot,
Pierrot rascal and infernal,
As a lass out of a kernel,
It is Pierrot, Pierrot, Pierrot!

Not as near high as Demeter,
The dear droll knows how in metre
From their eyes to shoot for thunder
That his subtle genius vicious
Makes more infinitely malicious
Than the grimacing Poet's wonder.

Lips red wounded with Insanity
Where slumbers lulling Luxury.
Pale faces all in agitation,
Long and very accentuated,
One might say habituated
To no serious contemplation.

Body slender and not thinner
Than a girl's who is a sinner,
Youth beyond all youth's surprising.
Voice in the head, festal feature
Of this singular mad creature
Made for sensual appetizing.

Go, beyond all Good and Evil,
Beat your feet and make the Devil
In your dream and over Paris,
That's the world, and be the soul there,
Infamous as any hole there
Where no fallen spirit marries!

Yet the custom is to greaten
To the huge height of our Satan
In an immense exaggeration,
Caricature and saintless faces,
Soulless symbols and Disgraces
Of our feverish agitation!

There is the clever parody of himself in "A la Manière de Paul
Verlaine."

C'est à cause du clair de la lune
Que j'assume ce masque nocturne
Et de Saturne penchant son urne
Et de ces lunes l'une après l'une.

Des romances sans paroles ont,
D'un accord discord ensemble et frais,
Agacé ce coeur fadasse exprès,
O le son, le frisson qu'elles ont!

Il n'est pas que vous n'ayez fait grâce
A quelqu'un qui vous jetait l'offense:
Or, moi, je pardonne à mon enfance
Revenant fardée et non sans grâce.

Je pardonne à ce mensonge-là
En faveur en somme du plaisir
Très banal drôlement qu'un loisir
Douloureux un peu m'inocula.

* * *

It is because of the midnight moon
That I assume this mask nocturnal
And of Saturn's urn and his power infernal
And of moon after moon in the hot mid-noon.

Songs without words have these romances,
That clash in discordant chords together
And hurt my sad soul in dusty weather.
O the shiver and sound of the dancer's dances!

Pardoned are these with their sins acquainted,
Thanks to the fiery sword in the garden:
As for myself I pardon
Not without grace returning painted.

I pardon this lie for its banality
In favour of an immensity of pleasure
Absurd enough in its lack of leisure
And not as sorrowful as Insanity.

There is "*Limbes*" with its duet between imagination and reflection.

L'imagination, reine,
Tient ses ailes étendues,
Mais la robe qu'elle traîne
A des lourdeurs éperdues.

Cependant que la Pensée,
Papillon, s'envole et vole,
Rose et noir clair, élancée
Hors de la tête frivole.

L'imagination, sise
En son trône, ce fier siège!
Assiste, comme indécise,
A toute ce preste manège,

Et le papillon fait rage,
Monte et descend, plane et vire:
On dirait dans un naufrage
Des culbutes du navire.

La reine pleure de joie
Et de peine encore, à cause
De son coeur qu'un chaud pleur noie,
Et n'entend goutte à la chose.

Psyché Deux pourtant se lasse,
Son vol est la main plus lente

Que cent tours de passe-passe
Ont faite toute tremblante.

Hélas, voici l'agonie!
Qui s'en fût formé l'idée?
Et tandis que, bon génie
Plein d'une douceur lactée,

La bestiole céleste
S'en vient palpiter à terre,
La Folle-du-Logis reste
Dans sa gloire solitaire!

There is the realistic "A Mademoiselle."

Rustique beauté
Qu'on a dans les coins
Tu sens bon les foins
La chair et l'été.

Tes trente-deux dents
De jeune animal
Ne vont point trop mal
A tes yeux ardents.

Ton corps dépravant
Sous tes habits courts,
—Retroussés et lourds,
Tes seins en avant,

Tes mollets farauds,
Ton buste tentant,
—Gai, comme impudent,
Ton cul ferme et gros,

Nous boutent au sang
Un feu bête et doux
Qui nous rend tout fous,
Croupe, rein et flanc.

Le petit vacher
Tout fier de son cas,
Le maître et ses gas,
Les gas du berger,

> *Je meurs si je mens,*
> *Je les trouve heureux,*
> *Tous ces culs-terreux,*
> *D'être tes amants.*

And there is the great poem to Rimbaud, *"Laeti et Errabundi."*
All his verses to or concerning Rimbaud have a power, a directness
and even a ferocity never found elsewhere in his work, as if something of Rimbaud possessed him as he wrote, but of all *"Laeti et
Errabundi"* stands surpreme. It is a complement or an answer to
the *"Vierge folle"* section of *Une Saison en Enfer*, and if the volume
had contained nothing else of value this alone would make it one
of his best. It is too long to print in full but the final two stanzas
have already been quoted; the last gives a faint idea of the quality of
the whole.

Parallèlement was an immediate success; it led to the appearance
of the profitable selection of poems two years later which by 1894
had gone into five editions and was still selling briskly. This in turn
led Verlaine back to rue Vaugirard and to comparative, very comparative affluence for a few months. And there, a few weeks after
settling in, he received an honor which, to the old guard at least,
came as an unpleasant surprise but which to the reader may seem
a rare case of the prophet honored in his lifetime: on the death of
Leconte de Lisle he was elected Prince of Poets by a decisive majority.
The affronted Hérédia, next best, polled less than half the votes
given to Verlaine; Coppée was at the bottom of the list.

Cheered by this refreshing gesture of sanity Verlaine promptly
spent every sou on a grand celebration in his rooms. As one would
expect he bore the honor lightly. "You have made me Prince of
Poets," he said in a mock reply to an address of welcome. "I'm
without a palace at the moment but my royal park is free to all"—
and he pointed grandly through the window to the Luxembourg
Gardens.

19.

THE LECTURER

1892-1893

[1]

One day late in October, 1892, Verlaine was to be seen in the Boulevard St.-Michel gesturing rather more vivaciously than usual and exposing a wealth of shirt front. He seemed to be inviting passers-by to examine his linen, and if one joined the crowd which gathered whenever he stopped, one would hear him say triumphantly, "Feel it; it's not just clean, it's new!" And he would shoot a pair of fairly spotless cuffs with an air.

Remaining a little longer one would hear the whole story: he had been invited to lecture in Holland; he or someone—it was not clear—had brought a white shirt, a hat, a jacket and trousers, a respectable shiny pair of boots; he would travel first class from Paris and back again; he was going to turn over a new leaf when he returned, save his lecture fees (he gave details, one thousand francs for six lectures, everything found) and lead a hard-working life, limiting his drinks, keeping his francs under the mattress. No more shortages, no more cadging of loans; probity, economy, respectability, order were to be the watchwords of the new Verlaine. *"Je vais me mettre dans mes meubles!"* he said again and again in sprightly tone "clicking his teeth like castanets," a habit of his in reforming mood.

As to all these last words, those who listened remained skeptical; he had said the same thing with similar emphasis before the publication of each book in turn. But no one wished to deny the significance of an invitation to lecture out of France; the lecture tour was a sign of renown and offered a chance of earning much more money than any book of poems could produce. Besides, one tour was apt to lead to another.

Before he managed to get himself onto the train on November 2, Verlaine's shirt had lost its first freshness but he arrived sober and cheerful at The Hague, a cheerfulness increased by his having watched from the window en route the pink walls of the prison at Mons passing by; a sight which he regarded benevolently and "almost triumphantly," as well he might, and which needless to say he made into a poem.

The tour had been arranged by the young Blok, a Dutch bookseller afterwards to become famous; he had visited Paris, listened to Verlaine at the cafés and, admiring and pitying in equal part, had secured sponsors. It was at the home of one of these, the painter Philippe Zilcken, that Verlaine made his headquarters. Verlaine, said Zilcken afterwards, "was neither black nor white but an impassioned, impressionable, versatile poet." He might have added, an unusual guest; he rose early, before anyone was astir; he retired after breakfast to the studio where he "surrounded himself with dictionaries," which astonished Zilcken as being quite out of reported character, prepared his lecture and, his host happening to comment on the incomprehensibility of Mallarmé's poetry, said, "But it's very easy, only a question of syntax," and proceeded by analysis of a poem to make everything clear. He won the heart of his hostess' small daughter, soon "the divine little Renée" and "my literary daughter"; and of his hostess whom he immediately approached with a "lots of things have been said about me and I want you to know exactly what kind of man you are entertaining"; this followed by a complete life history, nothing withheld and not too much excused.

After this all was plain sailing in the Zilcken home. The comfort of the house and for that matter of all the Dutch houses he visited overwhelmed him as did the amount of food they ate, and for a couple of weeks he lived like a lord, feasted, entertained with all the solemn-smiling thoroughness of that hospitable people. He loved their "sweet gravity" he said and took in good part their "unmalicious chaff"—for, taking immediately to schnapps, he was once or twice only just in shape to stand before his audience. He lectured at The Hague, Amsterdam and Leyden, his lectures consisting of a brief foreword on the Parnassians, Symbolists, Decadents and the latest school of poetry, Moréas' Ecole Romane, with readings from the best of them. His delivery was indifferent—"mediocre, negligible, almost voiceless," he said—and his hostess made him swallow a raw egg before he went off to the hall, but he could be effective as an onlooker remarks: "His voice, though rather heavy and slow, sometimes had a pleasant timbre and played on all the stops from oratory to invective; it had the hoarseness of one who takes a gloomy pleasure in making a sad avowal." His readings of his own poems were much admired by those who sat in the front seats, but the success of the tour was not in the lectures which were poorly attended but in the furor which his visit caused among the young literati.

After the first lecture Zilcken's house was filled with these young men and Verlaine was entertained at one dinner and soiree after another. His absolute absence of pose struck everybody and as he somehow managed to carry his drinks with discretion compliments abounded. "He's an artist from head to foot," one young poet enthusiastically told a friend, "a man who has made the most beautiful poems, a great and pure artist whose every look, every gesture conveys the unique personality"; and he enclosed a boutonniere worn by Verlaine at one of the dinners, which he had begged as a souvenir.

Verlaine returned triumphantly to Paris without having once blotted his escutcheon, with his thousand francs intact plus an advance from Blok on a Dutch edition of his *Quinze Jours en Hollande,* a little book which he retired to the Broussais to write—this because he immediately lost all the money he had made.

Of this more later; for the moment came another invitation, from Maeterlinck and the Belgian Catholic writer Jean Casier, to lecture in Belgium. Maeterlinck had spent several months in Paris a few years earlier, nominally to finish his legal studies, actually to haunt the cafés. His main center was the Brassière Pousset where Villiers recited his unwritten short stories and illustrated them in mime so vivid that one of his listeners, Mallarmé, was terrified that he would throw himself into the crowd in an epileptic fit. He would talk and act for six hours at a stretch and one of the crowd who never moved while he spoke was the young Belgian law student who forthwith abandoned the law and returned home to write with Villiers' voice still in his mind: "All I have done I owe to his conversation," he said later. He did not meet Verlaine who had then just embarked on his hospital period but he read his poems and pronounced him "the evangelist of dream and irony."

This highflown description notwithstanding, he heard enough about the evangelist to know roughly what to expect when the train steamed into Gand one morning in February, 1893. The window of a third-class carriage (no fares paid this time) opened with a great noise and the "faunesque" head of the poet protruded with a cry of "I take it with sugar!" This war cry Maeterlinck understood—the correct Casier, who stood with him on the platform, happily did not—to mean that Verlaine sugared his absinthe. All three "fraternized violently," Verlaine being already slightly the worse for wear. Maeterlinck mentioning lunch and a drink, the guest suddenly showed signs of restlessness and was quickly installed in a cab with his luggage, a much worn carpetbag. They drove to the Taverne St. Jean, the best restaurant in the city. Verlaine "wore the enraptured air and smile of a hairy angel" and, offered port, wisely chose gin to welcome the "magnificent lunch."

Verlaine's lightheartedness was due as much to relief at the sight and sound of Maeterlinck as to the flask of absinthe he had emptied during the night, for he had with a sinking heart read the work of his host before setting out. "A phenomenon, Maeterlinck a revelation!" he said afterwards. "From his plays and verse I expected to find a pale, thin, corpselike man swathed in flannel and drenched with herb tea. But not at all, a great big fellow greeted me most jovially, had a fine drink ready for me and said with a Flemish accent, 'Now, dear Master, we'll eat a good beefsteak.' This Maeterlinck had a formidable appetite. Afterwards he spoke of his bees while smoking his pipe." Verlaine breathed again: "I love mystics of this sort." His hosts were less enthusiastic, Casier worked up to reverence the greatest Catholic poet of modern times, Maeterlinck worried, knowing Casier and the "strait-laced and easily offended" Belgian audiences.

The lunch began inauspiciously; Verlaine was no sooner seated at the table decorated in his honor than he asked "with the simplicity of a Franciscan brother: 'Where are the latrines?'" A slight cloud passed over the table "the seraphic Casier gripping his chair with embarrassment." But Verlaine seemed to notice nothing; he went off and returned radiant; and as the gins followed one another, he explained with much laughter, bending forward confidentially, that "all that kind of thing was over long ago." As the meal progressed he began to tell anecdotes, charming some of them, Maeterlinck thought; but the maître d'hotel, anxious to do honor to the great man, was too zealous with the bottles, and before Maeterlinck could give him a discreet signal Verlaine was well launched. By that time

Verlaine at the François Premier, 1892

Verlaine, the Lecturer, 1893

he believed himself, Maeterlinck thought, to be in a bistro and almost imperceptibly the anecdotes changed character; into them "glided obscenities," which, fortunately, "our Saint Casier, comprehending nothing, took for subtle pleasantries."

Another matter was agitating Maeterlinck as he watched the gesticulating, talkative, hairy angel across the table. The new white shirt of the Dutch tour had long since been sold to the second-hand clothes dealer; Verlaine was wearing a gray-pink flannel shirt, "more gray than pink" Maeterlinck observed, closed at the neck by a colored cord with "alarming" tassels. Maeterlinck remarked that a white shirt and stiff collar would be considered de rigueur that evening; would Verlaine care to visit his shirtmaker? Verlaine agreed enthusiastically and off they drove when lunch was done. The shirtmaker laid out many elegant and expensive shirts but Verlaine, who had been nosing about the shop, pointed out a simple triangular shirt front and collar as worn by the waiters of lesser cafés: "That one's cheaper and easier." Nothing would dissuade him; he took it.

The problem then was to divert him until evening. Maeterlinck tried a round of "curiosities" but Verlaine showed an increasing tendency to stop en route at bars for 'a quick one'; he had, he explained, never before tasted "Haselt old style gin," the brand they had served as an apéritif in the restaurant; he believed that it held beauties undreamed of in the French gins; he would like to confirm this belief. What was more, he would obviously prefer to confirm it in the cheaper bars and not at the luxurious ones in which Maeterlinck tried to detain him by the lure of armchairs and illustrated papers.

At last evening came. Verlaine was still on his feet, he had put on his shirt front and carried his lecture notes purposefully but his bearing was such a blend of the jaunty and the confused that Maeterlinck prepared for a stormy session. He, Gregorie le Roy the poet and Georges Mince the sculptor, all big men and good boxers, arranged to police the lecture hall. The room was practically full when Verlaine was introduced by the president; as he approached the lecture table, inclining his head, a few stifled laughs came from the audience and Maeterlinck and his friends clenched their fists. Verlaine seemed not to have noticed (though he afterwards complained of the "snobbery" of the Belgians), put down his papers and read some dozens of verses with nothing more untoward than an occasional stutter.

Unhappily the arrangement of his papers had been imperfectly made—he had thrust them pell mell into the carpetbag in Paris and had not looked at them since—and he stopped in the middle of a line, fumbled ineffectually with the papers and began to improvise with no more than moderate success.

At this moment a door leading from the room to a billiards saloon opened, a man appeared shirt-sleeved with queue in hand, listened to the improvising Verlaine for a moment or two, said loudly, "That fellow is drunk!" and went back into the saloon, closing the door with a crash.

Maeterlinck and his friends, horrified, leaped forward to chastise the billiards player and to overawe the by then tittering section of the audience. But they reckoned without a Verlaine feeling well disposed toward the entire world: thanks to "the imperturbable calm of our old Master who lost the thread of his discourse without losing his head" the lecture settled down, continued eventlessly and ended without further hitch and to the sound of applause "scattered but distinguished."

The president handed a sealed envelope to Verlaine who was quickly surrounded by people demanding his autograph and asking "inane questions." He was rescued by Maeterlinck and his big friends and led outside. There he made straight for the nearest street lamp and feverishly tore open the president's envelope.

"Three hundred francs!" he cried, pale with emotion. "Where is the nearest bank?"

It was then an hour short of midnight. All the banks were closed, they assured him. "Then what shall I do?" he demanded. "You understand that I can't possibly spend the night with such a sum on me."

Maeterlinck promised him that if the money were stolen he and Casier would replace it; then, realizing that this was not exactly what Verlaine meant, he begged Le Roy, a nightbird himself, to look after the guest. Le Roy and Verlaine set off into the night and at Verlaine's request toward the still illuminated bars. Le Roy found his strength tested; he struggled for two hours, until the bars closed, to prevent Verlaine from drinking himself insensible and treating everybody he met. He succeeded to the degree that he was able to conduct Verlaine to the station that morning to catch the train for his next lecture town.

The lectures, at Charleroi, Antwerp, Liège, Verviers and Ghent, were unremarkable, saved as usual by Verlaine's readings of his own poems,

the poems rather than the readings being so much greater than anything else the audience had heard that evening. The audiences remained snobbish in Verlaine's eyes but he fell in love with one of
their towns, Bruges: "I should like to spend the rest of my life.
there," he said.

The last lecture was an unexpected triumph. It was held, of all
places, in the Palais de Justice where Verlaine had been sentenced to
two years' imprisonment. He rose to the occasion, threw aside his
usual notes, produced the proofs of *Mes Prisons* and read his account
of his sufferings in that very room twenty years earlier almost to the
month. The reading and his tears as he read moved his audience as
his lectures did not; he was loudly applauded and left Brussels in a
blaze of glory and with rather more than a thousand francs in his
pocket.

The glory perhaps went to his head for when, Taine dead, there
was a vacancy at the Academy and a journalist said, "Why not you?"
Verlaine promptly put his name down. Why not, indeed. Lepelletier,
who did not approve of Verlaine's young admirers on the Left Bank
or of anything that his old friend now did, explained why not in an
article in the *Echo de Paris:* Verlaine was not respectable. Meanwhile
the young poets and the journalists reveled in the situation: the
greatest poet in France and the most disreputable; what did the
Academy stand for, greatness or respectability? The answer when it
came was decisive; Verlaine did not get one vote.

This, however, was almost a year ahead. Before then, at the beginning of November Verlaine was on tour again, having been invited, to
his enormous gratification to give readings at Nancy and Luneville.
He was greeted with tremendous enthusiasm at both places and at
Nancy the production of a large plaque "Nancy for Metz" (Metz
having been incorporated in Germany since 1871) reduced the
proud Verlaine and the entire audience to tears.

Ten days later he left Paris for his last lecture tour, to his beloved
England.

[2]

In the past few years there had arisen in England a certain awareness that pleasures hitherto undreamed of lay just across the channel.
For the most part this awareness was confined to those who, tempted
by Louis Napoleon and the Parisian pleasure merchants, traveled

increasingly to Paris for the week end and for their holidays to sample the "Gay Paree" obligingly laid out for their benefit. In the eighties and nineties Paris of the Madeleine, the Place de l'Opéra, the Boulevard Montmartre and Montmartre itself was thronged with English and American tourists; all was ready for them, the glaring lights, the nudity, the vulgarity, while to reassure the timid were English bars, English hotels, English tea rooms, English beggars soliciting alms from the curbside in good honest cockney.

But there was also a small section of London intellectuals aware that English artists had much to learn in France. The appeal of French culture to the intellectual snob in England has been strong since the eighteenth century and remains powerful today but there were then as now a few men who appreciated the culture of France without denigrating the culture of their own country. Swinburne and his tiny following excepted, genuine appreciation was restricted almost entirely to the painter; it was pretty well established by then that if a young man wanted to paint seriously he would have to go through the Paris schools. And it was by the means of two young men whose interest was primarily painting that Verlaine was made known, first in print, then in public, to a select English audience.

The first of these, George Moore, though known now only as a writer, consorted in Paris with the painters, the Impressionists particularly. It does not seem that he had met Verlaine before he wrote about him in 1881, but he would have heard sufficient from Manet and his friends Mallarmé and Chabrier to provide a picture of this outcast Parnassian to accompany an appreciation of his work. In the same year another young Irishman, O'Shaughnessy, translated and published "Clair de Lune."

Neither the article of Moore nor the translation of O'Shaughnessy made the slightest impression in England, and it is probably true to say that Verlaine first became known to a few English people ten years later, in 1891, when Moore reprinted his article in Impressions and Opinions; Moore was just beginning to make a name as writer and the article might well have reminded the traveled reader of certain Paris newspaper snippets about the man pigeonholed by journalists as the reincarnation of Villon.

The first Englishman to make the acquaintance of Verlaine, in distinction to gaping at him in the Boulevard St.-Michel, was Arthur Symons in the early nineties. Symons was poet, essayist, critic and most Francophile of all English literary men. His interests, as it happened, took him more to Montmartre than the Latin Quarter, but for an intelligent man to know one set in Paris was to be known in practically all; there were no precise limits to sets or for that matter to the arts, many men trying their hand at several. Symons had heard of Verlaine, of course, but it seems that his knowledge of his work had been restricted to a chance reading of *Romances sans Paroles* in Coppée's house. He then met Morice, absorbed his enthusiasm and persuaded him to take him along to the François Premier.

This was one April night in 1892. Verlaine was sitting in the midst of a group of young men—Symons noticed the dark-featured Moréas with his blue-black hair and half-savage, half-sullen black eyes, and the tall thin painter Fernand Langlois with complexion almost gray and air of exhaustion. But Verlaine astonished him; he had expected something *"en diable* ending in a green tail" having heard many descriptions and seen many portraits "none pleasant"; he saw a shabbily dressed, collarless man, white scarf round his neck and gray soft hat pushed back on his head, a man with a "spiritual forehead, animal jaw, shifting faun's eyes . . . oblique, constantly in movement, with gestures of the lids and brows" and with a genial expression. Verlaine's air was "manly and gentlemanly." He was all gesture, face, hands, arms, body moving suddenly, violently, convincingly: "As he explodes into conversation his whole body seems to translate meaning into movement."

But what most surprised Symons was Verlaine's natural dignity; he conveyed unmistakably an "ineradicable refinement, impressive sincerity and simplicity with an entire absence of pose or deliberate extravagance—the extravagance when it came, often, being natural and on the spur of the moment."

Verlaine's conversation veered as violently as his movements. He began with natural courtesy to talk of England, how he admired the poetry of Tennyson and Swinburne, how he loved the English Sunday: "So religious!" he exclaimed, pulling imaginary bell ropes with his hands. Abruptly, having done his duty as host and expressing at the same time one of his thousand enthusiasms, he began to tell "rather shocking stories," interrupting himself from time to time, again courteously, to try to find the exact English equivalents for "unspeakable" French words—the quotes being Symons', of course.

Turning directly to the visitor he then told some "most dubious" experiences of his past life, told them "in a most matter of fact, impersonal manner with the good-humored tone of one who tells a curious story that may interest the listener." He wound up with an invitation to Symons and his friend Havelock Ellis, neighbor in his Fountain Court chambers, to visit him the following evening.

When the two young Englishmen climbed the stairs of the Hôtel des Mines in the Boul' Mich' the next evening, there was no Verlaine. Symons went out and came across Verlaine dragging himself along the boulevard on the arm of Bibi—la—Purée, the little man who had one day knelt before Verlaine in the Boulevard St.-Michel insisting that he be allowed to sew up the master's torn overcoat and who thereafter refused to leave him. Verlaine had forgotten his invitation, apologized several times with "tremendous" emphasis, and continued to excuse himself on the stairs, stopping every few paces to explain why he had to take his time.

The room was small, mean, frugally furnished. A portrait of Verlaine, a few books, a large Bible were the only personal possessions to be seen; two candles provided the only light. Verlaine was in expansive mood: "I have got *money*," he proclaimed in English. "I will have pleasure." He took out his purse, extracted two francs proudly and handed them to Bibi. Langlois came in and curled himself on the bed, Symons and Havelock Ellis occupied the two chairs, Verlaine limped about the room and Bibi, returning with glasses and a bottle of rum, perched himself on the chest of drawers. Verlaine dispensed the rum, sipping his own slowly, raising the glass halfway to his lips and holding it suspended while he talked "furiously," sometimes putting it down again untasted. He was "argumentative and explosive, his facial pantomime more frantic than ever."

He picked up the Bible, patted it fondly and showed it to his guests, pointing out the name of the Protestant translator. It was an excellent book, he assured Symons, and he was a religious man. "*Je suis Catholique!*" he exclaimed again and again, fondling the Bible in one hand, in the other grasping the glass of rum. "*Catholique du moyen age!*"

Recalling the nationality of his visitors he changed the subject and, laughing, quoted several examples of Cockney obscenities learned in London with Rimbaud. Finally, as the supreme compliment, he declaimed "in a weird accent" one of Hamlet's soliloquies.

Symons was a man of discernment; after these two short visits he cut through the gossip to a truth. He compared Verlaine with Villon —"picturesque vices, fell in with scum of society, whole nature waiting to turn into poetry"—that much was inevitable, but his summing up is solid. Drinks were offered to Verlaine all day long, he said, by people who said they were his friends (he would have added, had he known Verlaine longer, that the offers were not always accepted) but Verlaine sober "was the most delightful of companions —queer, rambling, confidential talk full of wonder, trouble and gaiety, a condensation of the mood of the moment and always on the verge of poetry." Back in London he promptly began to translate the poetry. Within two years he had published some translations and a critical estimate of Verlaine's work—criticism which compares favorably with anything written at that time by the French critics.

The pioneer work of Symons had its effect, and by 1892 a small band of intellectuals in London were aware that a great poet was living and writing in Paris. Wilde could write, "I look forward . . . to a talk about French art, the one art now in Europe which is worth discussing—Verlaine's art especially," and there grew up some sort of pilgrimage obligatory to any of the band who chanced to be in Paris. Not all were impartial, the young Edmond Gosse for example, an admirer of Leconte de Lisle, visiting Verlaine with preconceptions which Verlaine obligingly confirmed. So appears in the entrance to the cellar of the Restaurant d'Harcourt "a ghostly shape . . . a strange bald head" and, behind Moréas who went down to rout him out, "something flopped up out of the darkness like an owl—a timid, shambling figure in soft black hat with jerking hands." The figure, persuaded by a chorus of "Venez donc, Maître," at once explains (realizing by Gosse's surprised stare that he did not quite look the part) that his good suit was a legacy of the Belgian tour and, shooting his cuffs, "C'est ma chemise de conférence."

Another of the curious, John Grierson, hunting his quarry down to a café in the Place de l'Odéon, first saw Moréas playing dominoes, fixing his eye on his opponent from time to time and beating his chest with a "J'ai du talent! Moi, j'ai du talent!" An adequate summary of Moréas but the picture of Verlaine is less happy, a Verlaine who "to judge by the clothes he wore might have been a carpenter or bricklayer. But his face! Incarnation of Villon. Over two sleepy, waggish gray eyes a pair of Mephistophelian brows curved upwards . . . When he tipped his slouch hat back on his head he looked like a modern troubadour." He smoked incessantly, sipped cognac, raised his brows "and with an inimitable gesture of bonhomie passed a trivial remark." He praised English: "What a difference between *mère* and *mother!* The English is soft, homely and musical. Then there is the word *heaven*—how much more beautiful than *ciel.* English is made for sentiment and poetry. I love the English language." Then—Grierson again—we are back to the journalist after copy. He sees Verlaine and Bibi in the Boul' Mich' "looking like mendicants on their way home after having amassed a few sous at some church door." He lived, Grierson noted, near the Panthéon which, needless to say, was "where Villon lived five hundred years earlier."

There was much of this search after the picturesque figure of fun by English, Americans and others. They were right enough as far as they went, Verlaine was that too, but they did not go far enough. It remained for a young English painter, William Rothenstein, to harness the true admiration in England to some purpose. Rothenstein, then studying at Julian's, had a gift for admiration and a kind heart. He was struck by the beauty of Verlaine's poetry and by the injustice of such a man forever struggling to avoid starvation while his former friends flourished (Rothenstein was young, it must be remembered), and he wrote in this sense to Verlaine. Charmed, Verlaine invited Rothenstein to see him; and in September, 1893 they met at the Broussais. Rothenstein, who had already made himself equally at home in Montmartre and the Latin Quarter, had heard a great deal about Verlaine from De Sivry and Moréas: a great poet but impossible man, he was told. At first he did not find him so; he was clean and sober, which seems to have surprised his visitor; very pale with small candid eyes (brown to Rothenstein) heavy mustaches and beard turning gray. The Socratic nose, the comparison with Silenus were by this time automatic. He talked amusingly with a childlike humor of his leg which hurt, of the kind doctors and nurses, of the stingy Vanier, of his lectures in Holland and Belgium and, scenting money, of his poverty, pulling the stop full out. Not in vain; for Rothenstein, who was making a series of portraits of well-known men, asked permission to add Verlaine to the list, made three excellent lithographs of the bedridden poet, and then suggested a possible lecture tour in England.

Verlaine was enchanted; Symons, consulted, enthusiastic; and John Lane, the avant-garde publisher of the time, showed practical interest by commissioning two poems for one of his reviews, which he paid for in advance. *"C'est très honnête,"* commented the gratified Verlaine, pocketing the hundred francs. But he proved difficult to pin down, hard to find when out of the hospital, dubious about his health, uncertain about the times of trains, steamers and the like. Finally, when all had been settled and Verlaine had gone off to his short lecture tour in the northeast, Rothenstein, then in England, received an urgent demand for a hundred francs, without which the poet could not make the journey; some of this was apparently to "console" a certain person for his absence, the rest to pay his traveling expenses.

Symons, consulted again, advised against the sending of the money direct; it could melt before Verlaine ever reached the station. Instead, he sent it to an American friend in Paris with instructions to put the poet on the train. And on November 19 Verlaine "with a mildness, patience and charm reminding one of Jesus and Socrates" allowed himself to be taken to the station, given dinner and installed in his compartment, his portion of the hundred francs resting undisturbed in his purse.

In London the lecture had been arranged for the evening of November 21 in Barnard's Inn. Verlaine was to talk on contemporary French poetry; the tickets were ten shillings each and a notice circulated among the intellectual elite promised a good audience. Gosse made doubly sure by writing an advance "puff" in the St. James Gazette on the morning of the lecture, assuring readers that the price of the tickets would relieve a genuine poverty.

All, then, was ready, all but the principal actor. He was due in Symons' room for lunch on the 20th. Symons waited in vain. Forebodings gripped him; Verlaine alone with some seventy francs was a sobering thought. But Verlaine was better than his reputation; at that moment he was reposing himself at Dieppe as best he could after a shattering night of storm which had stopped all cross-channel sailings—a noisy night which reminded him unpleasantly of the bombardment of Paris more than twenty years before. He had spent part of the night on a bench in the waiting room until offered a sofa in the hotel opposite. On the evening of the 20th the sea had fallen sufficiently to allow a steamer to set off. He slept through most of the rough crossing and wrote a poem on the "immense caress" of the waves—he was always a good sailor—and arrived at the Temple in the early hours of the 21st, arrived full of good cheer and was at once enraptured by Fountain Court—the silence broken only by the small fountain—so enraptured that he could not tear himself from the fountain; and the anxious Symons, making yet another excursion in search of him, found his overdue guest, carpetbag in hand, drinking the water under the light of a pale moon.

Symons, radiant with delighted relief, made him welcome with gin and a box of crackers. As he ate and drank they talked "about everything under the sun"—Paris, the lectures, poetry, money, "poets think of nothing else—and with reason!"—talked for two hours. Verlaine found it "one of the best and gayest meals in my life." After a sleep he lunched with Symons and Gosse at a "sumptuous restaurant," dined à la française with Lane, Rothenstein, William Heinemann, Frank Harris, Herbert Horne, a wealthy sympathizer, and Henry Harland, the American novelist; then was escorted to Barnard's Inn where, the lecture being in French, a smallish audience had assembled.

He hobbled nervously, one foot in a carpet slipper, to "an immense chair at an immense table" and began by explaining that he was "not wanting" in experience as a lecturer. Then to the *Parnasse contemporain*, "an outpost of Romanticism, an advanced Romanticism in which thundered the formidable verse of Leconte de Lisle, flickered and twinkled that of Theodore de Banville while that of Baudelaire sighed and shone like a corpse candle." Following this "revered trinity" came Mallarmé, himself of the next generation, who showed sympathy and understanding of the generation then writing, the Ecole Romane of Moréas, successor to Symbolism, and the free verse *pléiade* of Tailhade "subtle, mystical, terribly, stingingly *méchant*—it is certainly a good thing to be counted among his friends!"

He dealt with the moderns in turn, then reverted to himself. A poet, he said, should be absolutely sincere, absolutely conscientious: "*L'art, c'est d'être absolument soi-même*"; his true dignity would show itself in attempt after attempt to reach perfection of form. "One poet has tried to do all this—myself."

Then he ran through his work, reciting poems from every book. *Poèmes saturniens* he rated as a youthful and even puerile affair "marked by imitations to right and left—Hugo, Gautier, Beaudelaire, Banville. And in addition, thanks to a mistaken taste for Leconte de Lisle, I was an impassible—*im-pas-si-ble* as the word was then pronounced in the passage Choiseul." He read "*Mon Rêve familier*" and "*Chanson d'automne*."

The only merit he could see in his first collection was a certain half-sensual, half-dreamy melancholy—a merit "confirmed with more mastery and deliberate intention in *Fêtes galantes*, a collection of poems costumed after the people of the Italian comedy and the fancy pieces of Watteau and including some piquant notes of velvety sharpness and sly malice." He read "*Crepuscule du Soir mystique*" and "*Le Faune.*"

La Bonne Chanson he rated "the most *natural*" of his works. This book led him into autobiography which he hoped the use of the third person would set at a safe remove: "Distress soon followed, not without faults on his side, to the household of the poet who suddenly threw up everything and went wandering in search of unsatisfying distractions. On the other hand, I will not say remorse (he did not experience it for he repented of nothing) but vexation and regret, with certain consolations, compensations rather, inspired him to write *Romances sans Paroles* in which the expression of *real* vagueness and want of precise meaning was part of his intention."

He read "*Spleen*" and "*Green,*" then: "A serious catastrophe interrupted these factitious pains and pleasures." He read "*Un grand sommeil noir.*"

His voice changed to another kind of solemnity: "Then divine resignation inspired *Sagesse*, which marked a new era in his poetry, and the motto of his life for many years." He read "*Beauté des femmes,*" "*Ecoutez la chanson bien douce*" and the Stickney poem "*O mon Dieu, vous m'avez blessé d'amour.*"

By this time he had lost track of the date sequence and showed every intention of slurring over the rest of his output. How explain the next comers to an English audience, even an "emancipated" one? He knew of only one way, continuing in his best moral and diplomatic manner—if a twinkle was in the eye it was safe from view: "Then, as was bound to happen, overstrained humanity resumed, or seemed to resume, its rights or fancied rights, whence came *Chansons pour Elle, Odes en son Honneur* and *Elégies* in which the new affections were celebrated in appropriate measures."

Possibly he felt that his explanation lacked force. At any rate he moved with appropriate dignity to a more serious and even apologetic note: "Then came troubles and sickness and the poet made a certain return on himself and resumed at times the sadness and severity of *Sagesse* with *Amour* and *Bonheur.*" But, a certain book resting unmentioned, he was constrained to add, "but not without an echo, but a rigorously diminished echo, of the sinful chants of *Parallèlement*, the most sensual, most reprehensible if you will, of his books." He recited, not one of the sinful chants but the ravishing "*Impression de Printemps*" written a few months before the lecture, which would effectively demonstrate to the audience that the great poet lived on.

There remained only the advance advertisement with which he concluded all his talks. His *Varia* soon to appear, he assured his listeners, "will provide evidence of the philosophic and serious side of what people are pleased to call my talent."

The next morning the press reported the lecture favorably with the exception of a complaint from the *Pall Mall Gazette* that his voice lacked eloquence and his subject matter originality and profundity; but the critic was obviously disappointed to find no trace of "the true Verlaine" in the sober lecturer. For the rest, all was good and Verlaine was soon telling Vanier exultantly, "A fine press, old chap."

The day was given to sightseeing, a visit to the French hospital to have his leg dressed, lunch with the young Francophile poets, dinner with Heinemann and an evening at the Alhambra. Symons drove about with him in a hansom and was constantly struck by his accurate recollection of the buildings they passed. Not much had changed in the general outline since the year with Rimbaud—Leicester Square had been tidied up and Shakespeare had taken the place of George IV, several restaurants had taken on a French air, the main streets were lit by electricity and the crude green and red of the women's lavatories had given way to pearl-gray and rose. This delighted Verlaine, but then everything delighted him: "the somber London of twenty years ago . . . is today an international and especially a French London." His one criticism was of the men's lavatories: why, he asked, hobbling painfully down and up the steps, were the English such prudes: everyone knew the lavatories were there, why pretend they were not?

He was on his best behavior all through the day, and in the evening whispered to Heinemann, who found him absolutely charming, that he must not, *absolument pas*, get drunk. Nor did he, thanks to a limited circulation of the wine, and was able more or less soberly to revel in the Alhambra, the same old Alhambra that he and Rimbaud had visited (but how differently as to seats, clothes and company!), the same old comic songs at which he roared, the same interludes of ballet. A novelty, a French one according to the English, was the tableaux of nudes. But the ballet was the thing: "I love Shakespeare but I love ballet better," he told Symons in the heat of enthusiasm, and no doubt at that moment he did.

The next morning he took the train for Oxford where he lunched with York Powell, the professor of history, Rothenstein and the French poet Charles Bonnier who lived in England. Some students tried to catch a glimpse of the famous man through the window and Bonnier, who knew the Verlaine of the Latin Quarter, was beside himself with amusement at the comical efforts of the poet to assume what he felt to be the manner appropriate to the venerable seat of learning. Verlaine too saw the farcical side of this pose of "the sage of Paris" and could not always keep a straight face. Then came a tour of the city in hansoms: "the streets rather like the prim and modest little streets of Boston" and, ravished by the beauty of the colleges, a contemptuous "our old Sorbonne . . . is pitiable compared with this exquisite Oxford," before repeating his lecture in the room behind Blackwell's shop. The audience was almost all students and Verlaine, in view of their youth perhaps, added to his description of what the poet must be and do an emphatic and profound *"le poète doit vivre beaucoup, vivre dans tous les sens,"* illustrating this from his own life.

The next morning he showed no sign of leaving and Powell, with an eye on Dodgson, the strict Master, and certain that Verlaine could not pass two sober days in succession, shadowed him fanatically from morning to night. Unnecessarily, as it happened; Verlaine, bewitched by Oxford and in no hurry to lose it, knew what was due to it, knew a good deal better than most of its inhabitants; besides he had given a promise; he arrived back in London the next day reluctant and sober.

Symons having gone to Italy, he was given a room in a boarding house on York Terrace, Regents Park, but did not see much of it, living for the next week "the life of a pasha and for nothing," an attractive thought—a form of assurance too, as will be seen—with "dinners *terribles*, theatres, *café-concerts*." Horne, Harland, Dowland and the young poets took over the role of Symons with gusto; he was invited to the Cheshire Cheese, the Francophile poets' rendezvous, he dined at the Constitutional Club (one's mind boggles at the thought of Verlaine in this milieu), recited his poems in luxurious drawing rooms; was, in short, lionized by a small and not very distinguished section of London society. But to him all was heaven, a rather wearing heaven: "I'm pretty tired of this game," he told Cazals, "although I take cabs too often. But when I say too often I'm wrong because I can only walk with great difficulty."

The week in London was unexpected. He had intended to return to Paris after the Oxford visit but Lane had produced a friend from the north, a young intellectual Congregational minister, Theodore London, who urged him to lecture in Manchester. After some hesitation—he was doing too much and doing it without the usual source of stimulation—and another visit to the French hospital he accepted, hoping to carry back to Paris a more substantial sum of money.

In this he was disappointed; the lecture at Manchester was badly managed, without advance publicity, and was held on December 1st in a dreary gaslit Congregational school in Salford, barely fifty people attending. But Verlaine began his day in determinedly optimistic fashion by praising St. Pancras Station, which he had last seen half built; remained cheerful through a Manchester fog; took to the interpreter, a Swiss schoolmaster, and was given a pleasant surprise at London's house before the lecture where he was offered a retiring room with a bottle of absinthe, procured heaven knows how, on the table. He emerged from the room after a prolonged interval, playfully punching his hat into clerical shape and regarding the Reverend Verlaine in the mirror from various angles, but repeated his lecture without incident. The one mischance occurred during the reception afterwards when his suspenders snapped. The alarming gap which developed being tactfully drawn to his notice, he gave his trousers a genial hitch and Lancashire susceptibilities were saved.

Returning to London the next day without as he wished seeing "Coin de Table," then at Manchester, or obtaining a photograph of it, he once more limped into a social round varied by treatment at the hospital. A second London lecture did not materialize; instead he gave a press interview, but his chief satisfaction came, it seemed, from the purchase of a splendid pair of suspenders: "otherwise I should keep my trousers up with a belt, a sure sign of moral disintegration." His view on the relative merits of English and French matches had turned a somersault; no longer could a bright manufacturer coin money by establishing a French match factory in London.

He remained indefatigably Anglophile even to the answering of impertinent questions by a journalist. The questions were for the most part of the usual inanity: was he the poetic descendant of Villon? for example, which Verlaine answered delightfully with a "I haven't killed anyone yet, nor am I a captain of industry. Villon was a great poet, but so was Racine, Corneille, La Fontaine, Victor Hugo. Why these odious comparisons?" The one intelligent question, Is it true that you take little notice of the rules of French poetry? he sidestepped with "It's possible to stretch that theory too far. The amateurs of free verse don't respect rhyme or rhythm. In short, one can't write a sonnet of fifty lines, a line of fifty feet."

He went back on the 6th. He was not to see England again although filled with hopes of doing so, and the various projects to cash in on the visit shrank in the end to little; a selection of poems which Lane was to publish retired into the vague after the Wilde trial, and Verlaine was paid for no more than a couple or so articles, on his visit and on a comparison of Racine and Shakespeare, and for a handful of poems. But he remained firmly attached to England and was visited by many Englishmen to whom he spoke atrocious English very happily, and notably by two Irishmen; by Wilde who omitted to offer him one of his special gold-tipped cigarettes, an omission which Verlaine observed; and by Yeats who extracted some second or third thoughts on Maeterlinck, "a bit of a mountebank"; on Villiers, "rather fanatical but wrote the most excellent French" and the meaning of whose *Axel* Verlaine claimed to comprehend as that love was alone of true worth; on Hugo, "a volcano of mud as well as fire"; and, most acutely, on "*In Memoriam*" which he had tried to translate but "Tennyson was too noble, too English and when he should have been broken-hearted had too many reminiscences." With which remark Verlaine can fitly quit the English stage.

He went back "over a sea like glass." He was disappointed with the financial result of the tour or said he was for reasons of tact; but something in the region of fifteen hundred francs was not to be despised and he changed his third-class return ticket via Dieppe for a second-class via Calais. This change he announced in a letter to Paris, announced apologetically and with a hint of bribery and corruption: "Perhaps I shall bring back some pretty little gift." And thereby hangs a tale, the last tale.

20.

CONJUGAL END

1890-1896

[1]

The life of Verlaine fittingly petered out in long-drawn comedy.
When he came back triumphantly from Holland in November, 1892
with his thousand and more francs and promptly lost the lot, the
"lost" was a kindly way of saying that it had been taken. Not stolen,
for the woman who took it believed it to be her due, and even in
the long run a kindness. The affair was a commonplace except for
the largeness of the sum.

Verlaine was, in brief, a family man and had been so for some
two years. There was no family and the one room (two in months
of exceptional luxury) in which he lived from time to time was an
apology for a home, not only miserably uncomfortable but always
changing; he had no fixed address. For that matter he had no wife;
but two women, at times three, had come into his life. Not on the
face of it an ideal existence, yet he had somehow reached a state
which exactly suited him.

The change came to public notice as it were on September 24,
1890, when a stocky middle-aged woman with short curly black hair
worn close over a low forehead called at Vanier's office with a note
from Verlaine promising a hundred lines of *Invectives* the next day
"against (I hope) a considerable number of *thunes*"—one of his
innumerable slang expressions for money—and introducing the
bearer as "Mademoiselle Krantz who is worthy of every confidence,
whom I love very much, who stops me doing foolish things, who
looks after me and my affairs admirably, and who has kindly agreed
to fetch from you a hundred sous which I simply must have."

Six months later, in March, 1891, another stocky middle-aged woman but more buxom, with a slight squint and reddish hair, called on Vanier and handed him a note from Verlaine in which he read, presumably with surprise, "Very unwell, I have asked Mademoiselle Philomène, in whom I have *justly* placed all my confidence, to be good enough to drop in at your office and collect the most money possible, one hundred francs at least."

The game continued. A year or so later it was "I am sending Mademoiselle Krantz to you to collect *everything you can spare* from the sale of *Mes Prisons*."

Three months later: "Here are some poems. Give all you can to Mademoiselle Philomène who will hand them to you . . . and who definitely has all my confidence and all my friendship—good sense, gracefulness, honesty, this one!—and is my faithful housekeeper."

One month later: "If Mademoiselle Krantz needs money I can thoroughly recommend this good creature to you."

Two months later: "A good thing I only sent Bibi with a letter purely *opportunist* and not pecuniary. I shall be much obliged if you would say nothing about it to Philomène. Though less beastly, she thinks everyone is spying for *the other*. But never mind! I love this good girl very much and don't want to lose her at any price."

Four months later: "Will you pay my *wife* Philomène for the two poems she will give you."

Vanier's relief can be imagined. After three years the man had at last made up his mind; the interminable procession of women would cease, and he would be spared the sight of Bibi's disreputable head round the door, a Bibi working impartially for the one who tipped him best or for a Verlaine trying to collect a few francs on the side; not to mention a Verlaine unable to trust any one of the three, limping painfully into the office with anxious looks to right and left before closing the door. What did Verlaine think he was? A charitable institution? A women's institute? He paid up because he could profitably print every line Verlaine wrote, good, bad or indifferent. But all the same . . .

But if Vanier's hopes rose uncertainly, they soon collapsed again. All that had happened was that Philomène had paid a visit of state, with a hat perched flowerily on her head, to a hospital-bound Verlaine. And at sight of this unprecedented honor the ravished Verlaine introduced her to the ward at large as his wife.

Five months later the game is resumed, for the moment in a third version: "I'm sending you most of my booty to look after *for me.* Neither 'authorization' nor 'messengers.' I'll draw on it myself from time to time but no one else, *not even Philomène.* Watch out!"

Six weeks later begins a series of "I authorize Mademoiselle Krantz to collect the money for the forty-nine lines herewith . . . for the enclosed poem . . . for the two productions she'll hand you" with a rider of familiar hue: "As you know, Mademoiselle Krantz is to be trusted."

As you know! But how could anyone know, least of all Verlaine, who six months later is writing "Please welcome Madame Esther, *still my best friend,* who is very happy to act just for once as my messenger and to collect the proceeds from you."

[2]

But to begin at the beginning. On some unspecified night in 1890 Verlaine picked up a streetwalker named Philomène Boudin who worked professionally under the name of Esther. He took a fancy to her, at first perhaps because she was an *Ardennaise,* later for several other reasons, and was soon living with her. What might at first sight appear as an obstacle to the romance—the presence in an adjoining room and at meals of Philomène's pimp who also happened to be her husband—turned out in practice a blessing. This man became greatly attached to Verlaine—he had never before met so helpless a creature, in his sense of the word, nor one so generous—and he soon constituted himself as unofficial guardian to the poet just as Bibi had made himself an unpaid fetch-and-carry. "If anyone so much as lays a finger on Monsieur Verlaine he'll hear from me," he would announce truculently; and, patting himself on the back, "Many's the time I've followed him home from a café without his knowing it, to make sure he got back safely."

Indeed had his wishes prevailed, the *ménage à trois* might have continued indefinitely. But Philomène, like Verlaine, splashed her money about royally and regarded him with disfavor when all was spent; in her cups she had a temper and did not hesitate to accuse her protector of withholding supplies for the benefit of others, demanding that all friends be left to their own devices. This Verlaine was unable to promise or, if a promise were extracted, to perform; he would slip out to the cafés from time to time and, returning empty, faced a woman of wrath. And when, as happened occasionally, Vanier drew in his horns, the scenes became longer and more painful.

Retiring from one of these to the bar on the ground floor Verlaine met at the counter a woman whose *Ardennais* accent at once aroused his interest. He outlined his grievances to her over a few mutual drinks, she sympathized, he accompanied her back to her room and, when morning came, decided to make it his home.

Eugénie Krantz was fifty, six or seven years older than Philomène, and had officially ended her occupation which she claimed had included spells with several moderately famous men. She was keeping herself alive by making shirts for the Belle Jardinière but was not adverse to a resumption of her true role and she perceived more clearly than the emotional Philomène that she had stumbled on a small gold mine; apparently it was only necessary for this queer customer to scribble a few lines on a piece of paper and the paper could be exchanged for cash in Vanier's office. She had a thirst which shirt-making could not quench; she also had vague ideas of providing for her old age; Verlaine, it seemed, could do both. She began to "organize" him; if he did not write so many lines a day he would hear from her; if he did he was rewarded by drink in plenty, a home of sorts and her favors in bed.

Verlaine settled down with her, escaping now and then to the cafés, but could not quite resign himself to the loss of Philomène. The problem was admittedly difficult, Philomène representing romance, Eugénie common sense; Philomène was a gadabout, Eugénie offered some prospect of a home of sorts; Philomène spent every sou, Eugénie talked of putting something by for a rainy day; Philomène didn't badger him into writing every hour of the day, Eugénie kept his nose to the grindstone; Philomène was jealous, Eugénie was close. One could go on forever; all these things were necessary or desirable at one time or another. What to do? But the problem was solved for him; after a month or two, sometimes a week or two, he was either driven out or walked out; he would not write his daily quota and Eugénie—"sometimes a bit of a shrew," he said with English understatement—would scream at him (rumor even spoke of a beating) until he fled in search of Philomène; he would slip off to a café once too often and Philomène, finding his pockets empty, would shout him into the street. And when both would have nothing to do with him he would search out his third string, Caroline Teiser, who, being made of weaker stuff, would share her all, which was not much, when he assured her that she, unlike those harridans he had lately made the mistake of consorting with, was his true muse and inspired him to write immortal poems. An astute move if he made it with intention, which he partly did, for as soon as Eugénie and Philomène discovered that their goose had found another pen in which to lay his eggs they sank their differences, wrenched him bodily away from the more or less gentle Caroline, demanded his money or his poems and gave him a bed under their eye. And the round began again.

[3]

The benefits of this somewhat stormy existence are not immediately obvious. What one chiefly sees at first is that Verlaine's life as the last great bohemian dispensing wisdom, good cheer and inspiration from his seat at the François Premier is merely the outward half of the man and that it was only possible because he had at the back of him a Philomène, a Eugénie and, in the dim distance, a Caroline. Also clear is the reason for his perpetual poverty. Even a Verlaine constitutionally unable to keep a sou in his purse could not unaided have got through the money he drew from Vanier and the others. But three women to be kept, two of them voracious females with a practically unquenchable thirst, and the position is reversed: how did he manage it? one wonders, and remembers the begging letters by the dozen which disfigure the last years.

Clear too becomes the reason for the falling away of his work. Not even a Verlaine can write poems of quality with a Eugénie standing over him day after day for years. The last books he wrote to celebrate the charms of Philomène and Eugénie, his *Chair* and *Odes en son Honneur*, make sad reading. He was too experienced a poet to write many bad lines as such, but the poems are nevertheless a travesty of the man; the enlivening bite of humorous irony has disappeared, the source of inspiration is not so much degraded as lifeless. The interminable thighs and breasts and buttocks read like a catalogue and the attempts to marry physical and spiritual in the persons of Eugénie and Philomène are the reverse of convincing. This late poetry, naïve in thought, unpassionate, inconsequential, reads like the poetry of an old man. As it was; twenty years of emotion, hardship, excess were having their effect even on Verlaine's strong body.

Nevertheless the poetry repays study; read carefully it reveals itself not as pornography, not as the maunderings of an old man but as the sleepy-ecstatic cries of a child snuggling against his mother. And therein lay the secret of the appeal, otherwise difficult to understand, of the two not particularly prepossessing lady loves. More than most men Verlaine declines to be summed up in a word or phrase; he was this, that and the other at various moments. But there were constants riding smoothly enough beneath that troubled sea and directing the passage of his apparently rudderless ship. He tells Cazals, for instance, when he hears of the death of Villiers: "His life was certainly more *worthy* than mine but not at bottom more proud. I've made greater efforts than he and I was—alas! I *was*—a more logical Christian. My falls are due to what? Shall I accuse my blood, my upbringing? But I was good, chaste . . . Oh! the drink which has developed the bug, the bacillus, the microbe of Lust to such a point in a body really built for the normal, the orderly! It's true that misfortune, a misfortune without equal I believe, did—for a time—temper me, then perhaps distempered me because I didn't practice the tempering wisely. With all my common sense I lack judgment. The moral of this I don't care for much because it smells of so-called physiology: I am a feminine— and this explains lots of things!" This shows some self-perception but he would have got nearer the target, though his life could scarcely have been much changed, if he had recognized that he remained above all a child. His future had been decided by the early years of indulgence, the petting, the caresses of two women, the withholding of all responsibility and practically all rebuke. He came out of this hothouse a nice boy because he had an unspoilably nice nature, but with an inclination not far from passion to be coddled through life. The absence of the maternal in the young Mathilde drove him to the unbending paternalism of Rimbaud, the revolt of Rimbaud drove him into the arms of the Church, to the soothing lullaby of English country life, to the masculine Lucien, Rimbaudish in face, with his strong athletic body like Verlaine's, his rigid moral code. Then, Rimbaud dead, Lucien dead, Nouveau insupportably righteous, the power of the Church reduced by the years, he turned to the hospitals where he was fed, dressed, undressed, reprimanded, praised like a baby, all responsibility, even the shadow of it removed, then to the brisk and

dominating Cazals and at the last reverted completely to the child
in the embraces and the reproaches of Eugénie and Philomène.

For his instinct, the one failure of Mathilde apart, was unerring.
He did not choose Philomène and Eugénie simply for their *Ardennais*
accent but because that accent stood for what he most needed. The
Ardennaises are a recognizable type, not only in their short, square,
firm, full-bosomed bodies and harsh faces but in their masculinity
of mind, their parsimoniousness and greed. The Ardennes has for
centuries housed preëminently a matriarchal society; almost everywhere the women rule, not with charm as in so much of southern
and central France but by force of character. Eugénie was typical
of her countrywomen, Philomène scarcely less so. Both were experienced in the arts of love, both knew well, as successful prostitutes
must know, how to deal with their most frequent customer, the
old or oldish man losing virility. Verlaine presented no problem to
them; they spoiled him in bed, ruled him in and out of it and
extracted every sou they could get from him, which was not
difficult. He responded with childish revolts and subterfuges but
at bottom always with alacrity and gratitude.

Their rooms were bare and cold but they were his homes; when
there was a fire in the tiny grate they had lit it but he warmed
himself at it, when the meal was put on the table they had cooked
it but he ate it. And the, on the surface, less pleasant side of the
relationship was at heart a consolation. When Philomène had
thrown him out and he came sheepishly back to Eugénie, she
would say grimly, "All right, I'll take you back, but mind, I know
you and if you don't make some money pretty soon I'll send you
away again." And when he had made some and they had spent it
she would shout at him, "Write ten lines so that I can cash them
at Vanier's." These are not the words of a woman to her lover,
they are the words of a mother to her son and as such Verlaine
accepted them. And in character he would sometimes revolt and
limp off with the air of one on a boyish escapade to what appeared
at a distance as the romantic charms of Philomène, a Philomène
who did not press him so hardly, who spent his money with florid
gestures, who was less dour, more lively, but who alas was even
more ruthless with him when his pockets had been emptied. Yet
even this was in line with the "bad woman" the boy had sought; and
he would make his way back to Eugénie with no hard feelings for

either, the first explosion over; and even the explosion having its pleasures.

Hard feelings—why should he feel them? They gave him what he wanted, to be cared for, to have excitement, safety, company, a home, discipline, sexual gratification, a certain mental activity and, in bed at least and on the spree, what could be interpreted by a fond man as affection. So, his poverty, his bad leg which was steadily growing more painful and all his other troubles notwithstanding, the appearance in his life of Philomène and Eugénie made his last years preëminently years of contentment; between them and his café life he could enjoy fame and domesticity, he could sit back happily as the Prince of Poets, fondle maternal limbs and cower contentedly under motherly whips. For these, to him, were all signs of that indispensable good feeling he lived for; disciples, women, all loved him, he was necessary, welcome and his heart warmed.

[4]

Not that these last six years were years of unalloyed bliss. Verlaine, it cannot be too often repeated, was a man of moods; he was not far behind Mrs. Welsh whom Carlyle described as indulging fifteen different humors within the hour. He had practical cause for discontent; he disliked poverty and discomfort but lived in both most of the time; he disliked, in principle, screaming women, but had them most of the time; he disliked pain but suffered it constantly; he disliked disapproval but endured it, at a distance, all the time.

But he was not only a man of moods, he was a man with a sense of sin, not the less strong because he successfully suppressed it most of the time. Not all the time, however. Thus for example he was found one night by a young disciple and some friends leaning over the Pont au Change staring into the Seine. Asked why he was there and alone he answered with a sob in his voice, "I'm bored. Oh I'm so bored! I've been thinking of throwing myself into the river." He was persuaded to dine but remained silent, pecked at his food and would not drink. They tried to cheer him by reciting *"Colloque Sentimentale."* He protested, then brightened as the poem proceeded; his eyes filled with tears at the end and he cried, "Encore! Encore." They recited *"Langueur"* and he became radiant and demanded that they recite the last poem of *Sagesse, "C'est la fête du blé."*

This done he rose, spread his hands wide with his familiar triumphant "Voilà!" and walked back to the bridge with his disciple. He fell silent again and the young man, trying to cheer him, asked what he could do. "Recite Rimbaud's *Derrières académiques*," said Verlaine, giving his own title to "*Les Assis*." The young man spoke the lines brilliantly parodying Coppée's "*Petit-Epicier*"; then, as Verlaine remained silent, began to walk away uneasily. At the end of the bridge he turned; Verlaine was looking after him with a smile "so sad and so nice" that he came back. Verlaine put a hand on his shoulder. "I owe you my thanks. Before you turned up tonight I thought of killing myself after an evening of thoughts I don't care to remember—my loneliness, my desultory life . . ."

The fact that Verlaine would never have found the courage to kill himself is beside the point. In these moods he had indeed "thoughts I don't care to remember"; thoughts of the dead Rimbaud, his inspiration and joy and bane; of Mathilde and Georges, dead to him; of Lucien, Valade, Cros, Glatigny, Nina, Villiers, Chabrier, all gone; of the rubbish that he was sending to Vanier day after day in the name of poetry; of what he had been and what he was. Cruel thoughts, hopeless thoughts, since time could not be turned back and the dead were dead, himself included.

But Verlaine was no tragic hero, a clown rather. Clowns have feelings but their clowning is the thing. The comedy went on with Verlaine for the most part resigned, in the grip of one storm after another which for him was a fruitful source of some after-amusement, for he had not lost his humor. What to be done, for instance, about the ladies' saints' days? One fell on the 14th, the other on the 15th of November. Both must be celebrated to the hilt. Each woman, well aware of the name day of her rival, took some pleasure in wrecking it, Philomène by delaying the agitated Verlaine beyond her span of twenty-four hours, Eugénie by tempting him to skip the preceding day. And whether he succumbed or resisted, the victim was in any event the lover. Verlaine moaned, laughed, dreaded the coming of November, blustered unconvincingly and more than once ended up with Caroline.

But it was not until the first lecture tour, to Holland, that the fun became really fast and furious. When Verlaine broke the news the women's eyes were opened and Verlaine bloomed into the great poet of all time. Never before had he been so kindly treated and his life during those preliminary weeks was a dream of delight, or would have been had he not been obliged always to leave one of the two in a flaming temper.

Unhappily, precise details of the negotiations immediately prior to and after the tour are lacking; it seems either that Philomène, always the less careful of the two, was unwise enough to quarrel with the lecturer just before he set off or, which is more likely, that he chose Eugénie as the most suitable guardian of his forthcoming treasure. If so he regretted it immediately, for she relieved him of the entire one thousand francs the instant he returned and after an unseemly fracas on the landing which brought the police in, the last time Verlaine was to have unfriendly dealings with them. He let out a large and dignified wail: "A false welcome awaited me in Paris, hypocrisy, lies, and finally the theft—skillful and crafty as well as plausible—of certain banknotes. . . . A most violent quarrel on my staircase led to the arrival of the concierge and the calling of the police who, mistaking my vehement and justifiable anger for the result of stopping too long in places where one drinks, carried me off to the police station for an hour or two, not without unnecessary brutality."

His tale of woe left Philomène so unimpressed that she slammed the door in his face, Caroline was either unavailable or out of funds, and he retired in dudgeon to the Broussais; just as well, this, since the tour had tried his leg to the utmost.

He soon discovered that he had done Eugénie an injustice; part at least of the thousand francs she had purloined was taken merely to prevent his spending it rashly elsewhere; so at least she said when news arrived of the Belgian tour. A fairly general harmony spread among the three in view of Belgian francs by the hundred, but with Philomène very much on the qui vive; and Verlaine, though privately instructing Vanier to whom he sent some of the profits en route, that Eugénie could draw on them, also sent some money direct to Philomène and behaved for the rest with the utmost tact, to the point of writing practically indentical letters to both women, the most striking difference being the opening "Bon chérie" to Eugénie and the no more than just "Ma grosse chéri" to Philomène who was renowned for her bosom. Tact even spread itself to the final promise "I shall send you a little more tomorrow and so on," Verlaine not wishing to look too far ahead, "until I can faithfully hand you, bon chérie, the entire proceeds." His last greeting, however, gave "thousands and thousands of kisses" to Philomène as against the "thousands" to Eugénie.

Not surprisingly both women were at the station to meet him. But Philomène was in some respects a frail vessel not always able to keep her eye on the main chance; though it may just be that in this instance she was simply unfortunate and, a big railway station not being the happiest choice for an appearance incognito, some admirer of the moment refused to be shaken off. However this may be, when Verlaine reached the barrier at the Gare de l'Est he saw Eugénie alone, Philomène accompanied. He did not hesitate, went off with Eugénie and, possibly shaken by what he had seen, handed over all his profits without a murmur.

There was some talk of banking the proceeds and of leading the life that Verlaine had been promising himself during the tour and for that matter ever since the publication of *Amour*; "*Je vais me mettre dans mes meubles!*" had simply become "*Nous allons*" in the course of the years. But the *nous* were little better able to hold to their gains than the *je*; in two months the money was no more. He was also homeless, romance having come belatedly to his companion who without so much as a by-your-leave set up house with a youthful barber's assistant.

Back to the Broussais went Verlaine where he was visited among others by Rothenstein and by Philomène, gorgeously hatted. This was the moment when she was metamorphosed into "my wife" and he introduced her to Rothenstein as such. Eugénie had become "that harlot" and "the cholera." And it was the temporarily victorious Philomène who insisted on the hundred francs advance before Verlaine went off to London a few months later, thirty francs of which she pocketed "just in case." In her miserable room in rue Broca, a room no bigger than an ordinary bathroom, a fire had been lit in honor of the American who brought the money—a single lump of coal.

The opening of the English tour was all Philomène. He kept in touch with Eugénie as a precautionary measure, but it was to his "*Chère femme*" that he sent money; from her that he begged a telegram, Yes or No, when the Manchester lecture was suggested; because of her that he abstained, with what effort can be imagined, from absinthe; and to her that after no more than five days' absence he proposed marriage or, to be exact, took up a chance remark of hers that it would be nice to be married, nice too if he returned from England with a certain begemmed bracelet which they had spoken of in exalted moments: "As for the bracelet, etc., I shall do your sweet will if at all possible. As for marriage, if you are speaking seriously it would give me *the greatest pleasure of my life* and we will go to Monsieur le Maire as soon as you wish. This would also be the best way of settling something on you after I die. O *chérie*, yes, let us do it, it was always my idea. I love only you and how greatly! Here I live the life of a pasha, for nothing, free. Dreadful dinners, theatres, music halls. But this scarcely amuses me and I would infinitely rather be near my Philomène even when she is naughty as can happen . . . sometimes! *And I don't drink* and I won't drink if my dear forbids me . . . sweetly." He thought to add later a reassuring "Don't worry about the women here. London did me great harm in that line twenty years ago. And then I love you too much."

It was to Philomène also that he wrote distractedly from London, Oxford and Manchester; distractedly because he had not spent one week in England before disillusionment set in. Eugénie's affair with the barber's assistant had lost its glamour the moment she heard of the new lecture tour; England, to her, was the land of riches; if Verlaine had made a thousand francs in Holland and in Belgium, what fortune might he not bring back from Albion! She brusquely threw off the hairdressing incumbrance and addressed herself to the work of countering the machinations of Philomène. She had met Rothenstein who caught a glimpse of her life with Verlaine, the fearful shouting matches when Verlaine accused her of robbing him, of keeping him so short that he could neither clothe himself nor buy a friend a drink, followed by the sudden silence, each walking apart "like two cats in a yard" and Verlaine continuing his talk on literature; she now wrote to Rothenstein at Oxford: "another person" was intriguing, she said mysteriously, he must on no account divulge Verlaine's movements or address.

The futility of this gesture no doubt struck her after she had mailed the letter. She followed it with a note of horrid warning to Verlaine; she had a word of advice to give him if he wished to hear it. Genially from his bed of roses he bade her speak. She did so and to some effect: Philomène was throwing away the money he was sending her, and not on herself alone; she was living openly with a young man. To clinch the revelation, she gave his name, Alfred, and, final humiliation, his age.

The news reached Verlaine incongruously in the midst of his lionizing. He received it with a mixture of panic and indignation: "If this is true," he wrote to Philomène after tearing up his first attempt, "tell me frankly. It would be frank and honest even though frightful. If it isn't true, prove it. That is to say, deny it strongly. Then pardon me, and the word marriage becomes a reality."

His correspondence became positively frantic; in every spare moment—and he was allowed few—he dashed off an appeal or a warning. When the preternaturally serious lecturer retired, at Oxford, at Manchester, in London "to prepare his notes," the notes took forms that would have surprised his audience: urgent "Say nothing! Not a word to a soul! Silence!" to a gratified Eugénie; wild "O don't deceive me! The shadow of that *man* torments me" to Philomène; and, the latter's denials lacking the substance he was looking for, a harassed call for aid to Cazals: "I am jealous in this country of Othello, jealous enough to die of it if I should decide to break with that too much loved, strange and delicious *middle-aged* woman! Is it true that she is deceiving and exploiting me up to the hilt? You can find out and must tell me. Or am I cuckolding and robbing myself?"

But Cazals' report was unnecessary: Philomène, badgered by daily letters, admitted that a man had visited rue Broca but, she explained, he was merely a young trussmaker fitting her out for a visit she intended to make to her home province in the near future.

At this Verlaine burst into a long lamentation to his "*Chérie, trop!*" as she had become. "I write this with death in my soul. When a fixed idea takes hold of a man all is over. I have the impression, everything tells me so, the past, the present, three thousand francs spent or put away without any profit to me, the hints of others—all indicate to me that you have a lover, that you are living with him, and that he couldn't care less about me or you. At your age one doesn't have lovers at twenty-nine *for nothing!* I am crushed by sorrow, I can't think of anything else."

Hope lingered on, however, and in the next sentence he explains that he is enclosing twenty-five francs, apologizes for not sending more, "for I must buy some clothes and linen," and suggests a compromise: "Let us remain good friends. We can meet each other and I shall never refuse to do you a service." Then he looked at her letter again and burst out afresh: "But live with you! From the very first we have never been able to manage it with your continual changing of address. It's you who mistrust me, is it—and I don't want to sleep outside a room I've paid for. That's really a bit too expensive. Some six hundred francs or thereabouts have disappeared and you want me to trust you with all my money. Thanks very much! and to Monsieur Alfred and to all the pimps who would lick their chops over it. You threaten to be angry with me. *Mon Dieu*, try it, but I have no more, in fact I have never had any confidence in you . . . and I know quite well, for instance, that your journey is imaginary, like your trussmaker, etc., etc."

But it was difficult to remain angry at a distance with the light creature: "Nevertheless I love you too much—one can love without trusting—to give you up." He tried the gentle reproach: "You who only love me—you told me so in the rue Pascal—for my money, because I am only a mug, only a client, only the man who keeps you while others are your lovers—you said it to someone, in front of me, in the rue Saint-Jacques—you ought to write nicely to me 'Well, yes, it's true, I'm living in furnished rooms with Alfred, 20 rue de la Glacière. I have some sous in hand. When I need more I will tell you.' Then we should remain good friends. Otherwise there will always be quarrels. That's dreadful (for me) but that's how it is."

Remembering the notes to Vanier which he had scattered in happier moments, he added a gentle threat: "All those notes you have, 'I authorize' etc., are useless. *I shall draw all money myself, alone.*"

But the thought would obtrude; suppose, just suppose . . . "For the rest, if you really haven't deceived me odiously, foully, ignobly . . . and if we are to live together, let us marry and I will make sure that you have something to live on after my death. . . . In any event, write quickly one way or the other. I'm due to leave Thursday but will come back earlier if you agree. And, given proof, my confidence will return and I'll make you the happiest of women."

He signed himself "Your too old, alas, it seems, P. Verlaine"; then, overcome again by the sadness of the occasion, added a wistful, or one could say pettish, "I can't bring myself to write either Madame Alfred! or 'Esther'! It's really too bad."

He waited one more day and, obtaining neither confession nor denial, recalled Eugénie, telling her to meet him at the Gare du Nord the next evening. "I am parting from Esther with great grief," he said and, with a frankness that the occasion seemed to demand, added, "I love and shall always love that woman. But she is dangerous for me and my mind is made up. I love you also. You have always been good for me and I only work well when I'm with you. I won't say any more of the other. If she had had a better character all would have been well."

This written, frankness seemed perhaps not the happiest way to regain Eugénie's regard; he hurriedly promised her a good dinner near the station before "making dodo" and assured her, and himself, "We can be happy if we are *wise*. Only it may be better to change our district. I *must* get as far away from Esther as possible. This poor girl has thrown a spell over me and things always go badly when I'm with her."

Evidently the spell was still working for he wrote at once to his "poor dear" to announce his decision with a "Farewell! It is better so. When you need me give me a sign and I'll do all I can. But to live together is impossible. You would always be paying for young men and that would end in pork butchery."

This sounded tolerably definite; too much so for Varlaine who made his decision appear rather less irrevocable by suggesting that "If you want to see me" she should meet the train in Paris when "I would have the greatest pleasure in embracing you, perhaps for the last time." This with the warning "But don't bring someone else with you as you did on the other occasion."

History does not record whether Philomène went to meet him. It seems unlikely since in his agitation Verlaine had given her the wrong day. In any event Eugénie carried him off in triumph and when the elections for the Academy came up a few months later it was Eugénie who, tickled by the thought of playing Aspasia to his Pericles, stopped all supply of drink for a week so that he could array himself in the frock coat with which to pay the necessary soliciting calls on the thirty-nine Academicians. Eugénie used afterwards to explain that he failed to become an Immortal because he had no top hat: "He had some but smashed them one day in a bad temper"—but this appears improbable since Verlaine, feeling unwell, excused himself when the visiting period arrived.

[5]

The race, needless to say, went to Eugénie. But the event was
hotly contested almost to the finishing post; Philomène came again
after the check by Alfred and for a time made all the running; Verlaine continued to alternate between the challengers, throwing in
another period with Caroline to whip them up; and when he retired
to the hospital for the last time at the end of 1894 Philomène and
Eugénie visited him on alternate days, both urgently requested be-
forehand to "Wear a hat!" and both were introduced solemnly to
the ward as *"ma femme."*

But when he left the hospital early in 1895 Verlaine was a really
sick man, scarcely able to walk. He needed a nurse rather more than
a lover and the still flighty Philomène scarcely filled the bill. He
therefore threw in his lot perforce with Eugénie "whom I love very
much and who despite her changeable nature is to some extent
indispensable to me as I cannot at the moment attend to my bad
leg myself." They set up house first in the rue Monsieur le Prince
and finally at 39 rue Descartes behind the Panthéon. The apartment
matched the dreary street and consisted of two small rooms and a
small kitchen; to the left of the main staircase was the bedroom from
which Verlaine rarely moved; to the right was the room where
Eugénie did her sewing. The rooms were clean but bare, the only
ornaments being an oil painting of Captain Verlaine and a cage of
canaries. To cheer the gloomy prospect Verlaine gilded all the
chairs and the bird cage.

Here came the visitors, Lepelletier and Cazals (on different days
and hours), Delahaye, De Sivry, Dierx, Blémont, a host of young
poets, Verlaine's English friends and as many of the crowd of curious
as could get past the maid. For Eugénie was determined that Verlaine should end his days in respectability; he and she continued to
quarrel violently, they drank themselves back to friendship, they
lived in an unsalubrious quarter, they dressed like beggars, they rarely
had a sou to bless themselves with but—they had a maid. Zélie was
not perhaps in the first flight of domestics, a blousy, bad-tempered
woman on the wrong side of fifty and as much addicted to the bottle
as her master and mistress. But as Eugénie had said, someone must
open the door to all these callers; it was not fitting that the wife in
all but name of the most famous man of his time, a man who would

have been in the Academy but for a fit of temper, should have to interview every Tom, Dick and Harry who tried to catch a glimpse of him, ask him to read poems, autograph books and the rest of the rubbish.

As for money, one is baffled. All Verlaine's books were selling, he could get a franc a line for anything he cared to write, he had at last been given a grant by the Ministry of Fine Arts, he was receiving a hundred and fifty francs a month from a committee including three leaders of Parisian society, Coppée, Prudhomme, Barrès and Montesquiou, and he had written a first installment (also the last) of his *Confessions* for *Fin de Siècle*, a beautifully written and hopelessly inaccurate account of his life to the coming of Rimbaud, which sold in vast numbers. Where, then, did it all go? No one knows. Drink was inexpensive, they had no other outgoings of moment, yet they were always hard up. One suspects Eugénie's mattress; Verlaine was obviously failing and she had fears for the future.

Toward the end of the year Verlaine received a letter from Georges, then apprenticed to a watchmaker in Belgium. This first sign from his son in fifteen years provides the most convincing proof of Verlaine's widespread fame. Mathilde had realized at last that it was no mean triumph to have been the wife of such a man and for the rest of her life his name was to take precedence of all others in her conversation, even of the vicomte she had refused. The ban on intercourse between father and son was relaxed and the twenty-three-year-old Georges promptly wrote, wrote in character; he would like to visit Verlaine but could not raise the fare.

Verlaine was overjoyed. The child's photograph was still stuck in the corner of his mirror, all his books had been sent to Georges as they were published, one had been dedicated to him. He sent the fare but Georges did not appear; he had been taken ill, had left the watchmaker and gone to his mother in Brussels. Verlaine wrote in vain to Mathilde; she too had moved; he asked a Belgian friend to search for them. All in vain; the boy did not come.

That winter was cold, the room scarcely heated, and a few days after he had heard from his son, late in December, he caught bronchitis. Feeling the approach of the end, he wrote his last poem. It showed that the poet lived in him still and with power:

Les Armes ont tu leurs ordres en attendant
De vibrer à nouveau dans des mains admirables

Ou scélérates, et, tristes, le bras pendant,
Nous allons, mal rêveurs, dans le vague des Fables.

Les Armes ont tu leurs ordres qu'on attendait
Même chez les rêveurs mensongers que nous sommes,
Honteux de notre bras qui pendait et tardait,
Et nous allons, désappointés, parmi les hommes.

Armes, vibrez! mains admirables, prenez-les,
Mains scélérates à défaut des admirables!
Prenez-les donc et faites signe aux En-allés
Dans les fables plus incertaines que les sables.

Tirez du rêve notre exode, voulez-vous?
Nous mourons d'être ainsi languides, presque infâmes!
Armes, parlez! Vos ordres vont être pour nous
La vie enfin fleurie au bout, s'il faut, des lames.

La mort que nous aimons, que nous eûmes toujours
Pour but de ce chemin où prospèrent la ronce
Et l'ortie, ô la mort sans plus ces émois lourds,
Délicieuse et dont la victoire est l'annonce!

He grew worse; when Delahaye called on the sixth day of the new year, he whispered, "I'm finished." The next day he was dressed and put into a chair so that he could lunch with two friends. He managed to eat and drink a little and talked proudly of Georges: "I shall leave him a name which will be as worthy as any other."

That night he fell from the bed; Eugénie and Zélie could not lift him back; he lay on the floor all night covered with a blanket and eiderdown.

By the time he had been put back into bed the next morning he was dying. Cazals was horrified when he saw him but one flicker of the old Verlaine showed itself; he overheard Eugénie's whispered "He's dying," opened his eyes and murmured with a smile, "Don't sole the dead man's shoes yet."

At eight o'clock that evening, January 8, he died muttering the names of Lepelletier and Coppée. None of the old friends sent for by Cazals had arrived before his death.

The next morning the papers were full of the news and rue Descartes was crowded with people trying to pay their respects at the bedside—poets of every age and school, old patients at the hospitals,

waiters from the cafés, neighbors from every street he had lived in for
the last eight years, even from the cour Saint-François, not to speak
of the mob of the merely curious.

There was no money in the house to pay for the funeral, or so
Eugénie declared, but the Ministry of Fine Arts contributed five
hundred francs and Verlaine's friends made up the rest. After a
service in the church of Saint-Etienne-du-Mont the procession slowly
crossed Paris to the family tomb in the Batignolles cemetery. The
coffin was hidden by a mass of flowers—roses, orchids, lilacs, carna-
tions—and the following crowd grew to enormous proportions by the
time the cortège began to climb the hill to the rue de Clichy, the
hill that Verlaine had walked so often as child, boy and man.

The chief mourner, Georges Verlaine, was absent. He had been
discovered doing his military service at Lille, notified, but to the
general surprise did not arrive. His place was taken by Delahaye,
Vanier, De Sivry and Cazals.

The four corners of the pall were held from the rue Descartes to
the church by Coppée, Lepelletier, Mendès and Montesquiou. After
the service Barrès replaced Montesquiou. Then Coppée, complaining
of fatigue, asked Mallarmé to take his place, hailed a cab and followed the procession at his ease, polishing up the notes for his funeral
oration. Mendès did not complain of tiredness but, showing obvious
signs of boredom, bought a paper en route and, still holding his cord
with one hand, made himself au fait with the day's news until the
long walk was done.

[6]

The funeral oration in France is a serious and lengthy business. So
while the old and young friends of Verlaine are showing their paces
before the largest assembly ever seen in the cemetery at Batignolles,
let us look for a moment into the future.

To begin with Verlaine's women. The victorious Eugénie, clothed
from head to foot in widow's weeds, rode in state in a carriage behind the four chief mourners. No doubt she gave an occasional
thought to the man in the coffin—Eugénie was far from being heart-
less—but naturally the future preoccupied her. Delightful preoccupation! The death chamber crowded every hour of the day, the enormous crowd following her carriage had given her ideas. What a life!
What a death too; for Eugénie, doing a roaring tourist trade in "the

pen with which Verlaine wrote his last poem" and "the last manuscript handled by the Master"—including the fragments of the
fragment of a play which she had torn to pieces and flung at Verlaine
in a fury—drank herself into the grave within a year.

Philomène was there too, in the crowd; and when all had gone
home, the speeches over, she knelt by the grave in tears and put a
bunch of violets on the heaped wreaths. Soon afterwards she went
back to her home in the Ardennes and Paris saw her no more. So
she really had intended to make that journey.

Caroline was not there. Caroline, stark naked, was hammering at
the door of the house in rue Descartes, shrieking that she was Verlaine's muse and must preach his fame throughout the world. She was
removed to an asylum where she died mad.

We have already glanced at Mathilde in her pension at Nice. Her
stories of the mighty were to be known and feared from one end of
the Côte to the other. Yet she was far from unhappy even though
both her marriages had failed; after all, what other woman could
claim to have been the wife of Paul Verlaine?

And where was Georges? Accusation and denial followed each
other briskly, and hard things were said of Mathilde in the literary
circles of Paris; unjust things, as it happened; she had not prevented
her son from going to the funeral. The explanation was less complicated; he was in a drunken stupor. Yes, Georges too; but Georges
was an alcoholic as his father was not; his end was certain. He did
not, of course, cut a great figure in the world; after trying his hand
at one thing after another he became a station master on the Métro
and died of delirium tremens in 1926.

Bibi, presented with Verlaine's clothes by a suddenly generous
Eugénie, proudly paraded them (for he, being small, was barely to
be seen) throughout the Latin Quarter until they fell to pieces. And
by that time he was ready to follow his hero.

Lepelletier, whose oration was so dull that we cannot possibly
repeat it, became a deputé and secured the inevitable ribbon across
his chest. When one talked to him of revolutions he would smile
indulgently, the kind of smile he gave whenever Verlaine was mentioned. He was indefatigable in trying to arrange for the erection of
a statue of "poor Paul," a statue cleansed of course of every trace of
riotous living. He died full of honors, respected by all; and if many
a hand was lifted to stifle a yawn during his lifetime not a voice was
raised against him afterwards.

Mendès remained the persistently golden-haired Apollo of a certain set for many years. He never precisely got anywhere though always on the verge of it, but his triumphs with women were prodigious. He produced in company many an anecdote of his old friend Paul whose genius he had spotted at a glance; the grain of truth in these anecdotes tended to become obscured by the years but he told them awfully well.

Coppée was rich in reminiscences too. He did not exaggerate much but grew sentimental with ease. He died rich, popular, hard working to the last. If one can barely restrain a shudder from time to time when contemplating the successful poetaster who was once a charming and imaginative young poet, that is merely kicking against the pricks.

Hérédia, who was not at the ceremony, was elected Prince of Poets in Verlaine's place and thereafter talked of his predecessor with majestic magnanimity. He was succeeded after two years by Dierx, melancholy to the last but a good poet.

Within a month of the funeral Vanier too was dead. He had earned his immortality.

[7]

But it is time to return to the grave. The orators, spurred by the size of their audience, had seized their chance. Eloquence of a kind rarely surpassed in the Batignolles cemetery flowed over the resting place of the dead man. Let us listen to a few extracts.

Coppée had polished to some purpose:

"Let us respectfully salute the tomb of a true poet and bow before the coffin of a child. Paul Verlaine and I had barely passed our twentieth year when we met each other, exchanged our first confidences and read our earliest verses. I see once more our two heads bent fraternally over the same page and once more I feel our admirations, our enthusiasms, our dreams in all their youthful ardor. We were two children marching confidently toward the future. But Verlaine never encountered experience, that cold and inescapable companion who takes us by the hand and leads us along the thorny path—he remained a child always. . . .

"Happy the child who, falling heavily and raising himself tearfully, immediately forgets his pain and trouble and whose eyes still wet with tears gaze eagerly and rapturously on nature and life. And happy the poet who like our poor friend here preserves the heart of a child, the child's freshness of vision and feeling and instinctive need of love, who sins without perversity, repents wholeheartedly, loves openly and believes in God. . . .

"Happy that poet! I dare to repeat it knowing full well how Paul Verlaine suffered in his sick body and sad heart. Child as he was he faced the world defenseless, and life wounded him often and cruelly. But suffering is the privilege of genius, a word which we must use when we speak of Verlaine, for his name will always stand for a new form of poetry which will always remain as one of the most important innovations in French literature. Yes, Verlaine created a type of poetry peculiar to himself, with an inspiration at once naïve and subtle, compounded of fine shades of feeling evoking the most delicate vibrations of the nerves, the most fugitive echoes of the heart, yet a most natural poetry fresh from its source and at times not far from the popular; a poetry in which the free and broken meter preserves a delightful harmony, the stanzas swaying and singing like the chant of the child, the exquisite lines filled with music. And in this inimitable poetry he has told us of the ardors, failings, remorse and tender dreams which have troubled his innocent heart.

"Such poems are made to live and I declare that the companions of Paul Verlaine's youth who have worked hard at their art would instantly renounce the pleasures and vanities of a happy life and accept the hungry days and shelterless nights of '*Pauvre Lélian*' if they knew that they would leave behind them, like him, pages that will never die and would see the immortal laurel bloom over their tomb."

Mendès had been reading his newspaper too earnestly:

"Paul Verlaine, you who are on the borders of night, my voice expresses the sorrow of the brothers of your youth with a last Adieu! and communicates to you their undying admiration.

"You passed away in suffering. Your martyrdom is ended. May God give you what you hoped for! But among us your fame remains imperishable, for you have erected a monument like unto none other. By shallow marble steps, through the melancholy whisper of roseate bays we mount to a great white chapel wherein fair wax tapers shine! And as the Kingdom of Heaven belongs to the meek in spirit, so the Kingdom of Fame belongs to the simple in genius. We love you and lament you, poor dead; we adore you, pure immortal."

Mallarmé:

"From generation to generation when youthful lips open, *Fêtes galantes, La Bonne Chanson, Sagesse, Amour* and *Parallèlement* will be poured out in a melodious stream quenching their thirst with an immortal flow of exquisite French. Paul Verlaine, his genius soaring into the future, remains a hero. . . . An example rarely furnished by the centuries, our contemporary faced all the terrors of the fate of the singer and dreamer, for solitude, cold, discomfort, poverty is the lot of him who with ingenuous hardihood walks through life at the bidding of his inspiration."

Kahn:

"I desire in the name of myself and of other poets younger than I to bid a last farewell to the most profound, most tender, most exquisite of French poets, the one whom we loved most of all."

Barrès:

"Paul Verlaine had neither official position, wealth nor influential friends. He did not belong to the Academy. . . . The essential part of him was his ability to feel and the accents which communicated these feelings, accents French to the core and imbued with those tender and thrilling beauties which have no analogy except in another art. . . . Verlaine, linked to François Villon by the freedom and charm of his genius, helps us to understand one of the principal facets of the French contribution to literature. Henceforth his ideas will take their place among those which form the national heritage— and this, thanks to the younger generation. It is by our constant propaganda, our generous love, our active clear-sightedness that the work of Paul Verlaine, repulsed by his friends and rivals save a few to whom public opinion renders homage, has triumphed over the obstacles which six years ago might have seemed insurmountable."

Moréas:

"I speak as one of Paul Verlaine's oldest friends among those who are called the poets of the new school. But let us leave schools alone. Today we think only of poetry; and from Victor Hugo to Leconte de Lisle, from Leconte de Lisle to the youngest among us, just as from Villon to Ronsard, from Ronsard to Malherbe and Jean Racine this poetry of the French bids us lament the loss of one of its greatest exponents. The author of *Sagesse, Jadis et Naguère* and *Amour* must be admired as an illustrious poet in the absolute sense of that word. . . . Adieu, Paul Verlaine . . . your name will not perish."

[8]

What is one to say of all this? Of the seven men who spoke at the graveside, Lepelletier had been almost unfailingly kind and helpful but understood next to nothing of the man he had helped and disapproved of the little he did manage to grasp; Mendès had shunned Verlaine for the last nine years; from the depths of his cotton-wool existence Mallarmé talked boldly of sufferings he had never experienced and had no intention of experiencing, he admired the poet but was so obviously distressed by the man that Verlaine kept away from him; Kahn admired the poet with reservations but made cruel and public fun of the man; Barrès admired the poet too but had long since drawn clear of the man, and his assumption that the poet was made by the younger generation, himself prominently included, was wildly far from the mark; Moréas, blown up with a vanity which time has not justified, admired neither poet nor man, he had quarreled with Verlaine, a quarrel of his own making, and had written of his work, "Verlaine, aged fifty, has published some little books; the earlier ones had some pretty, musical things in them. But these small poems of a page or two at most struck out at random are all so much wind. They don't make a work of art"; Coppée alone had an inkling of the man behind the poems and of the true stature of the poet, though his declaration that he would gladly have changed places with him was no more than poetic license—for Coppée had refused to vote for Verlaine's inclusion in the third *Parnasse contemporain*. Coppée, a visit or two to hospital excepted, had not set eyes on Verlaine for twenty-three years, Coppée had given him money but wanted nothing to do with him.

What, then, is one to say of these speeches? Rimbaud would have had a word for them but Rimbaud would have missed the point as he so often did. The subject of the eulogies would have seen the point as he usually did. How he would have chuckled! These seven men were following the tradition of their country in standing up and glorifying the memory of a one-time friend. "Today we think only of poetry," said Moréas. What he meant, speaking for the entire French nation, was, "Today we think only of the decencies." They had come to bury Verlaine and to praise him; neither they nor their audience looked for candor at the graveside; yet out of the mouths of these men, mouths filled with formalities, came, all unknown to them, truth.

Bibliography

MANUSCRIPTS ON OR
CONCERNING VERLAINE AT:

Bibliothèque Nationale, Paris
Bibliothèque Sainte-Geneviève, Paris
Musée des Archives de Police, Paris
Palais de Justice, Paris
Préfecture de la Seine, Paris
Musée Royale, Brussels
Musée des Archives de Police, Brussels
Musée Rimbaud, Charleville
British Museum
Bodleian, Oxford

WORKS BY VERLAINE

Oeuvres Complètes, Paris, 1899, 1911, 1926
Oeuvres Poétiques Complètes. Ed. Dantec, Paris, 1938, 1940, 1947, 1954
Oeuvres Posthumes, Paris, 1903, 1929
Oeuvres Oubliées, Paris, 1926, 1929
Confessions, Paris, 1895
Correspondance, Paris, 1922-1929
Mes Hôpitaux, Paris, 1891
Mes Prisons, Paris, 1893
Mémoires d'un Veuf, Paris Les, 1886
Quinze jours en Hollands, Paris 1893

BOOKS ON OR CONCERNING VERLAINE

VERLAINE, MATHILDE, *Mémoires de ma vie*, Paris, 1935
MORICE, C., *Verlaine*, Paris, 1888
CAZALS, F.-A., *Paul Verlaine. Ses portraits*, Paris, 1896
DELAHAYE, ERNEST, *Documents relatifs à Verlaine*, Paris, 1919; *Verlaine*, Paris, 1919
LEPELLETIER, EDMOND, *Paul Verlaine*, Paris, 1907
CAZALS, F.-A. & LEROUGE, G., *Les derniers jours de Paul Verlaine*, Paris, 1911
DONOS, C., *Verlaine intime*, Paris, 1898

ANON., *Paul Verlaine et ses contemporains*, Paris, 1897

NICOLSON, HAROLD, *Verlaine*, London, 1921

SECHE, A. & BERTAUT, J., *Paul Verlaine*, Paris, 1909

COULON, M., *Verlaine, poète saturnien*, Paris, 1933

PORCHE, F., *Verlaine tel qui'il fut*, Paris, 1933

FONTAINE, A., *Verlaine, homme de lettres*, Paris, 1937

ROBERTS, C. E. B., *Paul Verlaine*, London, 1937

RUCHON, F., *Verlaine. Documents iconographiques*, Paris, 1947

UNDERWOOD, V. P., *Chronologie verlainienne*, Lille, 1938

DELAHAYE, ERNEST, *Souvenirs familiers à propos de Rimbaud, Verlaine, etc.*, Paris 1925

ADAM, A., *Verlaine, l'homme et l'oeuvre*, Paris, 1953

MONTEL, F., *Bibliographie de Verlaine*, Paris, 1924

VAN BEVER, A. & MONDA, M., *Bibliographie et Iconographie de Verlaine*, Paris, 1926

UNDERWOOD, V. P., *Verlaine en Angleterre*, Paris, 1956

COULON, M., *Au coeur de Verlaine et de Rimbaud*, Paris, 1925

FONTAINAS, A., *Verlaine-Rimbaud. Ce qu'on presume de leurs relations; ce qu'on sait*, Paris, 1931

MOUQUET, J., *Rimbaud raconté par Verlaine*, Paris, 1934

CARRE, J.-M., *Autour de Verlaine et de Rimbaud*, Paris, 1949

BOOKS ON OR CONCERNING RIMBAUD

RIMBAUD, A., *Les Illuminations. Notice par P. Verlaine*, Paris, 1886
Poèmes. *Les Illuminations. Une Saison en Enfer. Notice par P. Verlaine*, Paris, 1892
Poésies complètes. Avec une preface de P. Verlaine, Paris, 1895

RIMBAUD, ISABELLE, *Mon frère Arthur*, Paris, 1920

DELAHAYE, E., *Rimbaud*, Paris, 1923
Les Illuminations et Une Saison en Enfer de Rimbaud, Paris, 1927

CARRE, J.-M., *La vie adventureuse de Rimbaud*, Paris, 1926

IZAMBARD, G., *Arthur Rimbaud. A Douai et à Charleville*, Paris, 1927. *Rimbaud tel que je l'ai connu*, Paris, 1946

RIMBAUD, I., & BERRICHON, P., *Rimbaud. Ebauches et correspondance*, Paris, 1937

STARKIE, E., *Arthur Rimbaud*, London, 1938, 1947. *Rimbaud en Abyssinie*, Paris, 1938

RIMBAUD, A., *Oeuvres complètes*. Ed. R. de Reneville et J. Mouquet, Paris, 1946

RIMBAUD, A., *Poésies*, Ed. H. Bouillane de Lacoste, Paris, 1947. *Illuminations*, Ed. H. de Bouillane de Lacoste, Paris, 1949. *Une Saison en Enfer*, Paris, 1951

ETIEMBLE, R., *Le Mythe de Rimbaud*, Paris, 1952, 1954

BOOKS ON OR CONCERNING
THE VERLAINE CIRCLE

AICARD, JEAN, *La Poésie de Jean Aicard*, Paris, 1909

ALQ, LOUISE D', *Causeries Familières*, Paris, 1882-4

BANVILLE, THEODORE DE, *Mes souvenirs*, Paris, 1882. *Nouveaux souvenirs*, Paris, 1890

BAUDELAIRE, CHARLES, *Maître et disciple, Charles Baudelaire et Léon Cladel* by

Judith Cladel, Paris, 1951. *Charles Baudelaire* by A. Sèche and J. Bertaut, Paris, 1910. *The Letters of Charles Baudelaire to His Mother*, London, 1928

BLÉMONT, EMILE, *Emile Blémont* by F. Clerget, Paris, 1906

BLOY, LÉON, *Vie de Léon Bloy*, by Bollery, Paris, 1938

CALLIAS, HECTOR DE, *Le Livre de la vie*, Paris, 1862

CHABRIER, EMMANUEL, *Emmanuel Chabrier d'après ses lettres* Ed. J. Desaymand, Paris, 1934

CLADEL, LÉON, *La Vie de Léon Cladel* by Judith Cladel, Paris, 1905

COPPÉE, FRANÇOIS, *Preface to Poèmes de Paul Verlaine*, Paris, 1904. *François Coppée* by M. F. A. de Lescure, Paris, 1889. *Lettres à sa mère et à sa soeur, 1862-1908*, Paris, 1914. *Souvenirs d'un Parisien*, Paris, 1910. *La Vie et l'oeuvre de François Coppée* by L. le Meur, Paris, 1932. *Toute une jeunesse*, Paris, 1911

CORBIÈRE, TRISTAN, *Tristan Corbière by R. Martineau*, Paris, 1925. *Tristan Corbière. Un essai par Jean Rousselot*, Paris, 1951

DESBORDES-VALMORE, MARCELINE, *Le Vie douloureuse de Marceline Desbordes-Valmore* by L. Descaves, Paris, 1911

DIERX, LÉON, *Léon Dierx* by E. Noulet, Paris, 1925

FANTIN-LATOUR, I., *Fantin-Latour: sa vie et ses amitiés* by Adolphe Jullien, Paris, 1909. *Fantin-Latour* by G. Kahn, Paris, 1927

FENÉON, FELIX, *Oeuvres de Felix Fenéon*. Intro. de Jean Paulhan, Paris, 1948

FORAIN, JEAN, *En écoutant Forain* by L. Vaillat, Paris, 1931

FRANCE, ANATOLE, *Le Vie et les opinions d'Anatole France by Anatole Thibault*, Paris, 1925. *Les Carnets intimes d'Anatole France* Ed. L. Carias, Paris, 1946. *Anatole France* by Edwin P. Dargan, London, 1937, *La vie littéraire*, Paris, n.d., 1937

GILL, ANDRÉ, *André Gill, sa vie* by A. Lods, Paris, 1887

GLATIGNY, ALBERT, *Lettres d'A. Glatigny à Theodore de Banville*, Paris, 1923. *Albert Glatigny: La vie-l'homme-le poète* by J. Reymond, Paris, 1936

GONCOURT BROTHERS, *The Goncourt Journals 1851-1870*, London, 1937

GOURMONT, REMY DE, *Promenades littéraires*, Paris, 1909

HÉRÉDIA, J. M. DE, *The Technique of the French Alexandrine: A study of the works of J. M. de Hérédia* by H. P. Thième, London, 1898. *Jose-Maria de Hérédia* by Miodrag Ibrovac, Paris, 1923

HUGO, VICTOR, *Olympio* by André Maurois, Paris, 1954

HUYSMANS, J.-K., *Souvenirs*, Paris, 1924

KAHN, GUSTAVE, *Silhouettes littéraires*, Paris, 1925. *Les origines du symbolisme*, Paris, 1936

LAFORGUE, JULES, *Jules Laforgue et ses poésies* by Léon Guichard, Paris, 1950. *Jules Laforgue and the Ironic Inheritance* by Warren Ramsay, London, 1953

LECONTE DE LISLE, CHARLES, *Leconte de Lisle* by Irving Brown, New York, 1929. *Leconte de Lisle* by P. C. J. Bourget, Paris, 1886. *Leconte de Lisle and his Contemporaries* by Irving Putter, New York, 1951. *Leconte de Lisle intime* by Jean Dormis, Paris, 1895. *Un Demi-siècle littéraire. Leconte de Lisle et ses amis* by F. Calmettes, Paris, 1902

LEMERRE, A., *Le Livre du bibliophile*, Paris, 1874

MAETERLINCK, M., *Life and writings of Maurice Maeterlinck* by Jethro Bithell, London, 1913. *Bulles bleues*, Monaco, 1948

MALLARMÉ, STÉPHANE, *Mallarmé* by Wallace Fowlie, London, 1953. *L'Amitié de Verlaine et Mallarmé* by H. Mondor, Paris, 1939. *Vie de Mallarmé* by H. Mondor, Paris, 1946. *Autobiographie*, Paris, 1924. *Stéphane Mallarmé 1842-1898. Poèmes et lettres*, Paris, 1948. *Les Miens*, Brussels, 1892. *Correspondance inédite de Stéphane Mallarmé*, Geneva, 1949. *Mallarmé par un des siens* by E. Dujardin, Paris, 1936. *Divagations*, Paris, 1897. *Verlaine, professeur à Rethel*, Paris, 1897

MENDÈS, CATULLE, *Le movement poétique français de 1867-1900*, Paris, 1903. *La légende du Parnasse contemporain*, Brussels, 1884. *La maison de la vielle*, Paris, 1914

MÉNARD, LOUIS, *Louis Ménard et son oeuvre* by P. Berthelot, Paris, 1902

MÉRAT, ALBERT, *Oeuvres Choisies, 1863-1904*. Paris, 1906. *Vers le soir. Impressions et souvenirs*, Paris, 1900

MERRIL, STUART, *Stuart Merril* by Majorie L. Henry, London, 1927

MORÉAS, JEAN, *Jean Moréas* by R. Niklaus, Paris, 1936. *Adieu à Moréas* by A. M. Barrès, Paris, 1910

NOUVEAU, GERMAIN, *La vie étrange d'Humilis*, Paris. *Valentines*. Preface by Ernest Delahaye, Paris, 1921. *Oeuvres Poétiques*, Paris, 1953. *Poésies d'Humilis et vers inédits*, Paris, 1924. *Germain Nouveau et Rimbaud* by Jean Richepin, Paris, 1927

RÉGAMEY, F., *Verlaine dessinateur*, Paris, 1896

RETTE, ADOLPHE, *Le Symbolisme. Anecdotes et souvenirs*, Paris, 1903. *Adolphe Rette* by W. K. Cornell, London, 1942

RICARD, L.-X. DE, *Ciel, rue et foyer*, Paris, 1866. *Mémoires d'une déclassée*, Paris, 1903. *Petits mémoires d 'un Parnassien*, Paris, 1898-1900. *Anatole France et le Parnasse contemporain*, Paris, 1902

RICHEPIN, JEAN, *Mes paradis*, Paris, 1894. *Recueil de morceaux choisis*, Paris, 1912

ROTHENSTEIN, WILLIAM, *Men and Memories*, London, 1931-9. *Paul Verlaine: Three Portraits*, London, 1931

SILVESTRE, PAUL ARMAND, *Portraits et souvenirs 1886-1891*, Paris, 1891

SUARES, ANDRÉ, *Cité, nef de Paris*, Paris, 1934. *André Suares et Paul Claudel: Correspondance*, Paris, 1951

SULLY PRUDHOMME, *The Technique of the French Alexandrine. A study of the works of Sully Prudhomme* by H. P. Thieme, London, 1898. *Sully Prudhome et sa pensée* by P. Flottes, Paris, 1930. *Journal intime. Lettres — pensees*, Paris, 1922

SYMONS, ARTHUR, *Collected Works*, London, 1924

VALADE, LÉON, *Léon Valade. Conference, etc.*, by Jules Truffier, Paris, 1904. *Oeuvres*, Paris, 1887

VALÉRY, PAUL, *Villon et Verlaine*, Paris, 1937

VANIER, LÉON, *Examen du manifeste*, Paris, 1889. *Les premières armes du symbolisme*, Paris, 1889

VIELE-GRIFFEN, FRANCIS, *Son Oeuvre* by J. de Cours, Paris, 1930

VILLIERS DE L'ISLE-ADAM, AUGUSTE, *Villiers de l'Isle-Adam* by R. Y. M. du Pontavice de Heussey, London, 1894. *Villiers de l'Isle-Adam* by F. Clerget, Paris, 1921. *Villiers de l'Isle-Adam* by M. Daireaux, Paris, 1936. *Faces et profils. Souvenirs de Villiers de l'Isle-Adam, J. Laforgue etc.*, by H. de Regnier, Paris, 1931

ZILCKEN, PHILIPPE, *Paul Verlaine*, Paris, 1897. *Souvenirs*, Paris, 1900. *Au jardin du passé*, The Hague, 1930

OTHER WORKS CONSULTED

ADAM, MME., *Chez les passants*, Paris, 1890. *Mes sentiments et mes idées avant 1870*, Paris, 1905

autour du Symbolisme, Lille, 1955

BEDIER, C. M. J. & HAZARD, P., *Histoire de la littérature Française illustre*, Paris, 1923-4

BERGERAT, A. E., *Souvenirs d'un enfant de Paris*, Paris, 1911-13

BERSAUCOURT, A. DE, *Au temps des Parnassiens: Nina de Villard et ses amis*, Paris, 1925

BONNIÈRES, R. DE, *Mémoires d'aujourd'hui*, Paris, 1883-8

BOURGET, P. C. J., *Quelques témoignages*, Paris, 1928-33

CAREL, A., *Histoire anecdotique des contemporains*, Paris, 1885

CASSAGNE, A., *Le théorie de l'art pour l'art chez les derniers romantiques et chez les premiers parnassiens*, Paris, 1906

DAUDET, ALFRED, *Alfred Daudet* by Léon Daudet, Paris, 1898

DÉMONT-BRETON, V., *Maisons que j'ai connues*, Paris, 1927. *Nos amis artistes*, Paris, 1928

DUFOY, P., *Chex Nina de Villard*, Paris, 1927

ELLIS, HAVELOCK *From Rousseau to Proust*, London, 1936

ELTON, OLIVER, *Frederick York Powell*, London, 1906

FORD, F. M., *Return to Yesterday*, London, 1931

FOUCHER, PAUL HENRI, *Les coulisses du passé*, Paris, 1873

GOSSE, E. W., *Collected essays: French profiles*, London, 1912

GRIERSON, J. FRANCIS, *Parisien Portraits*, London, 1911

HARRIS, FRANK, *Contemporary Portraits*, London, 1925

HOUSSAYE, ARSÉNE, *Mes confessions*, Paris, 1885

HURET, JULES, *Enquête sur l'evolution littéraire*, Paris, 1901

JADART, HENRI, *Souvenirs*, Paris, 1899

LE GALLIENNE, RICHARD, *The Romantic Nineties*, London, 1901

LELEUX, CHARLES, *Quand nous étions jeunes . . .* , Paris, 1930; *Mémorial du Collège Notre-Dame de Rethel*, Paris, 1933

MAY, JAMES L., *John Lane and the Nineties*, London, 1936

MARTINO, PIERRE, *Parnasse et symbolisme*, Paris, 1925

MOORE, G., *Impressions and Opinions*, London, 1891

MORICE, CHARLES, *Quelques maîtres modernes*, Paris, 1921

O'SHAUGHNESSY, *Songs of a Worker*, London, 1881

RAYNAUD, ERNEST, *Le bohème sous le seconde empire*, Paris, 1930. *La mêlée symboliste*, Paris, 1918

REGNIER, H. DE, *De mon temps*, Paris, 1933

SAINTE-BEUVE, *Correspondance*, Paris, 1877

SOURIAU, M., *Histoire du parnasse*, Paris, 1929

TAILHADE, LAURENT, *Quelques fantomes de jadis*, Paris, 1920

THEURIET, ANDRÉ, *Souvenirs des vertes saisons*, Paris, 1903
VERHAEVEN, EMILE, *Impressions*, Paris, 1928
WILSON, EDMUND, *Axel's Castle*, New York, 1931
ZOLA, EMILE, *Documents littéraires*, Paris, 1894

Index

V

Index of First Lines of Verlaine's Poems

ABOUT THE AUTHORS

With this eighth volume in their series of jointly written biographies, Lawrence and Elisabeth Hanson have again confirmed their ability to create studies of the artistic spirit which are perceptive in treatment and dramatic in effect. Lawrence Hanson was educated at Oxford and spent nine years with the British Broadcasting Corporation. His wife, Elisabeth, who studied at Edinburgh and St. Andrews Universities, is a classical scholar and pianist, with emphasis on Bach. Both Hansons have a continuing interest in theatre, opera and ballet. They make their home in one of the small hill towns of the French Riviera, leaving it each summer for an extended trip to their native England.